HISTORY OF INDIA

HISTORY OF INDIA

FROM THE EARLIEST TIMES TO *THE PRESENT DAY*

CAPTAIN L. J. TROTTER

EDITED BY

W. H. HUTTON, B. D.

GYAN

Published by

Gyan Publishing House
5, Ansari Road
Daryaganj, New Delhi-110002
Phone: 011-47034999, 9811692060
E-mail: books@gyanbooks.com

Distribution Network
gyanbooks.com
India, USA, Canada, UK, Australia, France

ISBN: 978-81-212-8886-6 (PB)
First Published, 1874

2nd Impression 2023

Printed at: Gyan Press, Delhi.

HISTORY OF INDIA
AUTHOR: CAPTAIN L. J. TROTTER

Emery Walker, Ltd., photographers

WARREN HASTINGS

FROM THE PAINTING BY SIR THOMAS LAWRENCE, P.R.A., IN THE NATIONAL PORTRAIT GALLERY

Frontispiece

HISTORY OF INDIA

FROM THE EARLIEST TIMES TO THE PRESENT DAY

BY THE LATE

CAPTAIN L. J. TROTTER,

AUTHOR OF
"JOHN NICHOLSON," "HISTORY OF INDIA UNDER QUEEN VICTORIA," ETC.

REVISED EDITION, BROUGHT UP TO 1911,

BY

W. H. HUTTON, B.D.

READER IN INDIAN HISTORY IN THE UNIVERSITY OF OXFORD AND
FELLOW OF S. JOHN'S COLLEGE; ARCHDEACON OF NORTHAMPTON;
HONORARY D.C.L., DURHAM

With 4 Maps and 22 Illustrations

SOCIETY FOR PROMOTING
CHRISTIAN KNOWLEDGE
LONDON: 68, HAYMARKET, S.W.
1917

EDITOR'S PREFACE

CAPTAIN LIONEL JAMES TROTTER was born at Chowringhee, Calcutta, in September, 1827. He died in Oxford on May 5, 1912.

He first came to England in 1831, and went to school in 1837, to Charterhouse in 1841, and thence to Merton College, Oxford, in 1845. In 1846 he obtained a cadetship in the Bengal Infantry, and in 1848 was appointed to the 2nd European Regiment. He served in the Punjāb campaign, October, 1848, to May, 1849, was present at Ramnagar, Chilianwala, Gujrāt, and the pursuit of the Sikhs and Afghāns up to Peshāwar, receiving the Punjāb medal with two clasps.

He served with the 2nd Bengal Fusiliers in Burma, 1853 (medal and clasp). After absence on sick leave he returned to India in 1857, and was in command of the depôt and station of Subathoo during the Mutiny. He retired on sick leave 1858, and left the Army on half pay in 1862.

Captain Trotter was a prolific writer. He contributed largely to the Anglo-Indian press, and to reviews at home. Among his many separate publications were the two volumes he wrote for the Clarendon Press series (edited by Sir W. W. Hunter) of "Rulers of India," on Warren Hastings and Lord Auckland. The present "History of India" was published by the S.P.C.K. in 1874, and was revised by the Author in 1899. Its freshness and vigour well deserve a re-issue, and an endeavour has been made to continue it on the same scale. Recent research has made it necessary to modify or alter several parts, especially in the earlier chapters, of the book ; but personal judgments of the author have almost always been left untouched, and no alteration has been made in any place where the writer's personal knowledge was concerned. The original work ended with 1898. Two chapters have been added by the present editor. For all statements of opinion up to the end of the viceroyalty of the Earl of Elgin in 1898, the late Captain Trotter is alone responsible.

THE VINEYARD,
PETERBOROUGH.
June, 1917.

EXTRACT FROM THE ORIGINAL PREFACE

THE following pages were written at the request of the Society whose name appears on the title page. Within the space allowed him the Author has done his best to give such an outline of Indian history as might serve to interest that large class of readers which lacks time, means, or will, for the study of larger works on the same theme. In beginning, as it were, from the very outset, he has sought to fix the reader's attention to the successive stages leading from the first Aryan settlements in India, up to the final conquest of the whole country by another people of Aryan race. It is well for many reasons that Englishmen should understand how much the nations of the West have in common with the dark-skinned children of their common forefathers. Nor is the wondrous tale of English conquests in India a thing to be studied apart from its connection with the previous conquests of the Mohammadans, and the great fight for empire between the countrymen of Sivajī and the Moghals.

In tracing, however rapidly, the history of so many centuries, the Author has availed himself of all the latest sources of information, many of which are pointed out in the footnotes. In no part of the book has he been content to follow slavishly in the wake of former historians and essayists. His treatment of Warren Hastings, for example, and his friend Sir Elijah Impey, however different from the picture drawn by Macaulay, is amply warranted by a careful study of documents which that great writer misread or overlooked. Throughout the volume he has striven to combine accuracy of fit detail with due breadth of handling and a clear, readable style; to give due prominence to leading events and characters, and to avoid the faults of a mere partisan. How far he has succeeded in any of these aims, the more critical of his readers must be left to judge for themselves, remembering only to make fair allowance for the mistakes which they are almost certain to find here and there in a work that deals with so many centuries of stirring life.

NOTE TO THE PRESENT EDITION

IN this edition the spelling adopted is that of the Imperial Gazetteer of India. Captain Trotter wrote thus as to the pronunciation of Hindustāni words.

"It will be seen from the following simple rules how many of the Indian vowel and consonant sounds correspond with those in our own and other Teutonic tongues.

"VOWELS—a broad as in 'father': a short as in 'America, or *u* in 'butter,' or *o* in 'son.'
e as in 'there,' or as *a* in 'pate,' or *e* in 'bell.'
íllong as in 'pique' or 'machine': i short as in 'bit.'
ó long as in 'tone,' or shorter as in 'obey.'
ú long as in 'rude' or *oo* in 'fool': u short as in 'full,' 'put.'
ai as in German 'Kaiser,' or English 'aisle.'
au as in German 'haus,' or the *ow* in English 'cow'

"CONSONANTS—g always hard, as in 'give.'
s hard, as in 'sin.'
ch always as in 'church,' 'chin.'
gh and kh guttural, as in Irish 'Lough,' and Scot 'loch,' or English 'loghut' and 'inkhorn.'
th and ph as in 'hot-house' and 'up-hill.'
y always as in 'yet,' 'young.'
w as in 'war.'

"The remaining consonants are sounded as in English save that *n* final is sometimes nasal, as in French 'bon.'"

CONTENTS

INTRODUCTION

BOOK I

INDIA BEFORE THE MUHAMMADAN CONQUEST

BOOK II

THE MUHAMMADAN PERIOD

BOOK III

THE MUGHAL DYNASTY OF BĀBUR

BOOK IV

THE RULE OF THE COMPANY

BOOK V

THE ENGLISH PARAMOUNT

BOOK VI

CONSOLIDATION OF ENGLISH RULE

BOOK VII

INDIA UNDER THE CROWN

LIST OF ILLUSTRATIONS

MAPS

INTRODUCTION

THE empire now ruled by the Viceroy of India includes not only the great Indian peninsula stretching under the shadow of the Himālayas, from the valley of the Indus to that of the Brahmapūtra, but also the broad regions watered by the Irrawady and the Salween. This vast area of nearly 1,700,000 square miles exceeds that of all Europe outside Russia. From the northernmost corner of the Punjāb to Cape Comorin in the south its greatest length is about 1830 miles, while its breadth eastward from Karāchi, near the mouth of the Indus, to the easternmost point of Burma, is even greater. The great mountain-wall of the Himālayas, which forms its northern boundary, curves away from the Yang-tse river westward to the Hindu Kush and the Sulaimān Hills, dividing India from China, Tibet, and Turkistān. The Sulaimān and Hāla ranges shut out the Punjāb and Sind from their western neighbours in Afghānistān and Baluchistān. On the east the new Burman frontier may be said to march with that of China, Laos, and Siam. The whole length of coast-line from Karāchi to the southernmost point of Tenasserim has been reckoned at nearly 4000 miles, while the extent of land-frontier is a thousand miles longer.

From the wild recesses of the towering Himālayas flow down the sources of the great rivers, the Indus, the Ganges, the Brahmapūtra, which find their several outlets in the Arabian Sea and the Bay of Bengal. Each of them on its long course to the ocean is fed by numerous streams, of a volume sometimes equalling its own. Two nearly parallel ranges of hills, the Vindhya and the Sātpūra, stretching eastward from the Gulf of Cambay to the valley of the Lower Ganges, divide India itself into two unequal parts, Southern India forming a kind of triangle whose point is Cape Comorin, with the double line of hills aforesaid for its base. At its western end the Vindhya range meets the Aravalli, a long, low chain of hills sweeping north-eastward across Rājputāna almost to Delhi. In the east it merges into the highlands of Orissa, Chota Nāgpūr, and Birbhūm. Again, from either end two chains of hills, the Eastern and Western Ghāts, pass southwards at varying distances from the coast, to meet at last in the Nīlgiri or Blue Mountains of Malabar, and to re-appear after a breach of twenty miles in the lofty hills that border Travancore and touch the sea at Cape Comorin. The Western Ghāts are much higher than the Eastern, and far more abrupt on their seaward face. Their eastern ridges slope into the table-lands of the Deccan and Mysore, or serve as outworks to the loftier Nīlgiris, even as the lower Siwālik range serves as an outwork to the Himālayas between the Sutlej and the Ganges.

From the wooded heart of the Vindhyas the Narbada winds along its rocky bed, past the rising city of Jubbulpore, through several hundred miles of rock and forest, until it reaches the Gulf of Cambay, below Broach. Enclosed between the Vindhya and Sātpūra ranges the Narbada valley separates Southern India from Hindūstān Proper. The Tāpti flows past the southern slopes of the Sātpūras into the same gulf a little below Surat. The Godāvari, on the other hand, after leaving the Western Ghāts near Nasik, crosses the Nizām's dominions, and, swollen by many tributary streams, empties itself by several mouths into the Bay of Bengal near Cocanāda. The Kistna or

Krishna also flows from the Western Ghāts near Māhābaleshwar, eastward to the Coromandel coast, receiving on its way the Bhīma and the Tungabhadra. India altogether abounds in rivers great and small, four of which, including the Irrawādy, are more than fifteen hundred miles long, while three of those in Southern India exceed 800 miles. It can boast, however, but few good harbours, chief among which are Bombay, Rangoon, and Moulmein. Goa, another good harbour, belongs to Portugal, and Karāchi, the port of Sind, has yet to prove itself a worthy rival of Bombay. Kārwar, Cochin, and Vijayadurg, would repay the cost of improving them. The approach to Calcutta on the Hūgli is rendered dangerous to large vessels by the "William and Mary" shoal.

Of the few lakes which India possesses nearly all are more or less salt. One of these, the great Rann of Cutch, is 190 miles long, and varies in breadth from two to ninety miles. In the dry season a waste of sand dotted with pools of salt water, it becomes in the rainy season an enormous marsh. From some of these lakes large quantities of salt are manufactured. A long tract of desert stretches from the southern border of Sind to the northern boundary of Rājputāna. Nearly all the country, indeed, between the Indus and the Aravalli Hills is a waste of sand, dotted with oases of varying size and fertility. The prevalence of sand and saltpetre in the soil of Upper India points to a time when all India north of the Vindhyas lay buried in the sea, which washed the feet of the Himālayas themselves. The fertile plains now watered by the Ganges and its affluents must have been the work of ages, during which the Himālayan rivers kept bringing down their yearly loads of earth from the mountains to the sea. It appears that the Himālayas themselves, whose snowy peaks now soar to a height ranging from 20,000 to 29,000 feet, have gradually been upheaved by volcanic agency from their ocean beds.

A broad belt of marshy jungle deadly to human life divides these mountains from the adjacent plains. The forests of this "Terai" afford ample means of smelting the iron found on the lower slopes of the hills. Many parts of India are rich in forest trees suited to almost every purpose of use or ornament. The teak of Burma, the Godāvari valley, and Malabar; the bamboo of Kaman, Bengal, Burma, and Southern India; the pines and deodars of the Himālayas; the sāl, ebony, and satin-wood of Central India; the sandal, iron, and blackwood of Coorg, Mysore, and other districts; the oak and walnut-wood of Sikkim; the India-rubber tree of Assam; the palm-trees of the Tropics, are far from exhausting the list. The noble mango-groves of Hindūstān give welcome shade to the traveller weary with marching over miles of sun-burnt plain, and the banyan-tree of Bengal grows into a forest by throwing out new roots from its spreading branches. Cottages are thatched with palm-leaves, and houses built with scaffolding made of bamboos. Cocoa-nut fibre makes excellent rigging, and cocoa-nut oil is highly prized for lamps. Bamboo fibre serves for mats and baskets; a bamboo stem yields the lightest of lance-shafts, while one of its joints does good duty for a bottle. Most of the houses in all parts of Burma are built entirely of wood. From the sap of the palm-tree is brewed the tāri or toddy which forms a favourite drink among certain classes. Another kind of palm yields the betel nut, which natives of every class and both sexes delight to chew. The sāl and deodar are largely used for railway sleepers, and in districts where coal is very costly forest timber serves as fuel for steamers and railway trains.

All over India there are two harvests yearly; in some places three. Bājra, jowār, rice, and some other grains are sown at the beginning and reaped at the end of the rainy season. The cold weather crops, including wheat, barley, and some other kinds of grain and pulse, are reaped in the spring. It is a vulgar fallacy that the people of India live on rice. The very opposite notion would be nearer the truth. Rice is grown mainly in the moist climate of Bengal, Burma, the Konkan, and Malabar. In Hindūstān and the Punjāb the staple food is wheat and millet; in the Deccan a poor kind of grain called rāgi. Berār, Khāndesh, and Gujarāt yield ample crops of cotton. The home of the sugar-cane is in Rohilkhand and Madras. The poppy-fields of Mālwa and Bengal yield the opium which swells the Indian revenue by more than seven millions a-year. Indigo and jute are mainly raised in Bengal. Coffee has become the staple product of the hill districts in Coorg, Wynaad, and the Nīlgiris. The tea-gardens of Assam, Cachār, Sylhet, and the southern slopes of the Himālayas from Kangra to Darjeeling, furnish most of the tea which now finds its way to English markets. The quinine-yielding cinchona is grown in even larger forests on the Nīlgiri and Darjeeling Hills. Another medicinal plant of great value, the ipecacuanha, bids fair to thrive in the Sikkim Terai. Cardamoms and pepper abound along the Western Ghāts, hemp and linseed are largely exported, and tobacco is widely grown throughout India.

Of fruits and vegetables there is no lack. Mangoes, melons, pumpkins, guavas, custard-apples, plantains, oranges, limes, citrons, and pomegranates, are common everywhere; figs, dates, and grapes thrive well in many places; and the pine-apple grows wild in Lower Burma. Cucumbers, yams, tomatoes, sweet potatoes, and many vegetables familiar to English palates, are raised abundantly for general use. Flowers of every shape and hue, and often of the richest scent, from the rose and jasmine to the oleander and the water-lily, spangle the plains, cover the surfaces of lakes and ponds, or glimmer in climbing beauty among the woods. The rhododendrons of the Himālayas grow like forest trees, and crown the hill-side in April and May with far-spreading masses of crimson blossoms. From the rose-gardens of Ghāzipūr is extracted the attar, a few drops of which contain the gathered fragrance of a thousand flowers.

The jungles teem with elephants, bears, wild buffaloes, tigers, leopards, panthers, and hyænas. Wolves and jackals prowl among the ravines in quest of deer and other prey. The lion is chiefly to be found in the wilds of Rājputāna and Gujarāt; the camel in the sandy regions of the North West; the one-horned rhinoceros among the swamps of the Ganges. Deer of many kinds abound everywhere. Snakes, poisonous and harmless, haunt the jungles and other lonely places. Wild boars are common. Monkeys abound in most parts of the country. The rivers swarm with fish, and alligators bask like huge lizards along their banks. Horses and ponies of divers breeds are used chiefly for riding, while the fields are ploughed and the carts and carriages of the country are drawn by bullocks of the Brahmani type. In many parts of India oxen still serve as carriers of merchandise. Buffaloes are usually kept for milk and ploughing. Sheep and goats are very common, and the Shāl goat of Kashmīr supplies the soft *pashmina* of which Indian shawls and other articles of clothing are made.

The woods re-echo with the harsh cry of the peacock and the lively chattering of parrots, woodpeckers, and other birds of gay plumage; to say nothing of various birds common to India and the West. Eagles and falcons are found in some places; kites, vultures, and crows abound everywhere. The great adjutant stork of Bengal plays the part of a scavenger in the most populous cities. Pheasants, partridges, ortolans, quails, snipes, and wild geese tempt the sportsman at certain seasons. The sparrow has followed the Englishman into the Himālayas. In one thing, however, India is sadly wanting: the voice of song-birds is almost everywhere mute.

India is fairly rich in minerals of various kinds. Her old wealth in diamonds, rubies, and other gems has well-nigh passed away; but new stores may be gathered from the mines of Upper Burma. Of less valuable stones, such as opals, amethysts, garnets, jaspers, cornelians, she still yields a goodly share. Gold in small quantities may be found in the gravels of many streams. Lead mines have been opened in the north-western Himālayas. Rich veins of tin have lately been discovered in Tenasserim and Martaban. Antimony and copper abound in the hill ranges. Petroleum is known to exist in Pegu and Assam. Vast beds of rock-salt occur in the Punjāb hills. The mountains of southern India are largely composed of granite, while excellent marble is quarried from the Aravalli range.

Iron ores have been found in many parts of the country, notably in Kaman, Bundelkhand, the Central Provinces, and Lower Bengal. In the Chānda district the surface of a hill two miles long and half-a-mile broad is covered with masses of pure iron ore. The iron beds in the Kaman hills extend for miles, and the clay of the Damodar coal-fields contains 39 per cent. of iron. From the growing scarcity of charcoal for smelting purposes the native manufacture of iron is fast declining, and the attempts of Englishmen in the same field have hitherto been baffled by the same and other causes. A substitute for charcoal, however, may yet be found in coal, large beds of which extend from Rājmahāl, on the Ganges, south to the Godāvari, and from the neighbourhood of Calcutta westward to the Narbada valley.

The coal-bearing rocks of the Damodar valley, covering 1500 square miles of ground, contain thick seams of coal, whose yield nine years ago exceeded half-a-million tons a year. From the Karharbāri coal-fields north-west of Rāniganj half that quantity could be supplied for 800 years. There are thick seams of coal in the Narbada valley. On the edge of the great sandstone tract watered by the Godāvari and the Wardha some promising beds have lately been examined; and over wide spaces in Berār and the Central Provinces seams of great thickness, and of a quality good enough for railway purposes, give fair promise of vast additions to India's store of fuel. The easternmost end of Assam also, where the Brahmapūtra emerges from the hills into the forest-clad wilds of Dibrugarh, contains several seams of excellent coal.

According to the census of 1911, British India, as apart from the tributary native states, contained an aggregate population of nearly 250 million souls, of whom about two-thirds live by husbandry alone. To this may be added probably 70 millions in all for the Native States. But the increase of population is so great between each census that we will not attempt to record statistics which would be out of date soon after they were written down. It may suffice to say, in regard to the density of population, that to each square mile we have an average which exceeds that of Great Britain. The 70 millions in the Native States are ruled by some two hundred chiefs and princes, great and small, whose joint possessions cover an area of more than half-a-million square miles from Kashmīr to Travancore.

Of the whole Indian population some 217 millions are Hindus by religion, and several millions more are probably Hindus by race. The Muhammadans of all races, Aryan, Semitic, and Mongol, may be reckoned at 66 millions, most of whom profess the Sūnni or Turkish form of Islām. The

Shiāh sect are chiefly to be found in the Deccan and Kashmīr. In Bengal the Muhammadans exceed 23 millions, the great bulk of whom are to be found in the Central and Eastern districts as husbandmen or landowners, while comparatively few inhabit the old centres of Muhammadan power. In Bengal, as in Kashmīr, the Muhammadan numbers seem to be largely swelled by former converts from among the low-caste Hindus. In the Punjāb there are now nearly 11 million, in the North-Western Provinces about 2 million followers of Islām. In the United Provinces of Agra and Oudh they number nearly 7 millions, and in the Central Provinces and Berar about half that amount. In the Punjāb, and along the frontier, there are about 10 million Muhammadans to about 6 million Hindus, and little more than two million Sikhs. The 12 million people in Burma are mostly Buddhists.

The aboriginal or prehistoric races scattered everywhere among the hills and forests are supposed to number about 10 millions, a fifth of whom people the highlands of the Central Provinces, while perhaps as many more are found in Mālwa and Khāndesh. In the hills of Orissa, Chota Nāgpūr, Birbhūm, Assam, and Cachār, they are also numerous. The Jains, an offshoot from Buddhism, number 1,248,000. The Parsīs, descendants of Persian Fire-worshippers, if few in numbers, fill a front place in the commercial doings of Western India. Christians of all sects and races may be set down at nearly four millions, about half of whom are Roman Catholics, owing allegiance to the Archbishop of Goa.

In a country which extends from the eighth to the thirty-fifth degree of north latitude the climate varies, not only with the differences of relative position, but with those also of local surface and surroundings. The dry heats of the Upper Provinces differ from the moist heats of Bengal and part of Southern India as a furnace differs from a vapour-bath. There are large tracts of country in Sind, the Punjāb, and Rājputāna, where rain seldom falls, and the thermometer rises to 120° in the shade. In the North-Western Provinces and Gujarāt the rainfall varies from 15 to 30 inches, most of it falling in about three months. A zone of light rainfall passes down the middle of Southern India. The eastern coast is generally hotter and drier than the western, which receives the full force of the south-west monsoon from June to September. From the Brahmapūtra valley down to Moulmein the heat in these months is greatly tempered by heavy and continuous rains, which fall in some places to a depth of more than a hundred inches, and convert the country into a sea studded with islands. In the Khāsi Hills 600 inches of rain have been measured in the year. In Lower Bengal and Orissa the rain-swollen rivers flood the country far and wide. On the table-lands of the Deccan and Central India hot days are followed by cool nights. Along the lofty slopes of the Himālayas and the wood-crowned ridges of the Nīlgiris, the rain pours heavily with few intervals for several months. Along the coast sea-breezes also serve to temper the heat. Over the sandy plains of Northern India the dry west wind blows from March to the middle of June with the fury of a sirocco, relieved at times by a simoom or sandstorm, which turns day into night for an hour or more, and cools the air for some days afterwards. From July to October the showers in these regions are followed by intervals of close, steamy heat, which finally give place to three or four months of clear, cool, bright weather, with frequent frost at night, and mornings often cold enough for a fire. In the hill-stations, where the summer heat is generally moderate, the resemblance to an English winter is heightened by frequent falls of snow. Within the tropics, on the other hand, the cold season, except on some of the higher mountains, answers on the whole to a mild September in our own country.

The languages and dialects used or spoken in India exceed in number and variety those of all Europe. The Aryan languages take the lead by right of their wide prevalence. Of the dialects which have grown out of the parent Sanskrit there are at least a dozen separate forms, of which Hindi, the most purely Aryan, and Urdū, the mixed language of the law-courts and the public services, are the most widely used. Each of the great provinces in Upper and Western India has its own dialect, which differs from the rest much as English differs from German or Swedish. In Southern India the Dravidian languages, such as Tāmil and Telugū, which belong in the main to some old non-Aryan type, are spoken by about fifty million people. In the Himālayan valleys, in Burma, and on the eastern frontier of Bengal, some form of Indo-Chinese or Mongol speech is generally spoken. Arabic, the language of the Korān, and Persian, the language of Mughal state officers and Anglo-Indian law-courts in former days, have enriched the Urdū of our day with a large stock of serviceable words and phrases.

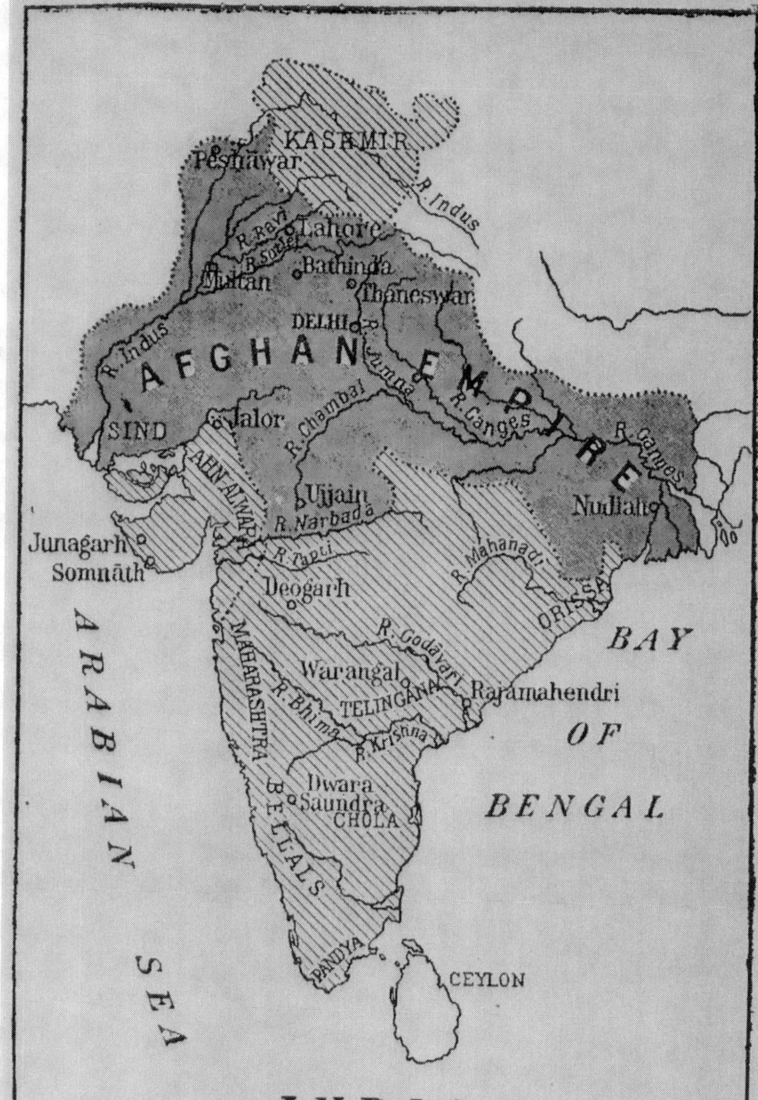

A MAP OF INDIA AT THE BEGINNING OF THE XIIITH CENTURY.

HISTORY OF INDIA

BOOK I

INDIA BEFORE THE MUHAMMADAN CONQUEST

CHAPTER I

THE ARYAN HINDUS

THE circumstances which mark the rise and progress of England's empire in Southern Asia have no precise parallel in any other page of the world's known history. Nowhere else has the world beheld so strange and fruitful an outcome from beginnings apparently so small. Macedon, Rome, Arabia, have each in its turn made mighty conquests in a wonderfully short space of time. Spaniards, in the course of one or two generations, became masters of half the New World. The hordes of Tamerlane, issuing from Samarkand, overran Asia in a few years. In our own century half Europe bowed her head for a season at the feet of the First Napoleon. India herself for more than two hundred years obeyed successive kings of the house of Bābur. In all these cases either the ground won at first by force of arms was speedily lost again, or else its further retention was mainly due to the settlements founded thereon by the conquerors themselves. British India alone presents the spectacle of a vast dominion conquered during the last two hundred and fifty years by the servants of a trading company, whose one great aim was to increase its dividends, and upheld by a few thousand Englishmen encamping in the midst of more than two hundred million natives. Nowhere else has so wide a sway over so many populous and civilised states been wielded with a grasp so firm by a mere handful of foreigners, strange alike in speech, manners, religion, sent forth from one of the coldest to one of the hottest quarters of the earth, and debarred by causes more or less invincible from founding families of their own or of a mixed blood in a climate peculiarly hurtful to English life.

How much of the seeming marvel sprang from sources in no way marvellous, the following pages may help to show. For that end it will not be enough to begin with the first days of British settlement in India. The true way to a clear understanding of later events leads far back through the Christian centuries into the twilight of prehistoric times. There is no real break in Indian history from the era of the Vedas until now. For all the changes that have been wrought by time and circumstance, the India of to-day reproduces in its main outlines the India of twenty or thirty centuries ago. Out of the two hundred and fifty millions who directly or indirectly obey our rule, more than a half may claim descent from those Aryan conquerors who, long before Hellas defied the Persian, were pushing the earlier races of Hindustān back into those sheltering hills and forests where their descendants may still be found.* The history of that olden civilisation has been written for us, not in chronicles like those which form the boast of Muhammadan India, but in the sacred

* The date of the events apparently recorded in the oldest Hindu epic, the Rāmāyan, is placed by Sir W. Jones in the 21st, by Tod in the 12th, and by Bentley in the 10th century before Christ.—Griffith's "Rāmāyan," translated into English verse.

writings of Sanskrit-speaking Hindus, and in poems which portray the social life of pre-historic India as vividly as Homer portrayed the social life of pre-historic Greece. From the Vedas, or religious hymns of the Brahmans, we learn what faiths were held, what gods were worshipped, what rites practised by the Aryan conquerors of Ancient India. The oldest Vedas, older by several centuries than the Homeric poems,* reveal to modern scholars the poetic sources of that purely natural worship which marks the childhood of all human races. They are full of the life-like symbolism in which imaginative minds love to embody their impressions of the outer world. They sing the praises of the "Deva," the bright divinities of Sun and Dawn, of Fire, Storm, Earth, and Sky. In them all nature is divine. Sūrya, the Sun-god, his car drawn by shining steeds, dispels the darkness, hurries after the Dawn as lover after love-maiden, and sheds light, health, and every blessing on all the world. "Let us meditate," says one famous verse, "on the desirable light of the divine Sun, who influences our pious rites."

Dyaus and Prithivi, Heaven and Earth—the Zeus and Demeter of the Greek Pantheon—are invoked as the great, wise, energetic parents of all the other gods. Aditi, "mother of the gods," stands one while for the sky, anon for the whole universe, and at times for something distinct from either. Ushas, the Dawn, the Homeric 'Ηώς, harnesses her purple oxen, calling all sleeping things to new life, enjoyment, or exertion, and sending her rays abroad like cattle to their pasture. Agni, the god of fire, the Latin Ignis, is a dear friend, who sits in the

* The true date of the Rig-Veda, or "Book of Praise," the oldest of the four Vedas, is still a moot question. It is safe, however, to assume, with Dr. Max Müller, on evidence of a very strong kind, that these old hymns and prayers, written in the oldest forms of a language probably older than that of ancient Greece, were composed between 1200 and 1500 years before Christ.

sacrificial chamber, diffusing happiness, like a benevolent man among mankind. Indra, the son of Dyaus and Prithivi, is the far-darting Apollo of the Vedas, the god of storms and rain, who rends the clouds asunder, gives vent to the showers, and frees the obstructed streams. He is invoked, as the Lord of Steeds, victorious in battle, whom neither earth nor heaven can contain. His horses are the scud that denotes the coming tempest. In his chariot rides Vāyu or Vāta, the rushing wind; he delights in drinking the sacred soma juice;* and the Māruts or storm-winds are his children, at whose approach earth trembles like a storm-driven boat, and in whose car ride the young lightnings. Varuna, the Vedic Ουρανος, represents the infinite wonder of the sky. He is the god who upholds order, who knows the place of the birds, the ships on the waters, the months of the year, and the track of the winds.

In this old Vedic Pantheon no one god is raised, like the Hellenic Zeus, to permanent kingship over the rest. Each stands for the moment highest in the minds of his own worshippers. "Among you, O gods," says Manu, "there is none that is small, none that is young; you are all great indeed." To each is offered his befitting sacrifice, each is marked off by his peculiar symbols; and symbol and sacrifice, both in their turn, come to be worshipped as divine. We have later hymns in honour of the horse, dear to Indra; of the ox or cow, that universal blessing to men who live by the plough; of the ladle and the post used for sacrifice; and of the soma plant, which yields a nectar beloved of the gods. To the Rishis, or bards who composed the Vedas,† all things

* The soma plant of the Vedas was the *Asclepias acida* of Roxburgh, now known as the twisting sarkostema, a twining plant with few leaves, and with clusters of small white fragrant flowers. It yields a mild, acid, milky juice, and grows in various parts of India.

† The Sanskrit "Veda" means "what is known"; from the same old Aryan root as Greek *οἶδα*; Latin *video, vates*; German *wissen*; Old English *witan* (to wit, or weet); and the old Norse "Edda."

appear divine, as symbols or expressions of the one supreme indwelling soul that quickens, moulds, and cherishes all alike. Sun, moon, and stars, the changes of night and day, the recurrence of the seasons. the trees, the flowers, the streams, the very means and processes of new growth, are clothed by these worshippers of nature with a divinity not their own. In the world's childhood "Heaven lies about them," as it lies about thoughtful children in all ages. They read the riddle of the universe with the eyes of poets whose natural language is that of worship. To them all life is a sacred mystery, an infinite marvel, to be studied only in a spirit of child-like thankfulness and pious awe. From glorifying the life around them they come in time to contemplate the life within, to speak of right and wrong, to yearn after union with the Immortal Being. In the later Vedas the troubled soul seeks closer communion with the Unseen Spirit; it expresses sorrow and implores forgiveness for its sins; it gives new names to the mysterious Power or Self which out of nothing evolved all things, and through which the good man's soul will find sure rest for ever beyond the grave.

Inevitably there comes a time when the beliefs of an earlier day harden, or are developed, into a fixed system. The poetic gods of the old Pantheon are replaced by the mystic trinity of Brahma, Vishnu, and Siva—the Maker, Preserver, and Destroyer—round whom revolve a host of smaller deities, whose numbers grow and whose features wax coarse with years. A race of philosophers and trained priests obscures the old imagery of the Vedic bards with the metaphysic subtleties of the Upanishads, the fantastic trifling of the Sutras and the Vedanta, and in time with the puerile grossness of the Purānas.* Old forms,

* The Upanishads were a kind of supplement to the Vedas; the Sutras were collections of philosophic aphorisms; the Vedanta, from *veda* and *anta,*

symbols, and figures of speech lose their old meaning; the attributes of godhead become distinct gods; the dim shapes of poetic fancy reappear as the sharply defined conceptions of an abtruse theology, or translate themselves into the uncouth, unmeaning objects of popular idol-worship.

Against this lower tendency Buddhism sprang up as a powerful but fleeting protest about the end of the sixth century before Christ. It was then that Gautama first preached a return to the purer doctrines which centuries of priestly rule and popular delusion had buried under a rank growth of debasing errors. His father was a prince of the Sākyas, and hence Gautama is often called Sākyamuni, the wise man of the Sākyas. Of this reformer—whose creed, if banished from its old birth-place at the foot of the Nepalese Hills, has since become the religion of nearly a third of the human race—not much is known for certain; and some years ago the very fact of his existence was called in question by one of the foremost Sanskrit scholars of our time. In spite, however, of Professor Wilson's doubtings, there is reason to believe that the Sākyamuni, afterwards more widely known as Buddha or The Enlightened, came of a race of kings who ruled at Kapilavastu, north of the modern Oudh; that having long sat at the feet of the Brahman sages in Magadha, or Bihār, and at Benāres, the Oxford of ancient India, he set forth with a few disciples to preach a purer gospel in Magadha, under the protection of its friendly king. The story of his after wanderings has been so beclouded with fable that time would only be wasted in trying to pick out the grain from the chaff. Before his death, however, the princely ascetic, whose own life and doctrines were in

end, were commentaries enforcing the purpose of the Vedas; and the Purānas from, *purāna*, old, embodied the whole round of legends, ritual, and philosophy, which had grown out of the Vedanta into the shape they first assumed about the ninth century of our era.

BUDDHA PREACHING. DISCOVERED AT SARNATH 1904

FROM A PHOTOGRAPH IN THE POSSESSION OF THE INDIA OFFICE

p. 6

open revolt from the debased religion, the pharisaic pride, and the social tyranny of the old Brahmanic order, had sown far and wide the seeds of a reaction, whose influence for mingled good and evil may still be found working in at least one province of British India, Burma, in one British colony, Ceylon, which was governed for a short time from British India, and among the numerous sect of Jains, who in various parts of India blend somewhat of old Buddhist traditions with the creeds and practices of modern Brahmanism.

Himself a prince of the Kshatriya or warrior caste, Sākyamuni held out the hand of fellowship to men of all castes and classes alike. Brahman and Sudra, priest, prince, and artisan, were all equal in his eyes. Breaking through the bonds of a religious system which had come to bring all things and beings under the yoke of an all-powerful priesthood, he strove to make men holy by teaching them to live pure and holy lives. Instead of sacrifices and severe penances he exhorted them to sin no more, to love one another, to forgive insults, to return good for evil, to bear patiently the ills of this life, to wage ceaseless war with their own lower natures. Life, he maintained, was full of sorrow, and the path to happiness could only be gained by mortifying the natural affections and desires wherein lie the sources of that sorrow. All virtue and well-being, in short, were summed up by the Sākyamuni in love and self-control. What else he may have taught, beyond the religious teaching of the Vedas and the metaphysics of their Brahman interpreters, remains for the most part an open question. That he aimed, for instance, at finding some new way of escape for the soul of man from its supposed liability to enter into new shapes of men and animals for evermore,* is a likely, if not quite a

* The metempsychosis, or transmigration of souls, was among the oldest tenets of Hindu philosophy.

necessary inference, from the doctrines afterwards preached in his name. The climax of his attainment is found when, described as "passing out of the state between consciousness and unconsciousness, he fell into a state in which the consciousness both of sensations and of ideas had wholly passed away." * Scholars have disputed whether the "Nirvāna," to which it is the highest bliss of the devout Buddhist to attain, means utter extinction or the calm that comes of absorption into the supreme soul. But "that Buddhism knows nothing of such absorption, if only because it admits no such Supreme Being, is now at last beginning to be understood." †

Be that as it may, we may hold it for certain that Buddha himself, like other great reformers, laid chief stress on that part of his teaching which would appeal most strongly to the popular heart. Some kind of hope for a happier future must have lain at the bottom of a religious movement which proclaimed the nothingness of human joys, and the need of deliverance from human ills and weaknesses. The idea of eternal rest beyond the grave may have meant for the multitude something very different from utter annihilation; even as to the Buddhists of modern Burma, Nirvāna means simple freedom from old age, disease, and death.

In due time the new revolt from caste-rules and Brahmanic traditions made its way over India and the neighbouring countries. Asōka, grandson of that king Chandragupta,‡ to whose court at the capital of Bihār Seleucus Nicator sent an envoy about 320 B.C., became the Constantine of the new creed. In his reign Buddhism spread over the whole of Northern and much of Southern India.

* Parinibb Sutta in "Sacred Books of the East," vol. xi., quoted by R. S. Copleston, "Buddhism," p. 144.

† Copleston, *op. cit.*, p. 215.

‡ The Sandracottus of Greek historians.

SARNATH CAPITAL (ASOKA PERIOD)
(FROM V. A. SMITH'S "STUDENT'S HISTORY OF INDIA")

p. 8

The stone pillars that mark his sway and still bear his edicts carved on their face, in characters first deciphered by Mr. James Prinsep, may still be traced from Bengal to the heart of Afghānistān. A great council held by him in 308 B.C., or as others reckon in 286 B.C., decreed the sending forth of missions to all the chief countries beyond India. In the first century of the Christian era Buddhism, having already struck firm root in Burma, Ceylon, Java, Tibet, and Kashmīr, was declared by a Chinese emperor worthy to take equal rank before the state with the religions of Confucius and Lao-tse. Losing its olden simplicity as its followers grew in numbers, it gathered strength from the very process of change and corruption which transformed its founder into its god and its very priests into heaven-born popes. Its temples were filled with images of the prince who had waged war against idol-worship, and its moral beauty was gradually marred by childish or grotesque superstitions, which culminated in the praying-wheels and the deified Lamas or high-priests of Tibet. In spite, however, of the changes wrought by time and circumstance, Buddha's spirit still lives in the religion that bears his name; his moral teachings still form the rule of conduct for millions of his present worshippers; and the yellow-robed monks of Burma still hold out to every Burman child such means of learning to read, write, and cipher as our English children enjoy.

In India the new religion seems never to have quite supplanted the old. For centuries they held between them a divided sway, each in its turn gaining or losing ground with the rise and fall of successive dynasties. At length came the inevitable conflict which ended by uprooting Buddhism from its very birth-place in favour of a religious system still dear to the bulk of modern Hindus. The stern simplicity of Sākyamuni's teaching had probably few abiding charms for his lively, sensuous, subtle-minded country-folk. Split up into opposing sects, the later Buddhists seem to have further weakened their cause by vain paltering with the popular taste for show and superstition. The old caste-system which Buddha had sought to demolish lent all its renewed strength to the Brahmanic reaction. From about the fifth to the tenth century of our era the long strife raged, until throughout all India Proper nothing was left of Buddhism but the grand old halls and temples which attest its former prevalence, and the mixture of Buddhist and Brahmanic usage which still marks the worship of the modern Jains.

Upon the Institutes of Manu,* the Minos of Aryan India, and the philosophic systems spun out of the Vedas by successive schools of Hindu thinkers, the victorious Brahmans built up the social and religious fabric of modern Hinduism. Every nation has its mythical lawgiver, its Minos or its Lycurgus, in whom it finds the sources of its social and political growth. Manu, the Adam or first man of the Aryan race, had given his name to a code of laws and customs compiled 900 years B.C. perhaps, but dating in its present form from between 200 and 300 A.D., by certain of the Mānavas, the oldest Aryan settlers in Upper India, who dwelt between the Sutlej and the "divine Saraswati." Their chief city, Hastinapur, the abode of the legendary King Bharat, renowned in old Hindu poetry, lay in Sind, to the north-east of the modern Meerut, and their settlements ere long covered the whole ground between the Ganges and the Indus. These were the men who founded that village-system and drew up those caste-rules by which Indian society is still in some measure kept

* *Manu*, the first man of the Sanskrit-speaking Hindus, is the same word as Gothic *mannus*, German *mann* and *mensch*, English *man*, and Welsh *mynw*. It comes from the same root as Sanskrit *mâna*, to think, *mânas*, the mind (Latin *mens*), and perhaps German *meinung*, "meaning."

from falling to pieces. Each village or township became the centre of a little commonwealth, governed in the king's name by a head-man of the conquering race, with the help of a council of its own house-fathers, or heads of families. Acting under these were a staff of village officers, maintained for various purposes at the common cost. Each village kept its own registrar, its own watchman, barber, schoolmaster, washerman, goldsmith, wheelwright. Every house-father obeyed the common laws and usages expounded or enforced by the village council; but within his own household he reigned supreme as any Roman father in the days of the Republic. Over the lands within and around his township his control was much more bounded. If, as head of a family, he might claim all but free and full ownership of the fields originally allotted to his family, the rest of his holdings belonged collectively to the whole village, and could only be used by him under certain fixed conditions. He had to sow the same crops as his neighbours, to let certain fields lie fallow in fixed succession, and to respect the right of other households to pasture their cattle on the fallow or stubble land. Each village, moreover, was fully equipped with tradesmen artisans, and so forth, whose relative place in the little commonwealth was determined by the several pursuits.

In the code of Manu all these members of the Aryan village community are arranged into four separate classes or "colours," each governed by its own usages and fenced off by strict rules and duties from every other. First come the Brahmans, the hereditary priests, the Levites of Aryan India, who sprang, says later tradition, from the head of Brahma himself, and whose time-hallowed rights were carefully guarded from all profane encroachments by the teaching of those holy books whose meaning they alone could rightly interpret. At once the religious and social leaders of their day, they found in the popular reverence for their order a willing accomplice in the building-up of a caste-system for which no real sanction can be found in the hymns of Vedic seers, nor in any writings earlier than Manu's code—itself the forged title-deeds of a class already supreme among the countrymen, by right of their general usefulness, their higher culture, and perhaps their purer lives. So firmly was their power established, that to kill a Brahman was accounted the worst of crimes, and to injure, or even insult him, a grievous outrage. No Brahman could wholly forfeit his divine birthright, nor could even kings take rank with Brahmans, the favoured children of the gods. To honour or befriend one of the heaven-born race was enough atonement for almost any crime. It was forbidden by the laws of Manu to take from a Brahman borrower more than two per cent., or half the interest that might be taken from a merchant. A Brahman might not stoop to trade or to earn money by other than purely intellectual pursuits; but he was always free to accept alms in food or money for the due performance of his priestly duties.

Next to the Brahmans in the social order of Manu, ranks the Kshatriya or soldier class. To this belonged most of the princes and nobles of Aryan India; and the Rājput tribes of modern India claim to be the purest living specimens of a class which seems once to have fought hard for social lordship with their Brahman rivals. Of the third or Vaisya class, tillage, trade, banking, law, and medicine were the chief pursuits, in most of which a very high degree of excellence had been already reached when the laws of Manu were first issued. These three classes embraced all men of Aryan race. To Brahman, Kshatriya, and Vaisya alike belonged the proud title of "twice-born" and the right of wearing the sacred thread. In the fourth or Sudra class, were comprehended all the "low-born," the people of mixed caste or of non-Aryan blood, whc followed trades and callings forbidden to the twice-born, or belonged by birth to any of the subject races. No Sudra was allowed to read the Vedas, to eat or intermarry with any member of a higher caste, or even to sit upon the same mat with a Brahman.

In course of time the system thus sanctioned by a mythical lawgiver, in behalf at once of an aggressive priesthood and a conquering race, underwent some noteworthy changes. Shattered, if not effaced by succeeding waves of Buddhism, it reappeared during the Christian centuries in a new and far more complex shape. Out of the four great castes there had grown some hundreds. The old sharp divisions of birth and calling had well-nigh vanished. Race no longer determined a man's pursuits. The Brahman ceased to be a born priest. In the struggle for life he and the lowly Sudra not seldom changed places, while both alike invaded the old domains of the soldier and the husbandman. Sudra dynasties ruled the land; Sudra priests sacrificed in the holy places; Sudra soldiers fought by the side of Brahmans and Rājputs; Sudra merchants, bankers, landholders, physicians, were held in equal honour with the Vaisyas, whose place they gradually filled. It was accounted no shame for a Brahman to cook the dinner of a wealthy Sudra, to become a clerk in a public office, to follow the standard of a Sudra captain, or to earn a livelihood by managing a farm. He might still, like a modern Polish noble, carry his head high among men of his own caste; but in the outer world his social importance came more and more to depend upon his worldly circumstances. As a priest or a Pandit he still enjoyed all the reverence which Hindus are wont to pay to their spiritual and intellectual guides. As a soldier or a merchant he continued to rank first among followers of the same calling. But a wealthy Sudra merchant or landholder paid small deference to the twice-born clerk who wrote his letters, or to the high-caste menial who prepared his food.

The Brahmans themselves branched off into a number of separate castes, each bound by its own rules, and few of them either claiming or conceding the right to eat or intermarry with any other. Alongside the old caste of birth and political standing there grew up also the caste of creeds and occupations; and the two processes got to be so intermingled that it is often hard to distinguish between them. Each group of persons following the same trade or calling in the same neighbourhood formed itself into a separate guild or brotherhood, held together by rules that often differed from those of corresponding guilds elsewhere. Like the trade-guilds of mediæval Europe and the trade unions of our own day, these Indian brotherhoods fenced themselves round with a network of moral and social observances, through whose meshes no one could break without risk of social outlawry. A kind of religious sanction was impressed on these rules by the priests or elders empowered to interpret and enforce them. The innate Hindu craving for self-government under strict conditions was carried down into the lowest circles and the smallest details of social life. The very Pariahs and utter outcasts, the scavengers, leather-dressers, conjurors, gypsies, thieves, adopted caste-rules of their own, behind which they loved to guard themselves from the approach of all outsiders, high or low. Caste in one shape or another found acceptance even with the Jains, the Sikhs, and the Muhammadans, to whose own inherited systems of life and worship it ran directly counter. Its influence for mingled good and evil continued to assert itself through all the changes which Indian society has from time to time undergone. Christianity itself has for the most part warred in vain against an institution not altogether unknown in the most civilised of Christian countries. Caste in India has many forms, most of which may be said to reproduce themselves in the class distinctions and social usages of every nation in modern Europe. It is not in India alone that certain trades, classes, or professions take precedence of certain others, that a halo of special sanctity surrounds the priest, that a wide gulf of social habit divides the nobleman from the shopkeeper. In England a barrister would incur deep social disgrace by stooping to practices admissible on the part of an attorney. A German noble would still be degraded by intermarriage with a mere plebeian. Even in the United States of America, where all classes are equal before the sovereign people, wealth has set up an aristocracy of its own, and the old pride of birth still rears its walls of separation between the old families and the new-made rich.

CHAPTER II

BRAHMANISM RE-ASCENDANT

WHAT the later forms of caste were to the earlier, the religion of the Purānas must have been to that of the Vedas. If the later Brahmans still professed to revere the teaching of Holy Books written in a tongue already strange even to themselves, they took care at any rate to amuse the people at large with scriptures better suited to the popular understanding. Somewhere about the ninth century of our era—the very time when Roman Popes were proclaiming the authority of those forged Decretals which gave a colour of old prescriptive right to their growing pretensions—the first books of the new Hindu Bible appear to have come into vogue. To these from time to time were added fresh Purānas, until their number had swollen to eighteen. In them were embodied the whole system of Brahmanic faith, worship, morals, philosophy, even law, as it grew up with the decline of Indian Buddhism. Borrowing alike from sources old and new, they contain a curious mixture of grotesque legends, gross superstitions, wild flights of reasoning and fancy, ennobling maxims, holy aspirations, flashes of shrewd insight, long trains of close and subtle thought. In respect of mental gifts the later Brahmans were still the true, if perhaps the degenerate, children of their Vedic predecessors. Learned in all the knowledge of their day, but blind perhaps to the poetic origin of the popular theology, they seemed to have aimed at strengthening their hold

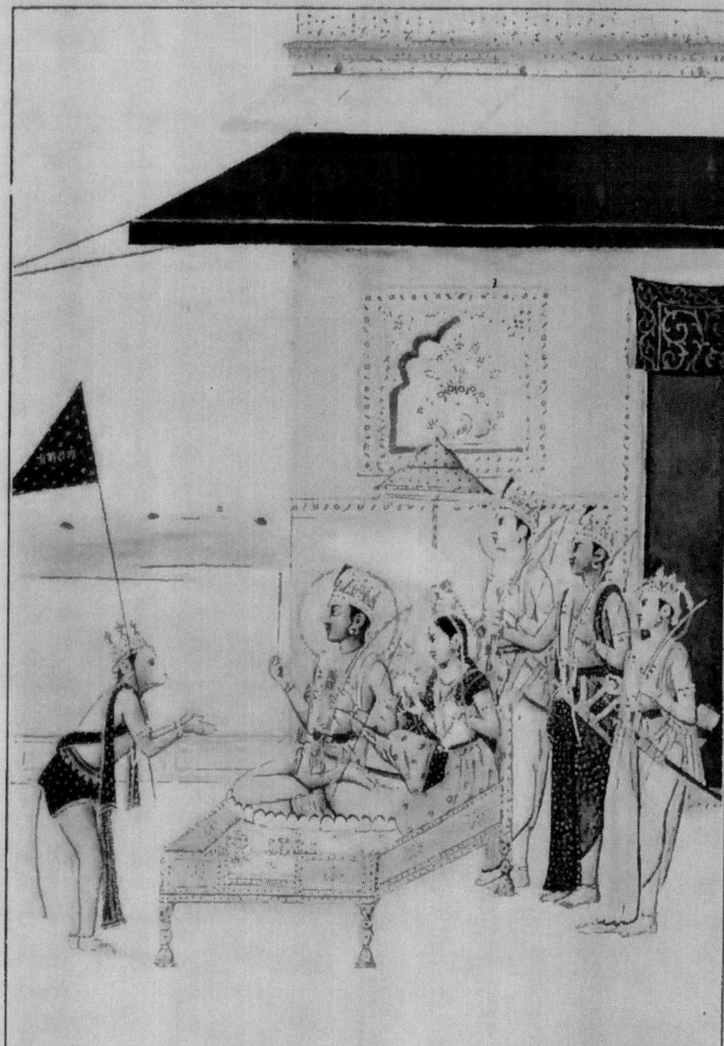

RAMA AND SITA ENTHRONED ATTENDED BY RAMA'S THREE BROTHERS AND THE FAITHFUL HANAUMAN RECEIVING HIS ORDERS

FROM AN ORIENTAL PAINTING IN THE BRITISH MUSEUM

p. 11

upon the people by sanctioning each new perversion of the old ancestral creeds. Under the working of the same law which evolved the later Greek Pantheon out of the simple nature-worship of the days before Homer, the religious poetry of the Vedas had blossomed out into a rank growth of monstrous-seeming legends, fantastic rites, and multiform idolatries. Whatever the Brahmans themselves believed, the popular worship had already hardened into a lifeless caricature of the religion bodied forth in the Vedic Hymns. If the Purānas held that Brahma, Vishnu, and Siva were but different attributes of one same godhead, the people at large were wont to treat them as separate and rival gods, the chief, perhaps, but not the only dwellers on the Indian Olympus.

Vishnu, the Indian Hercules, grew out of a Vedic synonym for the sun into the central figure of a new legendary circle, the divine embodiment of ever so many heroes renowned in song or fable. Hindu poetry is full of his Avatars or manifestations in the flesh. He is a little fish who swells and swells until he spreads for millions of leagues in one golden blaze over the ocean. In the shape of a boar five hundred miles high he plunges his mighty tusks into the waste of waters, and brings up the solid earth from its briny bed. In the memorable Churning of the Ocean, Vishnu as Narāyan recruits the fainting strength of gods and Titans employed in wresting from the deep the lost Ambrosia of the Immortals.*

* The Amrîta, or Drink of Immortality—answering to the Greek Ambrosia—had been lost in the great flood, which, according to Hindu legend, overspread the earth in the days of Manu—himself and the seven Rishis, or sages, floating on the waters in their ship of refuge, until, guided by the fish Vishnu, it rested on the highest peak of Himālaya. When the waters subsided, Brahma, at Vishnu's suggestion, proposed to churn the ocean until it yielded up the lost Amrît. How the Sûrs and Asûrs, the gods and the demons, tearing up the hill Mandar, wound about it the hundred-headed Shesha, the serpent king, for a churning-rope; how, standing on Vishnu's tortoise, they lowered the huge mass into the sea, whirling it round and round,

Again, in man's form with a lion's head, he comes like another Briareus to restore the Indian Jove to his lost throne, and defeat the giants who have conquered the earth. Anon, as Rāma the princely hero of the Rāmāyan, oldest and sweetest of Indian epics, he fights and slays the giant Rāvan, who had carried off to the isle of Lanka his beloved Sita, the faithful partner of his long exile from home and throne. As Krishna, the warrior king of Dwarka in Gujarāt, he is the foremost figure in many an Indian tale of love, war, or bold adventure. His last advent under the form of Buddha, the founder of a rival creed, seems to attest either the readiness of Brahman teachers to reverence old truths preached under new disguises, or else their politic desire to stand well with the people at large by admitting new gods into the old Pantheon; even as the deifying of the dark-skinned Krishna may point to the gradual fusion of old popular legends with those of peculiarly Aryan birth.*

If Vishnu owned and still owns millions of worshippers distributed among divers sects, Siva, the Destroying Principle, evolved from the Vedic Rudra, god of fire and storms, grew into the foremost rival, if not for a time the supplanter of his elder and more gracious brother-god. In some parts of India, temples that once bore the shield

with Vishnu's help, until treasure after treasure rose out of the troubled foam, from the horses of the Sun and the bow of Siva, to Lakshmi, the Indian Venus; how Siva betimes drank up the deadly poison that streamed from the mouth of the fainting Shesha; and how at last two maidens float up from the seething billows, the one bearing the heavenly Amrit, the other a flask of wine, which the heedless Asûrs drink off, to their own confusion;—all this Mr. W. Waterfield has well told in one of the most spirited of his "Indian Ballads." Of this wonderful story, which illustrates the mingled grandeur, wildness, sportive fancy, and tender grace of the best Hindu poetry, the original Sanskrit contains several versions, one of which, as given in the Mahābhārata, has been cleverly versified by Mr. R. H. Griffith, in his "Specimens of Old Indian Poetry."

* The Yādavas, or children of Yādu, were the brethren of Krishna, and the apparent forefathers of the modern Jats, who abound in Upper India.

and club of Vishnu have since been dedicated to the eight-armed bearer of the bow and crescent, whose necklace is threaded with human skulls, whose waist is girdled with serpents, around whose shoulders hangs a raw elephant hide, and whose third eye, placed in the middle of his forehead, betokens the sharpness of his mental vision. If Vishnu may be taken to embody the genial human side of the great World-Spirit called Brahma, the worship of Siva expressed the sterner, wilder attributes of the same unseen mysterious Fountain of all life and death. Stoical or ascetic natures found in the grave and gloomy rites that mark his worship that kind of spiritual comfort which others drew from the worship of the milder god. Chief among Siva's votaries are the Brahmans of Bengal, but it is in Southern India, where the pious Sankara Achārya preached and travelled nine hundred years ago, that the sects which honour Siva have made most way among the people. Of these not the least numerous are the Lingayats who worship Siva under the form of the Lingam, the male emblem of Nature's reproductive powers.

Siva-worship in its turn seems to have begotten new and strange outgrowths in the shape of the fierce goddess Dūrga and the elephant-headed god Ganesha. The former, herself in part evolved from the earlier Pārvati, Siva's queen, presently reappears in the yet sterner guise of Kāli, at whose bloodstained altars the robber tribes of India pay their special homage, and whose favour was besought by the murdering brotherhood of the Thugs. Sita, the faithful wife of Rāma, becomes merged in Sri or Lakshmi, the beautiful and bounteous goddess-queen of Vishnu. Sūrya, the sun-god, Kartikeya, god of war, Yāma, the Indian Pluto, Saraswati, goddess of learning, fill each a certain place in the later Hindu Pantheon. In the natural course of things, new legends, creeds, practices, sprang up to displace or absorb the old. Besides the deities common to all Aryan Hindus, each place or district followed its own rites and bowed down to its own local gods or demons, many of them borrowed from indigenous, or at least non-Aryan sources. In short, the popular worship took its colour and its grosser traits from all the changing circumstances, moral and physical, which have helped to shape the destinies of the Indian peoples.

Chief among the later off-shoots of modern Hinduism was the religious sect founded by the pious Kshatriya Nānak Shah, in the fifteenth century of our era. From time to time there arose in this or that part of India some earnest thinker, who strove to purify and regenerate the popular worship of his day. Buddha himself was not the first by many of those who essayed in India the kind of mission discharged towards their own countrymen by the Jewish prophets and the great religious teachers of Christian Europe. Of like stamp was Sankara Achārya, a native of Malabar, who in the eighth or ninth century of our era proclaimed anew the supreme bliss of perfect communion, through penitence, prayer, and self-sacrifice, between the human soul and the great unseen Spirit whence all things visible have their birth. Such, too, were the leading reformers of the fourteenth, fifteenth, and sixteenth centuries—Rāmanand, the St. Francis, and Vallabhā Swâmin, the Epicurus of India; Dâdu, the cotton-cleaner of Ajmēr, who taught that faith and a pure heart were better than fasting and sacrifice; Khabīr, who denounced the idol-worship and the corrupt doctrines of his day; and Tukārām, the Marātha poet, who preached a new gospel of love towards God and man, of child-like faith in all God's works and ways.

Khabīr, himself the disciple of Rāmanand, seems to have been held in equal honour by Hindus and Muhammadans. His follower Nānak, founder of the Hindu sect of Sikhs which afterwards became the ruling race in the Punjāb, proclaimed the religious brotherhood of the Hindu and the Mussulman in words which reflect the desire of benevolent minds in all ages : "He only is a good Hindu who is just and a good Muhammadan whose life is pure." His teaching was specially levelled against Brahman tyranny and the mixture of forms and superstitions which passed with the multitude for true religion. A succession of Gūrus or High Priests handed on his teaching and swelled the numbers of the new sect. In the Muhammadans, however, who then ruled India, the Sikhs found stern oppressors instead of powerful allies. After nearly a century of persecution they took up arms against the foe under the warlike Gūru Gofind, and after a long course of varying fortune, the peaceful followers of Nānak wielded military rule from the Indus to the Jumna, and held under a yoke of iron the crushed Muhammadans of the Punjāb.

A still later revolt from the popular creed was set on foot in the nineteenth century by the enlightened Hindu Raja, Rammohan Rai. He proclaimed a pure Theism founded on the religious teaching of the Vedas, and enriched with borrowings from the Christianity of the West. His mantle fell on the worthy shoulders of Dwarkanath Tagore, and the *Brahma Samāj*, or Church of Brahma, became the title of a sect which now owns several thousand followers. Some years later a fresh departure from the old faith was taken by the young Brahmist leader, Keshab Chander Sen, whose followers have disowned the last ties of social and religious habit that still bind the Brahmists of the older school to their unreformed countrymen. The Arya Samāj has now 1 per 10,000 of the population, the Brahma 0·1, Christianity 0·79. Later developments show that Brahmanism retains its assimilative power. It endeavours to absorb the most incompatible opinions. It preserves its vitality by what it takes from other religions. The old Hinduism is incapable of revival: it lives only by what it absorbs. And this is seen in the poetry which it produces. India has given birth to a great poet, Sir Rabindranath Tagore, the son of the religious leader Dwarkanath Tagore, who has learnt from the West to produce poetry which appeals to all the world, while it retains the character, embodies the feeling, and immortalises the history of the Indian peoples.

CHAPTER III

EARLY HISTORY OF INDIA

OF the early history of the Aryan Hindus very little is known for certain.* In the time of the older Vedas, they had already gained a firm footing in the broad plains that stretch from the Indus to the Ganges. Coming from the regions beyond the Hindu Kush, the classic Caucasus, they must have taken several centuries to win their way so far eastward; and a list of their old kings, as quoted by Arrian, the Greek historian, would seem to trace their early history as far back as the year 3000 B.C. Of the people whom they conquered or pushed before them we only know that they spoke a different language and belonged to a different, perhaps an older, to all appearance a less civilised race. These latter, the Dāsyus of

* The word Aryan, from Arya, Sanskrit for "noble," is now used to denote the Caucasian, Japhetic, or Indo-European races of men, whose languages, customs, and bodily traits may all be referred to one common type. From some central point in Upper Asia, one Aryan race after another appears to have wandered, either westward into Europe, or southward into Persia and Hindustan. The Celtic races made their way into Greece, Italy, Spain, France, and Britain; the Goths, or Teutons, into Germany, Scandinavia, and England; while the Slavs peopled Russia, Poland, and parts of the Austrian Empire. Persia was peopled by a Zend-speaking branch of the same Aryan family, and India became the heritage of the Sanskrit-speaking Hindus. None of these races can claim to be the parent of the rest; it is not even certain which of them was the eldest brother; but the fact of their common brotherhood, of their common distinction from the Semitic, Mongolic, and other types of men, has been clearly established by the researches of modern science. In the words of Dr. Max Müller, "The terms for God, for house, for father, mother, son, daughter, for dog and cow, for wail and tears, for axe and tree, identical in all the Indo-European idioms, are like the watchwords of soldiers."—"Chips from a German Workshop," vol. i. p. 64.

Aryan song, may once have covered the whole of ancient India; and their descendants, to the number of eleven or twelve millions, make up the various tribes of Bhīls, Gonds, Sānthāls, Kols, Mairs, Minas, Mangs, Kukis, and so forth, which still cleave to their ancestral hills and forests, or roam in quest of a livelihood from place to place. Dark-skinned, short, ugly-featured, with high cheek-bones and scanty beards, these rude, scattered remnants of some aboriginal race differ not more widely in outward shape and language than in tastes, habits, and ways of thinking, from the tall, light-skinned, full-bearded, comely-featured, subtle-brained Hindus of pure Aryan descent. They eat all kinds of food, are partial to strong drinks, know nothing of caste-rules, wear very little clothing, have no written language, no system of regular tillage, worship strange sprites and demons, and lead on the whole a wild, sequestered, unprogressive life. Some tribes however, have learned from contact with their civilised neighbours to move slowly forward in the same direction.

In the course of time the civilised conquerors of Upper India carried their arms and settlements across the great Vindhyan range, which walls off the Deccan, or Southern India, from the plains and deserts of the north. Meanwhile the conquered country had been parcelled out into several kingdoms, such as the Punjāb, Gujarāt, Kanauj, Tirhūt, Magadha, and Gaur or Bengal. It is hopeless trying to pierce the night of poetic fable which surrounds the history of those far-off days. The story of the great war between the Pāndus and the Kurus, as told in the Mahābhārata, the Indian Iliad, has probably as much or as little in it of the historic element as Homer's story of the Siege of Troy.* Not less baffling for historic purposes

* This war, memorable for a great battle, fought for eighteen days, nea[r] Delhi, in which all the tribes of Northern India are described as taking part,

are the events recorded in the yet older Rāmāyan, the Æneid or the Odyssey of Aryan India. Rāma, the hero of Valmīki's graceful epic, and rightful heir by birth to the throne of Ajodhya or Oudh, is doomed by a step-mother's wiles to wander in lonely forests towards the south. His faithful wife Sita shares and cheers his exile, until Rāvan, the demon king of Lanka, or Ceylon, bears her off through the skies to his own palace. Thither, with the help of an army of monkeys, who probably stand for the wild races of Southern India, the bereaved husband follows up the ravisher. A terrible fight ends in the death of Rāvan and the return of Sita to her husband's arms after she has proved her purity by passing unhurt through the ordeal of fire. Rāma, happy and triumphant, reappears in his late father's capital, to enjoy the kingly heritage which his faithful brother Bharat had so long held in trust for the rightful lord.*

What traces of historic truth may be gleaned from this fine old Sanskrit epic are slight and often uncertain. Rāma himself remains a heroic shadow, evolved, like Homer's Achilles, it has been thought, though improbably, from some dim poetic legend of the sun. The story of his wanderings and his southward march to Ceylon, if it has any historic meaning, may point to the progress of Aryan settlement in the regions south of the Narbada. At the time when Valmīki wrote his poem, his Sanskrit-speaking countrymen must have already gained some kind of footing in that part of the great peninsula. If

is supposed to have occurred about 1300 B.C. The poem itself, the work of many authors, contains matter which dates from periods of eight centuries, four before and four after Christ. The Mahābhārata—literally, the mighty Bharat—contains in eighteen books a series of legends concerning the adventures of the children of Pāndu and Kuru descended from Bharat the Great, who reigned at Hastinapur.

* The date of the Rāmāyan is very uncertain; but from internal evidence it would seem to have been composed for the most part before 500 B.C. Both these national epics are still widely read, or chanted, throughout Hindustan.

any trust can be placed in Hindu genealogies, a Pandyan dynasty of northern birth ruled part of Southern India in the ninth century before Christ, and a Chola dynasty, of like origin, sprang up a few centuries later in the modern Carnatic. Ere long Malabar also fell under the sway of Aryan kings; and before the Christian era all India had been colonised or conquered by Sanskrit-speaking Hindus.

They, or their Indian kinsfolk, had even carried their arms and settlement into the islands of Java* and Bāli, and may perhaps, under Buddhist princes, have already become masters of Ceylon, although the conquest of that island by a prince of the great Gupta line dates back only to the fifth century of our era.

Long before that time, in the first century B.C., another race of conquerors had overrun Saurāshtra, the modern Kathiawar. In the country once ruled by Krishna and his Jāt successors, the Sahs, an Aryan tribe from Persia, founded a dynasty which, about four centuries later, gave way to the prowess of the Gupta kings. These latter seem for a time to have wielded over the greater part of India a leadership akin to that which Athens, Sparta, and Thebes successively claimed over the rest of Greece, and which the Bretwaldas of the Saxon Heptarchy wielded over their fellow-princes. The strongest of the Indian rulers for the time being would win for himself the title of Maharaja Adirāj—Lord Paramount of the Old Empire—and that title his successor was free to keep, if he could. It was held from time to time by six of the Gupta princes, whose sway at one period extended from Kathiawar to Ceylon. In the middle of the first century before Christ it was held apparently by Vikram-Aditya, a prince of the Andhra dynasty, whose sway extended from Magadha, the

* Java seems to have derived its name from the Yāvanas; the Javan of Scripture, the Ionian Greeks of history.

erstwhile seat of King Asōka's power, through Central India to the modern Hyderabad in the Deccan. Descended from a powerful Rājput tribe, whom legend traces back to one of four Agnikūl brothers—"Sons of Fire"—evolved by Brahman spells from the sacrificial fires of Mount Abu in Gujarāt, in order to go forth and rescue India from the curse of Buddhism, King Vikram held his court at Ujjain * in Malwa, and became the Harūn al Rashid of Indian story. His great victory over the Shakas—the classic Sacæ—who had swooped down upon the plains of Upper India from the highlands of Kumaun, signalised the early years of a long and glorious reign. In him, after ages cherished the memory of an upright king and a steady partron of art and learning. Later Hindu fabulists were never weary of weaving legends in praise of Indra's god-like grandson, who "brought the whole earth under the shadow of one umbrella," whose court was adorned with the foremost poets and wisest thinkers of his day, and the beginning of whose reign has served to mark a new era in Hindu chronology.† Among those who had the largest share of Vikram's bounty were the "Nine Gems of Science"; one of whom, the poet Kālidāsa, still charms the hearts of his living countrymen with the honied tenderness of his "Messenger Cloud," and the thick-clustering fancies of his dramatic masterpiece, "Sakūntala."

In their victorious march southward the Aryan Hindus appear to have encountered a people almost as civilised as themselves, but speaking a language yet nearer to that primæval tongue of which even Sanskrit was only a later offshoot. These earlier settlers may have built the cromlechs and dolmens, and carved the funeral urns, of which

* Ujjain, one of the seven sacred cities of the Hindus, now belongs to Sindhia, the sovereign of Gwalior. The ruins of the old city lie about a mile to the north of its modern namesake.

† The Sambat era, as established by Vikram, dates from 56 B.C., and is still the recognised era of the Hindu calendar.

so many traces are found in the regions south of the Narbada, where some form of Tāmil is still the prevailing tongue. New invaders in their turn pressed from time to time on the first Aryan settlements in Northern India. Kashmīr, the ancient seat of a Kuru dynasty, was overrun by Scythian tribes, who appear to have mingled their own snake-worship with the Buddhism already imported thither.* Later still a Tartar dynasty ruled in their stead, and bequeathed to its own successors some noble monuments of architectural skill. Other tribes, whether of Scythian or Tartar origin, left their mark upon the country watered by the Ganges and the Brahmapūtra, and even made their way down the seaboard of Orissa. Tradition likewise tells of the Yāvans, whose name marks their Ionic or Greek extraction, as founding settlements in Kashmīr and Sind, and finally, in our own era, ruling Orissa for a century and a half.

Amid all such events, however, the candid historian must still grope his way with much care and many misgivings, content to rescue a few waifs of seeming fact from the darkness that everywhere broods around him. To trace events in their proper sequence becomes a hopeless task when the events themselves are shrouded in deceitful twilight, or lost in a tangle of decayed traditions. How much are we to believe, for instance, of that old story, which represents the Assyrian queen Semiramis as leading her myriads of horse and foot over the Indus, with thousands of camels disguised as elephants, whose panic-flight before the real elephants hurled against them by King Stabrobates caused the invading hosts to scatter in disastrous rout? The story itself, however, unknown to the travelled

* The term *Scythian* has often been misemployed as a synonym for *Tartar* or *Tibetan*. In point of fact the true Scythian belonged to a pure Aryan stock; perhaps to that branch of it, the Gothic, which furnished the forefathers of Saxon England.

Herodotus, and incredible in the shape traced out by the pens of Ctesias and Diodorus, need not perhaps be absolutely untrue. Nor is there anything quite impossible in the story of a much more successful inroad, accomplished in the tenth century before Christ by the troops of the Egyptian Rameses II.

There is surer ground for believing in a partial conquest of India by the troops of the Persian Darius Hystaspes, a near successor to the throne of Cyrus the Great. Fired by glowing tales of the rich and populous countries which his admiral Scylax had passed through on his memorable voyage down the Indus, that monarch carried his arms across the same river, as far as the great desert which divides Sind from Rājputāna. He created a satrapy out of the conquered province which must have included the whole of Sind and perhaps a large part of the Punjāb.*

About two centuries later a yet more famous conqueror stood upon the banks of the river, whence India has derived its name. Master of Persia on the defeat and subsequent death of Darius, the last king of his line, Alexander the Great of Macedon pushed his way steadily onwards through Balkh and Afghānistān, over the mountains of the Hindu Kush, through the rugged gorges of the Khyber, fighting and massacring as he went, capturing Massaga (probably near the Malakand pass) and the virgin fortress of Aornos, until his war-worn legions reached the Indus flowing in swift stream, which he crossed at Ohind, sixteen miles above Attock. Between the Indus and the Jhelum—the classic Hydaspes—he met only with friends, one of whom, the King of Taxila, appears to have offered his own aid against his powerful neighbour, Poros or Puru, whose sway extended from the Jhelum to Hastinapur on the Ganges. The youthful conqueror of Greece, Persia,

* See Mr. Vincent Smith's "Early History of India," 3rd edition, p. 38.

and Babylon, caught with his usual eagerness at a bait so tempting. Two hostile armies soon faced each other on the banks of the swollen Hydaspes, at a spot since memorable for the passage of the troops with which General Gilbert followed up Lord Gough's crowning victory over the Sikhs at Gujrāt. On the left bank of the river just below where it branches into several streams, Poros had arrayed his host, the flower of the warrior-tribes of Upper India. Alexander's strategy, however, served him well. Under cover of a dark stormy night, he carried a choice body of troops over the several branches of the main stream, and with the first streaks of morning bore swiftly down upon his opponent's flank and rear. Poros discovered the movement too late; but the courage with which he maintained a hopeless struggle, after half his troops had left the field, won for him the forbearance of a conqueror in whose ambition there was nothing mean. Treating the captive monarch, as Poros himself had asked to be treated, "like a king," Alexander took him into friendship, restored him to his throne, and even enlarged his frontiers with new conquests.

After founding two cities (Bonkephala, probably identical with the modern Jhelum, and Sikaia, perhaps Sukhchainpur) on the scene of his late successes, the conqueror led most of his troops across the Chenāb and the Rāvi or Hydraotes. On the left bank of the Hydraotes he encountered a large but ill-disciplined force gathered together, it seems, from the neighbouring hills. This he routed with heavy slaughter, in spite of a brave defence. Pushing on to the Sutlej—the classic Hyphasis—he would have carried his veterans even to Pataliputra the far-famed capital of Magadha, the Gangetic kingdom then ruled by a Takshak* prince of the Nanda dynasty,

* The word "Takshak" seems to imply the settlement of a Daco-Scythian people in the valley of the Ganges.

which had flourished there for nearly four hundred years. But the men who had followed him so far in quest of the world's easternmost bounds at length refused to go an inch further. Daunted by their attitude, or moved by their just complaints, Alexander unwillingly prepared to retrace his steps. He set up twelve great monuments, as altars to the gods, which may perhaps still remain by the ancient bed of the river Bias. Leaving Poros, it is said, in command of seven nations and two thousand cities and in alliance with the King of Taxila, he then led his tired soldiers back to the Jhelum. At the point where it receives the waters of the Chenāb, not far from Multān, he himself with part of his army embarked for a voyage down that river to its junction with the Indus, and then down the Indus to the sea, whilst his lieutenants, Hephæstion and Krateros, marched along either bank to the appointed meeting-place. A journey of several months, imperilled by the attacks of hostile tribes, and memorable for the storming of a stronghold defended by the Malloi, the people of Multān, brought the whole army to the sea-coast. Here Alexander once more divided his forces. While one wing, under Nearchos, sailed along the shores of the Indian Ocean and the Persian Gulf to the mouth of the Euphrates, he himself, with the other, marched along the coast amid the dreary sandhills of the Gedrosian desert, known to later times as Balūchistān. After his safe return to Susa, the great Macedonian still cherished the hope of one day planting his standard on the banks of the Ganges, of bringing the farthest marts of India into close commercial fellowship with the valley of the Euphrates and his new Egyptian capital on the Mediterranean. But the fever which slew him at Babylon, three years afterwards, in the thirty-third year of his age, cut short his career of conquest, and put off for many centuries the fulfilment of his schemes for the worldly advancement of the human race.

His work, however, was not destined to be all in vain. The voyage of Nearchos, itself in those days a feat of bold seamanship, prepared the way for new voyages of discovery, which finally laid the whole coast of Western India open to Greek adventurers from the Red Sea and the Persian Gulf. If Alexander's empire fell to pieces on his death, the ablest of his generals founded Greek dynasties which long held sway over its component provinces. If Babylon gave place to Seleucia on the Tigris, as the great mart of trade with the countries eastward of Mesopotamia, Alexandria, under the Ptolemies grew apace into the first commercial capital of the civilised world, the common reservoir for the trade of three continents. Greek art inspired some of the noblest, if not the earliest, efforts of Indian architects and sculptors, as traceable in the great Buddhist domes whose ruined masses still meet the eye, here and there, on the road from Kabul through the Punjāb to the banks of the Kistna. Greek coins discovered in Afghān, Punjābi, and Turkman cities, recall the days when Greek Seleucidæ and their successors reigned over a Bactrian kingdom, stretching at one time from Lahore to Samarkand.

When the first Seleucus had laid firm hold on the eastern provinces of Alexander's empire, he turned his arms against Chandragupta—the Sandracottos of Greek historians—who had annexed the kingdom of Magadha to the country erewhile ruled by Poros and the King of Taxila. But the able Greek soon found good reason to make peace with the powerful Sudra monarch, who remained master of all Alexander's conquests eastward of the Indus, in return for a yearly tribute of fifty elephants, and a marriage alliance with his late foe. A Greek envoy, Megasthenes, lived for many years at his court in Pataliputra,* and bore memorable witness to the peace, order,

* The site of this great city, ten miles long by two broad, with its sixty

ASOKA PILLAR

FROM V. A. SMITH'S "STUDENT'S HISTORY OF INDIA

p. 22

well-doing, and high enlightenment that prevailed throughout the realm. His son, Bindusara, renewed the treaties with Seleucus, and after a reign of twenty-five years handed on the sceptre of the Mauryan line to his like-minded heir Asōka, *c.* 273–232 B.C., the extent of whose sway is marked by the stone pillars engraved in Pāli, the spoken Sanskrit of his day, which have been traced from Orissa even to Kābul. During his long reign of thirty-seven years this wise and beneficent ruler made justice easy of access to the poorest of his subjects, and outdid even his grandfather in the success of his efforts to encourage trade, learning, and every civilised art. The first Indian monarch who openly embraced Buddhism, he may have presided also at the birth of that new architecture which tells its own tale of Greek example, moulding the handiwork of the earliest native architects in stone.*

He sent missions beyond the frontier of his territories, to Ceylon, as well as to the Tāmil kingdoms of the south. "In this way Buddhism, which had been merely the creed of a local Indian sect, became one of the chief religions of the world, a position which, in spite of many ups and downs, it still holds." †

Fifty years after the death of Asōka, which happened about 232 B.C., the great Mauryan dynasty gave place to that of the Sunga princes, who displayed their zeal for the faith of Buddha by building massive "topes" and hewing out majestic cave temples in many parts of their broad

gates, 574 towers, and moat thirty cubits deep, is placed by Mr. Vincent Smith at Patna.

* According to Mr. James Fergusson ("Tree and Serpent Worship"), the great Buddhist "tope" at Sanchi in Malwa is the oldest known specimen of pure stone architecture in Hindustan, and is one of many built by Asōka in honour of Sākyamūni. General Cunningham, however, would assign it a much earlier date. Be that as it may, its gateways were evidently built at a time when stone was beginning to supersede wood for building purposes; and its sculptures show clear traces of Greek influence.

† Vincent Smith, "Student's History of India," 1915, p. 68.

realm. These, in their turn, were succeeded about a century later by the Andhra line. Under its wide sway the greater part of India seems to have flourished for nearly five hundred years. It may have been a king of this line, perhaps Vikram himself, whom Strabo has described as sending an embassy to Cæsar Augustus at Antioch, a few years after Actium had made Julius' nephew master of nearly all the civilised world. Another embassy to the same potentate appears to have been sent about the same time by a certain "King Pandion," a prince, no doubt, of the old Pandyan dynasty whose reign of two thousand years over part of Southern India ceased only with the Muhammadan Conquest.

It was about a century later that some ripples from the wave of a new religious movement, whose birthplace was Judæa, first broke out upon the farthest shores of Southern India. Tradition, at any rate, points with some show of likelihood to Mailapur, or Mount St. Thomas, near Madras, as the last resting-place of India's first Christian teacher, St. Thomas the Apostle.* In the second century of our era Demetrius, Bishop of Alexandria, sent forth the eloquent Pantænus to visit and instruct the native Christians of Malabar, whose desire for further knowledge of the new Gospel some Egyptian sailors had brought to his ears. Two centuries later, we find John, Metropolitan of Persia, claiming authority over the Christian Churches in Southern India. In the sixth century a Christian bishop, consecrated in Persia, governs his Indian flock from Kaliānpur, near Mangalore, and Christian villages are discovered even in

* The tradition in question was already old in the time of St. Jerome, who in the fourth century A.D., speaks of the Divine Word as being everywhere present, "with Thomas in India, with Peter at Rome, &c." Long before then, in the second century of our era, happened the mission of Pantænus to the Christians of Malabar, as described by Clemens Alexandrinus. A useful sketch of the early Christian Church of Malabar may be found in Rev. J. Lobley's "The Church and Churches in Southern India," chap. iv. But see Mr. Vincent Smith's "Early History of India," pp. 233 seq.

Ceylon. In the latter part of the eighth century we see the Christians of Malabar living in peace and comfort under a king of the Chēra dynasty, and driving a busy trade with Persia and Egypt.

About a century and a half later two Syrian priests from Babylon reach Southern India on a mission from their Persian Metropolitan, and make new converts in the country ruled by the friendly Raja of Travancore. For some part of the tenth century a Christian raja seems to have reigned in Malabar. In the course of years the Churches of Southern India mixed up with their own simple doctrines some of the ideas and usages that prevailed among their neighbours, or were imported by missionaries from the Latin Church. In the last year of the sixteenth century the long struggle of the native Christians against the claims of the Portuguese Archbishop of Goa ends in the temporary triumph of the Roman rule. Fifty years later one-half of Rome's new subjects threw off the yoke they had never loved, and renewed their old allegiance to the Patriarch of Antioch. To this day the Church of St. Thomas, however shattered and defaced by time and human error, still owns many thousand worshippers who, whether in doctrine or discipline, have never bowed the knee to Rome.

Let us return for a moment to the Indo-Macedonian kingdom of Bactria. Among the kings of the dynasty which, about 256 B.C., succeeded that of the Seleucidæ, a prominent place is due to Demetrios, who reconquered the western provinces of the Punjāb ; to his successor Eukratides, who carried his arms still further eastward ; and to Menander, whose sway extended over the Punjāb and Sind. In the beginning of the first century before Christ, the Greek rule in Bactria and the adjacent provinces gives place to a succession of dynasties, Scythian, Parthian, Turkish, and Hindu, of all which some traces have been bequeathed to us in the coins discovered and deciphered by modern research. Each change of dynasty is marked by a change in the language of the legends borne upon the coins. Greek gives place to Sanskrit, which is followed in its turn by later forms of Aryan, Turanian, or Semitic speech. From some of these faithful witnesses to the past we learn that as late as the eighth century of our era Indian princes still reigned over the country westward of the Indus, from Sind up to Kābul.*

* See Professor Wilson's "Ariana"; Prinsep's "Historical Results," &c., and Mr. Vincent Smith's "Early History of India."

CHAPTER IV

CIVILISATION OF ARYAN INDIA

DURING the long period of which we have thus far spoken, Aryan India seems to have filled a commanding, if not the very highest place among the civilised races of that old time. In almost every field of mental, social, and political life, the early Hindus long kept ahead of their Western kinsfolk. Centuries before Pericles ruled or Plato wrote, their village communities had proved their extraordinary fitness for the work of governing themselves. In the sphere of philosophy they rose to heights of speculation hardly matched by the most daring subtleties of Aristotle, Spinoza, Berkeley or Kant. Their moral and religious theories involved some of the highest truths conceivable by human wisdom. As subtle thinkers and keen logicians they have never been surpassed. Their oldest poem, the Rāmāyan, teems with tender and holy thoughts, glows all over with examples of every virtue, is crowded with pictures of fatherly and fraternal love, of filial submission, of wifely purity, faithfulness, self-surrender, of manly tenderness, courage, firmness, long-suffering, of sexual love free from all earthlier taint, of domestic harmony, social well-being, of unaffected pleasure in the beautiful things of earth and air and human handiwork. Their earliest writings, whether in verse or prose, reveal the great progress made by a large-brained, supple-witted race in the arts that dignify, adorn, and sweeten life.

In astronomy the Hindus of the Rig-Veda had already

learned to mark out the moon's path through the constellations, to divide the zodiac into twelve signs or stations answering to the months, and seasons of the year, to measure time by weeks, months, and solar years, to follow the movements of the planets, and to fix with some precision the date of each recurring equinox and solstice. A few centuries later their wise men had begun to calculate eclipses, to mark the precession of the equinoxes, to measure the orbits of the moon and planets; and sought, not quite in vain, to account for the apparent rising and setting of the sun. Still later, in the sixth century of our era, Aryabhaṭa was perhaps the first in India who taught the spinning of the earth around its own axis, and who hit upon the true theory of solar and lunar eclipses.* He has been called, indeed, the founder of mathematical and astronomical science in India; and certain it is, that whatever help he may have derived from older Greek researches in those fields, his own discoveries and improvements more than repaid the debt.

In the twelfth century of our era Bhāskar-Achārya of Ujjain had forestalled by five hundred years the analytical methods of Newton and Leibnitz. Long before his day, centuries even before Aryabhata, the Hindus had begun to work out many of the higher problems in algebra. In arithmetic they invented decimals, and the letters of the Sanskrit alphabet supplied the numerals which modern Europe derived directly from Arabia. Their medical writings prove their early proficiency in the art of healing. They seem to have been clever surgeons, shrewd in detecting the sources and symptoms of disease, alive to the saving virtues of proper diet. They knew the value of human dissection,† and the medicinal uses of mercury

* He was born near Patna about A.D. 476.

† The practice of dissection was greatly hampered, of course, by the strength of religious prejudice.

and other minerals. Inoculation for small-pox seems to have been known to them from a very early age. Their chemical knowledge was far from despicable. Greek and Arabic physicians borrowed freely from the medical science of India; and the Khalifs of Baghdad, especially the far-famed Harūn al Rashid, set no little store by the Hindu physicians who visited or held posts in their court.*

From the days of Manu's Code, ancient India possessed a noteworthy system of law which, after weathering the Muhammadan Conquest, still guides and bounds the latest efforts of Anglo-Indian law-makers. In the study of grammar, or word-lore in its highest and widest sense, the Hindus were deeply versed as far back as the sixth or seventh century before Christ. Their grammar, like their astronomy, may have sprung from the depth of their religious instincts. If the need of fixing the exact time for a given sacrifice first made them astronomers, the duty of understanding what they prayed or chanted led them, it seems, to study the meanings, origins, and arrangement of words. Their oldest known lexicon, a work even now of acknowledged value, must have been written more than two thousand years ago. Their early literature, viewed as art-work, ranks second only to that of ancient Greece. The one bears to the other the same kind of relation which some great Hindu temple bears to the Parthenon. An old Sanskrit play, poem, or romance, if it lacks the severe symmetry, the classic grace of Homer or Sophocles, recalls the teeming luxuriance of an Eastern landscape, filled with the weird sheen of a tropical moon. At once the wildest dreamers and the most subtle of thinkers, the old Hindus produced great poets, philosophers, fabulists, story-tellers, but not one historian of even the smallest mark. "Sweet Sakūntala" was the

* Mrs. Manning's "Ancient and Mediæval India," vol. i. chap. 18.

delight of Germany's greatest poet. The "Hitopadesa, or Fables of Pilpay," have during the last twelve centuries been translated into almost every civilised tongue.* The epics of Valmīki, Vyāsa, and Kālidāsa; the dramatic, lyrical, and pastoral poems of Kālidāsa, Bhavabhūti, Jayadeva; the collection of prose stories preserved from an immemorial past, all attest the range and fruitfulness of the Hindu imagination, and abound with passages unsurpassed for beauty by any writings in the world. Only for the Muse of History does Aryan India provide no pedestal. Roaming childlike in a marvellous dreamland, gazing with rapt eye into the essence and the mystery of things, or clothing with ideal graces the scenes and characters of its pourtraying, the Hindu mind seems to have always spurned the cold rules of historic inquiry, to have treated past dates and events as mere aids to the weaving of poetic fancies, or religious fables. Indian chronology, such as it is, deals with myriads and even millions of years; while the kings and heroes of Indian story live to an age far beyond that of any recorded in the Jewish Scriptures.

Hindu plays were often accompanied by music of a sweet and plaintive kind, and the pathetic airs of Bengal have been likened by Sir William Jones to the wild but charming melodies of the Scotch Highlanders. In the sister arts of sculpture and architecture the old Hindus attained a pitch of excellence to which the ruined *topes* of Sānchi in Mālwa and Amrāvāti on the Kistna, the cave temples of Karle, Ajanta, Ellora, and Elephanta, the pagodas of Tanjore and Mahābalipur, bear memorable witness.† The carven pillars and gateways of Sānchi

* A still older version of the "Hitopadesa" was found by Professor Wilson in the *Panchatantra*, or "Five Sections," which coincides in the main with the work ascribed to Pilpay or Bidpai.

† The old Buddhist topes, of great but still undefined antiquity, were almost solid domes of brick or stone and plaster, rising out of a low basement, and crowned by a pillared *Thee* or relic-box, over which

come midway between the art of Greece and Egypt; and the friezes of Amrāvāti, a few centuries younger, have the rich variety and flowing life-like grace that mark the sculptures of mediæval Europe. In the rock-hewn halls and temples of the same or of somewhat later times, the massive pillars are often relieved with tasteful fretwork, and the broad flat roofs panelled out with carved and coloured scrolls, as graceful as those that adorn the Baths of Titus, and the best houses in Pompeii. The Vihāras, or convents of Ajanta, near Bombay, contain fresco paintings of high merit, whose age may be reckoned at fourteen hundred years. Grandeur of form, combined with no small beauty of detail, distinguishes many of the old temples in Southern India. The Great Pagoda of Tanjore, dating from the tenth century of our era, tapers upward through story after story to a height of two hundred feet. The wondrous temple of Halibēd in Mysore, built by a Brahman architect for a Jain king, is carved all over with designs of such exquisite beauty that they still form models for the carved sandal-wood of that province.* Orissa, famed for the worship of Jagannath, and rich in architectural remains, can boast of a temple at Bhubaneswar eleven or twelve centuries old, unsurpassed for lofty and solid grandeur. In Rājputāna the temples of Baroli and Chitōr claim special notice for the delicate fulness and classic grace of their sculptured details. The massive ruins of pillared temples in Kashmīr carry us back to the first centuries of our era, and seem to attest the influence of Greek upon Indian art. India, in short, abounds in architectural remains of exceeding

stood the mystic "umbrella." The tope, which served as a burial-vault, a relic-shrine, or a sort of temple, was usually surrounded by a rail of massive stone-work, richly sculptured, and divided by four tall gateways. (Fergusson's "Tree and Serpent Worship.")

* Bowring's "Eastern Experiences"; Fergusson's "History of Architecture."

beauty and great age, in the shape of temples, palaces, tanks, colonnades, bridges, castles, and fortified towns, many of which in the beginning of the fifth century charmed the gaze of the Chinese traveller Fa Hien.

In works of engineering skill, Southern India appears to have excelled from the earliest times. The tanks and reservoirs, which everywhere feed the country with water gathered from a thousand streams and from skies laden with tropical moisture, are often of vast size, with stone-faced embankments fifty feet wide, and sluices admirably fitted for their work. In old days, when iron was plentiful, India won the name she has not yet lost for skill in the making of fine steel. The best of the Damascus blades have been traced to the workshops of Western India. For skilful or artistic workmanship in gold, silver, and other metals, in ivory, earthenware, muslins, woollens, brocades, and precious stones, the artisans of India were renowned ages before our English forefathers landed in Britain. From the earliest recorded dates the Hindus appear to have been active merchants, neat-handed workmen, and patient farmers. It is probable that the gold of Ophir,* it is certain that the spicery borne by Arab traders to Egypt in the time of Joseph, came from Indian marts. The pepper of modern trade is still called by its old Indian name. It was out of Indian ivory that Phidias carved his statues of Minerva and the Olympian Jove.† Indigo, as its name denotes, was an old Indian product, known to Europe in the time of Pliny, if not before. From the same country came the sugar, which, introduced into Europe by Greek merchants, betrays its Indian

* According to Max Müller, Ophir was the same as Malabar.

† From the Sanskrit *ibha* came the Latin *ebur* and our *ivory*. The Greek *elephas* may be another form of the same word. "India mittit ebur," "Quicquid gemmarum prodiga mittit India;" "Præbet odoratas quia discolor India messes," are among the references that crop up in the Latin poetry of the Augustan age.

origin in the name it still bears throughout the civilised world.*

In the first century of our era rich streams of merchandise flowed from many a port of Western India to feed the growing luxury of Imperial Rome. Long before then, as we know from Manu's Code, Indian bankers issued their bills of exchange, and merchants insured their ventures by land and sea. Their character for enterprise, honesty, and shrewdness, stood high in the days of Marco Polo, who visited Southern India a few years before its great wealth in gold and jewels tempted the first inroads of Muhammadan conquerors. Then, as now, the fish-charmers on the Coromandel coast levied a handsome profit from the pearl-divers, whose safety they pretended by their magical arts to secure. Already Arab pirates were preying on the sea-borne trade of the country, and all direct intercourse between India and Europe had long since come to an end. But a busy trade had sprung up with China and Japan, while the cotton, indigo, hides, agates, and fine muslins of Gujarāt, the pepper, ginger, and peacocks of Quilon, the diamonds of Golconda, the "woven-air" muslins of Masulipatam, the pearls of Tanjore, still made their way through Egypt and Mesopotamia to the West.

The practice of Sāti or widow-burning, which Marco Polo found in full swing, appears to have been unknown in the days of Alexander. It was certainly unknown to the Hindus of the Vedic period. As far back as the reign of Chandragupta, the country was covered with thriving villages, relieved here and there by royal cities of vast circuit and stately adornment. Pataliputra, the capital of that monarch's realm, is said to have been ten miles long and two broad, with sixty gates, and more than five hundred

* Our word "sugar," German *Zucker*, Greek *saccharon*, evidently came from the Sanskrit and Persian "shakhar."

towers along its outer wall. According to the author of the Rāmāyan, the ancient city of Ajodhya, near the modern Fyzabad, had a length of twenty-four and a depth of three miles. Broad roads, some of them lined with canals, ran past noble squares, smiling gardens, well-built houses, stately temples, and palaces alive with splendid pageantry. Chariots, wagons, elephants, horses, streamed to and fro, bearing choice merchandise, "gay sleek people" in quest of pleasure, envoys from distant kings, or "bands of heroes skilled in every warlike weapon." Everywhere busy artisans plied their calling, holy men chanted the Vedas, damsels danced and minstrels sang their verses to the music of tabret and lute. The poorest man in the city earned for his day's labour a piece of gold. The women, says the poet, were fair to see, graceful, modest, of a charming wit; and each man was the loyal husband of one wife. Such are the leading strokes of a picture which, however coloured by the poet's fancy, may yet be taken for something like a fair presentment of Hindu life and manners thirty centuries ago.*

* The "Rāmāyan," translated into English verse by R. T. H. Griffith, M.A. Book I. cantos 5 and 6.

BOOK II

THE MUHAMMADAN PERIOD

CHAPTER I

EARLY MUHAMMADAN CONQUESTS, A.D. 664—1288

FOR several hundred years of our era no new invader seems to have gained a firm footing on Indian ground. In the middle of the sixth century, indeed, during the reign of Chosroes, or Nushirvān the Just, the greatest Persian king of the Sassanid line, who fought successfully against Justinian himself, the Persian arms were carried for a while into the Rājput territory of Surat. But Goha, the son of the Rājput queen, appears in due time to have regained his lost inheritance, and from his marriage with the granddaughter of the Persian king sprang a line of princes whose descendants still rule in Udaipur.

A hundred years later, when the Arab followers of Muhammad had already overrun Persia, conquered Egypt, Syria, Mesopotamia, and planted the standard of the crescent in a few years after Muhammad's death on the banks of the Oxus, they proceeded to turn their arms against the countries watered by the Indus.* In the

* "There is no God but Allah, and Muhammad is his Apostle." Such was the substance of the doctrine preached to his countrymen by Muhammad, the whilom hermit of Mount Hira, the high-born son of Abdallah, an Arab chief of the great Koreish tribe at Mecca. Born about A.D. 570, Mahomet—or more correctly Muhammad—began in his fortieth year to declare himself a messenger sent by God to turn his

year 664, the forty-second after the Prophet's flight to Medina, an Arab army marched from Basrah, on the Tigris, into Sind, while another, in quest of proselytes and plunder, set out for Kābul. The conquest of ancient Bactria seems to have been completed in fifty years, but Aryan India proved a harder morsel to swallow. Little, save the plunder of a few towns, was gained in this first inroad by the soldiers of Khalif Moāwiyah. A more successful attack on Sind was conducted in 711 by Muhammad bin Kāsim, who, in requital of some wrong said to have been sustained by the crew of an Arab merchant-ship, sailed up the Indus as far as Alōr, the capital of the Sindian Raja, slaying him and his bravest Rājputs in their last hopeless sally from the hard-pressed town, and storming several other cities by the way. Dahir's brave queen, preferring death to dishonour, perished in the flames of her own palace; but one of her daughters lived, it seems, to grace the haram of an Arab Khalif, and to avenge, as the story goes, her father's fall, by causing the disgrace or death of his conqueror, Muhammad bin Kāsim, who had meanwhile been carrying his master's arms and religion into the

countrymen back from their idol-worship to the true faith as handed down by Abraham, Moses, and Jesus Christ. Belief and thorough trust in one righteous God, who rewards each man hereafter according to his deserts, formed the groundwork of a new religion which, as developed in the Korān, became the one fountain of moral, social, and civil law to many millions of Muhammad's followers in every age. Reviled, persecuted, threatened with death by his fellow-citizens, the prophet of Islām in 622 fled with a few score kinsmen and disciples to Medina, where the growing numbers and strength of his converts ere long tempted him to draw the sword, at first in self-defence, presently for the wide extension of his spiritual sway. Before his death in 632, all Arabia had submitted to his rule, and the Byzantine emperor, Heraclius, had been threatened with an attack on his eastern provinces. Twelve years afterwards Persia was conquered by the generals of Khalif Omar, the second of Muhammad's successors, whose sway already included Syria and Egypt. A few years later Bactria shared the same fate, and the Muhammadan arms and faith were carried to the Indus. Early in the next century Spain itself succumbed to the Arab invader. In every case the conquered people had to choose between "the Koran, tribute, or the sword."

neighbouring kingdom of Gujarāt. Perhaps, however, his defeat by the Rājput chivalry of Chitōr, in Mewār, had more connection than Arab chroniclers might care to own with his disappearance from the scene of his first successes. Certain it is that by the middle of the eighth century not a trace of Arab rule was to be found in Western India.

Once more, in A.D. 812, the countrymen of Muhammad, under Mahmūd, governor of Khurāsān, a son or kinsman of the great Harūn al Rashid, crossed swords with the Rājput warriors of Chitōr. But Kāmrān, great-grandson of him who had routed Muhammad bin Kāsim, summoned to his aid the princes of Northern India, and once more the old Hindu prowess drove back the Muhammadan invader beyond the Indus and the Sulaimān Hills. Thenceforth for more than a century and a half the peace of India remained unbroken by enemies from without, and the Hindus might claim the honour of having been the first to roll back that tide of conquest which had hitherto marked the progress of Islām.

Their day of suffering, however, was to come at last; but not from the Arab masters of Baghdad. About the year 913 Ismael Samāni, a Turk of that race which has since ruled or roved from Constantinople to Pekin,* founded at Bokhāra a dynasty which for the next hundred and twenty years held sway over Khurāsān and other outlying provinces once ruled by the Khalifs of Baghdad. The fifth prince of this Samānid line had a Turkish slave named Alptigin, who won his way to the government of Ghazni, between Kandahār and Kābul, in Afghānistān. On the death of his master, Abd-al-Malik, in 961, Alptigin voted against the son's claim to succeed his father.

* The Turks of modern parlance are a mere branch of that Turanian race, which has given its name to Eastern and Western Turkestan, and furnished, in the forms of Attila, Chingiz Khan, and Timur, some of the greatest conquerors and most terrible scourges of mediæval Europe and Asia.

Suspected of intrigues against the new king, he retired to Ghazni, defeated the troops sent out against him, and finally carved out for himself an Afghan kingdom, which fell in 977 to his favourite slave and son-in-law, Sabuktigin.

At this time the country on the left bank of the Indus was ruled by a Hindu sovereign, whose capital was Lahore. In order to forestall the real or assumed designs of his Turkish neighbour, King Jaipāl marched a large army across the Indus to Laghmān, on the road from Peshāwar to Kābul. The hostile armies were face to face, when a sudden storm spread such dismay among his superstitious troops, that the Hindu monarch was driven to purchase a safe retreat by the surrender of fifty elephants and the promised payment of a large sum of money.

On his return to Lahore, however, Jaipāl refused to pay the price of his salvation, and put the Muhammadan envoys into prison. It was an evil hour for India when he preferred the crooked counsels of his priests to those of the high-minded warriors who urged him not to break his kingly word.

After disposing of his other enemies, the angry Tartar once more hastened towards the Indus, seeking vengeance for the insult offered him through his ambassadors. Once more the hostile armies confronted each other at Laghmān. On Jaipāl's side were arrayed the flower of the Hindu chivalry, their numbers swollen by contingents from Delhi, Ajmēr, Kalanjar and Kanauj. The abler general, however, won the day. An obstinate fight ended in the utter rout of Jaipāl's warriors, the plunder of their vast camp, and the subjugation of the Peshāwar valley.

Thus began that new career of Muhammadan conquest, which led in due time to the subjection of all India under the Mughals. Mahmūd of Ghazni, Sabuktigin's son and successor, was not long in gratifying alike his ambition and his religious zeal by a series of inroads amongst the rich idolators of Hindustan. In November, 1001, his fiery Turks and Afghāns once more overthrew with heavy slaughter the myriads of horse and foot that barred his progress through the Peshāwar valley. Their aged leader, the luckless Jaipāl, himself a prisoner at the close of that fatal day, was ere long set free on condition of paying his conqueror an annual tribute. But pride or reverence for the customs of his forefathers impelled the Raja to court an early death in the flames of his own funeral pile; and his son Anandpāl mounted the tottering throne of Kashmīr and Lahore.

One of his feudatories, the Raja of Bhatnaīr,* on the northern edge of what is now the Bikaner Desert, refused to pay his share of the promised tribute. Mahmūd turned upon him with his wonted energy; but Bijai Rai and his bold Rājputs fought with the desperate courage of their race, and not till after many repulses did the Iconoclast Sultān of Ghazni succeed in driving them into their last stronghold. At length the Raja slew himself in his despair, and his forfeit realm was annexed to the dominions of the conqueror. For the latter, fresh work had meanwhile been cut out by the rebel governor of Multān, which had passed some time before under the Muhammadan yoke. This business settled and a Tartar inroad from Kāshgar promptly repelled, Mahmūd once more set out to punish the Raja of Lahore for help given to the Sultān's foes.

Again a great Hindu army, gathered from all parts of Upper India, and equipped with the aid of money raised on the gold and jewels of patriotic Hindu women, crossed the Indus and spread out in magnificent array over the

* It was once the chief city of Bhatiāna, or the land of the Bhatis, an old Rājput tribe, traces of whose former civilisation are still found in the many ruined towns and villages scattered over the sandy wastes.

broad plain that stretches up to the Khyber. For forty days the armies faced each other. At length the Hindus advanced to the attack, or, as some say, to meet a feint attack on the part of Mahmūd, whose skilful soldiership made up for his inferior numbers. For a time fortune smiled on Anandpāl. His strong contingent of wild highlanders from Kashmīr soon drove the Turkish archers back to their entrenchments; the main line of Hindus swept forward as sure of victory over the hated Muslim, when suddenly the elephant ridden by Anandpāl himself took fright at the arrows and burning naphtha-balls, and fled. Other elephants followed his example. Quick to profit by the consequent disorder, Mahmūd hurled his Tartar horsemen in masses upon the foe. That day their swords drank deep of blood, if it be true that twenty thousand of Anandpāl's soldiers perished on the field.

The plunder of Nagarkot (Bhimnagar) and its richly-endowed temples sufficed the conqueror for that present. Three years later, however, he swooped down upon the yet holier shrines of Thanesar, in the Karnal district, only sixty miles from Delhi itself. Before the Hindu princes could rally to its defence, Mahmūd was on his way home, laden with untold wealth in gold and jewels, while two hundred thousand captives, say the Arab chroniclers, were sold as slaves among the people of Ghazni. Still thirsting for fresh plunder, the Muslim hordes, in the name of their Prophet, swept down the Jumna as far as Muttra, in the year 1017, and carried off the gold and silver idols from a hundred shrines, besides levying rich tribute from Kanauj and other cities in their way.

Mahmūd's heavy hand next fell upon Anandpāl, who seems to have leagued with other princes in punishing the Raja of Kanauj for making terms with the invader. Lahore, at any rate, was sacked in 1021, and its unfortunate monarch fled to Ajmēr. Two years later Gwalior opened its gates to the formidable Sultān. But the best remembered, if not the greatest, of Mamūd's Indian campaigns was that of 1024, which issued in the capture of Somnāth, on the coast of Gujarāt, one of the holiest and wealthiest shrines in all India. Endowed with the revenue of two thousand villages, and blest with the ministrations of as many Brahmans, to say nothing of the hundreds of barbers, minstrels, and dancing-girls, who waited on the presiding god, this far-famed temple-stronghold was for three days besieged in vain. At length, in one last despairing onset, led by Mahmūd himself, the besiegers stormed the place, slaying thousands of its defenders, and dealing havoc among the holy things. One huge idol the priests entreated and would have bribed their conquerors to spare. But Mahmūd, who gloried in the name of idol-breaker, struck the figure with his mace; the blows of his followers shattered it in pieces; and jewels of untold value rolled out in glittering heaps upon the floor.* Laden with these unforeseen spoils and the sandal-wood gates of Somnāth, the plunder-loving Sultān marched home a year later through the dreary deserts of Sind, where thousands of his followers perished by the way. Gujarāt itself, like most of the provinces overrun by Mahmūd, was left under the sway of a tributary prince.

In the year 1030, soon after Persia had fallen under the yoke of Ghâzni, death put an end to the terrible Sultān's career. For a century and a half his dynasty held its ground with varying fortunes in the country beyond the Indus. In India, however, it never gained any permanent footing eastward of Lahore. Mahmūd's expeditions, indeed, had been little else than enormous raids, and his successors were too busy in fighting foes nearer home to keep in order their Hindu tributaries

* Thornton denies the truth of this story about the jewels, as having been unknown to the earlier chroniclers.

between the Sutlej and the Ganges. Before the middle of the eleventh century the king of Delhi threw off the Muslim yoke, other princes rallied to his side, and but for the desperate defence of its starving garrison, Lahore itself would have been rescued from the grasp of its new masters. In the middle of the twelfth century that city became the last refuge of the Ghaznevid Sultāns, when the rest of their possessions had been torn from them by the Seljukian Turks and their own kinsmen, the Afghān princes of Ghor.

Thirty years later the descendants of Sabuktigin ceased tó reign in the Punjāb also. In the year 1186, Shihab-ud-din of Ghor, better known to history as Muhammad Ghori, crowned his former successes against Khusrū Malik, the Ghaznevid Sultān of Lahore, by seizing his capital and bearing the Sultān himself a prisoner to Ghor, where Muhammad's elder brother then held his court. Master of the Punjāb from Peshāwar to Multān, Muhammad presently led his warriors across the Sutlej to meet the allied Hindu hosts of Delhi and Ajmēr on the banks of the sacred Saraswati. A great battle, fought near Thanesar, ended in the rout of the invaders; and Muhammad, after a hot pursuit, was glad to place the Indus between his shattered forces and the foe. Next year, in 1192, the beaten prince, burning for vengeance, threw out fresh swarms of horsemen over the fair fields of Sind. Prithirāj, King of Delhi, his former foe, awaited him on the old battlefield, at the head of an immense array of horse and foot, marshalled under the foremost princes of Hindustān. The night before the battle which was to decide the fate of so many ancient kingdoms was spent by the Hindus in careless merriment, by the Turks in quiet preparations for attack. Before dawn Muhammad had crossed the Saraswati and well-nigh taken his opponents unawares. Still, with ranks hastily formed, they withstood for a time his most determined onsets. At length he ordered a retreat. The Hindus, in the eagerness of their pursuit, fell into disorder. Twelve thousand Turkish horsemen, led by Muhammad himself, thundered down into their broken ranks. The best and bravest of their leaders were slain or captured, and the shattered remnants of that proud army fled from a field reeking with the blood of their dead and dying countrymen.

On that fatal day Aryan India lost far more than thousands of precious lives and the accumulated treasures of a vast camp. From this second battle of Narāyan dates the true beginning of India's long subjection to Muhammadan rule. After staining his victory with the slaughter of his royal captive, Prithirāj, and of many thousand Hindus whom the storming of Ajmēr threw into his clutches, the resolute Ghorian made over his new conquests to his ablest general, Kutb-ud-din Ibak, who speedily carried his arms as far south as Koil, the modern Aligarh, and fixed the seat of his government in Delhi itself. Next year Muhammad, with a fresh army, returned from Ghazni to overthrow the immemorial kingdom of Kanauj and destroy or defile the temples of idolatrous Hindus at Benāres. On this occasion the Rhātors of Kanauj, one of the oldest Rājput tribes, sought honourable exile among the rocks and sandhills of Mārwār, where they founded the still-existent kingdom and dynasty of Jodhpur.

Year by year the Muhammadan arms were carried by Muhammad or his generals, with almost unvarying success, now westward of the Jumna to Gwalior, Chitōr, and even Gujarāt, anon down the valley of the Lower Ganges into the heart of Bengal. If the Rājput princes of Upper India fought long and manfully against their doom, it took Kutb-ud-din's soldiers but one year to bring the rich plains and populous cities of Bengal under the Muslim yoke. Nudiah, the Hindu capital, was given over to plunder, and the seat of the new government fixed at Gaur, on a branch of the Lower Ganges, a city whose vast circuit of verdure-covered ruins still reveals some noteworthy traces of Muhammadan genius in the domain of architecture. Ruthless in destroying the idols and pillaging the holy places of the Hindus, the Mussulman conquerors of India in the thirteenth and fourteenth centuries adorned their cities with mosques, palaces, tombs, and other buildings, conspicuous for bold outlines, square masses, and severe simplicity of detail. To the polished masterpieces of a later day, whose glories blossomed in the graceful grandeur of Bijapur, Ahmadābād, Jaunpur, Fatehpur Sikri, and bore ripest fruit in the buildings reared at Agra and Delhi by Shah Jahān, this old Pathān architecture bore much the same relation that the towers of Exeter Cathedral bear to those of Canterbury, or the nave of Gloucester to the chapel of Henry VII. at Westminster.*

On the murder of Muhammad Ghori in 1205 by some Punjābi hill-men, who thus requited him for his cruel treatment of their countrymen, Muhammad's faithful viceroy, Kutb-ud-din, was invested by the dead king's

* The monuments of early Pathan art in or near Delhi include the Kutb-Minār, one of the loftiest and most striking pillars in the world. The pointed arch first takes its place in Pathan buildings of the thirteenth century. At Bijāpur, in Satāra, the great dome of Muhammad Adil Shah's mausoleum, built in the first years of the seventeenth century, deserves special notice. The Jama Masjid of Ahmadābād, built by Ahmad Shah in the fifteenth century, with its fifteen domes upheld by 260 pillars, and the delicate lattice-work of its stone screens, may rank among the most beautiful of Eastern mosques. At Ahmadabād and Jaunpur the influence of Hindu on Muhammadan art is clearly traceable. The great mosque at Fatehpur Sikri, twenty miles south-west of Agra, with its glorious gateways, vast quadrangle, and majestic cloisters, attests from the hill on which it stands the piety and the splendid taste of the great Akbar, who also built at Delhi, in honour of his father Humāyun, a marble monument second only as a work of art to its younger rival, the Taj at Agra. The preservation of these magnificent monuments was made one of the chief cares of the Government of Lord Curzon.

successor with the sovereignty of Hindustān. The crown which he assumed at Lahore in 1206 he lived to wear but four years. His slave and son-in-law, Iltutmish, whom the nobles of the new kingdom chose for their next ruler, had a stormy reign of twenty-five years, during which he repelled an invasion from Ghazni, wrested Sind from a Mussulman rival, conquered Mālwa, up to that time ruled by a prince of the mythical Vikram's line, captured the strong fort of Gwalior, and re-established his sway over the rebellious governors of Bengal. Of all the old Hindu kingdoms in Northern India there remained scarcely one outside the Muhammadan rule. A few princes were allowed still to reign on condition of paying tribute; but far the greater part of the country was governed directly by rulers of the conquering race.

It was in this reign that the Great Khan of Tartary, Chinghiz Khan, the scourge of Asia, swept with his countless hordes of Mongol horsemen, like a lava-flood, over the vast regions between the Caspian and the Pacific, overthrowing the Turkish monarchy of Kharizm, and chasing the son of its Sultān, who had also reigned in Kābul, beyond the Indus. Had Iltutmish listened to the prayer of the fugitive prince, India might also have been involved in the general ruin. But Jalāl-ud-din had to flee elsewhither, and the terrible Tartar contented himself with a flying raid through Sind. Three centuries more had to elapse before a conqueror of the race of Chinghiz founded a new empire in Hindustān.

On the death of Iltutmish in 1236 his sceptre passed into the hands of a son, who was speedily set aside by his manly-hearted sister Raziyyat, whose only fault, says the historian Ferishta, lay in her being a woman. Her vigorous but troubled reign of three years collapsed in a rising among her nobles, who refused to submit to a woman. Carried off a prisoner to Bathinda, she won the heart of her captor, became his wife, and, with his help, took the field. Fortune, however, again deserted her arms, and her second imprisonment was speedily followed by her violent death.

In the six following years two princes of the house of Iltutmish successively exchanged the throne of Delhi for imprisonment and death at the hand of their restless or insulted nobles. Nasir-ud-Mahmūd, a younger son of Iltutmish, was then called to the throne, which he held for twenty years, dying peacefully in his bed after a series of successful struggles with the Hindu warriors of Rājputāna, Bundelkhand, and other revolted or independent states. His nephew, Sher Khan, even succeeded in driving the Mughal invaders out of Ghazni and re-annexing it to the throne of Delhi. His successor, Balban, a Turkish slave whose daughter had married the Sultān by whom he was raised to the post of Wazir, or prime minister, stepped without difficulty, but not without bloodshed, into his place. Having in true Turkish fashion got rid of his foremost rivals, he ruled the country for twenty years with a strong but by no means heavy hand, except when he had to put down a revolt in Bengal or to enforce his edicts against wine and open profligacy. His death in 1287, at a ripe old age, was hastened by grief for the loss of his favourite son Muhammad, who fell in the flush of victory over his Mughal foes. His splendid court, filled with poets, artists, philosophers from many lands, and refugee princes from the realms overrun by Chinghiz and his successors, furnished a congenial theme for the pens of fervid historians. It is worthy of remark, however, that the prince who thus opened his doors to high-born or accomplished strangers, had little mercy to spare for the subject Hindus. Not one of that race, we are told, was allowed by him to rise in the service of the State.

CHAPTER II

THE KHILJI DYNASTY OF DELHI, A.D. 1290—1321

THREE years after Balban's death, Jalāl-ud-din Firoz, a chief of the Khilji tribe that dwelt in the Afghān mountains founded a new dynasty in the blood of Balban's worthless grandson, Kai-kobad. In 1294 a Mussulman army, led by his nephew Ala-ud-din, began that series of invasions which was to end in the conquest of Southern India. Laden with the untold plunder of Deogiri, the modern Daulatabād, a famous hill-fort belonging to the Yādava kings of Māhārashtra, the victorious nephew returned home to plot, to compass in the most treacherous manner, the death of his confiding old uncle in the seventh year of his reign. This murder having been presently followed up by that of the king's two sons, Ala-ud-din mounted the vacant throne. His reign of twenty years was opened by the reconquest of Gujarāt and the capture of its Rājput queen, who lived to adorn the conqueror's haram. Next year his own strength and the courage of his troops were yet more severely tried in repelling the inroads of a vast body of Mughal horsemen, who swept Northern India up to the very gates of his capital. A great battle in the plains near the Sutlej issued in the rout of the invaders, but the victory was dearly won by the death of the Pathān monarch's ablest general. A second inroad took place in 1303, while half of Ala-ud-din's army was engaged in a fresh invasion of Southern India, and he himself was about to lead thither another army flushed with the recent plunder of Chitōr in Rājputāna.* The sudden retreat of the Mughals from the land they had wasted to their heart's content, was followed by their reappearance in 1305 and 1306. Once more the choicest warriors of Islam advanced, says their historian,† "like clouds and rain" against the infidel Tartars, and falling on them "like a raging storm" drove them with tremendous slaughter across the Indus. "Countless infidels were dispatched to hell," and many thousands were taken prisoners. With a cruelty not altogether unprovoked, the merciless Sultān ordered that his male captives should all be slain and beaten up into mortar for the fort at Delhi. A bastion or pillar was likewise formed out of their heads.

Free from further alarms on his Western border the energetic Sultān sent his general, Kafūr, a promoted slave, to enforce payment of the tribute due from the Raja of Deogiri. Yielding to necessity, the Raja sued for easy and obtained liberal terms. Three years afterwards the same general subdued the kindom of Warangal, to the south of the Godāvari, not very far from the modern Hyderābād. In besieging the walled town of Warangal the Mussulmans plied their "Western catapults" with such effect that the earthen walls were "pounded into dust" by the incessant shower of heavy stones. When the besiegers had stormed the outer works of the city,‡ its defenders lost heart and sued for terms. Little was

* During these centuries of trouble the Hindu princes, if they failed to avert disaster, knew at least how to die. Hopeless of resistance, the Queen of Chitor with the noblest of her ladies perished in the flames of their own kindling, while the Raja and his faithful followers were finding the death they sought on the weapons of the foe. A similar issue had marked the siege of Ranthambhor in 1299.

† Mīr Khusrū, author of the Tārīkh-i-Alāi, which narrates the History of Ala-ud-din down to A.D. 1310. See Sir H. Elliott's "History of India as told by its own Historians," vol. iii.

‡ According to another historian, Barni, the besiegers took the outworks by escalade.

granted them except their lives. Under fierce threats of a general massacre, the unfortunate Raja had to make all his treasures over to the conqueror, who returned to Delhi laden with the gathered wealth of a kingdom which for centuries had thriven peacefully under its Hindu lords. A hundred elephants, seven thousand horses, and treasure enough to load a thousand camels, were the visible tokens of Kafūr's success. His new conquest remained under the rule of its Raja, Laddar Deo, on condition of his paying a yearly tribute to the Sultān.*

The following year saw Maabar, the modern Carnatic, overrun by the same commander, who left his footmarks everywhere in plundered cities, ruined temples, and idols broken into pieces or carried off as part of the prize. On his march south-eastward across the highlands of Mysore he sacked the city of Dora-Samūdra, and defaced the beautiful temple which a king of the Bellāl line had just reared in honour of Siva.† After bearing his standard to Madura, if not to Cape Comorin, and building a mosque at some place on the sea-coast opposite Ceylon, Kafūr returned to Delhi in 1311 with a booty the like of which his countrymen there had never before seen. According to the native chroniclers, it included six hundred and twelve elephants, ninety-six thousand *mans* of gold,‡ several boxes of pearls and jewels, and twenty thousand horses. To each of his higher officers the Sultān distributed the gold in shares, ranging from half a *man* to four *mans*.

Once more, in 1312, Kafūr invaded the Deccan, to punish the refractory Prince of Deogiri, receive tribute

* Kafūr's army appears to have been reinforced by large numbers of Marātha horse and foot furnished by the Raja of Deogiri.

† Supposed to be the great temple of Halibēd in Mysore, a marvel of florid decoration.

‡ A *man* or maund equals about 80 lbs. weight English.

from Warangal, and send home fresh spoils from conquered countries. Meanwhile his master, Ala-ud-din, wreaked a fearful vengeance on the "new Mussulmans," or converted Mughals, who had been taken into his service or allowed to settle on his lands. Suddenly reduced by his orders to poverty and forced idleness, some of them plotted to seize, if not to slay, the ruler who was accused of grinding down his subjects with fines and heavy burdens, and enforcing with cruel penalties the prohibitions of the Korān against wine and other strong drinks. In meeting this new danger, Ala-ud-din gave full swing to his own bloodthirsty nature; twenty thousand Mughals, most of whom knew nothing of the plot, being by his orders slaughtered in one day.

Throughout his reign, Ala-ud-din seems to have betrayed in turn the most opposite workings of a strong but ill-balanced nature. A cruel tyrant, he yet gave heed at time to the counsels of his more outspoken advisers, and made some attempts to administer a rude sort of justice among his people. From a life of the grossest debauchery he could pass for some years into one of outward temperance and self-denial. Illiterate himself, he encouraged the presence of learned men at his court, and even deigned for their sake to master the rudiments of the Persian language.* Utterly ruthless towards friends or foes who might have stirred up his bile against them, he would sometimes listen with good humour, or at least with patience, to advice offered him under the faith of his kingly word. If he plotted the death of one of his bravest officers, he never tired of heaping favours on another who, all the while, was planning how to wrest the sceptre from his heirs. Fines, confiscations, and plunder went far to fill his treasury; but he checked the license of his nobles, tried to put down bribery and extortion among his revenue

* Barni, however, says that he "never associated with men of learning."

collectors, and punished with summary sternness every shopkeeper who was caught dealing in false weights or measures against the poor.*

In order to keep down the turbulence of his nobles, the exactions of his public servants, and to enforce obedience to his many stern decrees, Ala-ud-din maintained an army of spies and informers, who reported regularly whatever they might see or hear, even in the most private places. So great was the dread of them that many a noble dared hardly speak aloud in his own palace. A special edict, moreover, forbade the nobles and great men from giving feasts, holding meetings, marrying or giving in marriage without the Sultān's leave, or admitting strange guests into their houses. No wonder that feasting and hospitality fell into disuse, that the *sarais*, or public resting-places, were cleared of plotters, and that treason for a time became too perilous a game even for the boldest to play at, when his trustiest-seeming comrade might prove to be his direst foe.

Among other classes rebellion was to be disarmed by other means, such as heavy imposts, arbitrary fines, and sweeping resumptions of freehold estates. To the mass of the Sultān's subjects money became a thing unknown, and the people, says Barni, "were all so absorbed in obtaining the means of living, that the name of rebellion was never mentioned." For the millions of Hindus who had passed under the Muhammadan yoke this was indeed a time of bitter suffering. Like the Jews in Europe at that very date, they were fleeced and harried at every turn. From the *jiziya*, or poll-tax, to the rack-rent levied

* According to Barni, boys were frequently sent into the *bazar* to test the honesty of the shopkeepers. If one of these gave short weight, the inspector went to his shop, "took from it what was deficient, and afterwards cut from his haunches an equal weight of flesh, which was thrown down before his eyes."—Sir H. Elliott's "History of India," vol. iii. p. 196.

on the land in the shape of half the gross produce no effort was spared to reduce them to a common poverty. The poorest Hindu was taxed for the goat that gave him milk; his neighbour for the bullock that ploughed his bit of land. To ride their own horses and wear fine clothing were luxuries reserved for very few of the subject race. Threats and blows increased the tax-gatherer's merciless demands. No Hindu, says the historian,* "could hold up his head, and in their houses no sign of gold or silver or of any superfluity was to be seen." So hard became the struggle to live that the wives of Hindu landowners were often fain to serve for hire in the houses of the Mussulmans.

Nor did their troubles end here. It was the Sultan's ambition to keep up a large army on a low rate of pay—an achievement possible only if the price of provisions could be kept down. "The Second Alexander," as he delighted in calling himself, proceeded to fix the market-prices of various grains. A good deal of the "tribute" or land revenue was by his orders levied in kind. With the grain thus regularly accruing he filled his granaries. The grain-dealers were forced to sell again at a low uniform rate the corn which the *rayats*, or peasants, had been forced to sell them after satisfying the wants of the royal treasury. In times of drought and dearth the royal granaries threw open their stores at the market-rates. Regrating was punished by heavy fines and forfeiture of the stock held back from sale. Any attempt to raise the market-prices was further checked by the punishment of the market-overseer himself. Horses, cattle, slaves, fruit, vegetables, grocery, shoes, needles, everything, in short, exposed for sale in the *bazars* or market-places had its value strictly regulated and kept down by royal command. Nothing might be exported, while

* Barni, "Tārīkh-i-Firoz Shāhi.'

importation was freely encouraged. Hours were fixed for opening and closing shops. The monarch's will, in short, became law, overriding even the precepts of the Korān whenever these might clash with his own views of right and expediency. If his zeal for regulating everything led often to absurd injustice, or provoked repeated evasions of intolerable edicts, he appears at least to have succeeded in maintaining a cheap army, in keeping a tight hand on his unruly nobles, and in making life a sore burden to the mass of his Hindu subjects.

For some years of his reign Ala-ud-din governed vigorously and with fair success. Peace and order flourished everywhere; the nobles were quiet, the people outwardly loyal; life and property were pretty safe on the highways. Splendid buildings adorned his capital, and noble tanks stored up their water for the use of the dwellers in large towns. At length, however, the worst traits of his character and conduct began to bear answering fruit. The arrogance which had formerly shown itself in schemes for setting up a new religion, now tempted him to exchange his able ministers for worthless eunuchs and slaves who only pandered to his love of pleasure. A dropsy, brought on or heightened by self-indulgence, increased the violence of his temper. Mistrustful of most men, he yielded himself blindly into the hands of his cunning favourite—his partner in the foulest profligacy—Kafūr. Under this man's baneful influence he ordered the death of his brother-in-law and the imprisonment of his two elder sons. His nobles at length began to plot against him. Gujarāt broke into fierce rebellion. Chitōr was wrested from Muslim rule by the famous Rājput chief Hamir, and the son-in-law of Ram-Dēo drove the Muhammadans out of Māhārashtra. On hearing of these manifold disasters, the death-stricken monarch is said to have bitten his own flesh with rage. He died soon afterwards in the last days of the year 1316; and Kafūr, rightly or wrongly, was widely credited with a direct share in his death.

That he meant to profit by it was at once made clear enough by his seizure of the government, under a show of acting as guardian to the youngest son and pretended heir of the late king. The eyes of the two eldest sons were put out by his orders, and nothing but his own death at the hands of some officers of the palace-guard saved the family of his late master from the doom which so often follows a change of dynasties, or even of kindred rulers, in the East.

The third son of the late king, Mubārak, had no sooner regained his own freedom, and mounted the throne under the title of Kutb-ud-din, than he too proceeded to assure his hold of it by blinding his youngest brother and slaying the officers to whom he owed his life and sceptre. His short reign of four years opened well with the release of many thousand political prisoners, the restoration of much confiscated land, and the annulling of nearly all the harsh laws devised by his father. The Hindus breathed freely under a king who refused to tax them to the starving-point, and the Mussulmans once more took their pleasure without fear of spies and cruel tortures. While an able general suppressed the revolt in Gujarāt, the king himself marched into the Deccan, retook the stronghold of Deogiri, and hunted the rebel leader, Harapāla, out of his last hiding-place to a horrible death: he was flayed alive by order of the Sultan.

Leaving his favourite Khusrū, a converted Hindu, to overrun the Carnatic, Kutb-ud-din returned to Delhi. There, amidst his wine-cups, his women and his flatterers, he gave small heed to passing affairs, except when a plot discovered or a rebellion suppressed might rouse him into a burst of vindictive savagery. At length, in 1320, he too fell an unpitied victim to the treachery of his trusted follower Khusrū, who clinched his crime by slaughtering all those members of the royal family whom his master had spared. Only for a few months, however, did the renegade Hindu enjoy his blood-bought crown. Ghāzi Khan Tughlak, Governor of the Punjāb, led his veterans against the usurper. The victory of Indrapat, crowned by the seizure and beheading of Khusrū, opened Delhi to the conqueror, who was hailed by his Mussulman countrymen as their deliverer from the yoke of "Hindus and Parwāris." *

* These Parwāris were a body of retainers from Gujarāt.

CHAPTER III

THE TUGHLAK, SAIYID, AND LODI DYNASTIES, A.D. 1320—1526

NOT one of the house of Khilji being found alive, Tughlak mounted the throne of Delhi with the title of Ghiyas-ud-din. Under the mild rule of this son of a Turkish slave by a Hindu mother the country prospered, the Muhammadans breathed freely, and even the Hindus had little cause to regret the change. After setting his finances in order and lowering the land-rents to a pitch so moderate that fresh fields might yearly be brought under the plough, the new king proceeded to strengthen his frontiers against the Mughals. In 1322 his son Juna Khan was deputed to bring the refractory ruler of Warangal to terms. Repulsed with heavy losses on the first attack, he succeeded the next year in capturing the city and bearing its Raja prisoner to Delhi. The name of the city was changed to Sultānpur, and Mussulman officers were left in charge of the conquered province. The king's arms were equally successful against the Mughal invader on the north-west.

Next year the king himself marched into Bengal, where the son of his old master, Balban, still held an almost independent sway.* After bestowing on Karra Khan a royal umbrella in token of kingly rank, and reducing to obedience the revolted provinces of Dacca and Jaunpur, he returned homewards, only to be crushed to

* See page 56.

death, by design or accident, in the pavilion which his son had built for his reception at Tughlakabad.

Juna Khan, who succeeded him in 1325 under the title of Muhammad Tughlak, appears to have been one of the most gifted, wayward, wrong-headed, and merciless princes of his age. Deeply read in Persian and Arabic lore, equally at home in Greek philosophy and the physical sciences, a good mathematician, a renowned orator and letter-writer, endowed with a wonderful memory, of temperate habits, dauntless courage, invincible energy, in word and deed a pious Mussulman,* he bade fair to outtop the highest achievements of any former reign. But the curse of absolute power, working on a heated brain, a proud heart, and a fierce, unbridled temper, turned all that teeming promise to naught; and the wonder of his age lived to become its direst scourge.

His first measure, the payment of a heavy bribe to get rid of the Mughals who had invaded the Punjāb, was rewarded with a success it hardly deserved. The same good fortune, with better reason, followed his standard into Southern India, nearly all of which became thoroughly subjected to his rule. From Gujarāt to Chittagong, from Lahore to Madura, stretched an empire wider than that of Aurangzeb. But Muhammad hungered after new conquests. Three hundred and seventy thousand horsemen, according to Barni, were held for a whole year in readiness to enter Khurāsān. The cost of their maintenance, however, emptied his treasury, and the troops, collected for the conquest of Persia, repaid themselves on their way home with the plunder of their own people.

A few years later, in 1337, the restless Sultān sought

* "No learned or scientific man, or scribe, or poet, or wit, or physician, could have presumed," says Barni, "to argue with him about his own special pursuit, nor would he have been able to maintain his position against the throttling arguments of the Sultān."

to replenish a drained exchequer by throwing another large army somewhere across the Himālayas into Chinese Turkistan.* Checked in their advance by the courage or the numbers of the Chinese; wasted by hardships, disease, and the attacks of the hill-tribes in their rear, very few of the hundred thousand who set forth on that fatal errand survived the perils of a yet more ruinous retreat through fever-breathing forests and flooded plains.

Meanwhile Muhammad seems to have tried all manner of devices for recruiting his diminished revenues. New cesses on the land reduced the bulk of the *rayats*, or peasants, to utter beggary, thousands of them leaving their untilled fields to roam the jungles in quest of food or to lurk about the highways in hopes of plunder. Drought and high prices, the fruit in great measure of these exactions, brought on a famine which raged in the Ganges valley for several years, slaying "thousands upon thousands" of starving wretches, and breaking up many a household whose forefathers had dwelt for centuries in the same village. Large tracts of fruitful country were reduced to desert. In trying to mend matters the Sultān only made them worse. His scheme for circulating copper tokens of an artificial value in the place of gold and silver succeeded only in deranging the course of trade and enlarging the circle of popular suffering, without restoring the shattered finances of the state.

In this state of things, discontent, disorder, and rebellion grew more and more rife. Hardly had Mūltān been reduced to obedience, when the king's nephew rose against him in the Deccan, and a Mussulman noble drove the king's officers out of Bengal. With his usual energy

* Barni talks of a march towards "the mountain of Karājal," which "lies between the territories of Hind and those of China." The capture of this mountain was somehow to aid Muhammad in his still-cherished designs on Khurāsān.

Muhammad turned upon his assailants. His nephew was defeated, taken, and flayed alive. A popular outbreak in the Doab, or country between the Jumna and the Ganges, was suppressed with hideous slaughter of innocent thousands. The great city of Kanauj was given over to a general massacre. While one of his officers was putting down a revolt in Lahore, the king himself marched from Deogiri to deal with a like disturbance in the Carnatic. Cholera, however, made such inroads into his camp at Warangal that he withdrew his troops to Deogiri, himself half dead from the same disease; and presently Warangal also threw off the imperial yoke. It is mentioned as a master-flight of whimsical self-conceit, that a tooth he had lost on his way homewards was buried with great pomp under a stately mausoleum at Bhir.

It was about this time that Muhammad's liking for Deogiri issued in a rash and disastrous attempt to substitute that place for Delhi as the seat of his rule. He changed its name to Daulatabād. When his new capital had been adorned with new buildings and strengthened with new lines of defence, he commanded the people of Delhi to leave the city, whose growing splendour had kept pace with the growth of Muhammadan conquests, and to march with all their household goods to the homes he had chosen for them beyond the Sātpūra hills. The road thither had been planted with full-grown trees; but thousands perished from the toils of that long journey, and as many more filled the graveyards of Daulatabād. Ere long the survivors were allowed to return home, but once more, under pain of death, were they compelled to emigrate afresh. The new capital, however, was not fated to prosper on the ruins of the old. Delhi was again repeopled and Muhammad's last years were chiefly spent in the city that towers along the Jumna.

Those years were troubled with fresh storms, and fresh

disasters followed each other, in spite of the Sultān's high abilities and of the countenance bestowed upon him by the nominal head of Islām, the reigning Khalif of Egypt. Famine still raged in the Doab. His well-meant efforts to improve the revenue by bringing waste lands under tillage seem to have ended only in enriching a crew of official harpies at the public expense. Terrible punishments goaded his subjects into fresh outbreaks. The unprovoked slaughter of eighty "foreign Amīrs," or converted Mughal settlers, by his willing tool, the governor of Mālwa, roused their countrymen in Gujarāt into a rebellion, the scene of which was afterwards shifted to Daulatabād. After wasting the former province with fire and sword, Muhammad hastened into the Deccan; but while he was besieging Daulatabād, the news of a fresh rising recalled him into Gujarāt. Here he was again successful; but meanwhile the Deccan was slipping surely out of his grasp. With the help of the governor of Mālwa the insurgents drove the king's troops across the Narbada; and their new leader, Hasan Gangu, became the first king of an independent Bahmani line, whose sway was to flourish for the next hundred and eighty years.

Gujarāt reduced to order and desolation, the active monarch turned his arms against Sind, whose princes had given shelter to the fugitives from the neighbouring province. In spite of ill-health he was pushing on towards Tatta, on the Indus, when death, hastened by a hearty meal of fish, brought all his cares, schemes, and follies to a sudden close, in the twenty-sixth year of his unquiet reign. Seldom has a prince of like capacity laboured with a will so froward for his own undoing. The erewhile master of nearly the whole Indian peninsula had lived to see one province after another fall away from his sceptre. It was more than two centuries before an emperor of Delhi again held actual sway over the Mussulman lords of Bengal.

For nearly the same period Vijayanagar, cradled among rugged hills on the right bank of the Tungabhadra, remained the seat of a powerful Hindu realm, at one time reaching southwards to Madura. The Hindu Rajas of Telingāna fixed their capital for about eighty years at Warangal, and when that stronghold fell into the hands of a Bahmani prince, they continued for another century to hold the rest of their dominions on the Kistna and the Godāvari by right of their own strong arms. Gulbarga, in the valley of the Upper Kistna, became the chief seat of the Bahmani * princes already named, whose sway extended eastward from the sea to Berar, and from the Tāpti southward to the Tungabhadra. Several other provinces, such as Mālwa and Gujarāt, were either in full revolt or smarting under heavy punishment for past outbreaks, when Muhammad Tughlak breathed his last.

His nephew and successor, Firoz Shah, made a vigorous but vain attempt to reconquer Bengal. By the treaties afterwards concluded with that province and the Deccan, he accepted the issue he could no longer avert.† A subsequent expedition into Sind resulted in the nominal submission of the Jām of Tatta, a Rājput of the dynasty which had lately succeeded the old Sumēra line. With these exceptions and that of a temporary rising in Gujarāt, his reign for many years was peaceful and prosperous, and marked by not a few wholesome enactments. The savage punishments and tortures inflicted by former rulers

* Hasan Gangu, founder of the dynasty, is said by Ferishta to have been an Afghān husbandman, settled near Delhi on the estate of a Brahman whose favour he had won by handing over to him some treasure found on the estate. The Brahman seems to have had friends at court, to whose notice he recommended his tenant. Taking his patron's name, Hasan rose in the king's service, and when he too became a king, he added the name of *Bahmani* in honour of the friendly Brahman.

† The rulers of those provinces seem still to have paid tribute to Delhi, but were otherwise independent sovereigns.

were nearly all done away.* A great many small and vexatious imposts were removed. The victims of his uncle's cruelty he consoled with gifts or restored to their forfeit honours. Lands wrested from their former owners were given back to them or their heirs. The needy and the unemployed he supplied with work. Learning was encouraged, vice in its worse and more open forms sternly repressed, and luxury discountenanced by the King's own example.

A devout Mussulman, he gave alms freely to the poor, built many mosques, monasteries, and colleges, repaired the tombs of former sultans and nobles, and founded hospitals for high and low. With a grim sort of justice he refused to exempt the Brahmans, "the very keys of the chamber of idolatry," from the hateful *Jiziya*, or poll-tax, levied on all other Hindus. At the same time he remitted the tax on every Hindu who would make profession of Iṣlām, a stroke of policy which gained large numbers of converts to the dominant creed.† Gifts and honours further awaited these new soldiers of Muhammad; but for those who held fast to the creed of their forefathers he had little mercy to spare. Their temples were destroyed, their holy books, vessels, and idols publicly burnt, their leaders not seldom put to death.‡ If the Christian princes of that age were equally ruthless towards the heretic and the heathen, we cannot wonder at the

* "Amputation of hands and feet, ears and noses; tearing out the eyes, pouring molten lead into the throat, crushing the bones of the hands and feet with mallets, burning the body with fire, driving iron nails into the hands, feet, and bosom, cutting the sinews, sawing men asunder; these," says Firoz Shah himself, "and many similar tortures were practised. . . . Through God's mercy these severities and terrors have been exchanged for tenderness, kindness, and mercy."

† See the "Tārikh-i-Fīroz Shāhi" of Shams-i-Sirāj, a contemporary of Firoz, and that monarch's own brief memoir of his reign, the "Futūhāt-i-Firoz Shâhi"—both in vol. iii. of Elliot's "History of India."

‡ In spite of his own milder edicts, Firoz Shah had at least one poor Brahman burnt at the stake, according to the historian Shams-i-Sirāj.

intolerance shown by a believer in a religion which proclaimed the duty of converting infidels at the sword's point.

His religious training, however, bore fairer fruit than this. The historians of his day dwell with pride on the many public works begun or carried through during the reign of Firoz Tughlak. He is said, we know not how accurately, to have built two hundred forts and cities, forty mosques, thirty colleges, a hundred hospitals, a hundred and twenty *khānkas*, or public inns and caravanserais, twenty palaces, five tombs, a hundred tanks for bathing, a hundred and fifty bridges, and ten monumental pillars. To him also was Upper India first indebted for waterworks like those with which Southern India had long been blest. Besides damming fifty rivers and excavating thirty reservoirs, he carried a canal from Karnāl, on the Upper Jumna, through the thirsty plains round Hansi and Hissar, to the Kāgar river, and thence onward through once fertile Bhatind to the Sutlej.*

After a reign of thirty-six years, the good old king resigned his throne to his son Nāsir-ud-din. But a year had hardly elapsed before the new king was declared by his rebellious nobles unfit to reign; and Firoz, recalled from his hard-won privacy, was glad to seek it again after he had placed the sceptre in the hands of his grandson Ghyas-ud-din. A few weeks later he himself, at the great age of ninety, had found the deeper privacy of the grave.

For the next ten years the history of the Tughlak dynasty is one of continual disorder, unrest, and strife. In little more than a year one king had been murdered by a rival brother, who in his turn had given place to his exiled uncle, Nāsir-ud-din. For months more the strife between uncle and nephew raged with varying fortune,

* Of this great irrigation-work some two hundred miles have since been reopened by the English Government in India with excellent results.

before the twice-crowned son of Firoz Shah drove his nephew for the last time out of Delhi. His death in February, 1394, transferred the sceptre to his eldest son Humāyun, who, dying a few weeks later, was succeeded by his brother Mahmūd.

This prince's nominal reign of nineteen years began in trouble and closed in deep gloom. He was a mere boy when Muzaffar Shah, the son of a converted Rājput, set up an independent kingdom in Gujarāt. His example was quickly followed by the neighbouring governors of Mālwa and Khandēsh, while his own Wazir founded another kingdom at Jaunpur on the river Gūmti, not far from Benāres. Delhi itself was torn by incessant broils between the followers of rival claimants to the throne.

In the midst of these disorders a remote descendant of Chinghiz Khan swooped down from Samarkand across the Indus into the fair plains of Hindustan. At the Sutlej this new invader, known in history as Timūr or Tamerlane,* was met by his grandson, fresh from the conquest of Multān. Their march towards Delhi by the way of Bhatnair, Samāna, and Pānipat, was marked by the usual atrocities of their age and race. All these, however, were surpassed, if we may believe Timūr's own words, by the massacre of a hundred thousand prisoners in cold blood on his near approach to Delhi.† Mahmūd went forth to fight his fearful adversary, but his troops were no match for superior numbers, prowess, and military skill. The beaten monarch fled to Gujarāt, and his capital fell into the hands of a conqueror whose deeds were continually clashing with his pledged words. His promises of quarter

* A corruption of Timūr Lang, that is, Timūr the Lame. Timūr himself appears to have been more of a Turk than a Mongol by birth.

† See his autobiography, the Malfuzāti-Timūri, in vol. iii. of Elliot's "History of India." These "infidels and idolaters" were slain on grounds of alleged military expediency—a convenient excuse for the promptings of religious zeal.

to the people of Delhi issued in a tremendous carnival of blood and plunder, which lasted for five days, he himself feasting all the while in state outside the city, in seeming helplessness to avert or stay the horrors let loose by his "savage Turks" within. His own account throws little light upon the real origin of a disaster which he complacently ascribes to the will of God; the tone of his narrative betrays small regret; and his avowed attempt to seize all the Hindu refugees in the city provoked the tumults which his turbulent soldiery were so prompt to quench in blood.

Be that as it may, however, nearly the whole of Delhi was given up to plunder, its streets were piled with dead, and when the new Emperor of India, as Timūr now chose to call himself, set forth on his homeward march, a host of captives and an enormous booty of the richest kind followed in his train.

Having already, by his own account, slain some "lakhs" * of infidels, he resumed his holy war at Meerut, whose capture was attended by a general massacre. After raiding up the Ganges to Hardwār, at the foot of the Himālayas, and skirting that mighty range as far as Jammu, north of Lahore, he at length recrossed the Indus to renew elsewhere the horrors which had dogged his steps from that river to the Ganges. India at any rate saw him no more.

The exiled King of Delhi returned to his capital, but found little left him except the name of king over a sorry remnant of the empire once ruled by Muhammad Tughlak. For twelve years more he lived as a titled pensioner of one strong-handed noble after another. With his death in 1413 the house of Tughlak ceased to reign. A fight for the succession ended fifteen months later in the triumph of Khizr Khan, a Saiyid or descendant of Muhammad,

* A *lakh* is a hundred thousand.

whom Timūr had appointed Governor of the Punjāb. The founder of the Saiyid dynasty, he still claimed to govern as viceroy of the Emperor Timūr. After a prosperous reign of seven years, he was succeeded by his son Mobārak, whose uneventful reign of fourteen years was cut short by the assassin's knife.

In the days of his son Muhammad, Delhi was saved by Bahlōl Lodi, the Afghan Governor of Multān, from falling into the hands of the independent King of Mālwa. Ere long, however, Bahlōl himself was laying siege to Delhi, but in vain. Withdrawing to his own provinces, he had not long to wait before Muhammad's death and the helpless condition of his son Ala-ud-din, whose sway extended only a few miles round the capital, again brought him with fairer prospects to the front. Ala-ud-din retired on a pension to Budaun, and in 1450 the grandson of the ennobled Afghān merchant founded a dynasty which reigned at Delhi for about seventy-six years.

For half that period the throne was occupied by Bahlōl himself, who is said to have been "for those days a virtuous and mild prince, executing justice to the utmost of his knowledge." He treated his courtiers like friends, cared little for display, lived abstemiously, and enjoyed the company of learned men.* With the mingled courage and caution of his race, he put down one assailant after another, by fair means or foul, until nearly all the country between the Sutlej and the Ganges down to Benāres had been re-annexed to the kingdom of Delhi. His greatest achievement was the reconquest of Jaunpur after a war which, with varying fortunes and few pauses, raged for about twenty-six years.

Like so many Eastern sovereigns, his son Sikandar had to fight for his throne, first with the champions of his infant nephew, afterwards with two of his brothers.

* See Dow's "History of Hindostan," vol. ii.

Unlike most conquerors of his race, however, the new Sultān treated his fallen rivals with forgiving courtesy, sometimes even with brotherly affection. A just and vigorous ruler, he yet reserved his kindnesses for men of his own faith. Towards the Hindus he proved a merciless bigot, forbidding their rites of bathing and pilgrimage, destroying their temples, and building mosques in their stead. One poor Brahman, a probable disciple of the reformer Khabīr,* was put to death for having dared to maintain before Muhammadan doctors the equal claims of all creeds, if honestly practised, to acceptance in the sight of God.

After a reign of twenty-eight years, during which Bihār was added to his father's dominions, Sikandar was succeeded by his son Ibrahīm, whose pride and tyranny drove his subjects into frequent revolts, quenched by him in seas of blood. At length one of his tribesmen, Daulat Khan Lodi, Governor of the Punjāb, turned for aid to Kābul, where Bābur, a descendant of Timūr,† after a strange career of perils, defeats, and victories, had finally fixed his throne some twenty years before. He was only fifteen when he set forth, in 1497, from Firghāna, on the upper course of the Jaxartes (the river Syr), to conquer Samarkand. A few months later he left that city to fight for the recovery of his native kingdom, which had risen in revolt against him. Again, in 1499, he won his way by stratagem into the capital of Timūr, which had meanwhile fallen into the hands of a powerful Uzbek chief. Blockaded by the Uzbeks in Samarkand, he left that city a second time to find Firghāna also wrested from his grasp. For the next few years Bābur was the sport of untoward fortune, successful at one moment only to be

* See Book I. chap. ii.

† He was sixth in descent from Timūr and a remote descendant of Chinghiz Khan.

caught in sterner straits the next. Baffled at every turn, a wanderer hunted for his life, a prisoner in the hands of his worst enemies, the brave young chieftain never lost heart. Regaining his freedom he found shelter for a time in Kundūz, at the court of Khusrū Shah. Starting thence with an army chiefly recruited from Khusrū's troops, he marched on Kābul in 1504, and soon possessed himself of the country which his uncle had lately ruled.

From that time fortune, if still uncertain, smiled upon him in the main. After extending his dominions around Kābul, he crossed the Oxus in 1511, and for the third time conquered Samarkand. Driven thence in 1514 by his old enemies the Uzbeks, he at length turned his thoughts towards India. His first invasion of the Punjāb took place in 1519. Twice again in the next five years he crossed the Indus; and in 1524 he made his way into Lahore and Debalpur, at the invitation of the aforesaid Daulat Khan. But that shifty or ill-used Afghān failed to convince Bābur of his trustworthiness, and the latter again withdrew to Kābul, leaving Ala-ud-din, brother to the Sultān of Delhi,* in charge of the Punjāb.

The new governor, after fleeing from the hostility, was ere long enjoying the aid of Daulat Khan in his march upon Delhi. His defeat by his brother Ibrahīm before the capital at length roused Bābur, flushed with victory over the Uzbek invaders of Balkh, to one more decisive effort for the empire of Hindustān. In the spring of 1526 some ten thousand Mughal horsemen, with a smaller body of foot and a few field-guns,† emerged from the hills at Rupar, and, taking up fresh forces on their way, at length found themselves on the plain of Pānipat, face to face

* Some authorities call him uncle.

† Field-artillery are known to have been employed in India as far back as A.D. 1365, when the spoils taken by the Bahmani king of the Deccan from the Hindu hosts of Vijayanagar at the battle of Raichōr included 300 gun-carriages.

BABUR

FROM A MS. OF SHAH JAHAN NAMEH FORMERLY IN THE POSSESSION OF AKBAR III, NOW IN THE BRITISH MUSEUM

P. 78

with Ibrahīm's army, reckoned by the chroniclers, more or less wildly, at a hundred thousand strong. On a battle-field since famous in Indian history, Bābur entrenched his small army. His guns and infantry ranged in well-knit line behind their breastworks, while clouds of watchful horsemen covered their flanks, Bābur, with his son Humāyun, calmly awaited an attack from four times their own numbers. Impatient of delay, the hosts of Ibrahīm thundered down upon the foe. Their strength, however, was spent in vain upon that bristling barrier. Baffled and disordered, they were suddenly beset on their flanks and rear by Bābur's active horsemen, whose arrows seldom missed their mark. Repeated charges, one of them led by Ibrahīm himself, resulted only in heavier slaughter, in more confused retreat. Meanwhile Bābur, issuing from his entrenchments, led his unbroken troops steadily forward into the heart of the hostile ranks. Ibrahīm and five thousand of his best soldiers fell in one spot. Utterly dis-heartened by their monarch's fall, the Pathān army, says the historian, "recoiled like surges from a rocky shore and the torrent of flight rolled towards the banks of the Jumna,"* whither the Mughals kept up the pursuit, until Bābur, tired of useless bloodshed, gave the word to halt. Of the routed enemy he himself reckoned † that sixteen thousand died upon the field, and some thousands more must have fallen in their subsequent flight. On that fatal evening of April, 1526, the house of Lodi ceased to reign over the kingdom it had virtually recalled into being.

* Dow's "Hindostan," vol. ii.

† See Bābur's own Memoirs, translated by Mr. Erskine.

CHAPTER IV

THE CONTEMPORARY INDIAN DYNASTIES

AT the time when Bābur steps upon the stage of Indian history, it is well to pause for a moment and glance round over the great peninsula which his descendants were to bring for a season under their sway.

To begin with the cool, well-watered valley of Kashmīr, nestled in the heart of the north-western Himālayas. That country had been ruled by a long succession of Hindu, Buddhist, and even Tartar princes, when, in the early part of the fourteenth century, it fell into the hands of Shah Mīr, the Muhammadan wazir of its late raja, the last of the ancient Hindu line. The new king, under the name of Shams-ud-din, governed mildly and well for twenty-three years ; but one of his successors, about the close of the same century, proved a cruel persecutor of the prevalent Hindu faith. The long reign of Sikandar's nephew, Shādi Khan, brought better times to his Hindu subjects. From the day of his death to the battle of Pānipat was a period mainly of civil commotion and frequent change of rulers, one of whom, Muhammad, great-grandson of the wise and good Shādi Khan, was four times deposed during a nominal reign of about fifty years. On the last of these occasions, in 1525, he had been set aside in favour of his grandson by one of Bābur's generals ; but the timely departure of the Mughal troops opened the prison doors of the old king, whose few remaining years were spent in comparative peace upon his father's throne.

After its conquest by Muhammad Ghori, in 1186, from the Turks of Ghazni, the Punjāb, or Land of Five Rivers, commonly shared the fortunes of the Delhi kingdom. Harassed in the thirteenth century by the Mughals, it was ruled in the first years of the fifteenth century by Khizr Khan, in the name of his master Timūr. Hardly had the founder of the Saiyid dynasty won Delhi, when he began to lose his hold upon the Punjāb, which presently passed into the hands of Bahlōl Lodi, the destined supplanter of the Saiyid line. From the middle of the fifteenth century to the time of Bābur's invasion, the Land of the Five Rivers formed part of the dominions ruled by the house of Lodi.

Multān, like its northern neighbour, passed from one Mussulman conqueror to another, from the Ghaznevid princes to the house of Ghor, from thence to the Slave Kings of Delhi and their successors, down to the end of the fourteenth century. After Timūr's invasion, the country seems to have drifted away from its old allegiance, until in 1445 it fell into the guiding hands of the Afghān, Kutb-ud-din Langa, whose family during the next eighty years governed it without a master.

From the middle of the eighth century, when the Sumra Rājputs drove out the Arab invader, Sind throve under a native Hindu dynasty for nearly five hundred years. Early in the thirteenth century the Sumra princes were ousted by a Mussulman named Nāsir-ud-din. After his death Sind became the prize of another Rājput dynasty, that of the Jains, who paid some kind of tribute to the Sultān of Delhi, and towards the end of the fourteenth century embraced the creed of their Lord Paramount. A succession of Jain princes with Muhammadan names governed the country until, in 1520, the dynasty was displaced by that of the Arghūns from Khurāsān, who presently became masters of Multān also.

The old Hindu province of Gujarāt or Saurashtra, ruled by Ballabi princes for two centuries, passed in 524 under the sway of a Chaura dynasty, which flourished for about four hundred years, giving place in its turn to the Salonka or Chalukya line of Rājput princes, led off by Mulrāj, the warlike son-in-law of the last Ballabi king. Under these princes, who came from the Deccan, the land of Krishna prospered fairly on the whole for two centuries, suffering less than its neighbours from Muhammadan inroads, and bearing on its surface many noble monuments of its rulers' piety, splendour, and care for the common good. It still abounds in temples built by Jain architects, and the great reservoir of Kuran Sāgar—the Sea of Kuran—constructed in the eleventh century, was effaced by a flood so late as 1814.*

In 1228, this dynasty was replaced by a line of Waghila chiefs, who ruled the country during the rest of that century, until it passed under the sway of Ala-ud-din Khilji, then Sultān of Delhi. A hundred years later, about 1391, a new kingdom was founded in Gujarāt by the son of a Rājput convert to Islam. Sent thither from Delhi to displace the mild-hearted governor Farat Khan, whose kindness to the Hindus had roused the rancour of his own countrymen, Muzaffar Shah set up as king of the province entrusted to him as viceroy, and marked his reign by fierce persecutions of the people who still clung to his ancestral faith. His grandson, Ahmad Shah (1411–1443), the builder of Ahmadābād, was equally renowned for his wars, his splendid buildings, and his fierce zeal against idolators. The peninsula of Kathiawār, hitherto ruled in practice by its own Hindu chiefs, was now brought more closely under the Mussulman yoke. One of his

* The Jain temples of Mount Abū were built by Bhīm Dēo about 1030, and his successor Kuran built those at Girnar, as well as the reservoir that bore his name.

successors, Mahmūd Shah, turned his arms with success against almost every neighbour, and raised his kingdom to its highest pitch of greatness by land and sea. An embassy from Delhi bore witness to his power; and his fleets, in concert with those of the Mamlūk Sultān of Egypt, inflicted a signal check upon the Portuguese invaders of Western India. In the reign of Mahmūd's descendant, Bahādur Shah, the kings of Khandēsh, Berar, and Ahmadnagar paid formal homage to the king of Gujarāt, while Mālwa, after repeated struggles, became a part of his dominions.

The Mussulman kingdom of Mālwa had thus lasted about a hundred and thirty years. That province, lying between Gujarāt and Bundelkhand, with the Narbada for its southern boundary, had been governed by a long succession of Hindu princes, supposed to include the mythical Vikramaditya, and, some centuries later, the Raja Bhoj, before it passed under the Muhammadan yoke in the beginning of the fourtenth century. For nearly a hundred years its rulers were viceroys of the kings of Delhi. At last, in 1401, Dilāwar Khan of Ghor, a Pathān noble whom Firoz Tughlak had made Governor of Mālwa, threw off the last shred of allegiance to Delhi and founded a kingdom whose sovereigns were always fighting with this neighbour or with that. One of them, Mahmūd Khilji, besieged Delhi itself in the days of Saiyid Muhammad, but was driven off, as we saw, by the timely prowess of Bahlōl Lodi. Another Mahmūd fled to Gujarāt from the bondage prepared for him by his aggressive Hindu minister, Mēdni Rai. Restored to his throne by the help of King Muzaffar, he was taken prisoner by the troops of Raja Sanga of Chitōr, in a fruitless effort to drive Mēdni Rai out of Chandēri. The chivalrous Rājput forthwith set him free, a kindness which Mahmūd afterwards requited by wantonly attacking his son and successor, Rattan Singh. A fitting Nemesis, however, dogged his steps, in the shape of Bahādur Shah of Gujarāt, who listened the more readily to the Hindu's prayer for help, in that he himself had cause to complain of Mahmūd's treachery to the son of his old ally. Māndu, the hill-crowning capital of Mālwa, was stormed by the soldiers of Gujarāt, Mahmūd himself taken prisoner, and his kingdom annexed to that of Bahādur Shah.

South of Mālwa and south-east of Gujarāt, lay the little Muhammadan kingdom of Khandēsh, in those days a rich, smiling valley, watered by the Tāpti and a host of smaller streams, which successive princes, Hindu or Muhammadan, applied to the enrichment of the surrounding fields. Ruled for long centuries from Mālwa or Deogiri, it fell under the sway of its first Muhammadan governor in the reign of Firoz Tughlak. In 1399, Malik Raja was succeeded by his son, Nāsir Khan, who first claimed the rank and honours of an independent king. His reign was marked by the capture of the strong hill-fortress of Asīrgarh, one of the last remaining fastnesses of a Hindu dynasty, sprung from an old race of shepherd kings. The infernal treachery which issued in the seizure of a stronghold ruled by a friendly Hindu prince, and in the murder of the prince himself with all his family, was hailed by pious Muslims as a glorious triumph over the infidel. This noble deed was commemorated by the founding of Burhānpur, a city which one of Nāsir's successors, Adil Khan, enriched with buildings and waterworks of surpassing beauty or magnificent design.* Under its Muhammudan kings Khandēsh continued on the whole to prosper, until in the last days of the sixteenth century it passed under the wide sway of Akbar himself.

After his revolt from Muhammad Tughlak in 1338,

* Burhānpūr is still noted for the manufacture of rich and beautiful brocades, muslins, and other tissues.

Fakr-ud-din and his successors reigned for more than two centuries over Bengal. Of the events of that period not much is to be learned from the native chroniclers—a rare defect in the annals of any Muhammadan province. Frequent changes of dynasty happened of course in the usual violent way. One of the successful usurpers was Raja Kans, a Hindu Zamīndār, whose son became a Muhammadan, under the title of Jalāl-ud-din. Several of the kings who reigned in the fifteenth century were Abyssinian slaves or chiefs. At the time of Bābur's advent, their rule had been replaced and their power utterly broken by the house of Ala-ud-din, whose sceptre was ere long to pass into the hands of Humāyun's conqueror, the redoubtable Afghān Sher Shah.

Divided by the Great Desert from Sind and Multan, and spreading eastward nearly to the Jumna, rolls the broad sea of sandy rock-crested plain once called Rājāsthan, "the land of kings," but now generally known as Rājputāna, "the country of the Rājputs." Here reigned from century to century, hither from time to time fled with thousands of their followers and clansmen from neighbouring countries the high-souled, pure-blooded descendants of ancient Aryan lords. Century after century, from the days of the Arab Kāsim to those of the Mughal Bābur, these proud warrior chiefs defied the attacks or disowned in all but name the yoke of successive invaders. Some parts of the country were never conquered at all by the Pathān kings of Delhi. Others fluctuated between uneasy acquiescence and oft-recurring revolt. Foremost in bold, nor often vain resistance, were the Rājput princes of Mewār, whose capital, Chitōr, crowned the rugged hills that guarded their eastern frontier. At the end of the twelfth century, the Rahtōr clan of Rājputs left their early seats in Kanauj to wander westward across the Aravalli hills, and found a new kingdom in Marwār.

Under the feudal system which bound chiefs and followers together by strong ties of blood and fellowship, these Rājput races succeeded for the most part in maintaining a steady front against all assailants. A nation of born soldiers, who held their lands by a kind of joint military tenure, they mustered readily at the call of their hereditary chiefs, inflaming their courage with songs and tales commemorative of past glories, and betraying alike in victory and defeat the ancestral virtues of a proud, chivalrous, highbred, patriotic race; * virtues not wholly lost in their enfeebled, opium-eating children of the present day.

One of the foremost Rājput princes of the days before Bābur was the Rāna Sanga of Chitōr, who in the early years of the sixteenth century maintained a successful warfare against Gujarāt, and defeated in battle Mahmūd, the Muhammadan king of Mālwa. How courteously he treated his royal prisoner, and how meanly the courtesy was afterwards requited, we have already seen.

After the death of Hasan Gangu, founder of the Bahmani kingdom in the Deccan, his successors waged continual wars with the Hindu Rajas of Telingāna on the east, and of Vijayanagar on the south of their dominions. In 1421, Ahmad Shah dispossessed the former of their chief city Warangal, and made a savage inroad into Vijayanagar, part of which was added to his own broad realms. His son Ala-ud-din partially subdued the Konkan, lying between his western frontier and the sea, and removed

* "With them," says Elphinstone (p. 76), "the founder of a state, after reserving a demesne for himself, divided the rest of the country among his relations, according to the Hindu laws of partition. The chief to whom each share was assigned owed military service and general obedience to the prince, but exercised unlimited authority within his own lands. He in his turn divided his lands on similar terms among his relations, and a chain of vassal-chiefs was thus established, to whom the civil government as well as the military force of the country was committed."

his capital from Kulbarga (Gulbarga) to the heights where Bidar still towers in ruined majesty above the plain. In the reign of his grandson, Nizām Shah, the Deccan, overrun by the king of Mālwa, was saved from imminent ruin by the timely interference of the King of Gujarāt. In 1477, Nizām's son Muhammad exacted tribute from the Raja of Orissa, and carried his arms down the eastern coast as far as Kānchi, the modern Conjeeveram. On the western coast he completed the subjection of the Konkan, part of which had for about forty years defied the arms of successive Bahmani kings.

The real conqueror of the Konkan, Mahmūd Gāwan, the king's chief minister, one of the noblest men of that or any age, now fell a blameless victim to the plots of rivals who envied him his well-earned honours and commanding influence with the king. Too late Muhammad learned the innocence of the minister he had doomed to a hasty death. From that time the glory of the Bahmani kingdom began to fade away. His own death in the following year paved the way for the dismemberment of the Deccan under his child-heir. One large slice of his kingdom, from the sea to the Bhima and Kistna rivers, passed under the rule of Yusuf Adil Shah, who fixed his capital at Bijapur. The bought slave and faithful follower of Mahmūd Gāwan, he governed his new kingdom ably for twenty-one years, beating off assailants from every quarter, and attaching Marātha subjects to his rule by raising many of them to high civil and military posts. One of his successors, Ibrahīm, adopted the Marātha language, instead of Persian, for the public accounts. The dynasty, which survived the reign of Bābur and lasted into that of Aurangzeb, was involved in frequent wars, among others with the Portuguese, who steadily encroached upon its seaward possessions.

To the north of Bijapur grew up the rival state of Ahmadnagar, founded by Nizām Shah, who gave his original name of Ahmad to the city he built for his capital. He also appears to have favoured his Marātha subjects; and his successor, Burhān Shah, for the first time recorded in Muhammadan history, raised a Brahman to the post of Pēshwa, or prime minister. In spite of the Brahman's abilities, his master was compelled in 1530 to do homage to the King of Gujarāt; but the dynasty struggled on with varying fortune to its final overthrow by the troops of the Emperor Shah Jahān.

Out of the eastern provinces of the Bahmani kingdom, Imād Shah, a converted Hindu, who had risen high in the service of Mahmūd Gāwan, carved for himself the kingdom of Berar, which extended from the Indhyadri [Ajanta] hills to the Godāvari, with the highland city of Gāwilgarh for its capital. After a somewhat stormy existence of nearly ninety years, Berar was finally absorbed by its old rival Ahmadnagar.

A longer life, even to the days of Aurangzeb, awaited the kingdom of Golconda, founded in 1512 by Kutb Shah, a Turk whom Mahmūd Gāwan had appointed governor of the country between the Godāvari and the Kistna. During a reign of thirty-one years he made fresh conquests from the Rajas of Telingāna and Vijayanagar. His successors enlarged their dominions at the expense of their Hindu neighbours in Orissa and the Carnatic, and one of them in 1589 founded the city of Hyderābād, which became in after years the splendid capital of the Nizām's dominions.* Meanwhile, the diminished sway of the old Bahmani kings was still represented by the dynasty of Barīd Shah, which ruled at Bidar down to the middle of the seventeenth century.

One of the countries with which these Mussulman princes waged frequent war was Orissa, the Holy Land of

* It was called at first Bhāgnagar, the name it still bears among the Hindus. His son Haidar changed the name to Hyderābād.

successive Hindu creeds, and the seat for a century and a half of a powerful Yāvan dynasty, founded apparently by Greek invaders from the regions watered by the Ganges. In this land of forest-covered hills' and alluvial plains, stretching southwards from Midnapore to Ganjām, with the broad Māhāndi winding through it to the Bay of Bengal, a race of Sanskrit-speaking Aryans seems to have settled some centuries before the reign of King Asōka, pushing the aboriginal dwellers westward into the hills. Thither, from about the fifth century B C., a succession of Yāvan immigrants from the north brought with them the religion of Buddha, and the manners of a kindred but separate Aryan race, whom modern scholarship would identify with the Ionian Greeks. The worship of the sun, at any rate, came in time to be supplanted by that of Buddha, and the prevalence of the new faith for centuries afterwards is clearly attested by the rock-hewn caves, shrines, sculptures, and inscriptions, which cover the country with curious suggestions of Greek art applied to Buddhist purposes.*

Certain it is, however, that a Yāvan dynasty, entering Orissa from the sea, about A.D. 323, was expelled a hundred and fifty years later by a Hindu prince of the Kēsari line, whose advent paved the way for the gradual displacement of Buddhist by Brahmanic forms of worship. New temples everywhere arose in honour of Siva, whose worship in its turn succumbed in many places to the milder rites of the more genial Vishnu, best known to the myriads who yearly flock from all India to the priestly paradise of Pūri under his later name of Jagannath, the Lord of Heaven.

The Kēsari dynasty, which ruled Orissa for about six hundred and fifty years, was succeeded in its turn by the house of Ganga Vansa, in whose days the worship of

* See Hunter's "Orissa," vol. i. Sir William Hunter attempted to prove the identity of the Yāvanas in Orissa with the Ionians of Greek history and the Greek settlers in Kābul and Lahore.

Vishnu won its way into the headquarters of the Sivaite priesthood at Jajpur on the Baitarani. In the thirteenth century Hindu architecture reached its zenith, and the Orissa kingdom extended almost to the Godāvari. In the middle of that century the people of Orissa hurled back a Pathan invasion from Bengal, and ten years later another inroad was followed by a like defeat. In the middle of the fifteenth century the Raja of Orissa joined his Hindu neighbours in a league against the Mussulman invaders of Southern India, but some thirty years later he himself was paying tribute to a Muhammadan king. In the beginning of the sixteenth century the armies of Orissa were aiding a Mussulman ally against the great Hindu monarch of the South, Krishna Rāya Deva: but in vain. In 1563, the Orissa prince, no longer of the Ganga Vansa line, beat back a formidable inroad from Bengal; but this last flickering effort of native patriotism delayed for a few years only his country's doom. In 1567 the Afghān King of Bengal marched through Orissa at the head of an army which nothing could withstand, and for some unquiet years the country remained in the hands of its new masters. At last, when Bengal itself had acknowledged the superior might of Akbar, Orissa also was finally conquered by his great Hindu general, Todi Mall.

Krisna Rāya Deva, the Arthur of Southern India, mounted the throne of Vijayanagar in the first years of the sixteenth century. Ever since 1347, if not much earlier, the Hindu kingdom of Vijayanagar had played a leading part in the history of Southern India. From the usual want, however, of native annalists, our knowledge of the country comes to us in glimpses offered by the historians of the neighbouring Muhammadan states. The kings of the country, whose seaward frontier extended from Goa to Calicut, waged frequent wars with the Bahmani princes, and one of them, in 1493, suffered a heavy defeat from the ruler of Bijapur.

The glory and greatness of the kingdom culminated with Krishna Rāya Deva, whose sway extended over nearly all Southern India south of the Kistna, and whose arms were often successful against his Muhammadan neighbours.

So great at last grew the power of Vijayanagar, that the kings of the four Muhammadan states in the Deccan leagued together in 1565 against Rāmarāja, successor to Krishna Rāya. Their combined forces crossed the Kistna, and encountered the hosts of the Rāmarāja and his two brothers near Tālikōta. The Hindu horse charged boldly down upon the foe, with a fury which nothing could check until they came within reach of the guns brought forward by the King of Ahmadnagar. Against these Rāmarāja hurled the pick of his infantry, who fell in heaps under their deadly hail. A timely charge of Mussulman cavalry turned the disorder into hopeless rout. The brave old king himself was taken prisoner and mercilessly beheaded; one of his brothers died fighting; the routed troops were followed up with fearful slaughter; and untold treasures fell into the victors' hands. Vijayanagar was presently sacked and well-nigh destroyed; and the last great Hindu kingdom in Southern India thenceforth ceased to be.

CHAPTER V

THE PORTUGUESE IN INDIA

ABOUT thirty years before Bābur's victory at Pānipat, one of the smaller Christian states in Europe began to take an ambitious part in the affairs of India. As early as 1415, the success of the Venetians and Genoese in securing a monopoly of the carrying trade between Europe and India had fired Prince Henry of Portugal with the hope of diverting some part of a trade so enviable to his own shores. It was not, however, till the reign of John II. that Bartholomew Diaz fulfilled Prince Henry's previsions by rounding, in 1486, the Cape of Storms, which was afterwards to bear the more cheering title of the Cape of Good Hope. Eleven years later, King John's successor, Emmanuel, despatched a fleet which, under the famous Vasco da Gama, rounded the Cape, discovered Natal, and in May of the following year cast anchor near the city of Calicut on the Malabar coast. Courteously entertained by the Zamorin, the Hindu ruler of the province, Da Gama failed wholly to baffle the intrigues of the Moorish traders from Egypt and Arabia, who saw in these western strangers their likely rivals and possible supplanters. He sailed homewards in August, his three ships followed for some way in vain by a fleet of forty vessels sent out to capture them.

A fleet of thirteen ships and 1,200 men under Pedro Cabral appeared before Calicut in the autumn of 1500, less one ship lost with all its crew on the voyage thither.

The strangers were allowed to establish a factory, which the wrathful Muhammadans carried by storm. This outrage the Portuguese commander requited by setting ten Moorish ships on fire after their cargoes had been emptied into his own vessels, and cannonading the city itself. At Cochin, where he was kindly received, Cabral resumed the lading of his fleet, and took in some further cargo at Cannanore.

Soon after his departure homewards, the Zamorin of Calicut sent a powerful fleet to intercept the few ships which, under Juan de Nueva, were looking after Portuguese interests at Cochin and Cannanore. Careless of the odds against him, the bold Portuguese made ready for action, and used his guns to such purpose that the assailants speedily sheered off.

In 1502 a much larger fleet than Cabral's, carrying several hundred soldiers on board, sailed out of the Tagus under Vasco da Gama, who was empowered to take full revenge for the previous insults offered to the Portuguese flag.

Improving upon orders not perhaps too mild, the fiery Christian harried the Mussulmans wherever he met them, capturing a shipload of Mecca-bound pilgrims, and dooming hundreds of helpless prisoners to a cruel death in the flames of their own vessels. The Zamorin of Calicut being backward in making amends for the treatment of Cabral, the ruthless admiral hanged some fifty natives taken out of fishing-boats in the harbour, destroyed a great part of the town by bombardment, and set sail thence for Cochin, where his countrymen carried on a fair trade under the protection of its friendly Raja.

In 1503 Da Gama returned to Europe. Meanwhile another fleet from Portugal, under Affonso Albuquerque and his two brothers, arrived at Cochin in time to frustrate the Zamorin's designs against his vassal, the Raja of that place, who had dared to encourage the pushing strangers from the west. Once more defeated and compelled to sue for peace, the Zamorin availed himself of Albuquerque's departure to renew his attack upon Cochin, with a larger fleet than ever, and an army reinforced by the troops of his lord paramount, the Raja of Vijayanagar. In a series of hard-fought battles against fearful odds, the brave Pachēco beat back the invader with heavy loss; and a fresh fleet from Portugal under Soarez followed up his comrade's successes by the bombardment of Calicut, and the capture of all the Zamorin's vessels in fair fight.

Four years later, in 1507, a grand attack upon the rising Portuguese power in the Indian seas was concerted between the Venetians, the Sultān of Egypt, the Zamorin, and the Mussulman king of Gujarāt. Dom Francis Almeida, the first Portuguese Viceroy in India, had to meet this new danger as he best could. The allied fleets bore down upon that of Portugal, commanded by Lorenzo, the viceroy's son. A sharp engagement near Chaul, on the Konkan coast, issued in the defeat of the Portuguese and the sinking of their flagship with nearly all on board, including Lorenzo himself. For this disaster Almeida soon took his revenge. The port of Dābal destroyed by the guns of his fleet, he sailed northwards after the retiring foe, coming up with them off Diu, at the outer entrance to the Gulf of Cambay. The allied admirals at once accepted the challenge, and after a hard fight, in which all the best of the Muhammadan ships were burnt or captured, the remainder spread all sail in timely escape.

Almeida was ere long displaced as viceroy by Albuquerque, who raised the Portuguese power in the Indian seas to its greatest height, and won for it a noble and commanding seat by his final capture of Goa from the King of Bijapur. His conquests ranged from Ormuz in the

Persian Gulf to Malacca in the Malay Peninsula. Both towns were strongly fortified, and the whole sea-board of Western India became dotted with Portuguese factories. Baffled in his attempts on Aden and Calicut, he yet forced the Zamorin to sue for peace, crushed the Muhammadan trade in the Indian seas, and diverted the bulk of India's export trade with the West from the Adriatic to the Tagus. In spite, however, of these splendid achievements, Albuquerque fell into disgrace at Lisbon, and the news of his supersession by his foe Soarez broke his heart in the last days of 1515. With his dying breath the great viceroy, whose successes had been marred by no acts of wanton cruelty, bequeathed his son and a small estate to his sovereign's care, and appealed to his Indian career as the eloquent witness to his real deserts.*

Six years after his death, Diego Lopez de Siquēra, successor to Soarez, sailed against Diu with forty ships and three or four thousand men. But the bold front shown by the Gujarāti admiral cooled his courage, and not without heavy loss did his vessels make good their retreat to Chaul. In the following year Goa itself was besieged to no purpose by the King of Bijapur. In 1527 the fleets of Gujarāt were nearly destroyed in an unsuccessful attack on the Portuguese station of Chaul. Four years later Antonio di Silveira, with 400 ships and 22,000 men, made one more effort to capture Diu; but the genius and the guns of Rumi Khan, chief engineer to the King of Gujarāt, drove him out of the bay.

In spite of their fresh repulse, the Portuguese ere long

* Goa, the once splendid capital of the Portuguese in India, but now fallen into slow decay, lies in an island about twenty-four miles round. Its harbour, one of the noblest in India, is formed by an arm of the sea into which flows a small river. The old city still contains a number of fine churches, monasteries, and other buildings, the faded relics of former greatness. The Goa territory is about forty miles long by twenty broad, with a population of about 300,000, most of whom are Roman Catholics under a Portuguese archbishop.

gained a firm foothold on the long-coveted port, by means of a well-timed alliance with Bahādur Shah, the enterprising ruler of Gujarāt. That monarch's fears, however, were soon roused by the encroaching policy of his new friends, and his death in a chance affray between his attendants and the Portuguese gave rise to charges, not quite perhaps unfounded, of preconcerted treachery on both sides.*

Meanwhile a great fleet from Egypt, equipped by orders from Constantinople and commanded by a Turkish admiral, bore down in September, 1537, for the Gulf of Cambay, with intent to drive the Portuguese out of Gujarāt. But the brave Silveira, with only 600 men, prepared to defend to the last the new factory, which he had already turned into a little fortress. After eight months of imminent peril, of sufferings more and more enhanced by famine and disease,† the wasted garrison were gladdened by the approach of a fleet which the Viceroy of Goa had brought in the nick of time to their help. Sallying forth from their battered works, they drove before them the disheartened besiegers, and Diu was saved.

The history of the Portuguese during that century may as well be finished here. Two more futile attacks on Diu by Mahmūd Shah of Gujarāt, in 1545 and 1548, were followed by about twenty years of chequered warfare and much intrigue on land, and of supreme dominion by sea. No ship without a Portuguese passport could sail with perfect safety over Indian waters. In many articles of trade the Portuguese monopoly was complete; and of what trade was still open to ships of other countries, the Portuguese captains secured the lion's share by enforcing the right to load their own vessels first. If the frequent cruelty and

* See Elphinstone's "India," p. 678 (4th Edition).

† The ladies of the garrison bore no trifling part in the defence, and their heroic example went far to save the place.

arrogance of Portuguese commanders earned them many foes, their alliance was often courted by neighbours who had learned to dread their prowess in the field, or to take due measure of the strength that lay unseen behind the few ships and soldiers that guarded their factories. Whether from policy or national instinct, the Portuguese never pushed their way far from the sea-coast, confining themselves even at Goa to a narrow strip of land between the sea and the Western Ghāts. So long as their fleets ruled the ocean, nothing more was needed for the maintenance of their power. But the time was soon to come when stronger rivals pushed them from their watery throne, and their hold on India dwindled to a ruinous city, two small decaying seaports, Diu and Daman, and about 1,500 square miles of ground.

In 1570, however, the glory of Goa and the religious bigotry of its priesthood were at their height, when a great league was formed against it by the princes of Bijapur, Ahmadnagar, and Calicut. For ten months an immense army of horse and foot with 350 guns besieged in vain a city held by its governor, Dom Louis, with about 700 soldiers, aided by 1,300 monks and armed slaves. Wearied at last of a siege in which he lost 12,000 men alone, besides thousands of horses and cattle, and hundreds of elephants, the King of Bijapur withdrew his troops from what seemed a hopeless enterprise. A like repulse was all the Nizām Shah of Ahmadnagar obtained from his twice-attempted attack upon Chaul; and Chāle near Calicut was defended with equal success against the Zamorin. For the rest of the sixteenth century the Portuguese power in India remained unshaken.

But early in the next century new rivals appeared upon the scene. In 1604 the Dutch, who had but lately won their independence of Spain, wrested Amboyna from the Portuguese, and even made an attempt upon Malacca.

In 1612 a small English fleet defeated with heavy loss the Portuguese squadron which strove to bar its way into the harbour of Surat. Another English fleet drove the Portuguese, in 1622, from their flourishing settlement in the isle of Ormuz. Between the advances of two such rivals the Portuguese power in the Indian seas gradually declined, and the trade monopoly which the countrymen of Albuquerque had held for a century passed into other and stronger hands.

BOOK III

THE MUGHAL DYNASTY OF BĀBUR

CHAPTER I

BĀBUR AND HUMĀYUN—1526–1556

WITH the fall of Ibrahīm, and the rout of his army at Pānipat, dates the beginning of a new empire in Hindustān. The two great cities of Delhi and Agra speedily acknowledged their new master. But the task before Bābur was still formidable. The new Emperor of India had yet to make his way through the broad regions lying to the south, east, and south-west of his new capital. His soldiers and his nobles were equally unwilling to go further. Cheered at length by his brave words, or shamed by his earnest reproaches, most of them resolved to follow his standard, and in the course of a few months the old Mussulman provinces in the valley of the Ganges had nearly all submitted to his rule.

Westward of the Jumna, however, a mighty force was gathering against him, under the powerful Rāna Sanga, the Rājput sovereign of Mewār. Followed by all the chivalry of Marwār and Jaipur, and strengthened by the troops of Mahmūd, a prince of the dispossessed house of Lodi, the great Raja marched towards Delhi. At Sikri,* not far from Agra, he assailed and defeated the van of the Mughal army. Had he only dared to order a general

* Since called Fatehpur Sikri.

advance, the future of India might have been very different, for a panic had seized upon the bravest of Bābur's troops. But the right moment was lost. Bābur's stirring remonstrances touched the hearts of his officers. Dropping a few brave words here and there as he galloped along the line he had formed in order of battle, the light-hearted Mughal led his troops against the foe. The Rājputs fought with their usual courage, but nothing could withstand the charge of Bābur's veterans. Rāna Sanga's bloody defeat left Rājputāna at the victor's mercy, and cleared the way for fresh victories over Mahmūd Lodi, who at length, with the shattered remnants of his army, retired beyond the Sōn.

Next year Bābur attacked and stormed Chandēri, the capital of a small Rājput kingdom carved by Mednī Rai, out of the lands he had wrested from the kings of Mālwa. Once more Rājput heroism, hopeless of victory, preferred speedy death to the tender mercies of Muhammadan rule. As the Mughal troops were storming the city, the garrison slew all their women, and then rushed upon the foe to die. Chandēri captured, the fiery Mughal darted across the Ganges into Oudh, drove the Afghāns before him in all directions, and ere long added Bihār also to his sway. The Sultān of Bengal was glad to sue for peace on terms which included the surrender of North Bihār.

By this time Bābur's health was fast breaking under the heavy strain of so many and prolonged exertions. His end was probably hastened by anxiety for his beloved son, Humāyun, who now lay dangerously ill at Agra. With pardonable superstition, the war-worn father, walking thrice round his son's bed, solemnly besought Heaven to spare Humāyun, and take himself instead. "I have borne it away! I have borne it away!" were the joyful words that presently escaped him. From that moment, say the historians, the son began to recover, and the father to decline.

HUMAYUN

FROM A MS. OF SHAH JAHAN NAMEH FORMERLY IN THE POSSESSION OF AKBAR II NOW IN THE BRITISH MUSEUM

Be that as it may, it was Bābur's own conviction that he would shortly die; and it is certain that he met his end as cheerfully as he had battled through the darkest trials of his stormy life. After a few last words of wise and loving counsel to his sons and ministers, he died at Agra in December, 1530, at the age of forty-nine.

The best picture of the great Mughal is that which he himself has drawn for us in his own delightful Memoirs, replete with every charm of a frank, genial, yet manly nature, and a well-stored, inquiring mind. At once a poet, scholar, and musician, he had all the qualities which those words imply, mixed up with the tougher tissues that go to the making of the adventurous soldier and the hard-headed statesman. In a straightforward, lively, picturesque style, perfectly natural, yet never coarse nor inflated, he tells or suggests to us everything he did, saw, or suffered; how he wept for his boyish playfellow; how fond an interest he took in his mother and near kindred; how keen were his sympathies alike with the pleasures and the misfortunes of his friends; how lightly he bore his own reverses, riding a race with the only two friends who followed him, a houseless, half-starved wanderer, on his dreary journey from Samarkand. With equal ease and lightness of touch, he describes the hardships he underwent, the bursts of revelry in which he and his companions not seldom indulged; the scenery, climate, people, and products of the countries he passed through; the sayings and doings of his friends; his own successes, failures, and weaknesses; the sense of loneliness that came over him as he ate a musk-melon brought from Kābul. Violent sometimes, and cruel when the fit was on him, he endeared himself to his friends and followers by many kindly actions, and treated his enemies on the whole with wonderful forbearance. His high courage never failed him and his buoyant spirit nothing seemed to pull down. Fond of wine, and given to hard drinking, he eschewed both in his later years. No small part of his leisure hours was bestowed on public business, and his active habits were equally conspicuous in the camp, the council-room, and the hunting-field. In his last journey of 160 miles from Kalpī to Agra, in spite of failing health, he rode the distance in two days, and swam twice across the Ganges. Not content with the regular business of the state, his mind was always full of schemes for the public welfare, from the building of reservoirs and aqueducts to the introduction of new trade-products from abroad. No wonder that the memory of a king so lovable and so richly endowed should be cherished by the Muhammadans of India beyond that of all other princes, save Aḳbar, of the same great line.

Humāyun, heir to his father's Indian throne, seems to have inherited something of his father's chequered fortunes. Much against his own will, he weakened his empire by handing Kābul and the Punjāb over to his brother, Kāmrān. To another of his brethren he assigned the province of Sambal or Rohilkhand, while a third was appointed Governor of Mewāt, in Rājputāna. The first two years of his reign were employed in quelling revolts in Bundelkhand, Jaunpur, and Bihār. Then began a quarrel with Bahādur Shah of Gujarāt, who had given shelter to Humāyun's brother-in-law, and furnished the uncle of the last Pathān king of Delhi with the means of waging war against the new dynasty. Defeated at Mandasōr, and driven from place to place, the once powerful king of Gujarāt found shelter at Diu, in the farthest corner of his realm.

Humāyun's success was crowned by his daring capture of Chāmpanēr, seated on a lofty rock, up whose steep side he and 300 of his chosen followers clomb with the help of steel spikes. Leaving his brother, Mirza Askari, in charge of his new conquests, Humāyun marched back to Agra, in order to deal with a new rebellion got up by Sher Khan, an Afghān noble, who had already made himself master of Bihār, and begun the conquest of Bengal. The strong fort of Chunār on the Ganges taken after a stout defence, the Mughal monarch pushed on to Gaur, the capital of Bengal. Here, however, his troops were sadly thinned by sickness, consequent on the heavy rains and floods of an Indian monsoon.* In spite of the weather, his Afghān foe made his way up to Jaunpur, and threatened to cut off Humāyun's retreat. Leaving garrisons in his new conquests, Humāyun at length began his homeward march.

Once more, however, Sher Khan's skilful strategy turned his resources to their best account. After defeating a strong Mughal force at Monghyr, he suddenly fell about daybreak on Humāyun's army encamped at Chausa, near Buxār, on the road to Benāres, routed it with heavy slaughter, and drove its leader, with the shattered remnant of his host, in wild flight across the Ganges. Humāyun himself barely escaped drowning, his empress was taken prisoner, and the bulk of his best troops perished by the sword or in the river.

A like disaster befell him in the following year not far from Kanauj, where with fresh troops recruited from Kābul and Lahore he was again surprised by the same bold and crafty assailant. From this last crushing blow it took him many years to recover. Under the name of Sher Shah the victorious Afghān seated himself on the throne of Delhi, which he and his successors held for about sixteen years. While Humāyun, with a few faithful followers, was roaming perilously from place to place, from province to province, in vain quest of help, now from his brother Kāmrān at Lahore, anon from the rulers of Mārwār and Sind, Sher Shah was bringing province after province in

* The rainy season in Bengal lasts from June to the end of September.

Upper India under his sway, driving Kāmrān out of the Punjāb, overrunning Rājputāna, and wresting Chitōr from the discomfited Raja of Mewār.

His death before Kālanjar in the hour of victory transferred the crown to his second son Salim Shah, who, supplanting his feeble elder brother, reigned in peace for about nine years, and, like his able father, did much for the internal improvement of his dominions.* He was succeeded in 1553 by his brother Muhammad Shah, who secured his power by the murder of his child-nephew, and lost half his dominions through successful revolts in the course of his three years' reign.

By this time fortune, tired of persecuting the eldest son of Bābur, opened the way for his triumphant return to India and his father's throne. The first five years of Humāyun's exile had been a time of perilous adventures, cruel hardships, and hairbreadth escapes. Driven from Lahore by his brother's self-seeking policy, he had fled to Sind for the aid he was not to find there. Crossing the desert to Jodhpur with his household and a few followers, many of whom died of thirst and weariness by the way, he fared no better than before at the hands of a Hindu Raja, who had more reason to hate than help him. Thrown once more upon the dreary desert, with enemies behind him and before, each day's march bringing its own hardships, each halt a fresh fight for water with the unfriendly villagers, he lost all hope when the horsemen of Mārwār, led by the son of their Raja, closed in upon his small band. But Rājput chivalry still spared the helpless. Reproaching Humāyun for entering the Rājput country without leave, and for slaying the cattle which the Hindus held sacred, the son of the Raja supplied the fugitives with food and water, and bade them depart in peace. A

* The stern-looking Pathan fort of Salīmgarh at Delhi still bears his name, and was probably built in his reign.

few more days of wandering in the sandy desert brought Humāyun's diminished band to Umarkōt on the borders of Sind, where they found rest and a kindly welcome from its Hindu chieftain, Rāna Parsād. Here it was that Humāyun's beloved Hamīda gave birth, in October, 1542, to the son, who afterwards became the glory of India under the Mughals.

With the help of his new friend, Humāyun marched into Sind, and was making his way there against his old enemy, Husēn Arghūn, when Rāna Parsād, fired by some real or fancied affront, left the camp with all his followers; and Humāyun compounded with adverse fortune by retiring in 1543 towards Kandahar. Into that city his wife and child were admitted by his brother, Mirza Askari; but Humāyun himself gained no rest from wandering until he found an asylum at Herāt, then held by the Shah of Persia, who treated him on the whole with great, though fitful munificence, and agreed to aid him in wresting Kābul from his brother Kāmrān, on condition of his embracing the Shiāh tenets of Islam, and ceding Kandahār to his Persian ally.

These terms accepted, the royal exile set forth on his appointed task with a few hundred of his own adherents, aided by 14,000 Persian horse. In the autumn of 1545 Kandahār surrendered; but with the treachery of his race Humāyun took the first tempting occasion to turn out the Persian garrison and replace them by his own troops. Kābul, which he took at the beginning of that winter and lost again during his absence in Badakhshān, was recaptured in the spring of the year 1547.

His hold upon the country was still, however, uncertain. A reconciliation between the four sons of Bābur was ere long stultified by a fresh revolt on Kāmrān's part; fresh mishaps awaited the much-enduring Humāyun; and not till 1551 did he find himself once more master of Kābul and the surrounding country. Chased from one shelter to another, Kāmrān was at length betrayed into the hands of his long-suffering brother, who commuted with the loss of his eyes the death-sentence awarded by the Mughal officers of state.*

Humāyun's thoughts still turned to the scene of his early greatness and his father's renown. The new Pathān empire was already breaking up, but years of peril had taught him caution. Superstition, however, came to the aid of his natural restlessness; encouraging omens bade him venture on the path to which many friends and many circumstances were already inviting him. At length, in December, 1554, he marched from Kābul, made his way to Lahore, inflicted a crushing defeat on Sikandar Sūr at Sind,† and once more entered the gates of Delhi in July, 1555, after an absence of nearly sixteen years.

He was not, however, to enjoy his new-found throne for long. About six months afterwards, he was going down the stairs outside the terrace of his library, when the cry to prayer reached him from the nearest minaret. After praying like a good Mussulman on the spot, he was rising with the help of his staff, when it slipped on the smooth marble of the steps, and the king fell headlong over the low parapet. On the 25th January, four days after his fall, the brave but unlucky son of Bābur breathed his last, in the forty-ninth year of his age, after a career at least as stormy as his father's, set off by many of his father's noblest and most endearing, as well as some of his weaker traits.

* The "Memoirs" quoted by Elphinstone, book vii. chap. 4, say nothing of the previous sentence, but would lead us to regard the blinding of Kāmrān as an act of needless cruelty on Humāyun's part. That, however, seems to be an unfair view of Humāyun's character.

† Young Akbar, then but twelve years old, was in the thickest of the fight. Sikandar was a nephew of the great Sher Shah.

CHAPTER II

JALĀL-UD-DIN AKBAR, 1556–1605

THE throne to which Akbar succeeded in his fourteenth year was very different from that which he handed down to his successors. Enemies, open or secret, were plotting or rising against him on every side. He had hardly sent Sikandar Sūr once more flying to the mountains, and despatched some of his troops to the help of his ministers in Kābul, when Hēmu, the Hindu general who still fought for Muhammad Shah, the last king of Sher Shah's line, advancing from Bengal, captured Agra, occupied Delhi, and encamped on the fatal field of Pānipat. It was a trying moment for the new dynasty when Akbar's general, Bairām Khan, resolved, with the young king's willing sanction, to stake the hopes of the Mughals on the issue of a battle against tremendous odds. On the morning of the 5th November, 1556, the fight began which ended in the utter rout of Hēmu's army and the capture of its brave leader, badly wounded. Urged by Bairām Khan to win the title of "Ghazi"—Champion of the Faith—by slaying the captive with his own sword, the generous Akbar—so some authorities say—refused to strike a wounded foe, and the fatal stroke was dealt by Bairām himself.

A campaign in the Punjāb ended in the final surrender of Sikandar Sūr, who retired to Bengal, where the Pathāns still held their ground. For the next three years the government of Delhi was wielded by the able but too imperious Bairām, some of whose actions galled the pride and imperilled the authority of his young master. At length, in 1560, Akbar by a sudden effort took the reins of state into his own hands, and the unseated minister presently went into rebellion, in hopes of carving out a separate kingdom for himself. Foiled, however, by Akbar's promptitude, he had to throw himself on his sovereign's mercy. His prayers for pardon were heard by a prince who forgot his late offences in remembrance of his former great deeds. Raising the suppliant with his own hand, Akbar placed him by his side, and bade him choose between high office at court or elsewhere and an honourable retreat to Mecca. Bairām chose the latter, but was stabbed on his way through Gujarāt by an Afghān whose father he had slain in battle.

For many years to come Akbar's throne was anything but a bed of roses. He had still to reconquer the greater part of India, to control his unruly nobles, to win the goodwill or break the power of formidable Hindu and Muhammadan princes, to restore order and well-being throughout his dominions, to lay anew, in short, the foundations of a great and lasting empire. His own countrymen were mere strangers in the land, compared with the Pathans, who had been taking root there for three centuries past, and who, like the Norman settlers in Ireland, had lost many of their distinctive features by close and continual contact with surrounding races. It was Akbar's chief glory that he saw clearly what he had to do as a wise ruler of a distracted country, and did it steadily with all his might. Through all the warfare of his long reign he acted on the principle of treating his enemies as though they might become his friends, and this far-seeing policy was justified by almost unvarying success. His highest aim was to unite all classes, creeds, and races in India under one mild equitable rule; and his achievements in that direction have been rivalled by very few princes in any age or country.

In the first four years of his reign, Akbar extended his conquests over Ajmēr, Gwalior, Oudh, and Jaunpur. In 1561 Mālwa was wrested from the Afghāns by Abdullah Khan, an Uzbek leader, who afterwards sought to keep the province for himself. Akbar was not long in marching against the rebel, who fled to Gujarāt. The turbulence of commanders who tried to retain the government, or, at least, the plunder of the provinces they helped to win, would have reduced their young sovereign to a mere puppet, but for his boldness in dealing with so common a danger to the Muhammadan power. Zemān Khan, the conqueror of Jaunpur, had once already succumbed to Akbar's resolute bearing; but now he joined with the disaffected Uzbek lords in Mālwa in leading a formidable revolt, which Akbar, with hands full of other annoyances, could not for several years succeed in quelling. While the emperor was chasing his disloyal brother Hakīm out of the Punjāb, the Uzbek rebels pushed their way into Oudh and Allahābād. But Akbar's daring strategy served him well on this as on many another occasion. By a swift and sudden march, with only 2000 men he swooped down upon the rebel camp across the Ganges, slew or captured several of their leaders, and drove the scared troops before him in wild disorder. They never rallied again, and thus a revolt which had made head against his best generals was quelled at last by the brilliant energy of Akbar himself.

His arms were next turned against Chitōr, whose Raja, a son of the great Rāna Sanga, retired into the hills, leaving behind him a picked garrison of 8000 men. The siege of the fortress-city was carried on with patient skill by means of regular zigzags and well-laid mines. But the defence was equally stubborn, and not till their brave and skilful leader, Jai Mal, had fallen by a well-aimed shot from Akbar's own bow did the garrison lose heart. Then, with the usual wild courage of their race, they slew their women, and rushed out to meet their own fate from the Mussulmans who had already mounted the breaches. They perished nearly to a man, and the fall of their famous stronghold sent a shiver of dismay through all Rājasthān. Udī Singh himself remained untouched in his native wilds; but the hill-forts of Ranthambhōr and Kālanjar ere long fell to Akbar's arms, several of the foremost Rājput princes tendered their allegiance to the new power, and a few of them afterwards rendered it loyal service as soldiers, statesmen, or governors of important provinces. Princesses of the purest Rājput blood had already begun to enter the Imperial household as wives of Akbar, his sons, and kinsmen.* It is still the boast of the Rānas of Udaipur—the city founded by the son of Udī Singh some years after the capture of Chitōr—that the ladies of their house alone have never stooped to intermarry with the kings of Delhi.

Akbar's merciful treatment of the Hindus bore good fruit in his subsequent warfare against his cousins and their allies in Gujarāt. In 1572 the last king of that country had made him a formal tender of his crown, and Akbar at once proceeded to make himself master of his new kingdom. In one of his rapid marches he found himself with only 156 men in front of 1000 of the enemy. But his little band included the Raja of Jaipur and his nephew Mān Singh, and their steadfast courage not only saved his life, but enabled him also to beat off and scatter his assailants. One of his rebel cousins was afterwards routed by Raja Rai Singh of Mārwār.

Hardly had Akbar returned to Agra from the conquest of Gujarāt, when his cousin Mirza Husēn once more defied

* Akbar had married two queens from the houses of Jaipur and Mārwār, and a princess of Jaipur was already married to his eldest son.

him to the issue of battle. With a force of about 3000 picked men the prompt Mughal marched more than 450 miles in nine days, and suddenly confronted the insurgent troops near Ahmadābād. In a succession of bold charges he swept through and through the astonished foe; a successful sally from the city crowned his own efforts, and the siege of Ahmadābād was raised. Peace restored to the country, he again returned to Agra, the capital of his choice.

Two years afterwards he had entered upon the harder work of reconquering Bengal and the rest of Bihār from the Pathāns, whose ruler, Dāūd Khan, had never paid his promised tribute to the Mughals. Before Akbar's steady advance Dāūd retired into Orissa, where he held his ground for a time against Akbar's generals, including the renowned Todi Mall, his Hindu Minister of Finance. Driven at length into a corner, he made peace on condition of retaining Orissa for himself. In a few months, however, he was again tempted to try his fortune with Akbar; but his defeat and death in a pitched battle with the Mughal troops ensured the overthrow of the Afghān power in Bengal and Bihār. It was not, however, until three years later that these new conquests were brought into perfect order, after Todi Mall and his successor had put down a formidable rising among Akbar's own troops; and not till 1592 was the Afghān power in Orissa finally broken by Mān Singh.

Meanwhile Akbar himself had had to deal with his restless brother Mirza Hakīm, who in 1581 invaded the Punjāb from Kābul, and drove the governor, Mān Singh, into Lahore. After chasing him back to Kābul, and thence into the mountains, Akbar, with his usual nobleness, forgave his brother's offences, and left him in charge of Kābul until his death. This generous policy, however, was not always equally successful. At this very time the late king of Gujurāt, Muzaffar Shah, on whom Akbar had bestowed a jāgīr, or feudal estate, started a new insurrection in his former kingdom. Driven out of the inland provinces Muzaffar still held his ground in Kathiawar for a few years longer, until in 1593 he was given up to the imperial commanders, and slew himself on his way to the Emperor's court.

Master of Kābul, Akbar ere long set himself to conquer Kashmīr. The invading army made its way in 1587 to Srinagar, the capital; and the king, on making his submission, was compensated with a noble jāgīr in Bihār.

Meanwhile Akbar's generals were engaged in a vain attempt to subdue the lawless mountaineers of Swāt and the Khyber. In 1586 the Mughal troops got hopelessly entangled among the rugged hills and gorges of Swāt; the Raja Bīr Bal's division perished nearly to a man under the swords of the daring Yuzufzais; and his colleague Zain Khan was driven back with heavy loss to Attock, where Akbar had lately built the fort that still overlooks the Indus. Fresh troops sent into the mountains under Todi Mall and Mān Singh made some impression upon the foe by cutting off supplies and establishing a chain of strong posts in commanding positions. But the Yusufzais were never thoroughly subdued, and the legacy of trouble which Akbar bequeathed to his successors has not yet been exhausted even under the British rule.

It was about this time that Kandahar and Sind were annexed to Akbar's dominions;* the one conquest completing the range of his old hereditary possessions, the other leaving him undisputed master of all India northward of the Narbada, save perhaps the tract of country still held against him by the Rāna of Udaipur.

* In his war against Akbar the chief of Sind employed Portuguese soldiers and native *Sipahis*, dressed as Europeans.

Akbar's hopes were now turned to the Deccan, whither a way for his arms seemed to open itself in the offer made him by one of the rival claimants to the throne of Ahmadnagar. His troops marched upon the capital, but the brave woman Chānd Bībī, who held it for her child-nephew, maintained a defence so stout and heroic, that, after more than one attempt to storm the city, Prince Murad was fain to let her alone on condition of being allowed to occupy Berar.

A few months later war was renewed. Chānd Bībī had fallen into the power of her own minister, who forced her, in spite of the late treaty, to enter into a league with the other princes of the Deccan. Early in the next year Prince Murad encountered the allies at Sonepet on the Godāvari. A furious battle, which lasted two days, led to no more tangible issue than a protracted quarrel between the Mughal prince and his colleagues in command. At length Akbar himself resolved to interfere in person. Leaving the Punjāb, where he had long been staying, he reached the Narbada in 1599, and sent an army to renew the siege of Ahmadnagar. In spite of the murder of the brave Chānd Bībī by the agents of a hostile faction, in the midst of her efforts to treat for peace, the Mughals soon stormed the place with heavy slaughter; the young king was sent prisoner to Gwalior, and the final conquest of the whole kingdom might have been forestalled by many years had Akbar's return homeward not been hastened by unforeseen events. As it was, however, he stayed in the Deccan long enough to complete the conquest of Khandēsh, to betroth one of his sons to a princess of Bijapur, and to cripple beyond recovery the power of the Ahmadnagar kingdom.

The cause of his sudden return to Hindustan was the revolt of his eldest son Salim, who, left in charge of the home government, took advantage of his father's absence to seize upon Oudh and Bihār, plunder the treasury at

Allahābād, and proclaim himself a king. Cruel, violent, and revengeful, he had already, at thirty years of age, impaired his great mental powers and heightened his worst traits by hard drinking and excess of opium. Akbar, in terms of fatherly loving-kindness, entreated him to forego his unfilial projects, and all would be forgiven. In the very midst of their negotiations Salim was plotting the death of Abul Fazl, one of Akbar's most trusted friends and officers, and the chief historian of his reign. In happy ignorance of his son's share in the murder of so dear a friend, Akbar renewed his offers of reconciliation, and Salim, returning to a show of duty, took up his abode of Allahābād.

Fresh quarrels, the fruit of fresh excesses on Salim's part, were hardly appeased when Akbar, who had already lost his son Murad from illness, had to mourn the death of his third son, Prince Dāniyal, from chronic drunkenness. All these things preyed upon his own failing health, and his dying hours were further embittered by the intrigues of opposing factions at his court. Plans were formed for setting the unpopular Salim aside in favour of his eldest son Khusrū, the child of his Rājput wife. Akbar's influence, however, asserted itself in the jaws of death. The plot came to nothing; and in the presence of his weeping son and reconciled nobles, the dying king murmured his last injunctions to peace, goodwill, and loyal discharge of duties on the part of each and all there assembled. Entreating the forgiveness of any whom he might have offended, and commending to his son's care his own friends and the ladies of his household, Bābur's glorious grandson ere long passed away amidst the prayers of his chief Mullah, on the last day of his sixty-third year, in the fifty-second year of a reign which began two years before and ended two years after that of our own Elizabeth.

AKBAR'S ENTRY INTO SURAT

FROM A MS. IN THE VICTORIA AND ALBERT MUSEUM

p. 114

He died in outward seeming a better Mussulman than he had lived. His early devotion to the faith of Islam had long since yielded to a spirit of philosophical inquiry and large-hearted tolerance for all kinds of worship, as expressions of human yearning towards a common God. The same generous instinct which shrank from slaying the captive Hēmu afterwards led him, in the teeth of the prevailing bigotry, to show equal courtesy to men of every creed, and to encourage Christian priests and Brahman pandits in holding free discussion with the learned doctors of Islam. The Christians he treated with marked respect, paying reverence even to images of Christ and the Virgin Mary, and allowing his son Murad to study the Christian Gospels. His innate piety, guided by a powerful intellect, a tender heart and a romantic sense of justice, taught him to see good in forms of worship the most diverse, and to eschew the persecuting habits so dear to well-meaning zealots of every creed. In his hands the sword of Muhammad became a sceptre of upright and merciful dealing with all whom circumstances placed under his power. He entertained many Christian missionaries and discussed religion with them, but he never thought seriously of accepting the Faith.

In accordance with his love of evenhanded justice, he annulled all legal sanctions even for practices ordered by the Korān. No man was any longer forced by law to fast, attend public worship, go on pilgrimage, or abstain from wine and unclean meats ; and the rite of circumcision was put off till the age of twelve, in order that the young believer might be free in a measure to choose his religion for himself. In the same spirit he forbade the burning of Hindu widows against their will, the marriage of Hindu children before a fit age, and the Hindu practice of trial by ordeal.* The latest efforts of English legislation in

* On one occasion, hearing that the Raja of Jodhpur was forcing his

India were forestalled by a decree allowing Hindu widows to marry again. All taxes on pilgrims, temples, religious rites, and the hateful Jiziya or poll-tax so long exacted from the conquered Hindus were done away, and a stop was put to the cruel old Muhammadan practice of selling into slavery all prisoners taken in war. The more zealous Mussulmans shrugged their shoulders at these lapses from orthodox usage; but the reforming emperor held his own way, and their anger seldom broke into open remonstrance against changes decreed by "God's Khalif," with the virtual assent of doctors learned in Muhammadan law.*

In substituting a new era dating from his own accession for that of the Hijra, he may have been impelled by the same kind of vanity which led him to enforce the un-Muhammadan practice of prostration before the king. His extreme intolerance of the beards worn by all good Mussulmans appears to lack even the excuse of public policy, claimed for the war which Tzar Peter afterwards waged against the beards of Muscovite orthodoxy. But in the former instance it is only fair to credit him with the good results of a change, which at least included the more scientific method of reckoning by solar instead of lunar months and years.

Improving on the example of the Bijapur kings, Akbar gave high employment to Hindus of mark or promise. The Raja Mān Singh became one of his foremost generals and most trusty governors. Bīr Bal perished as we saw among the hills of Swāt. Bhagwān Dās of Jaipur, Akbar's brother-in-law, took a leading part in the conquest of Kashmīr; while Raja Todi Mall eclipsed his own renown as a successful soldier by his civil government of Bengal

son's widow to do *Sati*, he rode off to the spot to prevent the intended sacrifice.

* Akbar took care to obtain the legal opinion of his chief lawyers, that as head of the Church he had a right to govern it according to his own judgment. (Elphinstone's "India," book ix. chap. 3.)

Photo. by [illegible]erwood & Under[illegible]d

AKBAR'S TOMB AT SIKANDARAH

p. [illegible]

and the great financial reforms which, as Akbar's prime minister, he succeeded in carrying through.* Under men like these, thousands of Hindus fought in the Imperial ranks, or found a wide field for their talents in every branch of the civil service, except the judicial, which was still reserved for Muhammadans alone. In all suits, however, between Hindus, justice was dealt out by the Muhammadan judges in strict accordance with Hindu law.

At once among the bravest and most merciful of men, Akbar never took the field himself without chaining victory to his standard, nor ever stained his arms with needless cruelties. But the need for his presence over, he left his commanders to follow up his own successes; and enjoining them to deal humanely with the conquered, betook himself with unfeigned pleasure to works of peace, especially to the great work of establishing order and good government throughout the fifteen provinces of his empire.

For this end he found a fitting helpmate in Todi Mall, whose scheme for settling the land-revenue seems in the main to have developed the reforming policy of Humāyun's conqueror, Sher Shah. The land was divided into three classes, whose degrees of fruitfulness were measured by one uniform standard. For each bīgah—equal to about two-thirds of an acre—the average yield of its class was taken, and of the common average one-third was set apart for the government claim. The money value of that third was reckoned upon an average of prices for nineteen years back, and the husbandman was free to pay the State's share either in money or in kind. These assessments, at first made yearly, were afterwards revised only once in ten years, on an average of payments for the previous ten. All matters bearing on these settlements were duly entered from time to time in the village registers. No existing tenures were altered or ignored. Great care was taken to

* Todi Mall was a Hindu from Lahore.

respect the rights and redress the grievances of every husbandman. For revenue purposes the country was parcelled out into districts of a certain value, each placed under its own collector. A great many vexatious fees and taxes were removed, and the system of farming the revenue was done away. The net result of these measures was to lighten the land of many burdens without much reducing its fiscal value to the State. Reforms like these, however imperfect, went far to secure the happiness of the people, and served as the foundation on which our own countrymen were afterwards to build.*

In reforms of police and public justice the great emperor showed himself equally zealous, in his own despotic fashion, for his people's good. Criminals were punished without needless cruelty in certain prescribed ways; torture was wholly forbidden; and in ordinary cases no one could be judicially put to death until his sentence had been confirmed by Akbar himself. His troops were regularly paid in cash, their equipment carefully supervised, and false returns of men and horses checked by musters taken before each issue of pay. Each of the officers appointed by the king had to keep so many men, horse, foot, matchlock-men, and archers, ready for service at need. The army thus maintained, however fit for its purpose, was still a mere collection of chance levies, compared with the standing armies of modern Europe.

With a soldier's eye for defensive purposes, Akbar built the river-fortresses of Attock on the Indus, Agra on the Jumna, Allahābād at the meeting of the Jumna with the Ganges. In all branches of public business, his hand was visible, sweeping away old abuses, retrenching needless outlay, and devoting part of his great revenues † to works

* Elphinstone's "India," book ix. chap. 3. Colonel Meadows Taylor ("Manual of Indian History") points to the close resemblance between Akbar's revenue-settlement and the recent survey and assessment of Bombay.

† He is said to have drawn from India a revenue of thirty millions sterling,

DARGAH MOSQUE AT FATEHPUR SIKRI

of public usefulness or æsthetic grandeur. His piety reared near Delhi a noble tomb to the memory of his father Humāyun. His splendid taste in architecture shone out in the mighty gateways, broad quadrangles, and white marble domes of Fatehpur Sikri, whose ruined glories still fix the traveller's wondering gaze.* Nor did he fail to repair and extend the system of canals and waterworks begun two centuries earlier by Firoz Tughlak. To a Mīr-āb, or Chief of the Waters, he entrusted the supreme control of all such works, including the collection of water-rents and the even distribution of water to those who needed it, whether rich or poor. With kindly thought for his people's comfort, he ordered the planting of trees, "both for shade and blossom," along both sides of the canal first cut by Firoz between Karnāl and Hissār. †

Of this great and wise monarch little more remains here to tell. His tall but well-knit frame, mighty chest, and long sinewy arms, seem to hint something of that great bodily strength which delighted in walks of forty and in rides sometimes of a hundred miles a-day. His eyes were full and dark, his skin of a ruddy brown. Though (as the Jesuit tutor of his son Murad testifies) he could neither read nor write, he was equally at home in the battle-field, in the jungle hunting tigers or tracking wild elephants, in the palace weighing or refuting the arguments of rival priests or sages, in the council-room discussing points of statecraft with ministers like Abul Fazl and Todi Mall. Fond in his youth of wine and good living, in his after years he kept both these likings under stern control. Amidst the splendour of his public progresses and receptions, he astonished strangers from the

more than half of which came directly from the land. See Thomas's "Revenue Resources of the Mughal Empire."

* Its magnificent ruins cover miles of ground on the road from Agra to Jaipur. Their preservation and restoration were undertaken by Lord Curzon.

† Kaye's "Administration of the East India Company," p. 29.

West by his unstudied courtesies and simple tastes. He slept, we are told, but three hours a-day, spent hours together on public business, and took a keen interest in mechanical arts, especially in the casting of guns and the manufacture of other weapons. A steady friend, a generous foe, a forgiving father, a ruler merciful, upright, shrewd to select the fittest agents for his work, Akbar has left behind him one of the brightest names in the history of any country, a name whose lustre remains undimmed alike by the flatteries of indiscreet friends and the abuse of unsparing foes.*

[After this chapter was in type, the most valuable life of Akbar by Mr. Vincent A. Smith (Oxford, 1917) was published. It adds greatly to our knowledge, and should be read by all who wish thoroughly to understand the complex character of "the Great Mogul."—W. H. H.].

* One of these indiscreet friends was Abul Fazl himself, whose "Akbar-nāmah" is one long panegyric. The most valuable record of Akbar's home government is the Aīn-i-Akbari, or Code of Regulations, drawn up by Abul Fazl under his sovereign's direct supervision.

CHAPTER III

JAHĀNGĪR, 1605—1627

THE new emperor, Salim, under the sounding title of Jahāngīr, "Conqueror of the World," succeeded peacefully at the age of thirty-seven to his father's throne. His earlier measures went far to allay the fears engendered by his past shortcomings. His father's old officers were retained in their posts; some vexatious duties and barbarous practices which Akbar had left untouched were swept away; himself a notorious drunkard, he strictly forbade the use of wine and regulated that of opium. The Muhammadan creed reappeared upon the coinage, and the forms and ritual of the old religion resumed their place in the outward life of the imperial household.

The old nature of the man, however, soon revealed itself. In the spring of 1606, a few months after the emperor's accession, his son Khusrū broke into rebellion, but a month afterwards found himself a prisoner in his father's hands at Lahore. Seven hundred of his followers were forthwith impaled alive on a double line of stakes outside one of the city gates.* Along this ghastly avenue the wretched prince was borne upon an elephant, and compelled each day to witness the frightful agonies of the victims to his own ambition and his father's fierce revenge, so long as one of them remained alive. He himself was

* Elphinstone, quoting Jahāngīr's Memoirs, gives that number, which Dow reduces to three hundred.

carried to Kābul, where the discovery of a plot for his release again hardened his father's heart just as the emperor had begun to relax the closeness of his son's confinement.

The next few years were marked by the efforts of the imperial commanders to subdue the Rāna of Udaipur, and to complete the conquest of the Deccan, then ruled in fact by Malik Ambar, the great Abyssinian noble, who, for twenty years after the murder of the brave Chānd Sultāna, upheld the sinking fortunes of the house of Nizām Shah. Very little progress did the Mughal arms make against the Rājput highlanders of Mewār, until the emperor's third son, Prince Khurram, ere long to be known as Shah Jahān, took the field in person, and proved his generalship by compelling the Rāna of Udaipur to sue for peace. Mindful of his grandfather's policy, Shah Jahān raised from the ground his suppliant foe, placed him by his own side, and treated him with all kingly courtesy. The heir to the glorious memories of Rāna Sanga, the ruler of a kingdom independent for many centuries, now became the vassal of the great Mughal; but the country which Akbar had conquered from the kings of Mewār was restored to that vassal's keeping, and his son was raised to one of the chief posts of honour at Jahāngīr's court.

Two years after his successes in Rājputāna, Shah Jahān was sent to retrieve the mishaps of former commanders in the war against Malik Ambar. Abandoned by his ally, the king of Bijapur, the great Abyssinian was soon forced to surrender the provinces he had won back from the Mughals. Within four years, however, Shah Jahān was again marching towards the Narbada to drive Malik Ambar's Afghāns and Marāthas back to their appointed boundaries. In spite of his skilful soldiership, the champion of Ahmadnagar was brought to battle and again beaten by his former conqueror, who granted him the peace he asked for at a heavy price in territory and rupees.*

In the midst of these successes trouble was lying in wait for the victor himself at the hands of his stepmother, Nur-Jahān. Some time before his own accession Jahāngīr had seen and loved the beautiful daughter of a Persian gentleman, who, after many misfortunes, had taken service in Akbar's court. But her hand was already plighted to one of Akbar's nobles, the brave Sher Afgan, who led her away with him to his manor in Burdwān. Still bent on winning her for himself, Jahāngīr, soon after he came to the throne, would have bribed her husband into giving up his treasure. On Sher Afgan's refusal, high words seem to have passed between him and Jahāngīr's agent, the Viceroy of Bengal. The latter fell under Sher Afgan's dagger, and the murderer in his turn was slain by the Viceroy's followers. Nur-Jahān, removed to Delhi, still turned a deaf ear to Jahāngīr's addresses. At last, however, she yielded to his prayers or her own ambition, and in 1611 the marriage was celebrated with unusual pomp.

From that time Nur-Jahān wielded over her husband an empire which only ended with his life. He caused her name to be inscribed on the coinage; in all matters which attracted her notice her will became law. Her father was made prime minister; her brother was raised to an important post. Her taste enhanced the magnificence, her good management kept down the expenses of the Emperor's court. His vicious tendencies were so far held in check by her sweet influence, that he seldom gave way to savage outbursts, and never allowed himself to get drunk before the evening.

To Shah Jahān, the ablest and best beloved of his sons, the husband of her own niece, the Emperor's acknowledged

* One of Malik Ambar's chief followers was Shahjī, father of Sīvajī, founder of the Marātha power.

heir, she had hitherto given her powerful support. But the death of her father, followed by that of Prince Khusrū, the marriage of her own daughter to the Emperor's fourth son, Prince Shahryār, and the serious illness of the Emperor himself in 1621, all conspired to turn the ambitious woman's heart against the object of her former liking. The report of her altered feelings, of her intrigues in favour of her new son-in-law, reached the ears of Shah Jahān, who had just been ordered to retake Kandahār from its Persian conquerors. His manifest unwillingness to leave India on such an errand at a time so critical, brought him into conflict with his deluded father. A year passed away in fruitless interchange of messages between Jahāngīr at Lahore, and his mistrustful son at Māndu, then the capital of Gujarāt. At last the quarrel blazed out into open war, which told disastrously against Shah Jahān. Driven out of the Deccan by superior numbers, he suddenly turned northwards, led his troops boldly through Orissa into Bengal, and early in 1624 defeated the Governor of that province at Rajmahal.

For a short time he became master of Bengal and Bihār. But the imperial leaders followed him up; his own troops began to melt away, he himself fell sick, and at length, in spite of the help afforded him in the Deccan by Malik Ambar, the hard-pressed Shah Jahān was fain to accept the terms—surrender of his last strongholds, and of his two sons as hostages—on which alone his father would grant him peace and forgiveness.

By this time, however, a new quarrel of Nur-Jahān's provoking was about to involve the Emperor in new difficulties. Mahābat Khan, the Afghān general whom the Empress had employed to aid her against Shah Jahān, had aroused her jealousy by his late successes in the field and his growing influence at Court. False charges were brought against him, and by the Emperor's orders a cruel outrage was inflicted on his son-in-law.* Mahābat soon took his revenge. As the Emperor was marching towards Kābul, Mahābat, who had been ordered to accompany him, broke one morning into the tent where he lay sleeping off his last night's carouse. Jahāngīr awoke to find himself a prisoner, cut off from his troops on the other side of the Jhelum by a strong body of Rājputs, who guarded the bridge of boats. Baffled in a daring attempt to rescue her captive husband, Nur-Jahān resolved to share his confinement in the hope of ere long finding a way to set him free.

That hope was soon to be fulfilled. During a review of the Imperial troops at Kābul, a body of her own followers managed to strike in between the Emperor and his guards, and to bear the former away into the midst of assured friends. Mahābat Khan was pardoned on condition of restoring the Empress's brother, Asaf Khan, to freedom, and promising to go in chase of her enemy Shah Jahān. The fortunes of that prince, a fugitive in Sind, whom ill-health alone prevented from fleeing to Persia, had reached their lowest ebb, when the death of his brother Parvīz was followed by new disagreements between his father and Mahābat Khan. The prince and his late pursuer joined forces in the Deccan, and appeared to march towards Agra, when the death of Jahāngīr freed his son from further annoyances, and brought Nur-Jahān's power and plottings to a timely end. Thenceforth, until her own death in 1646, Jahāngīr's widow took no part in public affairs, devoting her life and the bulk of her magnificent pension to the memory of her uxorious husband.

It was during the last two reigns that our countrymen first made their way to the court of the Great Mughal. In

* A young nobleman, who had married Mahābat's daughter without the Emperor's leave, was stripped naked and flogged with thorns in Jahāngīr's presence.

1607 Captain Hawkins had been sent out by the East India Company with a view to obtain some footing for English trade in Indian ports. Some twenty years earlier two English travellers, Ralph Fitch and John Newbery, had found themselves, after many hardships and narrow escapes by land and sea, safe at last in Akbar's own city of Fatehpur Sikri. Little, however, came of this journey, whose quaint and interesting details are recorded in Hakluyt's Voyages,* save fresh encouragement to that spirit of English enterprise which the voyages and achievements of Drake, Hawkins, Raleigh, and other of Elizabeth's captains, had just called into active play. Captain Lancaster's first voyage in 1591, if it added little to our knowledge of India itself, whetted the greed or the curiosity of Englishmen at home. In December, 1600, the Earl of Cumberland and 215 knights, aldermen, and merchants were enrolled by royal charter into a company of merchants trading to the East Indies, and invested among other privileges with the monopoly of our Eastern trade for the next fifteen years. Their modest capital of £75,000 was at once laid out in five vessels freighted with goods and bullion, and placed under the command of Captain Lancaster, who in due time brought home a goodly cargo from Sumatra and Java, enriched with the spoils of a large vessel captured from the Portuguese. Fresh fleets were afterwards despatched under Middleton, Keeling, and other captains, who refilled their vessels, by fair means nor foul, with equal scorn for the feelings of native traders and the exclusive claims of their Portuguese rivals.

In company with Keeling went Captain Hawkins, who, after many adventures and much resistance from the

* Richard Hakluyt, Archdeacon of Westminster, first published in 1582 a small collection of Voyages and Discoveries, afterwards much enlarged in 1589—1600. He became the first historiographer to the old East India Company, founded in 1600.

Portuguese and their friends at Surat, met with a gracious welcome at Agra, in 1609, from Jahāngīr himself. For a time all went hopefully with the English stranger. He was promised a handsome salary while he stayed at court; an Armenian maiden was sought out and given him for wife; his pleadings on behalf of the new company were heard with seeming approval; and leave was granted him under the Emperor's seal to establish a factory at Surat. At last, however, his prospects began to change for the worse. The intrigues of his enemies at Surat and of Portuguese agents at Agra prevailed against him; his salary was left unpaid; his interviews with the Emperor grew less frequent; and at length, in November, 1611, Hawkins set out on his homeward journey with the main object of his mission unfulfilled.

A few months afterwards, however, Captain Best recovered the ground which Hawkins had won and lost. With his four ships he inflicted a signal defeat on a Portuguese squadron, which sought to keep English traders out of Surat. His victory taught the Imperial officers to respect those whom they had hitherto despised. In 1613 Jahāngīr confirmed by formal treaty the privileges first bestowed on Hawkins; and from that time Surat became the chief seat of English trade in Western India.

The footing thus gained by the East India Company was quickly followed up by the despatch of another embassy to the Mughal Court. In the last days of 1615 Sir Thomas Roe presented his letters from King James I. to Jahāngīr, who received him with marked distinction at Ajmēr, and treated him for two years as an honoured and even familiar guest. With very few exceptions, the great men and courtiers followed the Emperor's example. Their good-will indeed could not always be secured without heavy bribes; nor did Shah Jahān himself* look kindly

* Roe describes him as a tyrant and a bigot, who never smiled, nor paid

the new-comers who sympathized with his brother Khusrū, and shared, however innocently, in the drunken revellings at his father's court. In the end, however, Sir Thomas overcame all obstacles by dint of unwearied patience and cool address; and he returned to Surat armed with fresh powers on behalf of the Company, whose rights of trading were thenceforth extended to the whole of India.

It was one thing to secure these rights on paper, but quite another to enforce them against jealous rivals from the West, and unwilling servants of the Mughal. Little by little, however, the Company enlarged their outlay and found new markets for their trade. A few years of joint action between the Dutch and English companies in the eastern seas closed abruptly in 1623 with the torture and execution of twelve Englishmen at Amboyna,* on an utterly false charge of conspiring to seize the Dutch fort. Driven from the spice-bearing Moluccas, the English turned their attention more and more to India itself, where, besides their growing trade with Surat, they had already gained a footing on the Malabar coast. In 1625, their first settlement on the eastern or Coromandel coast was founded at Armagaon, a little to the south of Vellore. Within three years the new factory was armed with twelve guns and manned by a small body of factors and soldiers. Thither was removed the trade which some years earlier had flowed to Masulipatam. Ere long, however, the trade of Armagaon proved so unprofitable, that in 1639 Mr. Day got leave from a native chief to build a new factory at Madraspatam, the germ of Fort St. George and the populous city of Madras. But we must not further anticipate the events which have to be recorded in the following chapters.

court to any in particular; "flattered by some, envied by others, loved by none"; but the picture must be taken with large allowance for outward appearances and the force of personal prejudice.

* One of the largest of the Moluccas, or Spice Islands, in the Eastern Archipelago.

CHAPTER IV

SHAH JAHĀN, 1628–1658

ON the death of Jahāngīr, his son Shah Jahān hastened to Agra, where with the help of Nur-Jahān's brother, Asaf Khan, he quietly mounted his father's throne. Freed from present anxieties by the capture and death of Shahryār,* the new emperor gave the reins to his taste for splendid pageantry and architectural grandeur. In the midst of festivals costing millions of rupees, and of magnificent plans for rebuilding and adorning Delhi, he was suddenly called upon to put down a formidable revolt headed by Khan Jahān Lodi, one of his great lords and former opponents, who claimed descent from the Pathān kings of Delhi. Mistrustful of the emperor's feelings towards himself he suddenly broke away from Agra with his household and armed retainers, beat back the pursuing troops at the Chambal, and, plunging into the wilds of Bundelkhand and Gondwāna, made his way into the Deccan, where he counted on bringing many an old friend to his side, if not on raising the whole of Southern India against the Mughal. From the King of Ahmadnagar, who had just lost his able minister, Malik Ambar, he met with a warm welcome; but the Kings of Bijapur and Golconda held aloof; and the Marātha chieftain, Shahjī, soon saw reason to abandon his former friend, and enter into the service of Shah Jahān. Defeated, hunted from place to place, and

* Not only Shahryār, but the sons of Prince Dāniyāl also, were put to death by Shah Jahān's orders.

baffled in every attempt to make a stand, Khan Jahān fell at last fighting bravely near Kālanjar, at the head of a few of his remaining followers.

After his death the war which he had kindled in the Deccan blazed up afresh. The King of Bijapur at length took part with his neighbour of Ahmadnagar. On the murder of the latter by his minister, Fattah Khan, the son of Malik Ambar, his people made peace with the emperor, who turned his arms against Bijapur. For several years the king of that country defied the efforts of such able commanders as Asaf Khan and Mahābat Khan. Ahmadnagar, under its new master, Shahjī, again joined the conflict on the side of Bijapur; and not till 1636 did Adil Shah of Bijapur give up the doubtful game, on condition of paying a yearly tribute to Shah Jahān in return for a large slice of the Ahmadnagar state. Next year Shahjī also made peace, and thenceforth Ahmadnagar ceased to be an independent kingdom.

Meanwhile, in 1631, the Portuguese were finally driven out of Hūgli, near Calcutta, by order of Shah Jahān, who had not forgotten the refusal of the Portuguese governor to aid him in his hour of need against his father's troops. After an existence of nearly a century, the fort at Hūgli was stormed by the Mughals, a thousand of the garrison were put to the sword, besides several thousands taken prisoners, and only three out of three hundred ships in the river made their escape. Thenceforth the Portuguese power in Bengal was crushed for ever.

In 1637, Kandahār, the old appanage of the House of Bābur, was surrendered to the Mughals by its governor, Ali Mardan Khan. Ten years later, however, it fell again into Persian hands, and the bravest efforts of Shah Jahān's officers and men failed, after three sieges, in winning it back. Meanwhile, Ali Mardan had tried the mettle of his troops, including 14,000 Rājputs, in conquering Balkh for

Photo. by U[illegible]nderwood [illegible]

FATEHPUR SIKRI

Photo. by Underwood & Underwood

THE TAJ MAHAL

p.

Shah Jahān. After two years, however, of harassing warfare with the Uzbeks from beyond Oxus, Shah Jahān was glad to make over his new conquest to its former master.

For two years after the failure of the last attempt on Kandahār, the empire enjoyed unbroken peace. Shah Jahān employed that interval in extending to the Deccan the revenue system shaped out by Todi Mall. Emulous of Akbar's great example, his grandson governed well and justly according to Eastern ideas, treating his subjects, says Tavernier, as a father would treat his children, and choosing for his ministers men like Saad Ullah Khan, ablest and most upright of Indian wazirs. In spite of his lavish outlay on the court, on public shows, and the embellishment of great cities, he seems to have raised with ease a revenue of more than fifty millions, and he left as much as twenty-four millions behind him in his treasury. His people, on the whole, were prosperous and contented. The noblest streets in modern Delhi, the fortified palace with its marble halls and wide courts, and the Jama Masjid, or Great Mosque of that city, attest the splendour of his taste in building; while the exquisite Taj Mahal at Agra, with its taper minarets, soft-swelling marble dome, delicate trellis-work, and flowing mosaics has few, if any, rivals in the world for stately grace and symmetry of form, chaste brilliance of general effect, and finished beauty of rich but telling decoration. Reared in memory of his empress, Mumtāz-Mahall, it has since served to delight a long succession of strangers from the West.*

* Seen by moonlight, filling up one end of the cypress avenue leading from the outer gate to the marble terrace whereon it stands, the Taj gleams like a vision of fairyland. In March, 1904, Lord Curzon was able to state that as the result of his exertions the Taj is now approached through a beautiful park, and "the group of tombs, the arcaded streets and grassy courts, that precede the main building, are once more as nearly as possible what they were when completed by the masons of Shah Jahān. Every building in the garden

A yet costlier, if less noble, monument of decorative art was the far-famed peacock-throne at Delhi, adorned with a mass of diamonds, rubies, sapphires, and other gems, after the fashion of a peacock's tail.

Meanwhile, however, the ambition of Aurangzeb, one of the emperor's sons, and the intrigues of Mīr Jumla, wazir to the King of Golconda, rekindled the flames of war in the Deccan, with results that proved ruinous in the long-run to the Mughal empire. Appointed viceroy of the Deccan after his failure at Kandahār in 1653, Aurangzeb took up Mīr Jumla's quarrel with his master, and persuaded the emperor to let him work his will on the king of Golconda. Hyderābād was sacked by the viceroy's troops, and Abdullah Kutb Shah, driven in a corner, accepted the hard terms imposed by Aurangzeb.

At this moment died Mahmūd Adil Shah, the aged King of Bijapur, whose capital he had adorned with some of the noblest buildings to be seen in India. His death became the pretext for new aggressions on the part of Aurangzeb, who claimed for the emperor the right of naming an heir to the vacant throne. A Mughal army made a sudden inroad into Bijapur. Marking his progress with fire and sword, Aurangzeb at length besieged the city of Bijapur itself. The young king, whose troops were chiefly away in the Carnatic, was ready to accept such terms as his enemy might choose to force upon him, when news of the emperor's serious illness reached the camp of Aurangzeb. Concluding a hasty peace with his lately despairing foe, that crafty prince made ready to take all advantage of an illness which at any moment might end in death.

Then began a fight for empire between the four sons of

enclosure of the Taj has been scrupulously repaired, and the discovery of old plans has enabled us to restore the water channels and flower beds of the garden more exactly to their original state."

Shah Jahān. Dāra Shikoh, the eldest, who had for some time shared his father's power and duties, was now in his forty-second year—a frank, free-handed, open-hearted prince, of undoubted talent, marred by an overbearing temper and an utter want of common prudence. In religion a free-thinker of Akbar's school, he lacked one main source of the influence wielded by his abler, warier, more scheming, and far more bigoted brother, Aurangzeb. Between these two came Prince Shujā, viceroy of Bengal, whose talents were neutralised by his love of wine and pleasure. Aurangzeb's younger brother, Murad, viceroy of Gujarāt, was brave and generous, but dull-witted, gluttonous, and a drunkard. In him, however, the third of his father's sons found a convenient tool for the carrying out of his own plans. Leaving Dāra and Shujā to waste their strength against each other, Aurangzeb soon taught the credulous Murad to look upon him as a firm upholder of Murad's claim to their father's throne. They agreed to join forces against the free-thinking Dāra and his Hindu lieutenant, Jeswant Singh.

In April, 1658, Shujā, defeated by Suliman, the son of Dāra, withdrew from his fruitless struggle into Bengal. Meanwhile Dāra himself marched to his own defeat at the hands of Aurangzeb. Falling back from Ujjain to Agra, the beaten prince, impatient of his father's counsels, and trusting to his own superior numbers, staked his own and his father's fortunes on a battle fought near Agra in the month of June. The day was nearly his own, when a panic seized his troops, and Aurangzeb, pressing forward, drove them in wild flight from the field he had well-nigh lost. Pushing his advantage, he marched on to Agra, took his aged father prisoner, and, throwing off the mask he had hitherto worn, placed Murad also under close arrest. On reaching Delhi in August, he caused himself to be proclaimed emperor in the room of Shah Jahān. The deposed monarch lived for eight years longer, but his splendid reign of thirty years ceased with the entrance into Delhi of his undutiful son.

During these years the English made further progress in their Indian trade. In 1634 Shah Jahān gave the East India Company leave to trade with Bengal, and the first factory in that province was set up at Pipli, near the mouth of the Hūgli river. Two years afterwards a successful cure wrought on the emperor's daughter by Mr. Boughton, one of the Company's surgeons, was rewarded, at his own request, by new concessions to his employers. In return for a like service rendered by that gentleman to the household of Prince Shujā, his countrymen were allowed to erect new factories at Hūgli and Balasore.

Meanwhile a rival company, favoured, for his own purposes, by Charles I., attempted for about twenty years to trade on their own account in the Eastern seas. At length, however, the influence of the older body prevailed with Cromwell's councillors, and the two companies became one. Surat and Madras formed two presidencies; the former having control over the settlements in the Persian Gulf and Western India, while the latter held sway over the factories in Bengal and along the Coromandel coast.

CHAPTER V

AURANGZEB, 1658–1707

UNDER the title of Alamgīr, Lord of the World, the new emperor began his reign. In the midst of his relentless pursuit of his brother Dāra, he was called away to encounter Shujā, who had once more taken the field with a well-appointed army, and had already reached Benāres on his march up towards Agra. The two brothers encountered each other at Kajwa, a few marches to the north-west of Allahābād. In spite of a sudden attack upon his rear by his old opponent Raja Jeswant Singh, the emperor bravely held his ground, until by a mixture of cool courage, able generalship, and good fortune, the imminent defeat was turned into a crushing victory. Allahābād surrendered to the conqueror, and Shujā, hotly pressed by Mīr Jumla, fell back into the heart of Bengal. The rainy season compelled a pause in the pursuit; but by the year's end Shujā had been driven across the Brahmapūtra. A few months later he fled with a few followers into the Arakān hills, where all trace of him and his family very soon disappeared.*

Meanwhile Dāra, abandoned by Jeswant Singh, whom his crafty brother had at length bought over to his own side, led his recruited forces to a strong position near Ajmēr. Once more a hard-fought battle ended in his defeat at the hands of his abler and more determined

* It is supposed that they lost their lives through plotting against the Raja of Arakān. (Elphinstone's "India," book ix. chap. i.)

brother. Ahmadābād shut his gates on the princely fugitive; his wife died of fatigue and suffering on the way to Kandahār; and ere long Dāra himself, with one of his sons, was basely betrayed into the hands of his ruthless brother by a man whom he had once befriended, the chief of Jūn in Eastern Sind. Led in chains, on a sorry elephant, through the streets of that Delhi whose heart still yearned towards its recent master, the ill-starred captive was hurried to trial on the convenient charge of apostasy from the faith of Islam. When his head was brought to Aurangzeb, the emperor made a show of weeping over the fruits of his own unsparing ambition.

By a strange coincidence the two sons of Dāra and the son of his youngest brother Murad died shortly afterwards in the prison they had been sharing together in Gwalior. Murad himself, whose blind trust in Aurangzeb had been requited by a long imprisonment, was finally brought to trial on a charge trumped up against him by his heartless brother, and paid with his life the penalty of standing too near the throne.

Soon afterwards another source of possible danger was removed out of the emperor's way. His ablest general Mīr Jumla, had been ordered or encouraged to attempt the conquest of Assam. For a time Mīr Jumla carried all before him; but the rain-floods stopped him in mid-career; sickness raged among his troops; and a disastrous retreat to Dacca ended in their great leader's death. His memory was honoured by his son's promotion, and an expressive eulogy from the pen of Aurangzeb.*

By that time the emperor's alarming illness had for a moment threatened his life as well as his throne. As he lay in the last stage of weakness, he learned that his enemies were plotting to set up Shah Jahān, or one of

* "You have lost a father," he wrote to Muhammad Amīn, "and I have lost the greatest and most dangerous of my friends."

his own sons, in his stead. Propped up by pillows, he insisted on receiving anew the homage of his chief barons; and wrote out the orders which his tongue still refused to utter. By such means, with the help of his faithful sister, Raushanāra, he kept his enemies quiet until his recovered health put all hope of active resistance out of their heads.

About this time a new and more serious peril to the House of Bābur had begun to rear its head beyond the Narbada. The bold Marātha chieftain Shahjī, whom we lately saw carving a new kingdom for himself in the Deccan,* was son of Mālojī Bhōsla, a Marātha captain of horse under the orders of Jādu Rāo, a distinguished Rājput leader, who, after following the fortunes of the renowned Malik Ambar, had at length thrown him over for the sake of serving under Shah Jahān. In due time Mālojī won for Shahjī the hand of Jādu's highborn daughter, to which he had long aspired in vain. By fair means or foul Shahjī in his turn fought his way among the wrecks of fallen dynasties and dismembered kingdoms to the lordship of large estates lying between Poona and Bangalore.

His second son Sīvajī, the future founder of the Marātha empire, was brought up at Poona under his mother's care, by his father's Brahman agent, Dadajī Pant. Inured from boyhood to hardy exercises, and mingling constantly with the wild Marātha highlanders in his neighbourhood, Sīvajī ere long broke from his tutor's care, and became the leader of a band of lawless youths ready to follow him in any raid, whether against the wild beasts of their native hills or the Muhammadan dwellers in the plains. At the age of nineteen he contrived to seize the strong hill-fort of Torna, twenty miles south-west of Poona. In the following year he built a new stronghold on a neighbouring hill. Ere long several

* See book iii. chap. 4.

other forts were wrested from their Muhammadan masters, and placed under the charge of his Marātha followers. Emboldened by these successes, and enriched by the plunder of a convoy on its way to Bijapur, he swooped down upon the Konkan and brought under his sway a good deal of the rugged woody lowlands stretching westward from the Ghāts to the sea.*

At last the story of his exploits found its way to the court of Bijapur. His father, Shahjī, was seized as a hostage for the offending son; and a cruel death stared him in the face, when Sīvajī's appeal to the emperor Shah Jahān opened the prison door to Shahjī, if it failed as yet to ensure his perfect freedom. Four years later, when Shahjī's services were imperatively needed elsewhere, Sīvajī, by this time the eldest of his father's surviving sons, began to renew his old raids, with a steadiness of purpose heightened by religious zeal, and a boldness all the more successful for the tiger-like cunning that knew how and when to give it free play. A true Marātha in that wily daring and unscrupulous pursuit of a given end, which marked off his Sūdra countrymen from the high-souled thorough-bred Rājputs of the north, he had long since gathered, alike from the folk-lore of his native hills and the religious surroundings of his boyhood, abundant fuel for his ambition, and all needful sanction for his most unscrupulous deeds. Patriotism and piety alike impelled him on that path of conquest, which was to end the last great struggle for empire between the Marāthas and the countrymen of Lord Wellesley.

Before the end of 1655 Sīvajī had laid violent hands on the hill-country as far south as Satāra. During the three years of Aurangzeb's viceroyalty, the wily Hindu amused his powerful rival with loyal offers which he took

* The Ghāts, or Sahyadri Hills, from 3000 to 5000 feet high, run along the western coast of India from the Tapti southwards, thirty or forty miles from the sea.

care not to fulfil. On Aurangzeb's departure, Sīvajī renewed his old game against Bijapur. An army sent to punish him under Afzal Khan was lured into the woody ravines near his strong fort of Partābgarh, where Afzal himself fell treacherously murdered by Sīvajī at a peaceful interview, and his troops were slain or scattered by a sudden onset of Marātha bands.

Next year the bold outlaw, hard pressed by his pursuers, escaped by a clever trick from the fort of Panāla after a close siege of four months. For several months defeat and danger dogged his steps. It was not in Sīvajī, however, to despair. Fortune once more smiled on its daring follower; and before the end of 1662, with the aid of his father, Shahjī, he had won from the King of Bijapur a peace which left him master of the Konkan from Kalyān to Goa, and of the hill country between the Bhima and the Kistna, a dominion 250 miles long by nearly 100 broad. His troops at this time already numbered 7000 horse and 50,000 foot.

Freed from one enemy, Sīvajī presently dared the wrath of another, by raiding almost up to the walls of Aurangabād. In vain did Aurangzeb's generals bear down upon the foe, who gave way only to renew his attacks.* Driven out of Poona and shut up for a time in a neighbouring stronghold, Sīvajī suddenly burst away from his pursuers, and with 4000 light horsemen swooped down upon Surat. The English and Dutch factories beat off the invader; but the rich native city fell into his hands, and its plunder was safely lodged in his fort of Raigarh.

The death of Shahjī about this time threw into his son's hands a large tract of country on the southern

* One of Sīvajī's most daring exploits was the attempt to slay Aurangzeb's uncle, Shaysta Khan, who had taken up his quarters in Sīvajī's house at Poona. Entering the house in disguise, he so nearly effected his purpose, that Shaysta Khan lost two fingers in getting away, while his son and most of his guards were cut to pieces by Sīvajī's followers.

frontier of Bijapur. Armed with fresh means for mischief, Sīvajī began to worry the Mughals by sea. After capturing many of their ships and taking heavy ransom from rich pilgrims bound for Mecca, he sailed at the head of a large fleet down the coast to Barsalōr, in Kanāra, 130 miles south of Goa. Enriched with the plunder of that once busy seaport, the royal freebooter—he had just assumed the title of raja—made a fresh inroad into the Mughal dominions. By this time, however, the wrathful emperor had despatched a large army under Raja Jai Singh against his irrepressible foe, who deemed it best to purchase present safety by surrendering most of the forts he had wrested from the Mughals, on condition of holding the remainder as a jāgīr from Aurangzeb. Another claim which the emperor tacitly yielded, Sīvajī's right to the "chauth," or a fourth part of the Bijapur revenues, became a fruitful pretext for many a future inroad into the heart of the Mughal empire.

Under the standard of his countryman Jai Singh, Sīvajī's warrior's fought so bravely in the next campaign against Bijapur, that Aurangzeb in flattering terms invited Sīvajī himself to his court. So little, however, did the emperor's treatment of his new guest, whom he slighted as a mere adventurer and hated as a foe to Islam, appear to tally with his former promises, that Sīvajī, swallowing down his rage and disappointment, quietly prepared to escape from the snares which his wily host had seemingly begun to weave around him. His friends and followers once fairly out of Delhi, he himself in the dirt and rags of a Hindu fakir, made his way by baffling marches to the Deccan; and, nine months after his flight from the capital, was safely lodged in his own eyrie at Raigarh.

This period, which also marks the death of Shah Jahān, was perhaps the most prosperous of Aurangzeb's long reign. Little Tibet and Chittagong had just been

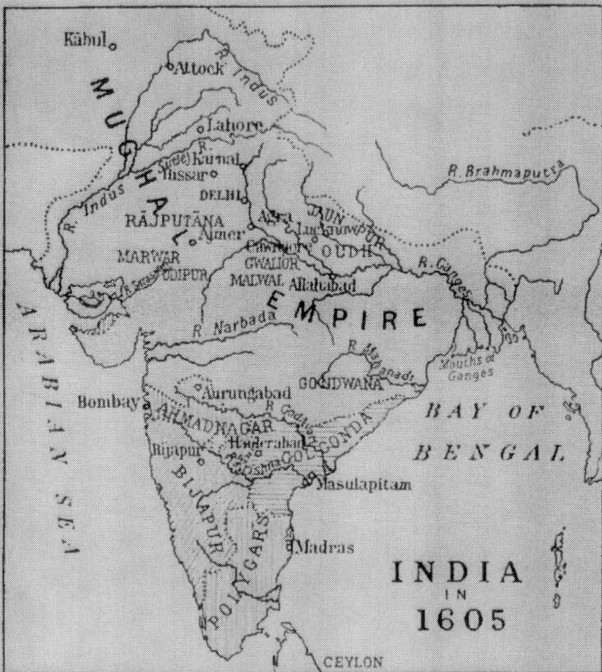
INDIA
IN
1605
MUGHAL EMPIRE
Kābul
Attock
R. Indus
Lahore
Hissar
DELHI
RĀJPUTĀNA
Ajmer
MARWAR
UDIPUR
GWALIOR
MALWAL
OUDH
R. Brahmaputra
R. Ganges
R. Narbada
GONDWANA
Mouths of Ganges
Aurungabad
Bombay
AHMADNAGAR
Bijapur
BIJAPUR
GOLCONDA
Masulipitam
POLYGARS
Madras
BAY OF BENGAL
ARABIAN SEA
CEYLON

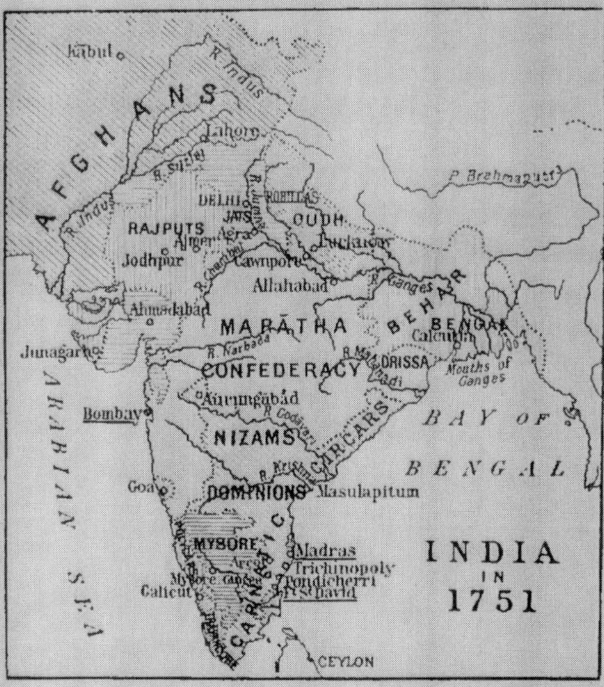
INDIA
IN
1751
Kābul
R. Indus
AFGHANS
Lahore
R. Sutlej
R. Brahmaputra
DELHI
ROHILLAS
JATS
OUDH
RAJPUTS
Agra
Ajmer
Jodhpur
Cawnpore
Allahabad
R. Ganges
BEHAR
BENGAL
Calcutta
Ahmadabad
MARĀTHA
CONFEDERACY
Junagarh
R. Narbada
ORISSA
Mouths of Ganges
Aurungabad
R. Godavari
Bombay
NIZAMS
DOMINIONS
CIRCARS
Goa
Masulapitum
MYSORE
Madras
Trichinopoly
Pondicherri
Calicut
CARNATIC
BAY OF BENGAL
ARABIAN SEA
CEYLON

p. 11

added to his dominions. His capital was thronged with envoys from Arabia, Persia, Abyssinia, and the Khan of the Uzbeks. The only clouds that darkened his prospects were the failure of his designs on Bijapur, and the renewed activity of Sīvajī himself. Even before the latter's return to Raigarh, his lieutenants had won back several of their master's former strongholds, and Sīvajī lost no time in bettering their example. Jai Singh's successor, Jeswant Singh, was bribed, or frightened into making peace with his Marātha opponent on terms which the emperor, for his own purposes, deemed it best to sanction.

Confirmed in his recent conquests, and endowed with a new domain in Berar, Sīvajī turned his arms against Bijapur and Golconda to such purpose, that the rulers of both those states were glad to buy off their old assailant with the promise of a yearly tribute. Two years of peace passed by, which Sīvajī devoted to the better government of his various conquests. Great in peace as in war, he ruled his subjects with a firm yet light hand, enforcing equal justice between high and low, choosing his agents from the ablest men in the land, and recruiting his treasury by fair and regular processes. His troops were highly paid and kept under the strictest discipline, and a well-ordered economy marked every branch of the public service.

Meanwhile the crafty emperor tried every art to lure into his hands the one foe whom he seems to have chiefly dreaded. Baffled at every turn by the wary Marātha, he at length gave orders for his forcible seizure. The peace thus broken, Sīvajī at once forestalled his enemies by a series of well-aimed and telling blows. By a daring night attack a choice body of his mountaineers recovered the strong fort of Singarh, near Poona. One of his generals overran Khandēsh, and levied the chauth on that province. He himself once more plundered Surat, and Janjira, on the Konkan coast, only escaped his clutches by placing itself under the protection of the Mughals. An army of 40,000 men, under Mahābat Khan, son of Shah Jahān's old ally, was sent against him; but half their number were routed in fair fight by Sīvajī's warriors, whose mettle had never before been tried against the Mughals in the open field.

For several years the war in the Deccan languished, while Aurangzeb was engaged in a series of struggles, now with the hill tribes of Afghānistān, anon with Hindu fanatics and Rājput princes nearer home. Not till 1675 did he succeed in patching up a piece with the unruly Khyberi and Yusufzai borderers, who had destroyed a Mughal army five years before. Next year the revolt of the Satnarāmis, a sect of Hindu devotees who had seized Narnōl and beaten back the troops at first sent against them, was quelled with heavy bloodshed and fearful massacres. For some years back the emperor had done his worst to estrange his Hindu subjects by a series of attacks on their religion, by forbidding the further employment of Hindus in the public service, and by lightening the burdens of the Muhammadans at their expense. At last the reimposition of the hated Jiziya, and the attempt to seize the widow and children of Raja Jeswant Singh, filled up the measure of his offences, and relit the flames of war in Rājputāna.

Overawed by the emperor's swift movements and powerful array, the Rāna of Mewār, or Udaipur, agreed to a peaceful compromise, which a few months later he appears to have set at naught. A long and uncertain struggle, embittered by mutual hate, by the ruthless ravages of the Mughals, and revived by the defection of Prince Akbar from his father's side, ended in a peace which enabled Aurangzeb once more to turn his whole attention to the Deccan. But the old ties which had held the Rājputs faithful to the empire for a hundred years past were rent for ever. Aurangzeb's bigotry had undone Akbar's work, and the strife, thus hardly allayed by mutual concessions, blazed up ever and anon during the rest of Aurangzeb's stormy reign.

Meanwhile Sīvajī had not been idle. The death of the King of Bijapur tempted him to renew his inroads on a country ruled by a weak ministry, in the name of a child-heir. Ere long nearly all the Southern Konkan had fallen into his hands. In June, 1674, he had himself crowned with all solemnity at Raigarh. Next year he was beating up the Mughals in Khandēsh, Berar, and the heart of Gujarāt. A well-planned alliance with Golconda opened the way for his long and successful march across the Kistna by way of Cuddapah, Madras, and Gingee to Vellore. Fort after fort, including Gingee and Vellore, fell to his arms, his father's domains in Mysore were brought under his rule, the chauth was levied through the Carnatic, and his half-brother, Venkajī, had to pay over half his revenue for the peaceful retention of Tanjore. By the middle of 1678 Sīvajī returned in triumph to Raigarh.

A few months afterwards Sīvajī was on his way to help Bijapur against its Mughal assailants, who were soon compelled, by his active efforts in their rear, to raise the siege of that city. The price of his timely succour was the cession of the Raichur Doab, between the Tungabhadra and the Kistna, and of full sovereignty over all Shahjī's domains in Bijapur. In the very flush of these last successes the great Marātha leader succumbed to a sterner foe than any he had yet encountered. A mortal illness carried him off in 1680, in the fifty-third year of his age, in the midst of a career not often paralleled in the history of any country. From a mere leader of banditti he had fought his way in thirty-four years, twenty of which had been spent in braving the might of Aurangzeb himself, into the very highest rank of Indian heroes, and the lordship of a kingdom strong enough to survive the onsets of, and ere long to break in pieces, the empire of the Mughals.

CHAPTER VI

AURANGZEB—(*continued*)

SĪVAJĪ'S eldest son, Sambhajī, had no sooner mounted his father's throne, than he took a cruel revenge on all who had favoured the cause of his half-brother, Raja Rām. Dissolute as well as cruel, he left the management of state affairs to his worthless favourite, Kalūsha, while he himself launched out into all manner of sensual excesses. From these he roused himself to renew his father's attacks upon Janjira; but the Sīdis or Abyssinians, who held that city, forced him to raise the siege, defeated his fleet in the harbour of Bombay, and laid waste a part of his own dominions.

He had not long returned to his favourite pleasures, when the advance of a Mughal army under Prince Muazzam called him again into the field. Aurangzeb himself was marching southwards at the head of a powerful array of horse, foot, and guns, followed by a train the most magnificent that even India had ever seen. The fine army which Muazzam led among the rocks and forests of the Konkan was so worried on its march by active Marātha horsemen, and so worn with hunger and disease, that only a disordered remnant emerged into the country eastward of the Ghāts. Prince Azam was equally unsuccessful in his first attempt against Bijapur. While the emperor himself in the following year was preparing to move forward from Ahmadnagar, Sambhajī's horsemen scoured the country in his rear, sacked and burned the great city of Burhānpur, overran Khandēsh, and threatened Berar. Next year the same tactics were employed with like success against Gujarāt; and Broach, at the mouth of the Narbada, shared the fate of Burhānpur.

The emperor, however, was not to be lightly turned aside from his long-cherished schemes of conquests in Southern India. Golconda having in the meantime been heavily punished for daring to accept aid from Sambhajī, he led his troops in person against the magnificent capital of the Adil-Shahi kings of Bijapur. A strict blockade forestalled the more hazardous issues of a direct assault, and on the 15th October, 1686, Aurangzeb was borne in triumph over the breach his guns had already made. Three years afterwards, the last Pathān king of Bijapur died a prisoner in his conqueror's hands, and the great city which his sires had embellished with mosques and palaces of surpassing beauty was consigned to neglect and its fatal follower, decay.

Within a year after the fall of Bijapur, Golconda also had succumbed to the arms and treachery of Aurangzeb. For seven months Abul Hasan, the last king of the Kutb-Shahi line, defended his capital with the courage of despair; but treason fought against him, and in September, 1687, he too passed away from his throne to a prison in the fort of Daulatabād.

No time was lost in continuing the work of conquest on which Aurangzeb had set his heart. Before the end of 1688, his rule extended to the borders of Tanjore; and Sambhajī, steeped in debauchery, saw one after another of his father's conquests fall away from his enfeebled grasp. At length he himself, in the midst of a drunken revel, was surprised by a body of Mughals, and borne off a prisoner to the imperial camp. Offered his life on condition of abjuring his creed, the proud son of Sīvajī spurned the bribe in terms of scornful ridicule, for which death alone was deemed too light a punishment by the enraged Mughal. After his eyes had been destroyed by a hot iron, and his tongue cut out for reviling the Prophet, he was at length beheaded along with his favourite, Kalūsha.

For a time it seemed as if all India lay helpless at the feet of Aurangzeb. So wide an empire had never been swayed by any former sovereign of Hindustan. But to the last his hold upon the Deccan remained insecure. Province after province, fort after fort, was wrested from the Marāthas, and the conquered people for the most part bowed their necks to the heavy burdens imposed by their new master. But the most peaceful among them chafed under the exactions of the imperial officers, and the levying of the Jiziya rankled deep in the hearts of the wretched Hindus. The disbanded soldiery of Bijapur and Golconda roamed the country in lawless troops, or offered their services to Marātha leaders. There was little either of peace or order in the new conquests. The spirit of the Marāthas also remained unbroken by passing defeats. After Sambhajī's death and the capture of his infant son, his brother, Raja Rām, upheld the fortunes of his line, first at Raigarh, and, when that place was about to fall, in the remote southern stronghold of Gingee. From that corner of the Carnatic he cheered the hearts and guided the movements of the Marāthas against their puzzled foes. His trusty lieutenants teased the Mughals with a kind of partisan warfare, in which the latter with their heavy accoutrements and luxurious habits were no match for the little, hardy, light-clad, ubiquitous horsemen whose usual food was a cake of millet with now and then an onion, who slept bridle in hand under the open sky, and whose strong, active, well-trained little steeds were always ready for the work required of them. Careful to avoid a charge from the heavy Mughal horse, they spread in countless bands over the country, plundering every district which refused to buy them off, hanging on the flanks of Mughal armies, cutting off their convoys, swooping down upon detached bodies of troops, and never losing a chance of doing their enemies the greatest possible harm.

To attack these hornets in their nests was a task which long baffled the best of the Mughal commanders. Not till after several years of bootless efforts did Gingee itself fall, in 1698, into the hands of Zulfikar Khan. Even then, however, the bold Raja Rām renewed the struggle from his next place of shelter at Satāra on the Western Ghāts, whence he himself at the head of a great army carried his ravages as far eastward as Jālna, in Berar, before the Mughals succeeded in driving him back. Soon after his own death in 1700, Satāra itself with several other strongholds was captured, after a brave defence, by the troops of the persevering emperor. But in spite of frequent reverses, of dissensions among themselves, and of Aurangzeb's amended plans for their suppression, the Marātha leaders rallied again and again round the standard of the manly-hearted Tāra Bai, who, for some years, ruled her people in the name of her late husband's heir, the boy Sīvajī.

For the next few years Aurangzeb tried hard to crush his daring foes in the Deccan. But for every fort he took he paid heavily with the lives of his own men; fresh swarms of Marāthas worried him at every turn; floods, famines, and deadly fevers weakened his resources or slew his troops. The untamable Rājputs of Mewār and the rebellious Jāts of Bharatpur kept drawing his attention beyond the Narbada, while a large force was sent against the Sikh insurgents near Multān. His own troops began to mutiny for want of regular pay from his failing treasury. The Marāthas in the meantime began to recover their lost forts; were ere long pouring into Mālwa, and carrying fire

AURANGZEB

[F]ROM A MS. IN THE BRITISH MUSEUM

p. 11

and sword through Gujarāt. They hovered like flies about the grand army which Aurangzeb himself had once more led against them; they derided his very overtures for peace; and worse and ever worse shame and disaster dogged his final retreat to Ahmadnagar, whence he had marched out twenty years before in all the pomp and glory of another Xerxes.

A few months later the aged emperor breathed his last in the city which sheltered the wrecks of his beaten army, after a reign of forty-nine, and a life of more than eighty-eight years. To the last he seems to have retained all the mental and much of the bodily vigour which marked his prime, and won him a foremost place among the princes of his own dynasty. His close attention to the smallest details of government may have been sharpened by his habitual distrust of all around him; but, in spite of the evils caused by his suspicious temper and narrow religious zeal, his people on the whole were well governed and lightly taxed.* One of his edicts forbade the raising of the land-rents on those who had improved their farms at their own expense. In anything that concerned the public welfare, from the tillage of the soil to the daily hearing of causes in the Hall of Audience, from the appointment of a clerk to the supervision of a great province, he displayed a keen and enlightened interest. His sense of justice failed him only when bigotry or personal ambition clouded his mental view. Merciless to his betrayed or defeated brethren, he pardoned and employed their followers, set his face as a rule against savage or

* His revenue from all sources has been reckoned, with seeming accuracy, at seventy to eighty millions sterling, at the rate of two shillings the rupee His land revenue alone amounted to thirty-four and a -half millions nett, about double that of Akbar's latter years, and twelve millions higher than that raised by Shah Jahān. His total revenue exceeded that of Jahāngīr by about thirty millions. These vast sums, equal then to about twice their present value, appear to have been collected with little effort.

severe punishments, and dealt mildly with all offences that touched neither his power nor his religion.

Of courtly manners, great personal courage, varied accomplishments, and some military skill, Aurangzeb failed to win the love of his own children, or the zealous co-operation of his chief officers. Never was a prince of his intellectual mark so often cheated or so badly served.* His best-planned enterprises were marred by the fruits of his fatally suspicious temper. Trusting no one, he was trusted in his turn by none. His son Muazzam he kept in prison for seven years. His favourite son, Akbar, joined in succession the standards of his Rājput and Marātha foes. Another son, Kāmbakhsh, was placed in arrest on a groundless charge of plotting with the Marāthas. His ablest surviving general, Zulfikar Khan, was driven by his worrying treatment to the verge of open rebellion. Even Prince Azam, best beloved of his sons after Akbar's defection, saw only treachery in his father's earnest-seeming efforts to retain his love.

Craft and cunning, indeed, were Aurangzeb's favourite weapons alike in the council and the field. "To succeed by art," says one historian,† "threw honour upon himself; to subdue by power acquired to others fame." This preference for crooked ways may even have gained strength in such a nature from the undoubted warmth of his religious zeal. Hypocrisy and devoutness often go together, and the true key to his conduct may be found, we think, in the bigotry which brought Prince Dāra to a cruel end, which estranged the hearts of the emperor's Hindu subjects, sanctioned the use of treachery against foes of a different creed, and blinded him to the fatal folly of crushing the old Muhammadan princes of the Deccan instead of helping them to put down the rising Marātha

* Elphinstone's "India," book xi. chap. 4.

† Dow's "Hindostan," vol. iii.

power.* A scholar and a poet, he banished poets from his court, abolished the office of royal historiographer, issued edicts against music and dancing, and turned every singer and musician out of the palace precincts. If his private morals were in keeping with the austere bent of his religious habits, he succeeded in uprooting the last traces of that wise and generous policy on which Akbar had sought to lay fast the foundations of the Mughal rule. If he neither drank, gambled, nor dallied with other than his lawful wives, he restored the old lunar year of the Muhammadans, maddened the Hindus with all kinds of petty persecutions, placed new weapons in the hands of his Marātha foes, and paved the way for the disruption of that broad empire which his own arms had helped to build up.

Two years after Aurangzeb's accession Charles II. mounted the throne of England. Among his first acts was the granting of a charter to the united East India Company, empowering them to make peace and war with the natives of India, to administer justice, and to expel interlopers from their ground. A year later, in 1662, the island of Bombay, with its noble harbour, formed part of the dowry which the Princess Catherine of Braganza brought over to her English husband. After six years of profitless possession Charles II. transferred the island to the East India Company, under whose sway it was destined to become the fitting capital of Western India, and the seat of a trade exceeding thirty millions sterling. In 1676 the Company were allowed to set up a mint in

* The kings of Bijapur and Golconda belonged, like the Persians, to the *Shiah* sect of Muhammàdans, who acknowledge and almost worship Ali as the true successor to his father-in-law Muhammad in the leadership of the faithful, and as the first of the twelve Imāms or Pontiffs of his line. Aurangzeb, like his forefathers and the bulk of Indian Mussulmans in these days, was a *Sunni* Muhammadan, one of those who ignore Ali's murdered son Husain as a true Khalīf. To this sect belong the Turks of the Turkish Empire.

their new possession, which had already been successfully defended against the Dutch. Nine years afterwards it displaced Surat as their chief station in the East Indies and the seat of the Western Presidency. In 1686 the President of Bombay was declared Governor-General of India. By that time ships of all nations had begun to anchor in the harbour of his new capital, and the Company's Indian trade had risen to a hundred *lakhs* of rupees, or more than a million sterling.

Meanwhile, in Bengal things had not gone smoothly between the English and the Mughals. With the French, Dutch, and Danish factories on the Hūgli, the English agents had no cause of quarrel. But the alleged exactions of the Mughals, and their Viceroy's refusal to let the English Company's servants fortify the mouth of the Hūgli against interlopers from England, provoked or became the pretext for a hostile movement against the masters of Bengal. In 1686 an English fleet sailed up the Hūgli, on its way to Chittagong. A quarrel between some English soldiers and the native police brought on a regular engagement, in which the natives were worsted. The English admiral opened fire on the town of Hūgli. An attempt to treat on the part of the Nawāb of Bengal came to nothing. At last Job Charnock, the chief of the English factory, withdrew to Chatanatti, the future site of the city which became in later years the chief seat of the English power in India.

Followed thither by the Nawāb's army, Charnock led his followers to the swamps of Hijali, an island at the mouth of the Hūgli. Here in the next few months half of his little garrison had perished from disease, and the rest were far on the road to a like issue, when matters began to take a more hopeful turn. Charnock was allowed to re-enter Chatanatti, and peace was all but re-established on the old footing; but Captain Heath, who had just arrived with a fresh fleet from England, disallowed the treaty, and Charnock, with all his countrymen in Bengal, sailed down the Hūgli for Madras. On its way thither the English fleet bombarded Balasore, and tried in vain to effect a landing at Chittagong.

Meanwhile, on the western side of India the Company had not gained much by the aggressive policy which its chairman, Sir Josiah Child, thought fit to pursue. The seizure of pilgrim ships on their way to Mecca was requited by the capture of the English factory at Surat, by a partially successful attack upon Bombay, and by the expulsion of the English from nearly all their settlements in Southern India. At last, in 1690, the Governor of Bombay was glad to renew the peace so rashly broken. His envoys returned from Bijapur with concessions easily granted by an emperor fully alive to the benefits of a growing trade with the foreigner; and Charnock once more sailed up the Hūgli to hoist his country's flag in the little hamlet of Chatanatti.

In 1695, three years after the death of Charnock,* his successor bought from the Mughals the three villages of Chatanatti, Govindpur, and Calcatta, out of which the modern Calcutta was to arise. To fortify their new possession was now the first thought of its owners, whose dreams of empire had already begun to mould their general policy, and whose agents had some years before been exhorted to look after the increase of their revenue at least as carefully as the growth of their trade.† It

* He was buried at Barrackpore, which the natives still call after him, "Achānak."

† "The increase of our revenue," wrote the Directors in 1689, "is the subject of our care as much as our trade; 'tis that must maintain our force when twenty accidents may interrupt our trade; 'tis that must make us a nation in India; without that we are but as a great number of interlopers, united by His Majesty's charter, fit only to trade where nobody of power thinks it their interest to oppose us."

was not long before the wish was gratified. During the height of a rebellion led by one of the old Pathān chiefs of Orissa, the French, Dutch, and English merchants on the Hūgli got leave from the hard-pressed governor of Bengal to put their several factories in a state of defence. Fortified works sprang up accordingly around the new settlement of Calcutta, and the flag of England was soon floating above the ramparts of Fort William, so called in honour of William III.

In the second year of the 18th century, another success—if the triumph of a monopoly may be so considered—befel the Company in its contest with younger rivals. For years past a host of "interlopers," licensed and unlicensed, had vexed the souls of the old chartered merchants by glutting the home markets with goods not seldom won by deeds of sheer piracy. The agents of rival companies intrigued against each other at home and abroad, their quarrels sometimes bursting into open warfare, while pirates like Captain Kidd * preyed impartially on all ships coming from India. At length the influence of the oldest company prevailed with the English Parliament to put an end to a rivalry so fraught with evil or unpleasant issues. In 1702 the chief of the rival companies were joined by royal charter into one "United Company of Merchants trading to the East." A few years later Calcutta itself, under the name of Fort William, became the seat of a new presidency. At this time, and for many years afterwards, the Company's servants, from the president to the lowest clerk, were free to eke out their small salaries with the profits which could then be gleaned from their private trade; profits so handsome, that ere long even the junior servants could sit down to dinner

* William Kidd, by birth a New-Yorker, had been sent out by William III. to cruise against the pirates; but ere long turned pirate himself. At last he was captured, tried in England for murder, and hanged.

with music playing, and ride out in a carriage and four.*

* The president's salary was then fixed at £300 a-year, while his eight members of council drew £40, the junior merchants £30, the factors £15, and the writers £5 a-year.

CHAPTER VII

SUCCESSORS OF AURANGZEB—1707-1740

In the will he left behind him, Aurangzeb had assigned the northern half of his wide dominions to his eldest son, Muazzam, with the title of emperor, and Delhi for his capital. Of the remainder, Azam was to rule from Agra all but the kingdoms of Bijapur and Golconda, which were reserved for Kāmbaksh. Prince Azam, however, took advantage of his brother's absence in Kābul to assume the sovereignty of all India. But it was not long before his pretensions and his life were put out together in a bloody battle fought near Agra between him and Prince Muazzam. The subsequent defeat and death of his youngest brother, Kāmbaksh, freed Muazzam from all present rivals, and left him, in fact as well as name, sole head of the Mughal empire, under the title of Bahādur Shah.

In the last-named victory, won at Hyderābād, a body of Marāthas fought on the conqueror's side, in fulfilment of a pledge obtained from Shahu, Sambhajī's lineal heir, on his release from the long, if mild, captivity enforced by the politic Aurangzeb. Shahu's gratitude to the Mughals seems to have survived the fall of Prince Azam, who had been first to set him free. At any rate, he transferred his services to Bahādur Shah, whose help enabled him to set up at Satāra a rival sway to that of the regent Tāra Bai. A further treaty empowered him to receive the chauth in the name of the new emperor, through the hands of Mughal officers alone.

Freed from anxiety on the side of the Marāthas, the emperor turned his arms against the refractory princes of Mārwār and Jaipur. Ere long, however, a new source of trouble drew his attention away from Rājputāna to Sind. Granting the Rājput chief almost as easy terms as the Rāna of Udaipur had won already, Bahādur Shah hastened to check the growing boldness of the Sikhs, who, early in the 17th century, had been driven by Muslim bigotry to employ worldly weapons in aid of the religious movement begun by Nānak more than a century before.* In the days of Guru Gofind, the tenth high priest in succession to Nānak, and grandson of Har Gofind, who had taken up arms to avenge his father's murder, the process of development, so common in like cases, from a body of religious reformers into a nation of armed fanatics had well-nigh become complete. From the highlands of the Punjāb the Sikh warriors issued to try their strength anew against their Muhammadan persecutors, but in vain. After a long struggle with Aurangzeb's soldiers, Guru Gofind became a lonely wanderer in the Deccan, and fell at last by the hand of a private foe near the monastery he had founded at Nāndēr.

To his old followers, however, remained a legacy of hatred and revenge, which a new leader, named Bandu, turned ere long to memorable account. Once more the Sikhs broke out from their highland shelter, to ravage Sind with fire and sword, and to repay, in the slaughter of *mullahs* and the destruction of mosques, the wrongs and insults which they and their fathers had suffered at Muslim hands. At length the emperor himself went forth to confront the danger which his officers on the spot had failed to put down. The Sikhs were driven back into the hills, and Bandu himself had a narrow escape from capture in the stronghold whose fall, after a brave resistance,

* See book i. chap. 2.

closed for that year a bootless struggle against overpowering odds.

A few months afterwards the emperor himself died at Lahore, in the fifth year of his reign and the seventieth of his age. With him the glory of the house of Bābur may be said to have departed. A fight for empire between his sons ended in the triumph of the eldest, Jahāndar Shah, a worthless debauchee, who begun by slaying all his nearest kinsmen, and, after six months of costly dalliance with fiddlers and mistresses, perished in his turn at the hands of his nephew, Farrukhiszar. Installed as emperor at Delhi by the arms of two Saiyid* brothers, Husain Ali and Abdullah Khan, that nephew began his reign with the murder of Aurangzeb's great general, Zulfikar Khan, the last emperor's able but overweening wazir.

After a few more murders, Farrukhiszar proceeded to abet some new favourities in plotting mischief against his Saiyid benefactors. Ajīt Singh, the Raja of Mārwār, was secretly encouraged to hold out to the last against Husain Ali, who had been sent to subdue him. This plot baffled by the Raja's timely acceptance of the peace offered by his opponent on liberal terms, the emperor next schemed to get rid of his powerful servant by making him viceroy of the Deccan, in the room of Dāūd Khan. The latter, too faithfully obeying his secret orders from Delhi, fell fighting at the head of his troops on the field which they for a moment had nearly won.

The same arts were employed by the emperor in the war which Husain Ali had to take up against the Marāthas. Once more, however, the wary Saiyid trumped his master's hand by concluding peace with Raja Shahu and his able minister, Bālajī Vishvanāth--a peace which left them masters of all Sīvajī's former conquests in Southern

* They were sprung from a family of descendants of Muhammad who had settled in the town of Bāra.

India, and acknowledged the Marātha claim to chauth upon the whole of the Deccan. Shahu's rival, Sambhajī, the son of Tāra Bai, was also acknowledged as Raja of Kolhāpur. For these concessions, Shahu agreed to pay a yearly tribute, and to furnish for the emperor's service a body of 15,000 horse.

Meanwhile Bandu, the Sikh leader, had once more led his armed fanatics into the plains between the Sutlej and the Jumna. In the midst, however, of their destroying career, they were checked, routed, scattered, hunted down by the victorious Mughals. Hundreds of their leading men were borne in triumph through the streets of Delhi, to the place where each in turn was beheaded, scorning to save his life by changing his creed. Bandu himself, after seeing his own child butchered before his eyes, was torn to pieces with hot pincers, exulting in the midst of his tortures at the vengeance which heaven at his hands had wreaked upon the wicked.

Unwarned by past failures, Farrukhiszar renewed his plottings against the Saiyids, one of whom, Abdullah, held the post of grand wazir. Some of his chief nobles would gladly have helped him to get rid of the two men whose greatness eclipsed their own; but the emperor's wavering policy broke up the league, and while he was yet dallying with a new favourite, Husain Ali, with 10,000 Marātha horse, marched up from the Deccan to his brother's rescue. The frightened emperor soon found himself at the mercy of men who had small reason to show him any. A tumult in the streets of Delhi sealed his fate. Dragged from his hiding-place to a prison, he was ere long put to death; two of his young kinsmen, raised in turn to the throne, died of consumption in the course of a few months; but at last a healthier successor turned up in Prince Roshan Akhtar, who took the name of Muhammad Shah.

The new reign began stormily. Risings in Allahābād,

the Punjāb, and elsewhere, might be quelled with small trouble by force or cunning; Chīn Kilich Khan, the future Nizām of the Deccan, was not so easily put down. Of a good Turkish family, the son of a favourite officer of Aurangzeb, he himself had risen under the same emperor to high military command in the Deccan, with the distinctive titles of Asaf Jah and Nizām-ul-Mulk. As governor of the Deccan for a few months after the death of Zulfikar Khan, he held the Marāthas in check until Husain Ali came to supplant him. Transferred to the government of Mālwa, Chīn Kilich waited for the moment when his turn might come to triumph over the hateful Saiyid pair, whose influence at court still worked unfavourably for his own ambitious ends.

It was not long that he had to wait. By the middle of 1720 he had crossed the Narbada, planted his standard on the fort of Asīrgarh, and defeated an army sent against him near Burhānpur. Another victory at Bālapār in Berar brought Husain Ali himself into the field. On his march southwards, however, the Saiyid fell by an assassin's dagger; his brother Abdullah, defeated in battle by the emperor he sought to dethrone, remained a prisoner in the hands of Muhammad Shah; and ere long Chīn Kilich Khan, already master of the Deccan, re-entered Delhi as wazir.

But the pleasure-loving emperor and his dissolute friends soon tired of the company of the grave old statesman to whom they chiefly owed their deliverance from the Saiyid yoke. They sent him to displace the governor of Gujarāt, who forthwith took up arms in his own defence. Chīn Kilich put down the rebellion and added Gujarāt also to his rule. His return to Delhi exposed him to fresh embroilments with the court. At length he threw up his post and retired to the Deccan, where Mobāriz Khan, governor of Hyderābād, was secretly encouraged to withstand him. Once more the arts of the Delhi cabal were foiled by the defeat and death of their new tool; and their intended victim was free to fix at Hyderābād the seat of a sovereignty which his successors have wielded to this hour. It is true that he covered the seizure of independent power by occasional gifts to his lord paramount; but the dismemberment of the empire had already begun.

It began indeed three years earlier, when Ajīt Singh, the Rana of Mārwar or Jodhpur, made up for his expulsion from Gujarāt by wresting the Rājput province of Ajmēr from the Mughals. If the Jāts of Bharatpur were once more quelled by the loyal Raja Jai Singh of Ambēr, more worthily remembered for his great love of science than for his success as a ruler,* the Marāthas were already gaining ground in Mālwa and Gujarāt. On the death of King Shahu's able Pēshwa, Bālajī Vishvanāth, in 1720, the sceptre he had wielded in the name of his puppet sovereign passed into the strong hands of his yet abler son, Bājī Rāo. With a keen eye for the inward weakness of the Mughal empire, the new Pēshwa soon carried the Marātha arms across the Narbada. "Let us strike," he said, "the withered trunk, and the branches will fall of themselves." His troops ravaged Mālwa and levied chauth in Gujarāt. Chīn Kilich Khan himself had to back out of his craftily planned alliance with the rival Marātha house of Kolhāpur. The head of that house, Samba, was forced to acknowledge Shahu's right to all the Marātha country except that which immediately surrounded his own capital. A great Marātha chief, Dabāri, who took up arms to depose the Pēshwa, was himself defeated and slain by his skilful opponent, and Gujarāt itself lay helpless

* Jai Singh, Raja of Dhundar, a descendant of Akbar's friend and Jahāngīr's father-in-law, Bhagwandās, was the greatest Hindu astronomer since Aryabhata. He erected observatories at Delhi, Muttra, Benāres, Ujjain, and Jaipur, his new capital, founded by him in 1728. From him is descended the present dynasty of Jaipur.

at the conqueror's feet. Pilajī Gaikwar, whose descendants still reign at Baroda, was set to govern the conquered province in the name of Dabāri's infant son. Two of Bājī Rāo's lieutenants, Malhar Rāo Holkar and Ranajī Sindhia, founders of still existing dynasties at Indore and Gwalior, were already engaged in the work of wresting Mālwa from the Mughals. In vain did the wily master of Hyderābād renew his old intrigues against his formidable neighbours. Loyalty to a tottering throne, filled by an ungrateful sovereign, formed no part of his political creed, nor had old age diminished his habitual caution. A compact formed between him and the Marāthas in 1731 left the latter free to push their conquests north of the Narbada, so long as they forbore from harrying the subjects of the Nizām-ul-Mulk.

The murder of Pilajī Gaikwar by the patricide son of Ajīt Singh brought fresh swarms of Marāthas into Gujarāt. Driven out of the province he had hoped to reconquer for the Mughals, Abhi Singh, the murderer, retired into his own country. Ere long Mālwa also was quietly surrendered by its governor, Jai Singh, into the hands of Shahu's Pēshwa. Grateful for help received from that quarter, the Raja of Bundelkhand had meanwhile placed the Marāthas in possession of his own domains around Jhānsi, on the Jumna.

Still hungering for fresh conquests, the daring Brahman kept making fresh demands on the emperor, who for some time could see no escape from further annoyance save in concessions which only whetted the greed of his insatiable foes. At length Chīn Kilich, repenting of his recent quietude, came forward to the rescue of his nominal master; while Sādat Khan, the Persian nawāb or governor of Oudh, marched forth to defend the empire on its north-eastern side. In spite of the check which Holkar's light horse received from the Nawāb on their raid towards

Agra, Bājī Rāo determined to show the emperor that he was still in Hindustān. Passing round the flank of a Mughal army encamped near Muttra, his swift-moving squadrons suddenly appeared before the gates of Delhi itself. After plundering the suburbs, beating back a sally from the city walls, and filling the citizens with utter dismay, they rode off again for the Deccan, laden with rich spoils, before Chīn Kilich, the emperor's new wazir, had time to intercept them.

In the first days of the next year the aged ruler of the Deccan, at the head of the strong and well-appointed army which he had led forth from Delhi, awaited near Bhopāl, on the Mālwa border, the approach of Bājī Rāo. But in the course of a few weeks his own position in the midst of active foes, who laid waste the country, cut off his supplies, and assailed his outposts, became so perilous, that he could neither advance nor retreat without heavy loss. Attempting the latter alternative, he was soon compelled to save himself from worse misfortunes by a treaty which assigned to the Pēshwa the whole of the country between the Chambal and the Narbada, besides pledging the emperor to the payment of fifty lakhs of rupees, or half-a-million sterling of our money.

But a yet more cruel blow was now impending over the Mughal power. In 1722 Husain Shah, the last of the Safavi kings of Persia, laid his crown at the feet of Madmūd, the Khilji chief of Kandahār, whose victorious Afghāns had for six months been closely besieging the Persian monarch in his own capital of Isfahān. On the death of Mahmūd two years afterwards, the crown thus won by him at the sword's point devolved upon his nephew Ashraf, whose wars with the Turks and Russians were followed by a sharper struggle with an enemy nearer home. His new assailant, Nādir Kūli, was the son of a Turkish shepherd in Khurāsān. Beginning, like Sīvajī, as a robber chief, he won his way to the leadership of an army which delivered his native country from the Abdāli Afghāns, drove Ashraf out of Isfahān, fought successfully against the Turks, and set Tahmasp, the exiled son of Husain, upon his father's throne.

Ere long, however, the new king had to make way for his abler protector, who began his reign by conquering Afghānistān. The internal weakness of the Mughal empire then turned his thoughts to the country beyond the Indus; and a joint letter * from Chīn Kilich and Sadat Khan is said by the native chroniclers to have spurred him on to the cheap and alluring task of heightening his own renown by the plunder of a defenceless people. On one plea or another he set forth from Kābul in the autumn of 1738, passed safely through the mountains that barred his way, crossed the Indus, and easily defeated near Karnāl the troops which Muhammad Shah had hastily brought up from Delhi to withstand him. Betrayed by his own officers, the luckless emperor sued in person for such mercy as the conqueror might deign to show. In the conqueror's train he returned to his own capital to collect the ransom which Nādir Shah was willing to accept.

But the worst for him and his people was yet to come. Two days after his return to Delhi, the rumoured death of his conqueror roused the citizens to sudden fury. They fell upon the few thousand Persian troops scattered about the city. The cowardly nobles made no attempt to stay the slaughter of those whom they had shrunk from facing in the field. Nādir Shah himself became a mark for stones and bullets as he rode next morning through the streets where lay the bodies of his murdered followers. One of his favourite officers fell dead by his side. Provoked beyond bearing by this last blow, he let loose his impatient

* Elphinstone doubts the truth of this story, which Mr. Keene, on the contrary, believes (Keene's "Mughal Empire," p. 36).

soldiers on the raging crowd. In the next few hours the massacres of Timūr's day were renewed within hearing, if not under the eyes, of Delhi's new master. Thirty thousand people are supposed to have perished, before Nādir Shah, moved perhaps by the emperor's humble entreaties,* ordered his obedient warriors to hold their hands.

It remained to continue the work of spoliation already begun. Every man of the least wealth or mark in the city, from the emperor and his nobles down to the smaller tradesmen, had to contribute his share to the general ransom. Every house was ransacked for hidden treasure. Torture was employed in aid of threats. Numbers of the people died of ill-usage or slew themselves to avoid it. Among the latter appears to have been the traitor Sādat Khan himself.† The native officers who had to collect the plunder filled their own pockets with untold sums at the cost of their helpless countrymen. Heavy fines were also drawn from the provinces. After two months employed on a quest so fruitful, the Persian conqueror marched out of Delhi laden with treasure in coin, jewels, and goods, whose value may have amounted to thirty crores of rupees, or more than thirty millions of our money. Conspicuous among his plunder was the famous peacock throne of Shah Jahān, the chiefest jewels in which were, more than a century after, to become the prize of a power

* According to Dow, Muhammad Shah himself, followed by his chief nobles, entered the Mosque of Roshan-ud-daula, in the Chandni Chauk, the Regent Street of Delhi, where Nādir was sitting in gloomy silence, and with tears besought him to spare the Emperor's subjects; whereupon he stopped the massacre.

† The story which Elphinstone quotes only to reject, is that Nādir sent for Chīn Kilich and Sādat Khan, and reviling them for their treachery to their king, spat on their beards: a disgrace which only death could wipe out. Chīn Kilich made a show of poisoning himself, and Sādat, deceived by his clever acting, took real poison and died. Whether the story be a myth or no, however, Sādat certainly killed himself on account of Nādir's behaviour towards him.

at that time owning but a few square miles of Indian ground.

A year after Nādir's return homewards, Bājī Rāo died in the midst of fresh plans for pursuing the work interrupted by the Persian monarch. Besides his northern forays, he had for some time past been engaged in warfare with the Portuguese, with the Sīdis or Abyssinians of Janjira, and with Angria, the pirate lord of Kolāba, near Bombay. The Portuguese his brother Chimnajī drove out of Salsette, Bassein, and other places in the Konkan ; but the Sīdis fought him on pretty equal terms, and the war with Angria, in spite of English aid, lingered on after the Pēshwa's death. Nor had Bājī Rāo succeeded in his latest essay against the Deccan, where Chīn Kilich's brave son, Nāsir Jang, had vigorously upheld the cause of his absent father. On the whole, however, in spite of partial failures abroad and dissensions among his own countrymen, the deceased Pēshwa's daring policy had raised the Marātha power to a height whence nothing but the incurable folly of his successors could afterwards bring it down.

CHAPTER VIII

THE MUGHAL EMPIRE TO THE BATTLE OF PĀNIPAT

BESIDES the plunder of a populous city and a broad province, Nādir Shah annexed the whole of the Mughal dominions in Kābul, Sind, and the Punjāb within the Indus. To the Mughal emperor he left a dishonoured crown, an empty treasury, and the wrecks of an empire already breaking to pieces. The closing years of Muhammad's reign were years of growing disorder, of ever-darkening prospects for the House of Bābur. Muhammad's court was rent with factions and filled with intrigues. Province after province slipped out of his feeble grasp. The Princes of Rājputāna disowned their allegiance with impunity. The Marātha Gaikwar reigned in Gujarāt. A bold adventurer, Mohābat Jang, best known as Alivardi Khan, had bribed the Court of Delhi to sanction his seizure of Bengal, Bihār, and Orissa. Safdar Jang, the son of Sādat Khan, governed Oudh as the equal rather than the servant of his liege lord. In Southern India remained not a foot of ground which the emperor could henceforth call his own, if his nominal lieges chose to deny the claim.

The very quarrels of Marātha leaders brought him no advantage. In return for help received from Bālaji Rāo, son and successor of the last Pēshwa, against the daring raids of his rival Raghujī Bhōnsla from Berar into Bengal, the emperor was fain to grant him full possession of Mālwa as a hereditary fief. A few months afterwards

Bālaji gave a new impulse to his countrymen's greed for plunder and conquest by granting his late opponent the right to levy chauth on Bengal and Bihār, if not on provinces yet further north. Thus free to push his own fortunes, Raghuji carried his arms and ravages into the heart of Bengal, to such purpose that neither the skill nor the soldiership of Alivardi Khan could long hold out against Marātha energy, backed by a mutiny among his best soldiers, a body of Afghāns under Mustafa Khan. The treacherous murder of Bāskar Pandit, the Marātha general, by the Mughal Viceroy himself, was requited six years later by the cession to Raghuji of half Orissa, and a promise to pay chauth for Bengal.

If Alivardi had looked for help to the aged Viceroy of the Deccan, he had looked in vain. After leaving his eldest son Ghāzi-ud-din as wazir at Delhi, Chīn Kilich on his return to Hyderābād had been for some time engaged in suppressing the revolt of his son Nāsir Jang. That misguided prince brought to his senses in 1742, his father's attention had next been called to the Carnatic, which one of Raghuji's officers, Morāri Rāo, was employed in wresting from its Mughal Nawāb. The old Tartar's presence at the head of a large army brought the Marāthas to a timely compromise; Morāri Rāo retaining Gūti and some other districts, while the rest of the country was shared between Chīn Kilich's grandson, Muzaffar Jang, and his faithful servant Anwar-ud-din. In 1748 Chīn Kilich himself, the wily and ambitious Nizām-ul-Mulk, died at Burhāupur at the age of seventy-seven; and his sons in the midst of their own quarrels could pay little heed to the affairs of remote Bengal.*

His death followed but a few weeks after that of

* According to some accounts, Chīn Kilich died at the fabulous-seeming age of a hundred and four. Elphinstone's estimate, however is probably much nearer the mark,

Muhammad Shah himself, whose path had latterly been cheered by a victory gained over Afghān insurgents in Rohilkhand,* and later still by his son Ahmad's defeat of Ahmad Khan, the formidable leader of a new invasion from Kandahar. An Abdāli Afghan, sprung from the sacred Sadduzai branch of his tribe, Ahmad Khan had no sooner fought his way to the headship of the Afghān race and the mastery of Sind, than he prepared to lead a small but resolute army across the Punjāb into Upper Hindustān. His skilful strategy baffled all attempts to oppose him until, in March, 1748, his soldiers found the Mughals under Prince Ahmad strongly entrenched near the city of Sind. A series of hard fights, continued for ten days, ended in the Abdāli's repulse with heavy slaughter; and Delhi for a few years longer was saved from further suffering.

A month after his victory Prince Ahmad mounted his father's throne, with Safdar Jang of Oudh for his wazir. It was not long before the latter, unable to cope by himself with a new Rohilla rising on a formidable scale, appealed for aid to the Jāts and Marāthas in the provinces skirting the right bank of the Jumna. With their help the invaders were driven back into Rohilkhand; but this success was more than balanced by a Mughal defeat in Mārwār, and by the conquest of the Punjāb by Ahmad Shah the Abdāli, or, as he now styled himself, the Durāni, king of Afghānistān. The defeat of the Rohillas moreover placed new weapons of attack in the hands of Sindhia and Holkar, who were free to ravage Rohilkhand under the cloak of levying their favourite black-mail.

Yet darker troubles awaited the luckless emperor. The streets of Delhi became the scene of a civil war between

* The Rohillas were a colony of Yusufzai and other Afghan tribes, which had lately conquered the country east of the Ganges, from Oudh up to the Himālayas.

the wazir and his new rival Ghāzi-ud-din, grandson of Chīn Kilich and son of the late wazir. For six months the battle-cries of Persian and Mughal, Shiāh and Sunni, resounded through the city. Holkar and his Marāthas fought for the Mughal leader against their Hindu countrymen the Jāts, whose Raja, Suraj Mal, had espoused the cause of Safdar Jang. At length the latter withdrew from a fruitless struggle into his own province beyond the Ganges. The emperor, however, soon wearied of the burden he had brought upon his own shoulders, when he plotted with the youthful grandson of Chīn Kilich against the murderer of his favourite eunuch. In the midst of an effort to shake off his new tyrant, he fell into the hands of Ghāzi-ud-din himself, who straightway put out his eyes, and set up as emperor in his stead a son of Jahandar Shah, under the title of Alamgir II.

Meanwhile the new Marātha Pēshwa, Bālajī Rāo, had been steadily building up the fabric of Marātha power with the mingled boldness, cunning, and perseverance of his caste and family. In 1749, the long reign of Raja Shahu, the grandson of Sīvajī, the prisoner of Aurangzeb, the patron or the puppet of three successive Pēshwas, came to an end; and Raja Rām II., grandson, real or pretended, of his dead namesake and the still living Tāra Bai, was installed as puppet sovereign in his place. While the titular heir of Sīvajī held at Satāra his phantom court, the Pēshwa himself at Poona wielded the virtual sovereignty of all Māhārashtra, and his orders were obeyed alike by Sindhia on the Chambal and by Raghuji Bhōnsla beyond the Kistna.

In spite of the intrigues of Tāra Bai, the turbulence of his cousin Sedāsheo Bhao, and the part he himself played in the affairs of the Deccan, Bālajī Rāo, with equal courage, skill, and good fortune, held his triumphant way through all snares and over all hindrances, until, by the time of Ahmad Shah's deposition, he had made the Marātha name a terror or a beacon throughout all India. In the fatal strife for power between the sons of Chīn Kilich, he contrived not only to baffle Salābat Jang and his French ally, Bussy, but to obtain the cession of West Berar from Salābat's eldest brother, Ghāzi-ud-din. In concert with the English Commodore James, his fleets in 1755 aided in capturing Angria's pirate stronghold of Savandrūg, which was forthwith made over to him in exchange for his seaport town of Bankōt.* To him also in the following year was transferred the old Marātha fort and town of Giriah, which the redoubtable Tūlaji Angria had vainly defended against Admiral Watson and his colleague Colonel Clive, already a soldier of mark in the service of the East India Company.

A year earlier Bālajī's brother Raghuba † had cleared away the last relic of Mughal rule in Gujarāt by the capture of the old Pathān city of Ahmadābād. Sharing the rich spoils with his lieutenant, Damaji Gaikwar, the conqueror carried his arms, and successfully asserted the Marātha claim to chauth against the Hindu chiefs of Rājputāna and Bharatpur. In 1751 his troops set forth from Mālwa on their way to Delhi at the prayer of the ruffianly Ghāzi-ud-din the younger.

That luckless city had just been taken and despoiled by a second Nādir, in the person of Ahmad Shah, the Durāni, who had thus revenged himself for the Mughal wazir's recent raid into Lahore. No sooner had he turned his back on Delhi, than Ghāzi-ud-din besought the Marāthas to aid him in getting rid of Ahmad's deputy, the able and honest Rohilla chief, Najīb-ud-daula. Under the wing of his new ally he re-entered Delhi in triumph, and Najīb-ud-daula

* A town in the Ratnagīri district, sixty-eight miles south of Bombay, at the mouth of the river Savītri.

† His proper name was Raghunāth Rāo.

retired northwards to his own domain near Sahāranpur. Emboldened by this success, Raghuba a few months afterwards crossed the Sutlej, drove the Afghāns out of the Punjāb, and set up a governor of his own choosing at Lahore. One of his generals overran Rohilkhand. To crown all, his cousin "the Bhao," as Sedāsheo Bhao was commonly called, was entering on a career of victory in the Deccan, which began with the taking of Ahmadnagar, and ended in 1760 with the conquest of half the country ruled by Ghāzi-ud-din's successor, Salābat Jang.

The Marātha power had now reached its highest point. From the Indus and the Himālayas down to the borders of Travancore, Bālajī levied the Marātha blackmail, or ruled the country through his own officers. The seed which Sīvajī had sown a century earlier had sprung up into a noble tree, whose branches, like the banyan-tree of the country, had struck fresh roots, until the single trunk had multiplied into a mighty forest overshadowing the whole peninsula, and threatening, as it grew, to kill off all rival growths. While the Hindu genius for civil government found free play in the countries which had been fairly brought under the rule of Brahman Pēshwas, the old swarms of mounted freebooters had been strengthened or replaced by regular armies of horse and foot, well paid, fairly disciplined, and equipped with guns, not wholly useless against ordinary foes.

But the shadow of a great disaster was already creeping over the Pēshwa's path. The pride that goes before destruction impelled his cousin, the Bhao, to supplant Raghuba as Captain-General of the Marātha armies in Hindustān. Meanwhile, a Marātha force in Rohilkhand had been driven back across the Ganges by Shujā-ud-daula, the Nawāb of Oudh. Ahmad Shah, the Durāni, had once more issued from the Afghān hills to punish the bold invaders of his son's domains in the Punjāb, and to drive the horsemen of Sindhia and Holkar across the Chambal. The murder of Alamgīr, by order of the blood-stained Ghāzi-ud-din, left Delhi without an emperor, but failed to arrest for a moment the issues dreaded by his murderer. Ahmad Shah marched on towards the Mughal capital, and an Afghān garrison ere long held the city in his name.

The Marāthas on their side were not idle. A mighty gathering of Rājputs, Jāts, and Marāthas swept up the country to complete the downfall of Muhammadan rule, and drive the Durāni across the Indus. Delhi itself was taken and once more despoiled by the soldiers of the Bhao, who would hardly wait to lead them against the Afghāns before proclaiming Bālajī's son, Wiswās Rāo, Emperor of Hindustān. Puffed up with his past successes and an overweening self-conceit, the Marātha leader gave no heed to the cautious counsels of his Jāt ally, Suraj Mal, but led forth his whole array of horse, foot, and guns, to attack an army of about equal strength commanded by the foremost general of his day.

The first hard blow in the coming strife for empire between the Muhammadans and the Hindus was virtually struck when Ahmad Shah plunged into the swollen Jumna above Delhi, and by fording or swimming landed his troops on the other side in the face of their astonished foes. Entrenching himself on the ill-omened field of Pānipat, the Bhao awaited an attack from the foe he had learned too late to value rightly. For two months the armies which were to decide the fate of India lay near each other, neither daring to move bodily out of its entrenchments, while outlying parties skirmished daily together, and flying columns beat up each other's quarters, cut off the enemy's convoys, or scoured the country for supplies. It needed all Ahmad's coolness and strength of will to curb the impatience of his Mughal and Rohilla officers, who were slow to see the wisdom of this long delay. But the far-seeing Afghān bade them sleep in peace, and trust all to a leader who knew what he was doing. "I will take care," he said, "that no harm befalls you," and he kept his word.*

At last the hour drew near when his patient watchfulness was to reap its due reward. Hemmed in on every side, their supplies cut off, their host of followers already starving, their huge camp reeking with the stench of dead bodies and the accumulated filth and refuse of near three hundred thousand souls, the Bhao's last efforts to treat with the double-dealing ruler of Oudh frustrated by Shujā's fears, and by the stern antagonism of the Rohilla chief Najīb-ud-daula, the whole Hindu army marched forth to battle in the early morning of the 6th January, 1761, with the courage less of hope than of sheer despair. "The ends of their turbans," says Grant Duff, "were let loose, their hands and faces anointed with a preparation of turmeric, signifying that they were come forth to die, and everything seemed to bespeak the despondency of sacrifice prepared instead of victory determined." On the side of Ahmad Shah were about 40,000 Afghāns and Persians, mostly mounted, 13,000 Indian horse, and 38,000 Indian foot, with thirty guns and many wall-pieces. Under the Marātha flag were ranged some 50,000 splendid cavalry, at least 15,000 irregular horse, with an equal number of foot, mostly trained in the Deccan by a Mussulman deserter from the French service, and 200 guns, besides a large number of wall-pieces. Both sides may also have mustered a large contingent of wild volunteer horsemen, whom the thirst for plunder and excitement had brought into the field.†

* "His orders were obeyed like destiny," says the chronicler Kāsi Rai; "no man daring to hesitate or delay one moment in executing them."

† The Pindāris, of evil fame, are recorded as flocking to the Marātha standard.

The centre of the Marātha line was led by Sedāsheo Bhao himself, with whom rode his young kinsman, Wiswās Rāo, and several chiefs of note in the Deccan wars. Mahājī Sindhia commanded the right wing, while the left, under the Gaikwar, was strengthened by the 9,000 disciplined Sepoys whom Ibrahīm Khan had brought up from the Deccan. Malha Rāo Holkar took post in the right centre. For one leader no place was to be found on that memorable morning. Suraj Mal, with many thousand Jāts and Rājputs, had already retired in dudgeon to his own land.

Hardly had the Marāthas begun their forward march, when the watchful Ahmad drew out his own array to meet them. His Grand Wazir, Shah Walli, held the centre, consisting chiefly of his own Afghāns. On his right were posted several Mughal and Rohilla chiefs, while the left was entrusted to the brave Najīb-ud-daula and the half-hearted Nawāb of Oudh. All day the battle raged with varying fortune. Overpowered by the steady onset of the Deccan Sepoys, the Afghān right gave way after a heavy slaughter. In the centre Bhao's Marātha and Rājput horsemen swept like a vast thunder-cloud upon the Grand Wazir's Durānis, and, in spite of Afghān prowess and the Afghān leader's bold example, drove them back in disorder on their reserves. On the Afghān left a more equal battle was waged by Najīb's Rohillas against the troops of Sindhia and Holkar.

In vain did the Grand Wazir attempt by repeated charges to retrieve the ruin that threatened his centre. The Bhao, whose courage far outstripped his generalship, still led forward his famished warriors into the heart of the hostile ranks. Round him and the hapless son of Bālajī the fight still raged with deadliest fury, and spears, swords, and battle-axes drank their fill of blood. At that moment of seeming defeat, Ahmad Shah by one supreme effort restored the fortunes of his hard-pressed troops. While every Hindu soldier was already engaged, his own reserves were still waiting the order to advance. Hurrying off a part of these to aid in turning the enemy's right, with the rest he rallied the fugitives from his own right and centre, and renewed the battle on that side.

The double movement soon bore fruit. Afghāns and Rohillas reformed their broken lines, large bodies of fresh horsemen thundered down upon the weary foe, and Najīb's reinforced warriors pushed back until they had rolled up the Marātha right. Still the fight raged under the hot afternoon sun, until Wiswās Rāo was seen to fall. Maddened at the sight, or aware of coming doom, the Bhao plunged into the thickest of the fray; Holkar, to whom he had last spoken, led his own troops from the field, as if all were lost already;* the Gaikwar followed his example; and presently the whole of that great army was flying in wild disorder from the swiftly advancing foe. The slaughter that followed in a chase of many miles completed the horrors of that eventful day. No quarter was asked or given. Of those who escaped the swords of their pursuers, a great many were cut up by the villagers themselves, and many more were afterwards slain in cold blood by their Durāni captors. Among these last were Jankojī Sindhia and the brave Ibrahīm Khan. The Bhao himself had found the death he sought for in the field. It is reckoned that only a fourth of the fighting men, and about the same proportion of camp followers, survived that fearful carnage. Thousands of women and children found in the entrenched camp and in the town of Pānipat, were sold as slaves; and the vengeance of the conquerors for

* He is said to have had a secret understanding with Shujā-ud-daula; but this is very doubtful. It is more probable, as Sir J. Malcolm thinks, that so good a soldier saw in a timely retreat the only hope of saving his own followers from the general wreck. In so doing he may only have obeyed the Bhao's last injunctions.

their own heavy losses was sated only when their victims had drained the cup of suffering to its last drop.

With the costly victory of Pānipat the league of Muhammadan princes against the common foe seems at once to have broken up. Ahmad Shah himself recrossed the Indus, leaving his late allies to settle their own affairs in their own way. If the Marātha power had received a permanent check, the Mughal Empire was never again to emerge from its late eclipse, although a nominal emperor might still hold his shadowy court at Delhi, and powerful princes were to offer him mock allegiance for kingdoms won by their own swords. Throughout Māhārashtra were heard the sounds of wailing for the carnage of Pānipat. The Pēshwa himself, who was marching towards Delhi, broke up his camp, recrossed the Narbada, and reached Poona only to die, bequeathing to his successors a broken sceptre and a losing struggle with a power already dominant in Bengal. How that power had meanwhile been advancing, the following chapter will show.

CHAPTER IX

THE FRENCH AND ENGLISH IN INDIA

FOR many years after the death of Aurangzeb the English in Bengal continued to play the part of peaceful traders, jealous of all rivals from the West, ready to grasp at any new concession which prayers, clamours, or timely services might win from native rulers, and careful to hold aloof from the wars that might rage around them. The good fortune which enabled an English surgeon, Mr. Hamilton, to cure the Emperor Farrukhiszar of an illness which had baffled the skill of native Hakīms, was requited, at Mr. Hamilton's own request, by an order exempting the Company's agents from all local charges on their merchandise, and by another which empowered the Company to buy over the lordship of thirty-eight villages near Calcutta. The help which the English afterwards received from the Viceroy, Shujā-ud-din, in their efforts to destroy the trade of an interloping company established at Ostend, consoled them for the dirt they had eaten under his unfriendly predecessor, Murshid Kūli Khan. During the troubles engendered by Alivardi Khan's long struggle with the Marātha invaders of Bengal, they obtained leave from the Viceroy to surround their settlement of Calcutta with an entrenchment afterwards known as "the Marātha Ditch."

On the opposite side of India, however, the English were sometimes less peacefully employed in defending their interests against the assaults of Marātha pirates, who became a terror and a nuisance to all vessels trading with the Konkan. The failure in 1722 of a joint attack by the English and the Portuguese on Angria's stronghold of Kolāba emboldened the pirates to fresh outrages; and not till more than thirty years after was the power of Angria's successors broken, by the combined attacks of English and Marātha forces on the rock-perched fastnesses of the pirate chiefs.

Meanwhile at Madras and in Southern India events had been happening which gave a new turn to the policy of the East India directors. While France and England were fighting at home, in India the merchants of either country had long been wont to follow peacefully, side by side, the business which took them so far away from their own land. Calcutta and Chandernagore, Madras and Pondicherry, were content to grow rich against each other, instead of taking an unprofitable part in the wars between the parent states. But in 1744, when France and England were once more at open strife, the bold Labourdonnais resolved, with the sanction of the French government, to fight his country's enemies in India also.* Returning to the Isle of France, of which he was then governor, he looked out in vain for the promised armament from home. But his amazing energy overcame all drawbacks. In one way or another he got together a fleet manned with sailors whom he himself, a sailor by profession and something of an engineer, had trained for their destined work. In July, 1746, after beating off an English squadron sent to intercept him, he anchored off Pondicherry, took counsel with its able governor, M. Dupleix, and set off again two months later for his long-projected attack upon Madras.

* A full and interesting account of this adventurer's brilliant career in India and the Mauritius may be found in Colonel Malleson's, "History of the French in India." During his rule, from 1735 to 1745, the Mauritius, or Isle of France, grew out of a wilderness into a flourishing colony. The best life of Dupleix is that by M. Prosper Cultru (Paris, 1901).

On the 18th September his ships and land-batteries began to bombard the fort, which Governor Morse with his three hundred Englishmen, of whom two-thirds only were soldiers, made a feeble show of holding. Three days afterwards the garrison surrendered as prisoners of war for the time being, with the power of redeeming the captured settlement after a specified term on payment of nearly half a million sterling. A large amount of booty fell at once into the conquerors' hands, besides the handsome present of £40,000 reserved by the governor for Labourdonnais himself.

The convention, however, displeased Dupleix, who found several reasons, including the powers entrusted to himself as Governor-General of French India, for afterwards setting it aside. In the midst of an embittered squabble between two men who, working together, might have driven the English out of India, a fearful storm so shattered the fleet of Labourdonnais, that he set sail from Madras, leaving the treaty he had just signed with the English Governor to be kept or broken at pleasure by Dupleix.*

Thus freed from a troublesome rival, Dupleix had now to deal with a new opponent in the shape of Anwar-ud-din, the Nawāb or Governor of the Carnatic,† who sent troops to enforce fulfilment of the Frenchman's promise to surrender Madras into his hands. If Dupleix had ever thought of keeping his pledge, he was now bent on keeping the fortified place instead. In vain did ten thousand of the Nawāb's warriors encamp around Madras, in hopes of punishing the insolent strangers who had cheated him

* At the Mauritius he found a new governor appointed in his place. On his way thence to France on board of a Dutch vessel, he fell into the hands of the English, was kindly treated in this country, and sent to France on his parole. There, however, he lay for three years in the Bastille, under charges of which he was at length acquitted. But he came out of prison penniless and broken-hearted, to die on the 9th September, 1753.

† Book iii. chap. 8.

out of his due share in the winnings gained from his English friends. With four hundred Frenchmen and Sepoys drilled in French fashion, and two guns, their leader sallied forth against the Mughals. The Mughal horsemen came thundering down upon the little band, but a few well-aimed discharges from the French guns checked them in mid-career, causing them to waver, halt, and turn back in headlong flight from the foe they had ignorantly despised.

This brilliant success was soon followed by another. A French force of 230 white men and 700 Sepoys was on its way from Pondicherry to succour Madras, when it found about 10,000 of the Nawāb's troops guarding with their guns the passage of the little river Adyar, near Madras. In a moment Paradis and his men were across the river, up the opposite bank, and pouring a volley into the astonished foe. A charge with the bayonet drove the Mughals into the town of St. Thomé.* Once more the French fire swept through their disordered masses, and sent them flying helter-skelter out of their last refuge. At that moment the victorious garrison of Madras came up to complete the rout, and chase the panic-stricken Mughals back towards Arcot.

Flushed with these victories, Dupleix proceeded to attack the English in Fort St. David, about fifteen miles to the south of Pondicherry. But the troops sent out by him were badly led, and a sudden onset of the Nawāb's soldiers drove them back in disorder to the French capital. An attack by sea on the Mughal town of Cuddalore was defeated by a timely storm. In March, 1747, Dupleix's best officer, Paradis himself, laid siege to Fort St. David, whose slender garrison were saved for the second time by the approach of an English squadron sent from the Hūgli to their relief.

* Or Mahapūram.

By this time the wily governor of Pondicherry had seduced the fickle Anwar-ud-din from his English alliance. But the Nawāb's friendship was short-lived. In 1748 he is again enlisted on the side of the English, who have got all ready for a grand attack on Pondicherry itself. By the end of June a bold attempt of the French to surprise Cuddalore had been baffled by the clever soldiership of Major Lawrence, the newly appointed commander of the English forces in India. It was not long, however, before Lawrence himself was taken prisoner by the brave defenders of Ariankopan, a kind of outwork to the defences of Pondicherry. Against the latter stronghold the renowned Admiral Boscawen opened his trenches on the 10th September with about 6000 soldiers, aided by a powerful fleet. So skilfully, however, was the defence conducted by Dupleix himself, after the fall of his ablest engineer and stoutest helpmate, Paradis, that after six weeks of fruitless effort, in which young Clive,* the future victor of Plassey, nobly bore his part, Boscawen carried back his armament to Fort St. David, leaving behind him a thousand of his best soldiers dead from wounds or disease.

The victorious Frenchman took care to trumpet the news of his success throughout India. From all quarters, even from Delhi, letters of congratulation came pouring in. It seemed as if nothing remained to him but the easy task of driving the defeated and despised English out of the country. But in the midst of the movements which Dupleix was planning for that end, came the unwelcome tidings of peace concluded at Aix-la-Chapelle on terms which obliged the French to give back their recent

* As a "writer" or clerk of the East India Company, Robert Clive shared in the fruitless defence of Madras against Labourdonnais. Carried off a prisoner to Pondicherry, he escaped thence in disguise to Fort St. David, and exchanging the pen for the sword, served as an ensign at the siege of Pondicherry.

conquests in Southern India. Madras was accordingly restored into English keeping, and the rival nations resumed the footing on which they had stood to each other five years before.

But neither of them was willing to let things remain as they were. The quarrels of the neigbouring native princes opened out new fields of enterprise to the servants of rival companies founded for the promotion of peacc-ful trade. On the plea of aiding the Marātha Raja of Tanjore to regain his lost throne, the English under Major Lawrence besieged and took the fort of Devikātta; the possession of which, with a strip of adjoining country, was afterwards secured to them by treaty with the Raja's brother and victorious rival, Partāb Singh.

Meanwhile Dupleix was busy weaving a larger web of the same kind, in concert with Chanda Sahib, son-in-law of a former Nawāb of Arcot, and for some years past a state prisoner at the court of Satāra. The recent death of the old Nizām-ul-Mulk, Chīn Kilich Khan, enabled the plotters to push their scheme. Set free by the Frenchman's intercession, Chanda Sahib made common cause with the Nizām's grandson, Muzaffar Jang, against his uncle Nāsir Jang, the rival claimant to the throne of the Deccan. At the head of a large force, aided by a choice French contingent these two princes entered the Carnatic, and gave battle to Anwar-ud-din, whose fall completed their victory. The chief honours of the day were won by M. de Bussy, whose name was soon to figure prominently in the wars of the Deccan. Marching on to Arcot, Muzaffar Jang proclaimed himself Subadār, or Viceroy of the Deccan, with Chanda Sahib as ruler of the Carnatic in his name. In proof of the latter's gratitude Dupleix himself was endowed with the lordship of eighty-one villages around his capital.*

* Malleson's "French in India," chap. vi.

Meanwhile Nāsir Jang was raising a mighty army for the purpose of crushing his rival; and Muhammad Ali, a son of the dead Nawāb, had not asked in vain for the help of English bayonets from Madras. When the opposing armies were near each other, a mutiny in the French contingent spread dismay among their allies. Chanda Sahib bravely covered the retreat of the French in the face of Morāri Rāo and his swift Marātha horsemen; but Muzaffar Jang surrendered to his uncle, who loaded him with irons after having sworn upon the Korān to let him go free.

Nothing, however, seemed to daunt or overthrow Dupleix. He brought the leading mutineers to a stern reckoning, and shamed their followers back into the paths of discipline. His envoys took high ground in treating with Nāsir Jang. His trustiest messengers held secret conference with discontented nobles in Nāsir's camp. A few hundred of his soldiers beat up the quarters of Morāri Rāo, and frightened Nāsir Jang himself into a swift retreat from the neigbourhood of Pondicherry. He shipped off five hundred Frenchmen and Sepoys to recapture Masulipatam from the Mughals. With a force no larger D'Auteuil dared the attack of Muhammad Ali's thirty thousand men, including two thousand English and Sepoys. When the latter had withdrawn in dudgeon from the camp of their headstrong ally, D'Auteuil himself, emboldened by the arrival of fresh succours from Pondicherry, moved out against the Nawāb, and drove his army like a flock of frightened sheep across the Panār. A few days afterwards some fifteen hundred Frenchmen and Sepoys, led by the skilful Bussy, scattered ten thousand of Muhammad Ali's warriors, who had rallied under the walls of Gingee; and, strengthened at the right moment by fresh troops, Bussy's heroes not only entered the town, but carried the rock fortress which Sīvajī had won through fraud, and Aurangzeb's best commander had retaken only after a long blockade.

Disturbed by these successes, the master of the Deccan began to treat with his daring assailants. But the terms on which Dupleix insisted were still too hard for his digestion. At the head of a combined host of Mughals, Pathāns, and Marāthas, he continued his advance on Gingee. But the traitors in his camp were numerous, and Dupleix was not a man to stick at scruples in pursuit of a given end. Ere long the Subadār was ready to yield all that the Frenchman had asked. But his offers came too late. Before a messenger from Dupleix could reach the French camp, a signal from the plotting nobles in that of Nāsir Jang had brought the French commander up to the scene of action. In the fight that ensued between his troops and the enemy the Pathāns and Marāthas took no part. Guessing too late the meaning of their inaction, the angry Subadār rode up to the traitor chiefs, and scolded one of them, the Nawāb of Cuddapah, for his cowardice. A bullet in his heart was the Nawāb's reply. In a few minutes the dead man's rival, Muzaffar Jang, found himself transformed from a prisoner in chains, under peril of instant death, into the newly-elected Subadār of the Deccan.

When the fight was over the new Subadār set off for Pondicherry, where Dupleix, with much pomp and pageantry, installed him in his uncle's place. Dupleix himself, decked out in the robes of a Muhammadan "Amrah," or baron of the highest class, was invested with the government of all the Mughal dominions to the south of the Kistna. Chanda Sahib, as Nawāb of the Carnatic, became the new governor's acknowledged vassal. The bestowal of a goodly *jāgīr* or fief on Dupleix himself, a handsome present in money to his officers and men, and the assignment of fresh districts to the Company under whose flag they had fought, filled up the ungrudging measure of the Subadār's gratitude to his French allies. At that moment the fame and influence of Dupleix had reached their highest point. Through his own skilful daring, seconded by a mere handful of his countrymen, the son of a French merchant had become the ruler of broad provinces and the patron of the lord of Southern India.

Accompanied by a small force of French and Sepoys under Bussy, the new Subadār set out in the first days of 1751 for his own capital of Aurangābād. But the Pathān chiefs who had compassed the death of Nāsir Jang were already plotting against his successor, who had stinted them of their expected rewards. Their treachery discovered, they were attacked and defeated by Bussy's soldiers; but Muzaffar Jang, in the eagerness of pursuit, was slain by the hard-pressed Nawāb of Kurnool, who a moment after shared his victim's fate. Amidst the confusion caused by this event Bussy showed himself equal to the need. With the consent of his Mughal allies, Salābat Jang, a younger brother of Nāsir Jang, was straightway advanced, like his late nephew, from a prison to the vacant throne.

CHAPTER X

THE FIGHT BETWEEN FRENCH AND ENGLISH

AT the time of Salābat Jang's accession to the throne of the Deccan, Muhammad Ali was intriguing with the English at Madras against his successful rival, Chanda Sahib. As soon as the hour seemed ripe for action, he threw off the mask of apparent readiness to make peace with his opponents, and refused to yield up Trichinopoly on any terms to the rival Nawāb. Once more, therefore, the French and English were arranged in arms under opposing flags. While Chanda Sahib, aided by a few hundred Frenchmen, was advancing on Trichinopoly, a small English force marched off to strengthen the native defenders of that place, and a somewhat larger body took the field in concert with their native ally. The latter force, however, crowned their defeat before Volkonda by an ignominious retreat upon Trichinopoly; and the troops of Chanda Sahib promised themselves an easy capture of his rival's last stronghold.

But fortune and the skilful soldiership of two brave Englishmen were to spoil their reckonings. Captain Robert Clive, who had already earned some laurels before Pondicherry and at Devikātta, now urged Mr. Saunders, the able Governor of Madras, to save Trichinopoly by making a dash at Arcot. It was a suggestion of Muhammad Ali, who knew the riches of the Arcot district. With 200 Englishmen, 300 Sepoys, and eight guns, Clive was allowed to save Trichinopoly in his own way. In the midst of a fearful thunderstorm his daring band presented themselves at the gates of Chanda Sahib's capital. The astonished garrison offered no resistance to men who could thus brave the wrath of the storm-god. Once master of the fort, which was more than a mile round, Clive set hard to work at strengthening its weak defences. He first thought of retiring to Trimidi, but Mr. George Pigot strongly urged him to hold on. The task seemed well-nigh hopeless, but a master-mind had taken it firmly in hand. In spite of Dupleix's entreaties, Chanda Sahib detached some thousands of his best troops, under his son, Raja Sahib, to deal with Clive. For seven weeks the little garrison of Arcot withstood the assaults of 10,000 men, aided by a powerful battering-train; their numbers reduced by disease and wounds to 120 Englishmen and 200 Sepoys. The succours which Mr. Saunders strained every nerve to forward from Madras were beaten back, and the supplies of the garrison were running very short, when Raja Sahib, learning that the Marāthas under Morāri Rāo were advancing to raise the siege, and foiled in his efforts to win the place by treating with Clive himself, gave the order for one last desperate assault.

On the 25th November, the fiftieth day of the siege, his troops rushed forward to the attack, drunk with bhang and religious ardour.* For many hours the fight raged at every assailable point, the Sepoys vying with their English comrades in the stoutness of their resistance to almost crushing odds. In their attempts to crown the breaches the assailants were swept down by an unceasing fire of muskets and guns, each man of the little garrison having spare muskets ready to his hands, while Clive himself worked like a common gunner. At last the attack died away, the town itself was abandoned during the night, and

* It was the day of the great Mussulman feast in memory of the martyred son of Ali.

the next morning saw Raja Sāhib's shattered forces retreating on Vellore.

The news of this heroic defence, maintained by a handful of men and half a dozen English officers, mostly raw volunteers, under a captain who had never before set a full company in the field, turned in favour of the English that tide of native feeling which had hitherto been setting strongly against them. Reinforced from Madras, Clive started off in pursuit of his late assailants, turned their flank with the aid of his Marāthas, and drove them, with the loss of all their guns, from the field. Another great victory over Raja Sahib and his French allies at Kāveripāk, on the road from Conjeeveram to Arcot, left Clive free to arrange with Mr. Saunders for the relief of Trichinopoly, then closely blockaded by the troops of Chanda Sahib and M. Law.

At that moment, however, another brave Englishman, Major Stringer Lawrence, the victor of Devikātta, who had meanwhile gone home to England, reappeared on the scene, as commander of the troops destined for the relief of Trichinopoly. With the hero of Arcot for his trusty lieutenant, he was not likely to fail without good cause. Trichinopoly was soon relieved; and the French, defeated or out-generalled at every turn, and cooped up at last in an island between two rivers, gave themselves up to Lawrence as prisoners of war. Forty-one guns, with heaps of warlike stores, were included among the spoils. Meanwhile the luckless Chanda Sahib, who had surrendered to the general commanding the native contingent from Tanjore, under a solemn promise that his life should be spared, was straightway put to death by order of his perjured captor, and his head was forwarded as a welcome present to Muhammad Ali.*

* Lawrence has been blamed by Colonel Malleson for conniving at this piece of treachery; but Orme's statement hardly bears out the charge.

Foiled in his best efforts, Dupleix would not be disheartened. The son of Chanda Sahib was at once proclaimed Nawāb in his father's stead. Morāri Rāo and the Regent of Mysore soon turned against their late ally. The repulse of an English attack upon Gingee encouraged the French and their allies to renew the siege of Trichinopoly. For two more years strife raged in the Carnatic, Clive and Lawrence losing no chance of adding to their old renown, while the prompt courage of an English subaltern, Lieutenant Harrison, saved the fort of Trichinopoly from almost certain capture.

Meanwhile Bussy's tact and boldness had served his country well at the court of Salābat Jang. In spite of secret foes and open assailants, he had not only upheld his own nominee on the throne of the Deccan, but had even won for himself the government of four fertile districts lying between the Eastern Ghāts and the Bay of Bengal, and stretching for nearly 500 miles from the Kistna northward to Ganjām. This valuable tract of country, since known as the Northern Circars, surpassed in extent and value the dominions which any other European power had hitherto swayed in India.

But a cruel blow was already being aimed at Dupleix's ambition and the power he had striven so hard to establish. While the siege of Trichinopoly was yet languidly going forward, there arrived at Pondicherry, in August, 1754, a special envoy empowered by the French Government to treat with Mr. Saunders for a speedy end to the strife between French and English on the Coromandel coast. M. Godeheu, himself a director of the French company, entered with a will on his appointed task. The truce to which both parties presently agreed was followed in December by a formal treaty, which bound both alike

The Nawāb surrendered not to the English, but to the forces of Muhammad Ali.

to refrain from mixing in the quarrels of native princes, and virtually to accept Muhammad Ali as the rightful Nawāb. Each side was to retain its present winnings until arrangements could be made for readjusting their several shares. Godeheu, in short, surrendered almost everything for which Dupleix had so long fought and schemed, with varying fortune, but with unflinching zeal. But more to the English than all their other gains was the recall of the daring statesman who had dreamed of building up a great French empire in Southern India. The supplanted Governor of Pondicherry went home poor and in debt, to meet with a chilling welcome from the company he had served so well, to plead in vain for repayment of the great sums he had spent out of his own fortune on their account, and to die at last in disgrace and almost beggary, with the debtors' prison already staring him in the face.

The treaty thus concluded was soon broken. The Regent of Mysore, on the strength of a promise once made by Muhammad Ali, pressed his claim to Trichinopoly, which the English refused to render up. An English force set out early in 1755 to help Muhammad Ali in exacting tribute from the Pālikārs of Tinnevelly and Madura. The French in their turn gathered rents on behalf of the Regent of Mysore, and even threatened Trichinopoly itself. Early in the next year a movement of the English against Vellore was thwarted by the firmness of De Leyrit, who had succeeded Godeheu as Governor of Pondicherry. Before the year's end it was known that France and England were again at war, and De Leyrit lost no time in acting upon that knowledge. While the English were engaged elsewhere in helping the Nawāb against his own subjects, a strong force of French and Sepoys once more endangered the safety of Trichinopoly. But the brave Captain Calliaud, by a skilful movement, circumvented the French commander, and forced him to retire to Pondicherry. For this repulse the French consoled themselves by a series of successful raids elsewhere, and the last days of 1757 left them masters of nearly all the strong places in the dominions of Muhammad Ali, while Bussy easily maintained his hold on the Northern Circars.

Meanwhile Bengal had become the scene of a struggle on whose issue rested the future of all India. In April, 1756, Alivardi Khan, the able and stout-hearted Subadār of Bengal, was succeeded by his favourite grandson, Sirāj-ud-daula, a youth whose feeble intellect and imperious temper had not been improved by a long course of debauchery and freedom from all control. One of his first acts as Subadār was to demand from Mr. Drake, the Governor of Fort William, the immediate surrender of a Hindu refugee, son of the wealthy governor of Dacca, and the destruction of all the new defences which Mr. Drake was accused of having erected round Calcutta. Enraged at the Englishman's evasion of the former demand, he led an army of fifty thousand men against a settlement in every way ill-prepared to defend itself. A garrison reduced by neglect to 174 men, weak defences, bad gunpowder, cowardice among the leaders, disorder and mismanagement everywhere, all combined to render the fort and city an easy prey to the furious Subadār. On the 19th June a general rush of men, women, and children, to get on board the shipping in the river, was followed by the flight thither of Mr. Drake and the military commandant.

Thus shamefully abandoned, Mr. Holwell, the ablest civil officer left behind, took command of the weakened garrison, and prepared to defend the fort. But everything was against him. Blind to all his signals of distress, the captains of the vessels, which had dropped two miles down the river, made no attempt to succour their deserted

A STREET IN OLD CALCUTTA, SHEWING MARTYRS' MEMORIAL
FROM "ECHOES OF OLD CALCUTTA"

p. 19

countrymen. The soldiers, who for two or three days had repulsed the enemy's attacks, at length broke into the liquor-stores, and became too drunk for further resistance. While Mr. Holwell was yet parleying with the besiegers, some of the latter rushed into the scene of disorder, and in a few minutes Fort William, with all its surviving defenders, fell into the conqueror's hands.

But the survivors had yet to taste the full measure of their misfortunes. On one of the hottest nights in the year, when the climate of Bengal had changed from the heat of an open furnace to that of a well-warmed hot-house, a hundred and forty-six prisoners, including one or two women, were shut up in an old guard-room, or black-hole for soldiers, less than eighteen feet square, into which the air, yet further heated by the flames of burning ware-houses, crept through two small windows strongly barred. None but the strongest and those who kept nearest the windows, had a chance of living through that awful night. In the fight for life that went on from hour to hour, few heeded other tortures than their own. The living trampled on the dying and the dead in their efforts to reach the windows, or to get at the water handed in to them through the bars. Mad with thirst, fever, pain, and the fearful stench, many of them sought to end their sufferings by provoking the guards outside to fire upon them. But their inhuman jailors laughed the louder at their revilings, held lights to the windows the better to enjoy the dreadful scene within, and gloated over the sight of thirsty wretches fighting for the water with which they were kept supplied.* Next morning, when the Subadār had slept off the effects of last night's debauch, there crawled out of that den of horrors Holwell himself, with twenty-one men and one

* Mr. Holwell, one of the survivors, wrote a detailed account of the horrors of that memorable night in language all the more powerful for its unadorned simplicity.

woman,* most of them hardly more alive than the dead who lay heaped up in noisome ghastliness within.

Holwell and four others, including the woman, were carried off, in irons, to Murshidābād; but the rest were allowed to make their way to the ships, which forthwith dropped down to Falta, near the mouth of the Hūgli. Three months afterwards Holwell and three of his fellow-sufferers were finally set free. It was not till the middle of December that the English refugees at Falta descried the fleet which Admiral Watson had led out from Madras two months before, laden with the troops destined to retrieve the disasters of the previous June, and to pave the way for the conquest of Hindustān. Their commander, Colonel Clive, who had returned to India in 1755 as Governor of Fort St. David, and had since shared with Admiral Watson in the taking of Giriah, lost no time in adding to his old renown. The fort of Baj-baj, a little way up the river, was soon taken by his troops and a body of seamen. On the 2nd of January, 1757, Calcutta and Fort William fell once more into English hands. Hūgli itself was stormed on the 10th by Clive's best subaltern, Captain Eyre Coote, the future opponent of Haidar Ali.

Enraged at these unforeseen reverses, Sirāj-ud-daula led a large army towards Calcutta, masking his purpose by a show of listening to the peaceful overtures from the Calcutta Council. At length, impatient of further dallying with a treacherous foe, Clive on the 4th February, made a determined assault on the Mughal camp. A heavy fog marred the full execution of a well-conceived movement, and after some hard fighting Clive withdrew his troops. But the frightened Subadār had no mind to renew the struggle with such foes. Drawing off his army to a safe

* Mrs. Carey, whose husband, a sea-officer, died in the Black Hole. When the survivors were released, she herself being, in Holwell's words, "too young and handsome," was reserved for the Prince's haram at Murshidābād.

distance from Calcutta, he offered, this time sincerely, to make peace. On the 9th February was concluded a treaty which restored to the English all their former privileges and factories, gave them full permission to fortify Calcutta, to coin money at their own mint, and promised in some measure to make good their recent losses.

CHAPTER XI

THE ENGLISH TRIUMPHANT—1757–1761

By this time Calcutta had learned the news of another war in Europe between France and England. Instead of returning to Madras, Clive at once resolved to attack the French settlement of Chandernagore, on the Hūgli. The faithless Subadār, on the other hand, was already plotting with Bussy against his new friends, while the Calcutta Council, led by the wretched Drake, were bent on pledging their countrymen to remain strictly neutral towards the French in Bengal. But Clive's forecasting energy overrode all obstacles, and the way was further cleared for him by a threatening letter, in which Admiral Watson told the Subadār that, if any more plottings went on with the French, he would "kindle such a flame in the country as all the waters of the Ganges should not be able to extinguish." A humble answer from the frightened Sirāj-ud-daula removed the last scruples from the mind of the honest sailor, who forthwith went heartily to work in aid of his less scrupulous colleague.

On the 14th March Clive made his first movement against the fort of Chandernagore. On the 17th his batteries opened their fire, to which the defenders kept up for some days a spirited reply. It was not till the 23rd that Watson could bring two of his men-of-war alongside the fort; but a few broadsides from the *Kent* and *Tiger* wrought such havoc that the French were driven to treat for a surrender, and before evening Chandernagore, with its brave garrison and much treasure, had passed into Watson's hands, not without heavy loss to the conquerors.*

The Subadār was furious, but he took care to dissemble his rage and hatred of the victorious English. Cringing and insolent by turns, now bribing Bussy to come and help him against the common foe, anon seeking to lull Clive's suspicions by letters full of high-flown compliments, now threatening the English factory at Kāsimbazār, anon sending to Calcutta a large instalment of the promised indemnity, he furnished Clive with ample pretexts for treating him as an enemy in disguise. The Englishman, however, for all his courage and his past achievements, would commit himself to no rash movement against the ruler of a rich and powerful province and the commander of countless legions. He preferred to meet cunning with cunning, plots with plots; and his opponent's folly lent itself to all his schemes. A plot for the Nawāb's dethronement was carried on between the English leaders and some of the foremost statesmen and richest bankers in Bengal. It was agreed that Mīr Jāfar, brother-in-law of the late Subadār, should be raised to the forfeit throne, in return for vast sums of money payable to the English Company and their troops.

The plot was well-nigh ripe when Amīn Chand, a rich Hindu banker, who had long played a doubtful part both towards the English and his own sovereign, threatened to disclose to the latter all that he had somehow learned, unless his silence could be purchased on his own terms. Clive at once resolved to outwit him with his own weapons. Two copies of the secret treaty with Mīr Jāfar were drawn up, in only one of which was inserted the agreement made

* Among the troops employed in the siege were the Bengal Battalion, afterwards the 1st Bengal European Fusiliers, and the Bengal Sepoy Battalion, afterwards the 1st Bengal Native Infantry. The latter regiment had been raised, armed, and drilled like an English regiment by Clive himself. (Broome's "History of the Bengal Army," pp. 92 and 116.)

with the treacherous Hindu. Among the names affixed to this document was that of Admiral Watson, forged apparently by Clive himself with the assent of his more scrupulous colleague. In excuse for the part borne by Clive in these crooked proceedings, it must be remembered that many lives of Englishmen and natives in Bengal were staked on the good faith of a self-seeking scoundrel, who would else have sold to their worst enemy the secret he had ferreted out for himself.

By this time Sirāj-ud-daula had heard of Ahmad Shah's retreat from Delhi into Afghānistān. Danger from that quarter he no longer feared; but the signs of danger nearer home had begun to attract his notice; and the flight of Watts, the English agent, from Murshidābād seemed to confirm his worst suspicions. While his own troops were once more mustering at Plassey, about forty miles to the south of Murshidābād, Clive was preparing to strike the blow which was to make him virtual master of Bengal. On the 13th June, 1757, he marched from Chandernagore at the head of 1000 Englishmen and about 2000 Sepoys, and ten guns. On the 17th the fort of Katwa was carried by his troops after a brief resistance. Here the monsoon or rainy season burst upon them with a violence which for a moment damped the spirits of their bold leader himself. The news that presently reached him from Mīr Jāfar did little to allay his new-born doubts and misgivings. Defeat at that distance from all support meant utter ruin to his little army and to the hopes that centred in them. He wrote for help to the Raja of Burdwān. For the first and last time in his life he called a council of war. His own vote, the first given, was in favour of halting at Katwa until the close of the monsoon. In spite of the counterpleadings of bold Major Coote, twelve officers out of nineteen voted with Colonel Clive.

But a few hours later the cloud had passed away from

his soul, and the order was given for his troops to cross the river next morning. A long march of fifteen miles through mud and water brought them, at one in the morning of the 23rd June, to a grove of mango trees beyond the village of Plassey, within easy hearing of the enemy's drums. The left of his little army rested on the Bhagirathi river. A mile in front of him lay the enemy, 50,000 strong in infantry alone, besides 18,000 horsemen from the north, and fifty-three guns, mostly of great size.

Soon after daybreak the hosts of Sirāj-ud-daula advanced from their entrenchments to the attack; a small party of Frenchmen with four light field-pieces leading the way. By eight o'clock the latter were engaged with a small body of English well posted in front of their main line. When the enemy's fire became too hot for his little force, Clive withdrew to the safer shelter of the grove. For some hours a cannonade was kept up on both sides, with little damage to the English, who from behind their own breastworks took leisurely aim at the masses in their front. At noon the enemy's ammunition was nearly all spoilt by a heavy shower. A charge of the enemy's horse was easily repulsed, and the fall of their leader himself struck the Subadār with sudden terror. By two P.M. the great bulk of his troops were already moving from the field, while their panic-striken commander led the way with 2000 horse to his own capital of Murshidābād. The French withdrew their guns into the entrenched camp. Mīr Jāfar Khan, whose movements had hitherto puzzled the English commander, at length drew off his own men from Clive's right flank. No longer doubtful of the issue, Clive pushed boldly forward against the entrenchments, where the French still bravely held their ground. Ere long they also had to retire without their guns. By five o'clock the victors were in full possession of the enemy's camp with all the vast wealth it contained in baggage, cattle, guns, and warlike stores. The victory which was to seal the fate of India had been won with a loss of only twenty-three soldiers killed and forty-nine wounded on the winning side.

Arrived at Murshidābād, Sirāj-ud-daula took counsel with his officers of state. For a moment the bolder policy recommended by some of them revived his courage ; but his old fears and suspicions speedily returned, and the next night he fled in disguise from his palace, only to fall a few days later into the hands of his enemy Mīr Jāfar, whose son, impatient of his father's kindlier leanings, caused the grandson of his father's benefactor to be privily put to death.

Six days after the rout of Plassey, Clive entered Murshidābād. Mīr Jāfar was formally saluted as Nawāb of Bengal, Bihār, and Orissa, and steps were taken to fulfil the compact which had placed him on his kinsman's throne. A large sum of money was at once sent down to Calcutta in part payment of the promised compensation for the losses suffered in 1756. On the East India Company was bestowed the fee simple of the land for six hundred yards around the Marātha Ditch, together with revenue rights over the country south of Calcutta. The members of the Calcutta Council, and the forces, naval and military, received handsome presents. The conqueror of Plassey, who might have helped himself to untold wealth out of the royal treasury, was content to accept a thank-offering of about two hundred thousand pounds.*

It was now time to undeceive the wretched Amīn Chand. The genuine treaty was produced and read. On discovering the trick which had been played upon him,

* To those who afterwards upbraided him with his greed, he indignantly replied, "When I recollect entering the treasury at Murshidābād, with heaps of silver and gold to the right hand and to the left and these crowned with jewels, I stand astonished at my own moderation."

Amīn Chand fell senseless to the ground. The shock to his avarice may have weakened his wits; it certainly sent him on a pilgrimage to a famous Hindu shrine; but it did not afterwards keep him from mixing again in public affairs.*

Clive had now gained for his countrymen that pre-eminence in Bengal which Dupleix had once secured for the French in Southern India. As Governor of Fort William in reward for his brilliant services, he lost no time in following up his late achievements. The French were hunted out of Bihār into Oudh by the dogged pertinacity of Major Coote. Several risings against the new Nawāb of Bengal were promptly suppressed. Colonel Forde, one of Clive's best officers, was sent off to fight the French, no longer led by Bussy, in the Northern Circars. By a series of bold movements and well-delivered blows that dashing commander wrested Masulipatam from the French, and frightened the Nizām, Salābat Jang, into ceding a large tract of adjacent country to the conquerors of his late friends. Shah Alam, son of the puppet Emperor of Delhi, sought, with the help of the Nawāb of Oudh, to carve out a kingdom for himself in Bengal. But the mere sound of Clive's coming forced him to raise the siege of Patna; the army he had got together melted away before the swift approach of Clive's warriors, who cared nothing for heat or superior numbers; and the prince himself, deserted by his ally, was glad to obtain from his pursuer the means of continuing his homeward flight. For this fresh service Clive was rewarded by Mīr Jāffir with a *jāgīr* worth about £25,000 a-year.

But the new Nawāb of Bengal had not yet learned the lesson of passing events. He began to intrigue with the

* He is said by Orme to have become a drivelling idiot; but the story is quite untrue. See Broome's "Bengal Army," p. 154, and "Catalogue of the Orme MSS." (S. C. Hill), p. xxxi.

Dutch at Chinsura against the power to which he owed everything. A Dutch fleet from Java, laden with troops, appeared in the Hūgli. There was then no war between England and Holland, and Clive had some private reasons for avoiding a quarrel.* But he met the danger with his wonted readiness, and Dutch outrages provoked the struggle which, as a statesman, he had no wish to avert. On the 24th November six out of seven Dutch men-of-war were taken, after two hours' hard fighting, by three English ships of small burden,† and the seventh was afterwards caught near the mouth of the river. On the same day the bold Colonel Forde drove the Dutch, with heavy slaughter, back into Chinsura; and on the morrow another force of Dutchmen, Sepoys, and Malays, was well-nigh destroyed on the plain of Bidāra by about half the number of English and native troops under the same leader. Thoroughly humbled, the Dutch at Chinsura sued for terms, which issued in a treaty binding them to pay the expenses of the war, to discharge the bulk of their troops, dismiss the vessels which Clive engaged to restore, and to resume the footing on which they had hitherto traded in Bengal.

Early in the next year Clive sailed for England, in the flush of his well-earned fame, at the age of thirty-four, to receive fresh honours from his admiring countrymen. Meanwhile in Southern India also the tide was turning fast and finally against the French. Lally, a brave but headstrong soldier, who had fought in the Irish Brigade at Fontenoy, strove hard but vainly to stem that tide. Fort St. David and Devikātta fell before his arms. The siege of Tanjore was raised by the timely intervention of an

* The bulk of his wealth had just been remitted to Europe through the Dutch East India Company.

† The largest, the *Calcutta*, measured only 761 tons. Four of the Dutchmen carried thirty-six guns a-piece, and two more twenty-six guns. (Broome's "Bengal Army," chap. iii.)

English force; and a French fleet, which might have done Lally good service, sailed off at a critical moment to the Isle of France. Arcot, on the other hand, was surrendered to the French by Muhammad Ali; and Bussy, who had been summoned in an evil hour to Lally's aid from the scene of his own successes, vainly attempted to dissuade his headstrong chief from undertaking the siege of Madras itself. In the last days of 1758 Lally's soldiers took up their posts in front of a stronghold defended by the veteran Colonel Lawrence. For two months they held their ground in spite of the resistance offered by the besieged, and the spirited efforts of Major Calliaud to annoy the besiegers from behind. In February, 1759, a breach was made in the walls of the Fort, and Lally was preparing to storm it if he could, when, on the 16th, an English fleet laden with succours anchored in the Roads. Next day the French were in full retreat on Arcot, leaving behind them fifty-two guns and many of their sick and wounded.

For yet another year the fight for empire in Southern India went forward to issues which grow daily clearer. The failure of the English in their first attack on Wandiwash was brilliantly retrieved a few months later by Coote's capture of that place, and the crushing defeat he afterwards inflicted on a French force which ventured to renew the siege. Bussy himself, who was among the prisoners, was generously allowed to return to Pondicherry. One strong place after another was taken or retaken by the victorious English. With the fall of Karikal in April, 1760, the French had little more to lose in Southern India besides Pondicherry itself. Hampered at every turn, now by want of stores and money, anon by the interference of his civil colleagues, or the mutinous conduct of his own ill-paid, starving troops, Lally saw his prospects growing darker and darker, until in September he and his countrymen were closely besieged in their Indian capital by the foe whom he had so lately thought to drive into the sea.

In vain had Lally looked round among the native princes to help him in his hour of need. Neither from Haidar Ali, the usurping ruler of Mysore, nor from Bālajī Rão, the Marātha Pēshwa, could any help be obtained. Week after week saw his chances grow more desperate, as the English drew their circles closer around him, and the stock of food for his garrison melted away. Even the great storm of December, which destroyed the English batteries and sank or disabled many of the English ships, brought no relief to the despairing garrison and their sick commander. At length, on the 15th January, 1761, when his stock of food was on the point of being exhausted, Lally offered to surrender. Colonel Coote would listen to no conditions, and Lally could only bow to his fate. Next day, when the English marched into the surrendered stronghold, the wasted forms and wan faces of the soldiers drawn up to receive them told their own tale.

Pondicherry was afterwards levelled to the ground. Lally, hooted by its ungrateful citizens, withdrew to Madras, from thence to Paris, where misfortune still dogged his steps. The men who had persistently thwarted him in Pondicherry sent home their own version of past events. Bussy himself made common cause with De Leyrit's party against the man who had bravely done his best to save French India. In 1766, after languishing for three years in the Bastille, the luckless Irishman paid upon the scaffold the penalty in France so often awarded to ill-success.

With the fall of Pondicherry the French power in India passed away. Three months later the last of the French garrisons surrendered to an English force; and three years after the death of Lally, the Company, which had made no effort to save one of its ablest servants, was itself consigned to extinction. Thenceforth the history of India becomes the history of British struggles and achievements in the path marked out for England by the victory of Plassey and the rout of Pānipat.

BOOK IV

THE RULE OF THE COMPANY

CHAPTER I

THE ENGLISH IN BENGAL—1761–1774

WITH the fall of Pondicherry and the battle of Pānipat, two leading events in the history of the same year, a new power has begun to raise its head among the peoples and princes of India. Before tracing the further growth of that power, it is well to take a rapid survey of Indian affairs about the year 1761.

If the strength of the Marāthas was cruelly broken by the slaughter of Pānipat, the empire of Delhi had already dwindled away to a few districts around the capital. The Punjāb was ruled by the Afghan Ahmad Shah. In Sind the Tālpur chiefs acknowledged no master. Rohilkhand obeyed the orders of Najīb-ud-daula. Shujā-ud-daula, the Nawāb Wazir of Oudh, paid the merest show of obedience to his titular lord at Delhi. The Hindu princes of Rājputāna had won for themselves an independence tempered only by the need of paying now and then the Marātha chauth. The Marātha power, if its unity was broken at Pānipat, still swayed under separate princes a vast tract of country, from Gujarāt in the west to Tanjore in the south. The Gaikwar reigned in Gujarāt, Sindhia and Holkar divided Mālwa between them, the Bhosla dynasty was firmly seated in Nāgpur, Marātha princes held Tanjore and part of the Carnatic, the Rajas of Kolhāpur and Satāra were still supreme along the Western Ghāts, and the Pēshwa of Poona reigned over a long stretch of country from the borders of Mysore to Kalpī and Jhānsi on the Jumna. Orissa itself obeyed the Marātha rule, and nothing but Clive's firmness had deterred the Marāthas from continuing to levy chauth in Bengal.

The Jāts, a warlike tribe of Hindu origin from the banks of the Indus, who had greatly troubled the officers of Aurangzeb, had already under the daring Suraj Mal founded a strong state between Jaipur and Agra, with Bharatpur for its fortified capital. Salābat Jang, as Nizām of the Deccan, ruled over a dominion sadly crippled by the conquests of his Marātha neighbours. In Mysore the ambitious Mussulman soldier, Haidar Ali, had already won the virtual sovereignty of a kingdom hitherto swayed by a long succession of Hindu rajas. Muhammad Ali, under English protection, held independent rule over the Carnatic from the Panār river to Tanjore. The little states of Travancore and Cochin were still governed by Hindu rulers. Goa and its few dependencies belonged to Portugal. Besides their old settlements on either coast, the actual possessions of the English were confined to certain districts around Calcutta and in the Northern Circars. But the rich and populous provinces of Bengal and Bihār were ruled by a sovereign of their own choice, upheld on his throne by British bayonets, and liable at any moment to be set aside by those who had placed him there. It was, in short, the same tenure on which the Nawāb of the Carnatic held the dominions he had won with English aid from the French and their native allies.

Soon after his bootless raid into Bihār, Shah Alam, whose real name was Ali Johar, mounted the tottering throne of Delhi in the room of his murdered father. Still hankering after Bengal, and afraid to enter his own capital, he marched with his new wazir, Shujā-ud-daula, and a large force upon Patna in the first days of 1760. Defeated, followed up, and checked at every turn by the active Colonel Calliaud, he made a bold rush back from the neighbourhood of Murshidābād to Patna; and that city, closely besieged for nine days, was on the point of falling, when Captain Knox with 200 Englishmen, a regiment of Sepoys, and a few troops of horse, came up to the rescue after a long hurried march in the hottest season of the year. The rout and final scattering of Shah Alam's troops was followed up by a yet more daring attack on the 30,000 men and thirty guns, which the Nawāb of Purnea had brought up too late to the emperor's aid. A fight of six hours ended in such a victory for the handful of Knox's warriors, as clinched the hold already won by like feats of prowess on the native mind.

Meanwhile the government of Mīr Jāfar was falling into worse and worse confusion. The death of his son, the cruel, profligate, but stronghanded Mīran, brought matters to a speedy crisis. Mīr Kāsim, the old man's son-in-law, opened the way for his own advancement by settling out of his own purse the arrears of pay demanded by the mutinous soldiery of Bengal. His schemes for the dethronement of his weak father-in-law found ready countenance at Calcutta, where Mr. Vansittart was ruling in the place of Clive. In due time Mīr Jāfar agreed, however reluctantly, to make way for Mīr Kāsim; and English help in the unpleasant business was repaid by the addition of Midnapore, Burdwān, and Chittagong, to the realms of the East India Company; besides a gift of twenty lakhs of rupees, or £250,000, to Vansittart, Holwell, and their fellow-councillors.

But the bargain thus concluded bore little fruit for good. It was not long before the new Nawāb began to aim at gradually shaking himself free from British control. He transferred his seat of government from Murshidābād to Monghyr. His troops were disciplined on the English model and armed with muskets better than those which bore the Tower mark. A foundry for casting cannon was secretly set at work. A faithful friend of the English, Rāmnarain, Governor of Patna, was plundered of all his wealth with the assent of the feeble Vansittart, in spite of the efforts made by English officers in behalf of one whose safety had been guaranteed by the Calcutta Council.

At length the smouldering quarrel between the English and Mīr Kāsim blazed out into open war. A dispute concerning the undue extent to which the Company's servants had carried their right of exemption from transit duties on their own goods was inflamed by acts of violence on both sides. One Englishman was slain in a scuffle; Mr. Ellis, head of the Patna factory, and several other gentlemen were taken prisoners after a vain attempt to seize upon the city; some of the leading natives in Bengal shared the fate of their English friends; and before the middle of 1763 the troops on both sides were ready to take the field.

In the midst of the heavy July rains the campaign was opened by the English, who drove the Nawāb's army before them at Katwa on the 19th, entered Murshidābād a few days later, and replaced Mīr Jāfar, now old, leprous, and half-imbecile, on the throne he had been forced to abdicate three years before. A second victory, won at Giriah on the 2nd August after a hard fight, enraged Kāsim beyond all bearing. Rāmnarain and the great Sett bankers of Murshidābād were thrown into the Ganges. Raja Rājballab, another old friend of the English, was put to death with all his sons; and an order was issued for the murder of every Englishman imprisoned at Patna. When Kāsim's own officers declined to do such butcher's work, he found a ready instrument in Walter Reinhardt, a native of Luxemburg, who had deserted from one service into another until, escaping with Law's small band of Frenchmen from Chandernagore, he rose to high command under Mīr Kāsim. The nickname of Sombre, which his Swiss or English comrades at Bombay had given him for his dark complexion and sullen looks, his Bengali followers had turned into Sumru, the name by which English writers have handed him down to lasting infamy. This merciless ruffian, whose hatred of the English had helped to endear him to his new master, carried out so thoroughly his savage errand, that more than fifty gentlemen and a hundred soldiers with a few women were shot down or cut to pieces in cold blood.

This happened in October, a few weeks after Major Adams with 3,000 men had utterly routed 50,000 of the enemy near Rājmahal, with the loss of 15,000 men and a hundred guns. On the 6th November Patna itself was stormed in the most brilliant style by Adams' unquailing heroes; English and Sepoys vying with each other in deeds of daring against formidable odds. A week later Adams set out in chase of the disheartened Nawāb, whose myriads were fast melting away from him under the spell of so many defeats. Before the year's end, however, Mīr Kāsim and the ruffian Sumru had found shelter in Oudh under the wing of his old enemy Shujā-ud-daula.

Worn out with toil and exposure, Major Adams now threw up the command of the little army which in less than five months he had led from Calcutta to the Karamnāsa, defeating many times his own numbers of disciplined troops in two pitched battles, carrying four strong places by siege or assault, and capturing more than 400 pieces of cannon. It is sad to think that the foremost hero of a campaign, perhaps the most brilliant ever fought in India, was fated never to enjoy the honours he had so richly earned. Major Adams had hardly reached Calcutta on his way home, when he died amidst the unfeigned regrets of every Englishman in Bengal.*

Next year the struggle was renewed by the Nawāb-Wazir of Oudh, who marched down towards the Ganges with the wandering Shah Alam and the ousted Mīr Kāsim in his train. Chased out of Bengal in 1760, and shut out by the Marāthas from his own capital, Shah Alam had lingered in Bihār, where early in 1761 he was twice encountered and defeated by Major Carnac. Among the prisoners taken in the well-fought action at Suan, near the city of Bihār, was the brave Frenchman Law, Clive's old opponent at Plassey, who surrendered only on condition of keeping his sword. The beaten emperor at length made peace, on terms which left him free to mend his tattered fortunes further north, with the help of a modest pension from his late foes. On his way up the country, however, he had fallen into the hands of Shujā-ud-daula, who kept guard over his titular sovereign as a kind of prisoner at large.

On the approach of the Nawāb-Wazir's army, the English retired into Patna, which on the 3rd May, 1764, was attacked by the enemy for several hours with more of daring than success. As the rainy season drew near Shujā-ud-daula fell back to Buxār. During the pause which followed the outbreak of the monsoon, the mutinous spirit which, earlier in the year, had spread for a time from the European soldiers to their native comrades, broke out again among the latter with such violence, that Major Munro, a king's officer who had just replaced the feebler Carnac in the chief command, was driven to quell it by blowing the ringleaders away from the cannon's

* Broome's "Bengal Army," chap. 4. "What," asks the author, "were the boasted Indian triumphs of Darius, of Alexander or Seleucus Nicator, with their powerful and disciplined armies, opposed to unwarlike barbarians, divided amongst themselves, compared to this single campaign?"

mouth. His timely firmness nipped the new danger in the bud. The mutineers, who seem to have behaved like pettish children, returned at once to their duty, and Munro set forth in October towards Buxār with a force of about 900 Europeans, 6,000 native horse and foot, and twenty-eight guns.

On the 23rd he fought and won the famous battle of Buxār against an army about 50,000 strong, including Sumru's disciplined brigades, and thousands of Afghān horsemen who had fought under Ahmad Shah at Pānipat. A hundred and thirty guns, mostly of large calibre, enhanced the odds against the English commander. Nothing, however, could withstand Munro's skilful movements and the unfaltering prowess of his troops. After a day's hard fighting the English saw themselves masters of a field strewn with thousands of the enemy's dead. Thousands more perished in their headlong flight across a neighbouring stream, and but for the breaking of a bridge by Shujā's order a vast amount of treasure would have swelled the victor's gains. As it was, however, the enemy's camp and a hundred and thirty guns fell into their hands. For a victory which placed the whole of Bengal and a great part of Upper India at their mercy, the English paid with a loss of 847 in killed and wounded.

Shujā-ud-daula fled across the Gogra into Oudh, while the English marched upon Allahābād. Want of money kept them from advancing further, and time was wasted in fruitless negotiations with Shah Alam, who had now had enough of Shujā's protection, and with the Nawāb-Wazir, who declined to yield up Sumru and Mīr Kāsim, but proposed, of course in vain, to despatch the former by underhand means. Two brave but unsuccessful assaults upon the rock-fortress of Chunār, a few miles above Benāres, close the record of English failures and successes for this year.

Once more in 1765 the Nawāb-Wazir, with the help of a Rohilla force from Rohilkhand, took the field, while Malhar Rāo was bringing up his Marāthas from Gwalior to attack the English on that side. But Carnac, who had taken the command vacated by Munro, soon drove the Marāthas back across the Jumna, and, after beating Shujā himself in several encounters, forced him to make peace at any cost with his conquerors. The treatment he received was merciful enough, for Clive had once more appeared upon the scene. In the month of May the victor of Plassey sailed up the Hūgli, Lord Clive, Governor and Commander-in-chief of the Company's possessions in Bengal. The years he had spent in England were years of frequent warfare between him and the Court of Directors, who begrudged their ablest servant the estates conferred on him by their Indian allies. But Clive's great influence, and the course of later events in Bengal, had at last compelled them to lay aside their private jealousies, in favour of one marked out by the common voice for the work of restoring order and good government on that side of India.

One of Clive's first acts in India was to conclude with the suppliant ruler of Oudh a treaty which surrendered to the Mughal emperor the districts of Kora and Allahābād, assured the payment of fifty lakhs of rupees as a fine to the Company, and empowered them to trade free of duty throughout the Nawāb's dominions. He next proceeded to ratify the agreement already made in effect with Shah Alam. In return for the revenues of the districts ceded by Shujā-ud-daula, and for twenty-six lakhs a year from the revenues of Bengal and Bihār, the emperor on the 12th August formally endowed his English friends with the Diwāni or virtual government of Bengal, Bihār, and Orissa—provinces which then contained about twenty-five million souls, and yielded a revenue of four millions

Emery Walker, Ltd., photographers

LORD CLIVE

FROM THE PAINTING BY NATHANIEL DANCE, R.A., IN THE NATIONAL PORTRAIT GALLERY

p. 214

sterling. The English, on the other hand, agreed to furnish the titular Nawāb of Murshidābād with the means of supporting his mock sovereignty, and a household suited to his rank. A new nominee of the Company, Najm-ud-daula, had just been raised to the unreal throne, whence death, hastened by the insolence of English greed, had finally removed his aged father, Mīr Jāfar. As for the discrowned exile, Mīr Kāsim, he had already exchanged the cruel guardianship of Shujā-ud-daula for a life of unheeded poverty near Benāres; while the infamous Sumru, scenting danger from a prolonged stay in Oudh, had just hired out his services to the Jāts of Bharatpur.

Thus in less than ten years, the merchant-company whose life-struggles seemed to have been quenched in the Black Hole of Calcutta, had gone so far on its new career of conquest as to dictate terms to half the princes of India, to make the Mughal emperor himself a mere pensioner and footstool of his English lieges, and to thwart the greatest native power in India, the Marātha League, in all its efforts to retrieve the disaster of Pānipat. "We have established," wrote Clive to the India House, "such a force that all the powers in Hindustān cannot deprive us of our possessions for many years." Yet Clive himself could not or would not see the goal to which events were already bearing the foreign masters of Bengal. He assured the Court of Directors of his firm resolve and hope always to confine their possessions to the provinces he had just obtained for them. To go any farther was "a scheme so extravagantly ambitious that no government in its senses would ever dream of it."

The work of conquest was not, however, to be resumed by Clive. Far other tasks devolved upon him during the brief remainder of his Indian career. A serious mutiny among his own officers, caused by a reduction of their extra pay in the field, had to be encountered with a strong hand; but Clive was equal to the need. The mutiny was promptly quelled with the aid of his faithful Sepoys;* and after some of the worst offenders had been cashiered by court-martial, the rest in all penitence returned to their duty.

A yet fiercer lion stood in Clive's way. The Company's servants in Bengal had been wont to eke out their small salaries by all manner of indirect gains, by means which made them a byword among their own countrymen, and a terror to the people at whose expense their ill-gotten riches were mostly earned. Intent on winning large fortunes in a few months, they overreached, plundered, oppressed their native customers, allies, and subjects at every turn. "The people under their dominion," said a native chronicler of those times, "groan everywhere, and are reduced to poverty and distress." Nearly the whole inland trade of the country passed through the all-grasping hands of the Calcutta Council and their like-minded agents. No one, high or low, was safe from their unscrupulous greed. Their demands and exactions had hastened the death of Mīr Jāfar. Twenty lakhs of rupees from the exhausted treasury at Murshidābād was the sum distributed among nine of the leading men at Calcutta, as the price of their agreeing to set up his infant son in his stead. While Bengal was going to ruin, and the Company at home grumbled over their small dividends, the Calcutta factors kept filling their own purses in utter disregard of justice, decency and common patriotism. Clive mourned over the eclipse of his country's fame, and declared with honest scorn that "there were not five men of principle left at the presidency." †

* One Sepoy regiment marched 104 miles in fifty-four hours, reaching Surājpūr in time to prevent an outbreak among the Europeans.

† For a striking if somewhat exaggerated picture of Bengal at this period, the reader may turn with profit to Macaulay's masterly essay on "Lord Clive."

He had gone out again, however, determined, as he said himself, to "destroy these great and growing evils, or perish in the attempt." In less than two years, the task entrusted to him was fairly accomplished. Armed with the chief civil and military control, he cared nothing for the intrigues, clamours and open resistance of his colleagues and subordinates. The taking of presents from the natives was forbidden under stern penalties, and the private trade of the Company's servants put down. Some of his opponents were turned out of office, and their places filled with gentlemen from Madras. Debarred by his instructions from raising the pay of the civil servants to a point commensurate with their official standing, Clive sought to check the tendency to make money through indirect and underhand means, by reserving the monopoly of salt, betel-nut, and tobacco, for the special use of the chief civil and military officers. After a certain sum had been set apart for the Company at home, the balance was parcelled out in so many shares among the members of council, colonels, senior merchants, factors, and other gentlemen, to each according to his rank. It is strange to think that a measure which at least succeeded in uprooting the worst abuses of a faulty system, was afterwards quoted against its author as the very wickedest of his alleged misdeeds.

In the beginning of 1767 Clive quitted for the last time the scene of achievements which, however blurred by a few acts of doubtful justice, entitle him to a foremost place in the hearts and memories of his countrymen. No other man of his age and mark, beset with like temptations, overcame them, on the whole, with loftier courage and cleaner hands. One of his last acts in India was to make over to the Company, in trust for invalided officers and soldiers, a sum of about £60,000, which Mīr Jāfar had left him in his will.* In broken health he returned to England poorer than he had left it, although untold wealth from many quarters had lain within his reach.

The rest of his life-story is soon told. It was not long before his foes at the India House renewed their attacks on a hero, whose worst delinquencies were less intolerable than the good deeds of his latter years. To the blows he had struck at official knavery in Bengal, Lord Clive was mainly indebted for the storm of obloquy and personal slander, disguised as zeal for the public good, which embittered, if it did not even hasten, the close of his eventful life. Every bad act of his countrymen in India, whether done in his absence or against his express commands, was laid upon his shoulders; and the founder of our Indian Empire was held up to popular hatred as a monster of every vice and crime. The dreadful famine of 1770 in Bengal gave his enemies a fresh plea for venting their rancorous spite on a nobleman whose friends in Parliament were growing daily fewer. But Clive met their attacks with all his old courage and proud self-respect. From his place in the House of Commons he defended himself in a speech which for the moment silenced his accusers, and won from old Lord Chatham, who happened to hear it, the tribute of his highest praise. Before a committee of inquiry into Indian affairs he underwent an unsparing scrutiny into every act of his public life, claiming credit for the very things which his questioners sought to prove against him. He had deceived Amīn Chand, but in the same circumstances he would certainly do once more the same thing. He had taken money from Mīr Jāfar; but what then? Why should he feel ashamed of an act which was neither mean

* Lord Clive's Fund was given up to his heirs a few years ago, after having done good service for nearly a hundred years.

nor wicked? All things considered, he could only wonder that he had not taken much more.

At last, in 1772, a vote of censure was formally brought before the House of Commons. Once more Clive spoke with telling earnestness in his own defence; and the Commons, refusing to brand with infamy a name so worthy to be held in proud remembrance, resolved that Clive had rendered great and meritorious services to his country. But their verdict came too late to undo the effects of illness aggravated by years of mental anxiety. In November, 1774, the conqueror of Plassey, who had already won for his countrymen a kingdom larger and much more populous than their own, died by his own hand at the age of forty-nine.

CHAPTER II

EVENTS IN SOUTHERN AND UPPER INDIA—1761–1775

THE progress of events in Southern India after the fall of Pondicherry now claims our attention. With the expulsion of the French from India their English rivals found themselves charged with the military defence of the Carnatic on behalf of its nominal ruler, Muhammad Ali. But they had no money to spare for that purpose, and their spendthrift ally had even less. To replenish his own and the Madras exchequer by making war upon the Raja of Tanjore was Muhammad Ali's ready thought. But a peaceful settlement made with the Raja under English prompting enabled the Madras Council to pay their way for that present, and in time the surplus revenues of the Carnatic passed entirely into their hands.

By the treaty of peace concluded between France and England in 1763, the factories taken from the French in India during the late war were given back to them, and both nations agreed to acknowledge Muhammad Ali as Nawāb of the Carnatic, and Salābat Jang as Subadār of the Deccan. The latter, however, had been dethroned a year before by his brother Nizām Ali, who straightway put him to death as soon as he heard of the treaty. Not long afterwards the usurping fratricide invaded the Carnatic, ravaging the country as he passed along, until the bold front displayed by a small English column at Tirupati compelled him to retrace his steps.

In pursuance of the treaty made by Clive with Shah

Alam, the Madras government in 1766 sent troops to occupy the Northern Circars. But Nizām Ali, who had meanwhile turned his arms against Jānoji Bhōsla, the Marātha sovereign of Berar, ill brooked the loss of further territory; and the English at Madras had no Clive at their head. Yielding to the threats of the prince they had so lately defied, they at length agreed to hold the ceded province as tributaries of Nizām Ali, and to make common cause with him against common foes.

One of these foes was Haidar Ali Ḳhan, the Muhammadan soldier of fortune, whose stout arm and strong will backed by a matchless talent for intrigue, had made him the foremost officer, ere long the self-chosen ruler of the old Hindu state of Mysore.* For some ten years past he had fought with varying success against the Marāthas, the Nizām, and the Nawāb of the Carnatic. But for the perils which then came near to overwhelm him in Mysore, he would have aided Lally in his last struggles against the victorious English. A few years later he had overcome all antagonists at home, had thrown into prison his old patron and ablest rival Nanjirāj, and dethroned the last and weakest of the princes who for several centuries had ruled Mysore. Since then he had carried his arms as far as Calicut and Bednōr, until his growing power provoked the Pēshwa Mādhu Rāo to make war upon him in concert with Nizām Ali.

Early in 1767 the Marāthas invaded Mysore, and carried off rich plunder before the Nizām and his English allies were ready to fulfil their share of the compact. A few weeks later Colonel Smith, the English commander, saw too good reason to mistrust the good faith of his professed ally. At last the Nizām, who had succeeded in

* Haidar Naik, as he was first called, was born in 1702, the son of a Mughal officer in the Punjāb, where Haidar himself served as a naik, or captain, before he took service with the Raja of Mysore.

selling himself to his late foe, threw off his mask entirely, and marched with Haidar Ali against Smith, who had withdrawn his troops from Nizām Ali's camp. On the 3rd September the allied armies, reckoned at 70,000 men with more than 100 guns, attacked about 7,000 English and Sepoys with sixteen guns at Chengām in South Arcot, but were signally defeated with heavy loss. Retiring to Trinomalli for supplies and reinforcements, the victors, now 10,000 strong with thirty guns, were again attacked on the 26th by numbers nearly as great as before; and again their stubborn courage and steady discipline drove their assailants in disorder from the field. On that day and the next more than 4,000 of the enemy were killed or wounded, and half their guns taken by the victors, whose own loss was only 150 men. Ill supported by his ally, the resolute Haidar still kept the field; but his efforts to take the fort of Ambūr, on the road from Bangalore to Madras, were gloriously repulsed by the brave Captain Calvert, and Smith's timely appearance on the 7th December forced Haidar Ali to raise the siege and withdraw the bulk of his army into Mysore.

Early in the next year the Nizām's just fears of English vengeance were allayed by a treaty which bound him to help the Madras government in subduing his late ally, on condition of receiving tribute for the country which his new friends might conquer for themselves. Nizām Ali on his side agreed to acknowledge Muhammad Ali as ruler of the Carnatic; and the right of the Company to hold the Northern Circars under the Imperial grant of 1765 was virtually admitted. Haidar himself was to be treated as a rebel and an usurper, who ought to be suppressed at any cost. By this bold if hazardous move against the ruler of Mysore, the Madras Council committed themselves and their unwilling masters at home to a deadly struggle with the boldest, fiercest, ablest, and most determined foe whom our arms encountered in Southern India.

Meanwhile the Bombay Government had done their best to cripple Haidar's naval power in the west, by sending a fleet to take Mangalore and other places on the Malabar coast. It was not long, however, before the dreaded Mussulman won back his lost towns, including Mangalore, whose cowardly commander abandoned a large number of wounded English and Sepoys to the tender mercies of a ruthless and embittered foe. On the other side of his dominions, however, that foe kept losing so much ground before Colonel Smith's steady advance, that he was glad ere long to offer terms which the Madras government would have done well to accept. But the demands of the latter rose with their late successes, until Haidar, scorning to humble himself any further, and alive to every chance of bettering his own position, resolved to fight on and teach his enemies a lesson of wise forbearance in the hour of their seeming prosperity.

Before the year's end he had forced Smith to raise the siege of Bangalore, had defeated the English under Colonel Wood, had recovered the districts he would have ceded to the Company, and begun to ravage the borders of the Carnatic with fire and sword. Ere long, in spite of Smith's watchfulness, Haidar's active horsemen outflanked their opponents, and swept forward in full speed for Madras. Smith followed them, eager for revenge and victory; but it was too late. Frightened at Haidar's sudden appearance within a few miles of their own city, the Madras Council readily agreed to treat with the foe whose offers they had so lately spurned. Smith was ordered to halt his troops, while Haidar leisurely proceeded to dictate the terms of a treaty which left him master of all his former possessions, and bound both parties to help each other against all assailants. For this lame conclusion to their former menaces, the rulers of Madras excused themselves by pleading want of money to carry on the war.

About this time the Pēshwa of the Marāthas had sent forth a mighty army to levy chauth on the princes of Upper India, in the name of a power still bent on retrieving the losses of Pānipat. When the Jāts and Rājputs had been duly plundered, the invaders swept over Rohilkhand, but were induced by timely overtures from Shujā-ud-daula to spare Oudh. Masters of Delhi, they invited Shah Alam thither from his temporary capital at Allahābād. In spite of the warnings of his English friends, that weak but ambitious scion of the house of Bābur suffered himself to be escorted into Delhi by Marātha sabres, and installed by his Hindu patrons in the throne of Akbar and Aurangzeb.

But the foolish Mughal soon began to chafe under the protection of his new masters, whose little finger was heavier than the loins of the Nawāb-Wazir. In the latter part of 1772, when the Marāthas were engaged to the eastward in exacting fresh tribute from Rohilkhand, the Mughal Minister, Najaf Khan, was defeated by Tukaji Holkar in his attempt to ward off an attack of the Jāts upon one of the Emperor's feudatories. In vain did Najaf Khan rally his troops for yet another stand before Delhi. The Mughal capital opened its gates to the victorious Marāthas, and the fickle Emperor made his peace by disowning his brave defender, and yielding up the districts which Clive a few years before had transferred into his charge.

But the English were in no mood to suffer Marātha aggrandisement at their own expense. The presence of an English force deterred the Marāthas from entering the ceded provinces, which were afterwards handed over to the Nawāb of Oudh, from whose charge they had been wrested by the English after the battle of Buxār. Meanwhile the death of the Pēshwa, Madhu Rāo, in November, 1772, gave the Marātha general a good excuse for withdrawing his army, laden with the plunder of many provinces, across the Narbada before the middle of 1773.

While one great army had been thus engaged in the north, another, led by Madhu Rāo himself, had struck some heavy blows at the power of Haidar Ali, in return for his open defiance of claims pressed under former treaties. Fort after fort in his eastern provinces fell into the invaders' hands. A large part of Mysore was ravaged by clouds of Marātha horsemen. Trimbak Māma, who took over the command from the ailing Pēshwa, caught Haidar at a disadvantage on his retreat towards Seringapatam, and nothing but the Marātha greed for plunder saved Haidar's routed troops from utter annihilation. In vain did the stout-hearted ruler of Mysore appeal to Madras for the succour which under recent treaties he had perhaps some right to claim, although he might seem to have forfeited that right by his wanton invasion of Marātha ground. The Madras Council would have given him the needful aid; but Sir John Lindsay had been sent out from England as King's envoy to the Court of Muhammad Ali, and the ruler of the Carnatic would hear of no friendly movement in behalf of his hard-pressed neighbour. Sir John himself shared the Nawāb's feeling; and the Council, hampered by their conflicting duties, abandoned Haidar to his fate. Before the end of 1771 the turbulent sovereign of Mysore was glad to obtain peace on conditions which stripped him of nearly half his kingdom, and saddled him with the payment of a heavy tribute to the Court of Poona. He never forgave the English for what he considered a cowardly breach of faith, and his son Tipu took up the legacy of revenge.

By this time a fit successor to Clive was about to

assume the office which Clive's retirement had left for some years past in much weaker hands. During those years many things had gone wrong with the East India Company and its servants in Bengal. In Clive's absence the old abuses began to crop up again more and more thickly; the revenues, handsome in themselves, were wasted in the collection by all kinds of jobbery and mismanagement; the people of Bengal suffered from heavy and unfair exactions on the part alike of English supervisors and native deputies. Immense grants of land enriched a few native jobbers at the expense of their English rulers. On the top of all this broke out the dreadful famine of 1770, when the husbandmen sold their cattle, their farming tools, their very sons and daughters for food, when the living were fain to eat the dead, when pestilence added its ravages to those of hunger, and tender women, laying aside all their wonted privacy, rushed forth unveiled into the streets to beg a handful of rice for their starving children. More than a third of the people in Bengal are reckoned to have died of famine or disease, and for years to come large tracts of once fertile country lay waste or overgrown with rank jungle.* From these and such like causes it happened that the Company was already deep in debt, at the very moment when its directors were declaring dividends of six per cent. on the half-year.

Conscious of the dangers that beset them in India, and frightened at the outcry waxing loud against them at home, the Court of Directors at length announced their resolve "to stand forth as Dewān, and to take on themselves the entire care and management of the revenues through the agency of their own servants." Hitherto the government of Bengal in all its branches had been carried

* Hunter's "Annals of Rural Bengal"; Macaulay's Essay on "Lord Clive"; Girdlestone's "Report on Past Famines," etc.

on mainly through native officers, most of whom had woefully abused their powers. To the strong hands of Warren Hastings was now entrusted the execution of the desired reforms. That great, if sometimes erring statesman, had first gone out to India at the age of eighteen. Seven years later, in 1757, his talents had won the notice of the hero of Plassey, who placed him in the difficult post of Resident at the Court of Murshidābād. In 1760 he rose to be a member of the Calcutta Council, where his great abilities and his upright dealings stood out in sharp relief against the shortcomings of profligate or blundering colleagues. Returning to England in 1764, with a good name and a purse but poorly stocked, he went out again five years later as second Member of Council at Madras. While he was doing his best there to retrieve the financial disorders consequent on the war with Haidar and the spendthrift rule of Muhammad Ali, he found himself appointed President of the Calcutta Council; and in April, 1772, Warren Hastings took charge of the post with which his name was to become inseparably linked for praise or blame in the minds of his countrymen at large.

The new Governor of Fort William lost no time in carrying out the orders he had received from home. It was to him a painful but necessary duty to begin by dealing harshly with Muhammad Reza Khan, the Mussulman Governor of Bengal, and with his Hindu helpmate, Raja Shitāb Rai, who had fought like a Rājput hero under Captain Knox twelve years before, in the memorable rout of Shah Alam, under the walls of Patna. Both these nobles were removed from office, and afterwards brought to trial for alleged misdeeds which their accusers wholly failed to prove. Both, in due time, were formally acquitted, the Hindu with especial honour and every token of regret for the wrong unwittingly done him.

His chief foe, however, was the wily Nand Kumār, who had been Governor of Hūgli under Mīr Jāfar, and made himself a byword for perfidy and intrigue, gaining nothing by his unsparing efforts to supplant his worthier rivals. The powers which Hastings took out of their hands were not to be entrusted again to native overseers. Thenceforth the real government of Bengal and Bihār was handed over to the acknowledged servants of the Company. The seat of rule was finally transferred, with the Treasury and the Courts of Justice, from Murshidābād to Calcutta. The little Nawāb himself was to retain nothing of his father's crippled sovereignty, save the name and social state of Nawāb. A son of Nand Kumār was appointed treasurer of his household. The courts of civil and criminal justice in each district were placed under the charge of English officers; and courts of appeal were established in Calcutta, under regulations drawn up for their guidance by the clear-headed governor himself.

Hand-in-hand with these reforms proceeded the task of settling the revenues of the country. After a close but often baffling search into the rights of existing Zamindars or land-holders, the land of Bengal was farmed out to the highest bidders, by way of experiment, for five years.* In keeping with the immemorial usage of the country, with the practice alike of Hindu and Muhammadan rulers, Hastings looked to the land revenue as the mainstay of his new fiscal system. Several taxes which bore hard on the people, or yielded little to the Treasury, were abolished. In each district an English collector, aided by a staff of native officers, was appointed to collect the revenue, to settle all disputes between land-holders and tenants, to protect the Rayats or husbandmen from the extortions of Zamindars and native underlings, and to use

* Kaye's "Administration of the East India Company," part ii. chap. 2.

his best efforts in furthering the trade and industry of his own district. To each group of districts was assigned its own commissioner, who travelled about the country as overseer or controller, and sent in his reports to a central board of revenue sitting in Calcutta.

While the new governor was thus engaged in Bengal, the process of reform was being applied by Parliament to his masters' affairs at home. The Select Committee of 1772 issued a report which became the groundwork of the Regulating Act passed in the following year by the ministry of Lord North. An important change in the terms of admission into the Company and of election to the Court of Directors, reduced the number of stockholders greatly for the better,* and secured to each director four years of office at a time. The Governor of Fort William became Governor-General of India, with a salary of £25,000 a-year; and four members of Council, whose joint salaries amounted to £40,000 a-year, were to aid or check his movements. A Chief Justice and three puisne judges, appointed by the Crown, were to form a Supreme Court of Judicature, wielding large but ill-defined powers over all persons except the Governor-General and his Council. The clamours of the Company against these inroads on their chartered rights were partly allayed by a loan of a million sterling from the Royal Exchequer; but the thin end of the wedge had been fairly driven into the fabric of their rule.

Meanwhile Hastings, urged by an empty treasury and the prayers of the Directors for more money, had been doing his best to set things financially straight in Bengal. The tribute to Shah Alam, a quarter of a million sterling, was no longer paid. For twice that sum he agreed to make over to the Nawāb-Wazir of Oudh the districts of Kora and Allahābād. For another large sum he agreed

* The qualification for a Proprietor was raised from £500 to £1000.

to lend the ambitious Shujā-ud-daula a body of English and native troops to aid in the conquest of Rohilkhand. His policy in this matter has often been denounced, by none more eloquently than Macaulay himself. But Hastings, handling the question as a statesman and a financier, paid small regard to the sentimental claims afterwards pleaded in behalf of a race of Pathān nobles too weak to bar out the Marāthas, and too turbulent to keep the peace among themselves. He knew that their leader, Hāfiz Rahmat Khan, owed Shujā-ud-daula, for help given against the Marāthas, a sum which he could not or would not pay. He knew that the Mughal emperor had bestowed on our good friend, the Nawāb-Wazir, the government of a province which a predecessor of Hāfiz Rahmat had wrested from a Mughal emperor thirty years before. He knew that his own masters were sadly in want of money, that the troops lent out to a useful neighbour would cost his own treasury nothing in the meantime, and that a sure way of keeping the peace in Bengal was to be found in the maintenance of a strong government on its northern frontier. As for the bulk of the people in Rohilkhand, it was not likely that they would lose on the whole by a change of masters which bade fair to rescue them alike from internal troubles and foreign raids. They were Hindus and they certainly rejoiced at being freed from the Muhammadan Afghāns.

In accordance with these views an English force under Colonel Champion marched into the doomed province. On the 23rd April, 1774, his little army had to bear the brunt of a hard fight against 40,000 Rohillas, led by Hāfiz Rahmat himself. In spite of these odds, enhanced by the cowardice of their allies, the English won the day, leaving 2000 Rohillas with their brave leader dead or dying on the field. Bitterly did Colonel Champion inveigh against those "banditti," the men of Oudh, who looked on at the fight from a safe distance and then hastened to plunder the enemy's camp. This victory sealed the doom of the Rohilla Pathāns. Faizulla Khan indeed retained his father's fief of Rāmpur as the price of his timely submission to the Nawāb-Wazir;* but some 20,000 of his countrymen were driven out of the conquered province. It is certain, however, that the mass of the people in Rohilkhand, mostly of Hindu descent, suffered neither in purse nor person from the downfall of their late masters; and the stories of their cruel fate, as afterwards raked up in England by private and political foes of the great Governor-General, were little better than idle tales.†

Had Hastings been left free to pursue his own plans for the better government of Bengal and the safeguarding of its frontiers, some dark passages in the history of this period might have remained unwritten. But with the landing of the new councillors in October, 1774, his powers of independent action were to be sadly crippled by the malice or the misconceptions of men who combined to outvote him at every turn. Of the four members of his remodelled Council one only, Mr. Barwell, took the part of Hastings against a majority led by Philip Francis, one of the ablest, fiercest, wrongest-headed, most rancorous statesmen of his day. Francis set himself at once to the congenial task of hampering the ruler whom he had already learned to hate. Under the guise of patriotism, of upright scorn for wrong-doing, he gave full vent to the workings of a narrow mind and a thoroughly malignant heart; and in such a climate as that of Calcutta the

* His descendants still hold their place as Nawābs of Rāmpur (Keene's "Mughal Empire").

† "The Hindu inhabitants, about 700,000, were in no way affected," writes Captain Hamilton in his "History of the Rohilla Afghāns," founded on the works of Rohilla historians. Sir John Strachey's "Hastings and the Rohilla War" has entirely freed the Governor-General from all the charges against him.

natural sourness of his temper was pretty sure to derive fresh poison from the fierce summer heats.

His evil influence soon began to bear fruit. The Governor-General's agent at the Court of Shujā-ud-daula was replaced by another of his own choosing. In spite of Hastings' remonstrances, the English brigade was recalled from Rohilkhand. On the death of the Nawāb-Wazir his successor, Asaf-ud-daula, was forced to make over the district of Benāres to his English allies, and to pay a larger subsidy for the use of his borrowed Sepoys. Francis and his friends in the Council thwarted and overrode Hastings at every turn. They interfered with a high hand in the affairs of Bombay and Madras; their meddling fingers left unseemly marks on the government of Bengal itself. They listened with greedy ears to every charge which the enemies of Hastings were but too ready to bring against a governor fallen into manifest disgrace. In India it is always easy to complete the ruin of dishonoured greatness by means of false witnesses and forged papers; and the friends of Francis in the Calcutta Council became ready dupes of all who owed Hastings a grudge or deemed it politic to win the favour of his opponents.

Foremost among the crowds who hastened to peck at that wounded vulture was the wily Hindu Nand Kumār. He had never forgiven Hastings for cheating him of his hoped-for succession to the post of Muhammad Reza Khan, and now it seemed as if the hour for his revenge had struck at last. This man, a master of intrigue and falsehood, openly charged the Governor-General with having taken bribes from the widow of Mīr Jāfar, from Muhammad Reza Khan, and several others. In the Council he found a ready hearing. Scorning to defend himself against such a man before such a court, Hastings left the Council-room, followed by his friend Barwell.

But Francis and the other two voted themselves a Council, went into the charges put forth by Nand Kumār, and declared Hastings guilty of having amassed no less than forty lakhs of rupees—£400,000—in two years and a half by all kinds of underhand means.*

For a moment Nand Kumār could revel in the sweetness of gratified revenge. Courted by many of his own countrymen, and believing himself strong in the support of Francis and his English partisans, he little knew what an undercurrent of disaster was about to drag him down into its lowest depths. Scorning defeat at the hands of such a foe, Hastings turned for help to the Supreme Court. A charge of false swearing and conspiracy was lodged against the villainous Brahman. While the trial was yet pending one Mohan Prasād renewed on his own account an old action for forgery against the Raja, who had once been saved from impending danger by the timely intervention of Hastings himself. The case thus suspended a few years before was now transferred to the Supreme Court. Convicted on the clearest evidence, Nand Kumār was condemned to death in accordance with the law which Sir Elijah Impey and his brother judges were bound to administer.

It was not the first time that a native of India had been doomed to the same punishment for the same offence. Ten years before a Hindu of rank had only escaped hanging by a timely reprieve;† but since then at least two natives had been less fortunate. With the arraignment of the guilty Raja, Hastings had nothing whatever to do;

* The whole charge was afterwards proved to be a wilful falsehood, founded on letters forged by Nand Kumār himself.

† "Memoirs of Sir Elijah Impey," by his Son, pp. 99 and 299, etc. The reprieve of Rādachand Mithra had been owing to the fact that he was the first Hindu condemned for forgery under English law. Sir James Stephens, "Nuncomar and Impey," has fully vindicated Hastings and Impey from the charges against them made by Macaulay and James Mill.

still less, if possible, with his execution. He had been fairly tried before an English jury, and all four judges had concurred in dooming him to a felon's death. From that fate neither Francis nor his colleagues made any effort to save the prisoner. No prayer for respite was presented by any of the prisoner's friends, native or English, to the Supreme Court. One petition, indeed, was forwarded by Nand Kumār himself to General Clavering of the Supreme Council; but that petition was first presented at the Council Board eleven days after the writer's death, and Francis it was who proposed to have it burned as a libel by the hands of the common hangman.

On the morning of the 5th August, 1775, Nand Kumār underwent the doom which, as a British subject amenable to the stern English law of that day, he had richly deserved. The most brilliant of English essayists has drawn a powerful picture of the horror, grief, dismay, which the hanging of so eminent a Brahman, for an offence in native eyes so venial, produced upon the minds of his countrymen in Calcutta and elsewhere. More than one historian of British India has dressed up in his own words the lurid fiction which Francis was the first to circulate many years after the event. In plain truth, however, the sentence of the law was carried out before spectators moved far more by curiosity than concern.

Of the Hindus who thronged at the gallows' foot few gave any signs of wild excitement. No loud shriek of horror and despair went up to heaven from the gathered mass; but an audible hum of satisfaction went round the Muhammadans as the drop fell upon "the worst man in India," the perjured persecutor of Muhammad Reza Khan. As for the alleged rush of sorrowing Hindus to wash out the pollution of witnessing such a sight in the sacred Hūgli, it was simply a natural movement from the scene of a tragedy already complete to the wonted bathing-ghāts of a river that rolled hard by.*

* It is a pity that Macaulay's splendid essay on Warren Hastings should have been marred by his rash adoption of the slanders circulated by Sir Philip Francis against both Hastings and Sir Elijah Impey. The whole story of Nand Kumār's trial and execution, as told in his pages, betrays a curious want of insight into the character of Francis, a perverse blindness to the legal questions involved in the case, and an unaccountable ignorance of the documents whence Mr. Impey drew the means of clearing not only his own father but Hastings himself from the groundless inventions of a spiteful partisan.

CHAPTER III

WARREN HASTINGS—1775–1786

THE troubles of Hastings were not over with the death of Nand Kumār. His wiser policy was thwarted at every turn by the mischievous meddling of Francis and his partisans. In Oudh their chosen agent, Bristow, supported the ladies of the late Nawāb's household in their seemingly unfounded claim to all the treasure, about two millions sterling, which Shujā-ud-daula had left behind him. In spite of his own empty treasury, of his growing debts to the Bengal Government, and of the Governor-General's earnest remonstrances, the new Nawāb-Wazir was compelled to forego his just share of the property in dispute. A fearful mutiny among his unpaid troops, quelled at last with heavy loss of life, was the natural, if sad result of the measures sanctioned by the Calcutta Council.

Nor was the outlook for Hastings much brighter elsewhere. If he had many friends both in India and in England, the Prime Minister, Lord North, and a majority in the Court of Directors sided with his opponents in the Bengal Council. His measures were condemned by the Directors, who, under Lord North's prompting, sought to remove him from his post; but the Court of Proprietors flocked to his support, and quashed, by a large majority, the vote of their own Directors. Thus encouraged, Hastings struggled on at his thankless task. At last, in September, 1776, the death of Colonel Monson gave him the casting vote in his own Council. Once more he found himself free to govern in his own way, unchecked by the ignorance or the malice of inferior men.

But a new danger ere long confronted him. During the previous troubles he had lodged with Colonel Maclean a conditional offer to resign his post. This offer, in spite of its subsequent withdrawal, the Directors chose to accept as final, and Mr. Wheeler was ordered out to replace him. Before his arrival the senior member of Council, General Clavering had installed himself as acting Governor-General, and commanded the troops in Fort William to obey no other orders than his own. Francis, of course, was ready to follow up any blow aimed at his hated rival. But Hastings had no mind to throw up a doubtful game. His own orders to the troops were cheerfully obeyed. Colonel Morgan at once closed the gates of Fort William against Clavering. A like answer came from Barrackpore. An appeal made by Hastings to the Supreme Court clinched the defeat of his opponents. Impey and his fellow-judges ruled that Clavering had no power to assume an office which Hastings had not yet formally resigned, The General and his followers had the wisdom to accept the award, and Hastings, who had promised to accept it for worse or better, at once withdrew from all further action against his defeated colleague.*

Two months afterwards Clavering died, and Wheeler, who had gone out to replace Monson, usually voted with Francis against the Governor-General. Hastings, however, had still the casting vote, and the gallant Sir Eyre Coote, who presently took his seat in Council as successor to Clavering in the chief command of the troops, gave small encouragement to the factious Francis.

* See letter from Sir E. Impey, quoted by his son. "Memoirs," pp. 162–5. Captain Trotter himself wrote an excellent Life of Hastings in the "Rulers of India" series.

During the lull which followed this passing squall, Hastings carried on the work of government with a firm and skilful hand. Before the last settlement of the land revenue expired in 1777, he had sent out commissioners to collect the means of renewing it in a better form, with especial regard for the just claims of the Rāyats or husbandmen to protection from the demands of encroaching or needy Zamindars. The latter also were to be assessed at a lighter rate, for many of them had suffered heavily under the assessments of 1772. For the next four years the revised leases were renewed yearly, with such corrections as policy or justice might demand. Meanwhile the enemies of Hastings at home still found fault with everything he did or planned; but in spite of all their railings, the services of such a ruler were not to be lightly dispensed with at a time when England, hard pressed by a war with her American colonies and threatened on all sides by European foes, had special need of all her ablest men. At the end of his term of office in 1778, Hastings found himself reappointed for another five years.

At that time a new danger was met by the dauntless Viceroy with his usual readiness of resource. In 1775 the Bombay Government had somewhat rashly pledged itself to uphold the cause of Raghuba, the erewhile conqueror of Lahore, and sometime prisoner of his nephew Madhu Rāo, against a rival claimant to the headship of the Marātha League. On the murder of Madhu's brother, the young and promising Narain Rāo, in 1773, his restless uncle and suspected murderer, Raghuba, had declared himself Pēshwa, while another party headed by the able Brahman Minister, Nāna Farnavīs, presently set up a posthumous son of Narain Rāo on the throne of his murdered father. The Marātha leaders took different sides according as their interests or jealousies might lead them. Raghuba turned for help to the English at Bombay, who were nothing loath to turn his needs to their own advantage. Without consulting the Government of Bengal, they agreed to help him with a body of troops in return for the cession of Salsette and Bassein, an island and a port near Bombay itself, and for a handsome yearly payment to the Bombay Treasury. Colonel Keating led his troops into the Marātha country, routed an army tenfold stronger than his own at Arras, near Barōda, and drove the enemy across the Narbada, while a heavy defeat was inflicted on the Marāthas by sea.

If Hastings condemned the Treaty of Surat as an impolitic measure which he had never sanctioned, he was not for rashly setting it aside in the face of these successes. But in these days the party of Francis had its own way in the Bengal Council; and the Bombay Government was ordered to withdraw all its troops forthwith. Colonel Upton was sent from Calcutta to undo the work so promisingly begun. But the insolence of the Poona Regency had well-nigh renewed the war, when Nāna Farnavīs at length accepted the compromise offered by the English envoy. By the Treaty of Purandhar the English retained possession of Salsette, which they had already won; their claim on the revenues of Broach was also acknowledged; but the rest of their agreement with Raghuba was formally annulled, in return for a pension allotted by the Poona Government to the late ally.

New causes of quarrel, however, soon arose. A despatch from the Court of Directors confirmed the former treaty with Raghuba. Neither at Bombay nor Poona was the new treaty carefully observed. From mutual bickerings the quarrel proceeded to words and acts of mutual defiance. Surat was occupied by troops from Bombay. Raghuba himself was welcomed to the former city as an honoured guest. On the other hand, a French adventurer was received at Poona with open arms as an accredited envoy from the King of France, who was just on the point of declaring war with England. Hastings also was now free to act according to his own judgment; and the timely secession of Sakharām Bāpu from the Poona Regency furnished a new plea for returning to the policy always favoured at Bombay.

At length, in the cold season of 1778, an English force took the field from the western capital, while a Bengal column under the skilful Colonel Goddard pushed on through Bundelkhand and Mālwa, to cross the Narbada before the close of the year. Meanwhile the Nāna had struck some hard blows at his Marātha assailants; and Raghuba's prospects were already darkening when Colonel Egerton advanced towards Poona across the Ghāts. They were now to become still darker. At Talegāon, within a forced march of Poona itself, a strange panic beset the Commissioner, Mr. Carnac, whose powers entirely overruled those of the English commanders. The order for retreat was given, the guns were hastily thrown into a pond, and nothing but the cool courage of Captain Hartley and his rear-guard of Sepoys saved the whole force from annihilation at the hands of an enemy who had hitherto shrank from barring its advance. Two days later, on the 13th January, 1779, the English leaders crowned their disgrace by bargaining for a safe retreat for an army which under better handling might have borne Raghuba in triumph to the Marātha capital.

A new gleam of hope, however, was soon to shine for that luckless prince. Neither at Bombay nor at Calcutta was any respect shown for the disgraceful Convention of Wargāom. Its English authors were dismissed the Company's service. Colonel Goddard brought his troops in safety to Surat. His proposals for a fresh treaty falling through, he took the field at the beginning of 1780, captured among other places Ahmadābād, the stately capital of Gujarāt, and twice defeated the Marātha troops of Sindhia and Holkar. The gallant Hartley pushed his way in the Konkan. Meanwhile, another Bengal column under the daring Major Popham, which had been sent by Hastings across the Jumna, drove Sindhia's Marāthas before them, stormed the fort of Lahore, and carried by a well-planned escalade the formidable rock-fortress of Gwalior, which Coote himself had deemed it madness to attack.* Before the year's end Bassein had surrendered to Goddard, and the dashing Hartley crowned his former exploits by signally defeating 20,000 Marāthas who had been pressing him hard for two days.

These successes were followed by the surprise and rout of Sindhia,† in March, 1781, at the hands of Popham's successor, Colonel Camac. On the west, however, Goddard was less fortunate. A mighty gathering of the Marātha hosts barred his way to Poona from the top of the Ghāts and went near to cut off his retreat. To advance was hopeless, to stand still was little better. It only remained for him to attempt a hazardous retreat before 60,000 pursuers, keen for his destruction. Thanks to their own courage and their leader's skill, his troops succeeded in the attempt, but not without paying dearly for their success.

By this time evil tidings had come to Hastings from Madras. Ever since their rejection of his prayers for help against the Marāthas, Haidar Ali had been nursing his revenge against the English. For some years, however, he contented himself with trying to repair his crippled

* It was taken by Captain Bruce and twenty Sepoys.

† Māhadajī Sindhia, a younger son of Ranoji Sindhia, had escaped, with a wound which lamed him for life, from the rout of Pānipat, to become the head of the house of Sindhia.

fortunes at every turn. Before the end of 1772 he had subdued the brave highlanders of Coorg, hundreds of whom were murdered by his orders in cold blood. In little more than a year later he had made good all his former losses, and before the end of 1776 new provinces had been added to his widening frontier. Two years later his northern frontier had been pushed up to the Kistna.

Meanwhile Haidar's fear of the Marāthas had tempted him more than once to renew his overtures to the English at Madras. But the latter, taken up with their own schemes, quarrels, and perplexities, paid little heed to the advances of a neighbour whose power for mischief they underrated, or whose friendliness they would not trust. Balked by the Home Government in their unjust designs on Tanjore, overruled continually by orders from Calcutta, hampered by their relations with the Nawāb of the Carnatic, and pressed by a chronic want of funds, the Madras Council filled up the measure of their weakness by reckless quarrelling among themselves. One governor was sent home in disgrace; another, Lord Pigot, was held prisoner by his colleagues for several months; and his successor, Sir Thomas Rumbold, became from the first a mark for the many slanders which were destined long to survive him.

Hardly had Rumbold taken up his office, when he learned that war had already broken out between France and England. This became the signal for a prompt attack on the few places still held by the French in Southern India. With the fall of Pondicherry in October, 1778, Mahē alone, a town on the western coast, remained in French hands. In the following March, Mahē also fell to our arms, and very wroth thereat was Haidar Ali, some of whose troops had aided in the defence. His anger at the blow thus dealt to his secret friends was increased by the march of English troops through his newly conquered province of Karpa into the Guntūr district, which Nizām Ali's brother Basalat Jung had lately rented to the government of Madras.* Now, if ever, had come the time to drive his old enemies into the sea. His own army, 90,000 strong, well-equipped, and trained by French officers, might alone suffice for that purpose. Backed by the hosts of Nizām Ali and Nāna Farnavīs, its shock would be irresistible.

A willing listener to a tempting offer did the envoy from Poona find in the fierce old sovereign of Mysore. If Haidar loved the Marāthas little more than the English, he had no objection to make use of either for his own ends. Turning a deaf ear to the counter offers now made by Sir Thomas Rumbold, he prepared, in his seventy-eighth year, for a campaign which might end in leaving him master of all Southern India. Happily for us at this critical moment, Nizām Ali's quarrel with his English neighbours, regarding the tribute claimed from them for the Northern Circars, was allayed by the timely interference of the Governor-General, enforced perhaps by his own fears of the danger involved in furthering the secret schemes of so ambitious a plotter as the Sultan of Mysore.†

If Rumbold was dimly aware of coming danger, neither his own councillors nor Hastings himself, at the beginning of 1780, seems to have guessed how near and terrible that danger was.‡ Sir Hector Munro himself, as head of the Madras Army, made no effort to meet the storm whose warning murmurs already filled the air. In every mosque and pagoda of Mysore Haidar's agents were busy preaching

* Haidar had long marked out Guntūr for himself.

† It was given out that Haidar had obtained from the puppet Emperor of Delhi a formal grant of sovereignty over all the Nizām's dominions.

‡ In reply to Rumbold's warnings, Hastings declared himself "convinced, from Hyder's conduct and disposition, that he will never molest us while we preserve a good understanding with him." See Marshman's "India," vol. i., Appendix.

a *Jihād* or holy war against the infidels from the West. At length, in July, 1780, the hosts of Mysore poured like a lava-flood through their mountain-passes over the Carnatic; their progress marked by burning villages, whose smoke ere long became clearly visible to scared spectators from the heights near Madras.

To meet this formidable inroad, Sir Hector Munro, with about five thousand men, set out from Conjeeveram, while Colonel Baillie had to lead about half that number round from Guntūr. Precious days were lost to the latter by a sudden flood; and on the 6th September, when he was only a long day's march from Conjeeveram, his little force was fiercely attacked by Tipu, the brave son of Haidar. A timely reinforcement, under Colonel Fletcher, enabled Baillie to press onwards until the 9th, when only two or three miles divided him from Munro. But between them lay the bulk of Haidar's army, and next morning Baillie saw himself beset on all sides by overwhelming odds. All that day his men fought on under every disadvantage, vainly hoping for the help that never came. The victor of Buxār proved utterly false to his old renown. Unmoved by the sounds of the heavy firing which was dealing havoc in his subaltern's ranks, Munro never budged an inch to rescue him. At last, in despair of maintaining a hopeless struggle, Baillie surrendered, and three hundred English soldiers, the feeble remnant of his shattered force, laid down their arms. But for the timely interference of Haidar's French officers, even these, in spite of their surrender, would have all been butchered where they stood. As it turned out, few of them were destined to survive the wasting effects of wounds, sickness, and prolonged ill-treatment in the noisome prisons of Mysore.*

* Out of Baillie's eighty-six officers, thirty-six were slain or mortally wounded, and only sixteen surrendered without a wound.

Munro himself, who seems to have been paralysed by the impending failure of supplies for his own army, fell back at once to Conjeeveram. Thence, after throwing his heavy guns into a tank, and sacrificing much baggage, he hurried off in quest of supplies to Chingleput. Disappointed there also, he retreated on the 14th September to St. Thomas's Mount, near Madras, leaving Haidar to waste the Carnatic at his leisure, and to bring the siege of Arcot to a successful close.

When tidings of these disasters reached Calcutta, Hastings met the occasion with his wonted fearlessness. A fresh quarrel with his old enemy Francis, who had broken his pledge to oppose none of Hastings' larger measures after the return home of Mr. Barwell, had just issued in a duel, from which Francis bore off a wound that did not tend to improve his temper. Backed, however, by Sir Eyre Coote, Hastings kept the upper hand in his Council. Not a moment did he now lose in developing his own plans for the salvation of Madras at any cost. Sir Eyre Coote, with a choice array of Bengal troops, was at once despatched to the scene of danger in supersession of Munro. The acting Governor of Madras was removed from his post. Even the Company's remittances to England were held back for the better carrying on of war against Haidar Ali.

Arrived at Madras, Clive's old comrade hurried off to the relief of Wandiwash, the scene of his former victory over Lally. The news of his approach frightened the enemy away from a place which Lieutenant Flint, with the aid of a hundred men, had been defending with the courage of a second Clive. The relief of Chingleput and the capture of Karangāli had marked the first stages of Coote's advance. Coote's repulse in June before Chilambram encouraged Haidar to make a dash on Cuddalore, while Coote was resting his troops at Porto

Novo. But the fiery veteran made haste to grapple with his powerful opponent, and on the 1st July his eight thousand men hurled themselves against ten times their number with a force that nothing could long withstand. After six hours' fighting the enemy fled, leaving ten thousand on the field, while Coote's loss amounted only to three hundred, so well had his guns been served.

Again the two armies came together in August near the scene of Baillie's great disaster; but this time the victory was less complete. On the 27th September, however, Haidar was utterly defeated at Sholimgarh, with the loss of five thousand men. By this time Lord Macartney, the new Governor of Madras, was preparing another force for the capture of the Dutch possessions in Southern India; Holland also having been added to the number of our foes. The fall of Negapatam in November was followed in January of the next year by the capture of Trincomali in the neighbouring island of Ceylon.

Before Coote took the field again, Muhammad Ali, the worthless ruler of the Carnatic, had been forced to make over to the Company for five years the revenues he had hitherto squandered on himself, while the men who fought for him were in perpetual risk of starving. Thenceforth the movements of our troops would not be hampered by the want of those supplies which the Nawāb had so often failed to furnish at the right moment.

In the beginning of 1782 Coote hastened to the relief of Vellore, which, but for his timely movement, must soon have fallen into Haidar's clutches. A few days later the arrival of succours from Bombay enabled Major Abingdon, the bold defender of Telicherry, in Malabar, to rout the army which had vainly besieged him for eighteen months. Calicut, on the same coast, next fell to the English arms. But these successes were soon to be balanced by failures and mishaps elsewhere. Forty thousand of Tipu's soldiers fell upon Colonel Braithwaite's little force of two thousand men—nearly all Sepoys—in Tanjore; and after a fight, prolonged with matchless heroism, for twenty-six hours, the wasted remnants of Braithwaite's band were saved from utter extinction only by the generous efforts of Tipu's French allies. French fleets appeared from time to time on the Madras coast, to be encountered with small result by English admirals. Cuddalore was taken at last with the help of Suffrein's sailors, and Admiral Hughes was too late to save Trincomali. If Coote's dashing energy once more rescued Wandiwash, and dealt Tipu another defeat at Arnī, his movement against Cuddalore failed for want of timely succour from the fleet; and the close of that year saw him trying to recruit his shattered health in Bengal. What with the desolation of the Carnatic, the famine raging around Madras, the daily expected landing of French troops led by the renowned Bussy himself, the losses caused to English shipping by gales on the eastern coast, and Humberstone's retreat before Haidar on the Bombay side, the outlook for our countrymen in Southern India at the end of 1782 was almost as dark as ever.

One gleam, however, brightened it even then. On the 7th December Haidar Ali died at the great age of eighty, worn out by an illness which had never kept him from sharing like a common trooper in the toils of the past campaign. Earlier in the same year Hastings had succeeded in detaching the last of the Marātha leaders from their alliance with the Sultan of Mysore. The first to make peace with him was the Raja of Berar, who, early in 1781, had sanctioned the march of a Bengal brigade through Orissa towards Madras.* His example was followed by Sindhia, after his defeat by Colonel Carnac;

* This brigade suffered heavily on its march from cholera, the disease which has since become endemic in many parts of India.

and at length, in May, 1782, was concluded the Treaty of Sālbai, which left Mysore to fight on single-handed against the English power. By this treaty Sindhia regained his lost possessions, all but Gwalior, besides new territory about Broach; the Gaikwar of Gujarāt became an independent prince; Raghuba was to retire into private life on a handsome pension; and Bassein, with some other districts, was surrendered to Nāna Farnavīs as regent for the young Pēshwa. It was not, however, till after Haidar's death that the Nāna set his seal to a compact which further bound him to aid in rescuing the Carnatic from the yoke of Mysore.

The news of his father's death brought Tipu back for a time from the western coast to his own capital, to make sure of his succession to the vacant throne. Ere long death relieved him of his stoutest foe, the war-worn Coote, who barely lived to reach Madras once more. In April, 1783, Bussy himself landed on the eastern coast and led his Frenchmen to the defence of Cuddalore. By that time, however, Tipu was far away to the westward, opening his batteries on the hill-fort of Bednōr, held by some of the troops whose valour had hewn a way for General Matthews into the highlands of Mysore. After a brave defence, Bednōr was surrendered a heap of ruins, and its luckless garrison, in breach of Tipu's pledged word, marched off in irons to the neighbouring fortresses. Yet more protracted was the defence of Mangalore by Colonel Campbell. At last, however, the wasted garrison, cheated of the supplies assured to them under an armistice, were fortunate in being allowed to march out with all the honours of war at the end of January, 1784.

Meanwhile neither Bussy nor General Stuart had made much progress in the Carnatic. Two sallies ordered by Bussy from Cuddalore were repulsed with heavy loss.*

* In one of these actions Sergeant Bernadotte, the future King of Sweden, was taken prisoner by the English.

The fleets of Hughes and Suffrein fought and parted without result. At length came tidings of peace between France and England, when all hostile movements on either side were stayed by mutual agreement, and the French officers in Tipu's army left him to carry on the war alone.

By this time another British force under Colonel Fullarton was steadily advancing into the highlands of Mysore. Before him lay the road to Seringapatam, and a fair chance of finishing the war by a few bold strokes. But the Governor of Madras, unheeding the counsel and the commands of Hastings, stooped to sue for the peace which Fullarton was eager to dictate under the walls of Tipu's capital. That brave officer was ordered to fall back, in compliance with a truce which Tipu was openly breaking. Lord Macartney's messengers were received with studied insolence by a monarch bent on turning their master's folly to his own profit. Not till Mangalore had fallen into his hands did the wily sultan deign to consider the object of their errand, or even to let them enter his camp. At last, on the 11th March, 1784, the long series of scornful insults was crowned by the sight of two English envoys standing for two hours before Tipu, with heads bare, beseeching him to sign the treaty they held in their hands. Their prayers were finally granted at the intercession of envoys from Poona and Hyderābād. By this act of needless self-abasement the Madras Government purchased a peace which restored to each party their former possessions, and rescued more than a thousand Englishmen from the slow torture of prison life in Mysore. At the best, however, it was only a hollow truce, which Tipu, at once a fanatic, a restless schemer, and a born foe to the English, was pretty sure to break at the first opportunity.

CHAPTER IV

WARREN HASTINGS—(*continued*)

In the midst of his anxieties concerning the war in Southern India, Hastings found himself involved in fresh troubles nearer home. The conflicting claims of the Company's civil servants and the Crown judges in Bengal to jurisdiction over the natives beyond Calcutta, had brought him for a time into direct collision with the Supreme Court, headed by his best friend, Sir Elijah Impey. A war of writs on the one hand, of proclamations on the other, raged between the two parties. Arrests, resisted by the Company's soldiers acting under Hastings' orders, were enforced by the Calcutta judges with the help of sailors and policemen hired for the purpose. Hastings forbade the Bengal Zamindars from obeying the decrees of a court whose claims appeared to clash with the higher interests of the State. The Chief Justice in his turn issued summonses against the Governor-General and his Council, a proceeding which the latter laughed to scorn. Stories of outrages committed on either side were rife throughout the country, and the whole machinery of government was fast approaching a dead-lock.

Happily, just before the departure of Francis, the quarrel was appeased by a timely movement on Hastings' part. The Sadr Dewāni Adālat, or chief civil court of Bengal, as reformed by Hastings a few months earlier, was placed before the end of 1780 under the charge of Impey himself. The wisdom of this step soon became clear. An able lawyer and an upright judge, Impey at once drew up a simple and serviceable code of rules for the better administration of civil justice throughout Bengal. The young English judges in the lower courts soon learned to mend their ways and shape their judgments in careful accordance with the principles laid down by their new chief. The old broils between rival authorities came to an end; law and order reigned once more throughout the province; waste lands were brought again under the plough; and revenue began to flow with its former freedom into the Company's treasury.

This stroke of policy on the part of Hastings was hailed at the time by the Court of Directors with their hearty approval. But ere long their ears were poisoned by slanders emanating from the spiteful Francis, who, leaving India at the end of 1780, had carried his rancour and a goodly fortune home. In the course of 1782 they decreed the removal of Impey from a post whose burdens he had meanwhile borne with signal credit, at his own unaided cost.* A few months afterwards, his enemies at home had succeeded in carrying through the House of Commons a vote for the absolute recall of a Chief Justice who had ventured to take office under the Company while yet a servant of the Crown.

Meanwhile Hastings, pressed for money to carry on the war with Haidar, had demanded from his feudatory, the Raja of Benāres, a special aid of £50,000 and 2000 horse. Chait Singh's evasive answers failed to soften the heart of a Governor who had good reason to believe in the Raja's power to meet so moderate a demand. Not till Hastings approached Benāres in August, 1781, did Chait

* Through his acceptance of this further office, "the Chief Justice," says Macaulay, "was rich, quiet, and infamous." Unluckily for the brilliant essayist, the fact is that Impey refused the additional £5000 a-year which the Calcutta Council would gladly have paid him for the additional work.

Singh strive to avert his anger by begging him to take twenty lakhs of rupees—£200,000—in payment of all claims. Hastings sternly insisted on fifty lakhs. A few days afterwards, on reaching Benāres with an escort of native troops, he placed the Raja under arrest. The people of the city rose upon the Sepoy guard, and slew them almost to a man. Chait Singh, escaping across the river, called his followers to arms. In that hour of supreme peril, with only half a hundred Sepoys between him and the insurgent rabble of a great city, Hastings quietly gave the last touches to his treaty with Sindhia. Faithful messengers, stealing out of Benāres, carried his orders to the nearest military posts in Bengal. At the first opportune moment, he himself withdrew to the fortress of Chunār, to await the issue of his plans for suppressing the revolt.

Defeated in the field, Chait Singh fled at last into Bundelkhand. His stronghold of Bijagarh fell into the hands of Major Popham, the conqueror of Gwalior, and the booty found there was divided among our troops. The bulk of Chait Singh's wealth, however, had followed him into his place of exile; and the Governor-General, balked of his prey, consoled himself by exacting a larger tribute from the prince whom he set up in his uncle's room.

Hastings was yet at Chunār, when a new way of replenishing his drained exchequer was opened to him by the treaty which he concluded with Asaf-ud-daula, the Nawāb of Oudh. By this arrangement, the one dark spot, perhaps, in a bright career, the property which the Oudh Bēgams, the widow and mother of the late Nawāb, had unjustly retained for their own use six years before, was now escheated to its rightful owner, the Nawāb himself. Of this sum at least half a million was paid into the Bengal treasury in acquittal of the Nawāb's debts to the

Bengal Government. It was believed, indeed, by Hastings himself that the despoiled princesses had conspired against him with Chait Singh; but the grounds for such an indictment have only recently been fully ascertained, and the harsh measures taken by the Nawāb to enforce his claims redounded, unfairly, to the discredit of Hastings himself.* The money thus obtained, on whatever pretexts, enabled Hastings to carry on the war with Mysore and to complete his successful dealings with the Marāthas.

By this time the reign of the great Governor-General was drawing to its close. Censured by the Court of Directors for his share in the dethronement of Chait Singh and the plundering of the Oudh Bēgams, opposed once more by the members of his own Council, Hastings at length prepared to throw up his thankless post. Before carrying out his purpose, he visited Lucknow in 1784, and, in compliance with orders received from England, compelled the Nawāb-Wazir to reinstate the Bēgams in the forfeited jāgīrs. When all the more pressing affairs of his government had been duly settled, he issued farewell letters to all the native princes, handed over the keys of Fort William to his successor, Mr. Macpherson, and on the 8th February, 1785, sped by the good wishes of admiring thousands, he sailed away from the country which he had ruled for thirteen years, amidst every kind of danger, vexation, and discouragement, with a vigour, wisdom, self-reliance, and general mastery of his means, unsurpassed, if it has ever since been equalled, in the annals of British India.†

* One of the Bēgams was alive, hearty, and "very rich" in 1803, when Lord Valentia visited Lucknow. ("Memoirs of Sir E. Impey," p. 236.)

† In Hastings the scholar was largely blended with the statesman. A steady patron of Eastern learning, he spoke the languages of India with ease, and was deeply versed in Arabic and Persian literature. Ignorant himself

The welcome which Hastings at first received in England was not unworthy of his high deserts. At Court he was treated with every mark of respect. Of His Majesty's ministers, Pitt alone viewed the great Viceroy with unfriendly eyes, and declined to recommend him for the peerage he had so fairly earned. His services were acknowledged by the Court of Directors in a formal sitting, at which no voice was raised against him. He soon found a seat in the House of Commons. But rest from further trouble was not yet to be his lot. Pitt's Ministry had just succeeded in carrying the famous India Bill of 1784, which placed the Court of Directors under the general control of a board composed of privy councillors, headed by a Minister of the Crown. If any traces of political power still remained in the hands of the Directors, the Court of Proprietors ceased to have any direct voice in the government of India. Under this arrangement Hastings lost the help of his most serviceable friends; and in Parliament his enemies were neither few nor powerless. At their head was the eloquent and high-souled Burke himself, supported by Fox, Sheridan, and all the strength of the Whigs. In the background stood his inveterate foe, Sir Philip Francis, who furnished the Whig leaders with an ample store of arguments, fair or foul, for the coming attack. What friends Hastings might still number on the Tory side of the House were all too weak to make head against the hostile influences wielded by their great leader, Pitt.

Early in June, 1785, Burke opened his campaign against the late Governor-General, who had landed in England but a few days before. In April of the following year his list of charges was laid before the Commons'

of Sanskrit, he encouraged the study of it among his countrymen, and his influence led the Pandits of Bengal to teach English scholars the classical lore of ancient India.

A VIEW OF THE TRIAL OF WARREN HASTINGS, BEFORE THE COURT OF PEERS IN WESTMINSTER HALL.

P. 254

House. In the matter of the Rohilla war, Pitt sided with the friends of Hastings; but when the treatment of Chait Singh came up for discussion, he was found voting with the majority in favour of the motion brought up by Fox. On the charge concerning the Oudh Bēgams, memorable for Sheridan's masterpiece of fiery rhetoric, Pitt once more threw his vote and influence into the scale against Hastings.

At last, in February, 1788, the final impeachment of the great English proconsul was begun before the assembled peers of England by Burke himself. For seven years the trial dragged on, until in April, 1795, Hastings found himself acquitted on every charge by a majority always large, sometimes overwhelming, of the twenty-nine peers who came to record their votes. He left their presence with a clear character, but an almost empty purse, the great bulk of his moderate savings having gone to meet the expenses of his long trial. But the timely grant of a liberal pension by the Court of Directors enabled him to spend his declining years in comfort and scholarly ease on the ancestral estate of Daylesford, which had been lost to his family for more than seventy years. Long afterwards, in 1813, when the charter of the East India Company was to be renewed, Hastings, now in his eighty-second year, once more presented himself at the bar of the House of Commons. This time, however, he came, not as an arraigned criminal, but as a witness who had weighty things to say on many questions of Indian Government. The Commons, who had greeted his entrance with admiring cheers, rose and uncovered when he withdrew. Other tokens of respect and honour awaited him elsewhere, in London, Oxford, and at Court. He was made a member of the Privy Council, a doctor of laws; the Prince Regent presented him to his royal guests, the Emperor of Russia and the King of Prussia, in whose train he went to

Oxford; and the hope of yet higher honours once more dawned upon him. But the half-promised peerage was still deferred; and in 1818 the white-haired statesman quietly breathed his last at Daylesford, in the eighty-sixth year of a life whose peaceful ending could hardly have been foregathered from its stormy noon.

Before his departure from India, Hastings had ordered the Government of Madras to annul the agreement which placed the revenues of the Carnatic at their entire disposal. Against this act of well-meant but doubtful policy, Lord Macartney fought for a time with much success. But a fresh order from Dundas, the first President of the new Board of Control, overrode the policy upheld by Lord Macartney and sanctioned by the India House. Sir John Macpherson, who was acting in the room of Hastings, shrank from disobeying the commands of Dundas; and the revenues, which in English hands would have been turned to good account, were at length surrendered into those of a spendthrift prince who owed everything he had to English support and forbearance. The result of this step was to enrich a number of greedy adventurers, native and European, who had lent money to the Nawāb at enormous interest, and screwed untold profits out of the large estates assigned them in partial payment of their claims.

Sir John Macpherson continued to hold office until the autumn of 1786, when Lord Cornwallis, a statesman and soldier of some merit during the war with our American colonies, took up the reins of power at Calcutta. Sir John's government, if not otherwise eventful, had been marked by his stern refusal to pay chauth to the Marāthas for Bengal, and by his undoubted success in reducing the public outlay. In Southern India a brief war between Tipu and the Marāthas ruffled for a time the general peace; and Sindhia in the north was already scheming to overthrow the last relics of Mughal rule around Delhi. But not till after the landing of Sir John's successor did the old storm of war and general tumult burst forth again with a fury which English guns and bayonets alone could check.

CHAPTER V

LORD CORNWALLIS—1786–1793

LIKE many of his successors, Lord Cornwallis landed in India full of wise resolutions against war and conquest, and eager only to ensure peace and good government in the dominions entrusted to his charge. For a time his efforts were rewarded with success. Armed with powers which Hastings would have envied,* he put down abuses with a stern hand, raised the salaries of the civil servants and set his face like a flint against every kind of jobbery and crooked dealing. The Nawāb-Wazir of Oudh was sharply lectured for his shortcomings as a ruler; but his future payments to the Calcutta treasury were curtailed by more than a third, and his general right to mismanage his own affairs, and waste his revenues, if he chose, in riotous living, was carefully respected.

By this time Cornwallis availed himself of the peace lately renewed between Tipu and his neighbours, to enforce his claim to the Guntūr Circars, in pursuance of a treaty made with the Nizām in 1768. For several years after the death of Basalat Jung, his brother, on this or that pretext, had kept the province in his own hands. At length, in 1788, seeing that Cornwallis would brook no further trifling, Nizām Ali yielded up the disputed territory, with a blandly expressed reminder of his own claims

* Cornwallis was empowered by Pitt's "Declaratory Act" to disregard the votes of his Council.

under the treaty of 1768. At the same time, the wily son of Chīn Kilich sounded the Sultān of Mysore about forming a league against the English. Tipu's ready assent was burdened by an offer of marriage with the Nizām's daughter. Wrath at the very notion of such an alliance with the son of a low-born adventurer gave the Nizām a timely motive for withdrawing from a perilous path, and making the best terms he could with the English Government. It was idle to hope for immediate possession of a province conquered by Haidar, and firmly held by his son: but Cornwallis undertook to hand the Bālaghāt over to the Nizām, whenever it might fall into English keeping, and promised to aid that monarch at need, under the terms of the old treaty, against all common foes.

Tipu's hatred of the English was not lessened by this new proof of their readiness to meet his movements half-way. To blame Cornwallis for taking these precautions would be alike unfair to his known character and the circumstances of a critical time. He knew that the fierce bigot who inherited all Haidar's schemes of conquest was only waiting for the right moment to avenge himself on the power which had thus far prevented him from carrying his arms all over Southern India. His attack on Travancore in the last days of 1789, in defiance of the treaty which placed its Raja under our protection, compelled Cornwallis to take up the challenge thus flung in his very face.

A joint treaty for defence and offence between the English, the Nizām, and the Pēshwa, was the answer promptly given to that challenge. Fifteen thousand Englishmen and Sepoys, under General Meadows, opened the campaign on the side of Madras. In spite of hindrances caused by the wretched Madras Government, Meadows worked his way round by Coimbatore into the Mysore highlands, and carried in September the strong fort of Pālghāt. The

Marāthas on their part had not been idle, nor the English column despatched from Bombay. Tipu, on the other hand, watched with a tiger's cunning for the moment when he might catch his foe unready or asleep. Such a moment came when Colonel Floyd's column, too far from its supports, was driven backwards with the loss of several guns. But the wily Sultān was already overmatched in fighting-power. A strong division from Bengal reinforced Meadows in November. On the Malabar side, Colonel Hartley added to the laurels he had won ten years before by routing the Mysore troops, many times his own numbers, under the walls of Calicut. The reduction of Cannanore by Abercrombie cut Tipu off from his last stronghold on the western coast.

Next year Cornwallis himself, displacing the worthy but not too brilliant Meadows, set out at the head of a powerful army from Madras. Misleading Tipu by a series of feints, he made his way into Mysore without firing a shot. On the 21st March, Bangalore surrendered, in spite of Tipu's efforts to relieve it. The Nizām, who had hitherto done little for the common cause, now joined the English with 10,000 horsemen, gaily apparelled but nearly useless. As for the Marāthas, they never appeared at the right moment. Cornwallis, however, pressed on towards Seringapatam, through a country stripped beforehand of all supplies. On the 13th May he confronted Tipu strongly posted on the ridge of Arikēra with the Cauvery on his right. By a well-planned night-march he turned the enemy's flank, and the battle of the following day resulted in a victory which might have placed the capital of Mysore at the victor's mercy. But the troops were already starving, disease was fast thinning their ranks, and of the Marāthas nothing had been heard. At last, on the 26th, the victorious army began its retreat towards Bangalore. A few hours later our Marātha allies came up with the retiring columns, in good time to assuage their hunger, but too late to check their backward march.

The rest of that year was spent by our troops in conquering the Bāramahal on the eastern frontier of Mysore, and in the capture of Nandidrūg, Savandrūg, and other hill-forts which native armies had been wont to besiege in vain. Our native allies were also busy worrying Tipu's northern frontiers. Coimbatore, on the other hand, after a long and manful defence under Lieutenant Chalmers, fell at last, a mere heap of ruins, into the hands of the Sultan, who rewarded its brave defenders by carrying them off to prison in wanton breach of his pledged word.

At length, in January, 1792, Cornwallis led a fine army of 22,000 men with ninety guns against Seringapatam. Reinforced by contingents from his native allies, he planted himself on the 5th February in front of Tipu's last great stronghold. A night-attack, skilfully planned and brilliantly carried through, left him master of the outworks on the morning of the 7th, and gave his troops a commanding foothold on the island in the Cauvery, where stood the city itself. On the 16th, Abercrombie's Bombay column came up to complete the circle of attack; and the fierce Sultān, already frightened at the progress made by the English batteries, and disheartened by the panic among his own followers, saw no escape from utter ruin save in accepting such terms as the English General might choose to enforce. On the 22nd February Tipu learned his fate. The price of his submission was to be the forfeiture of half his kingdom, the surrender of two sons as hostages, and the payment of three crores of rupees—about £3,000,000—towards the expenses of the war. His proud spirit fought for a time against his better judgment; but every voice in his council urged submission, and Tipu sullenly gave way. On the 24th he put his seal to the first draft of the treaty which was to cripple his power for ever. Next day his sons were received with all honour in the English camp.

A sudden check to the progress of the treaty was caused by the Governor-General's somewhat tardy effort to rescue the friendly little state of Coorg from Tipu's clutches. For some days it seemed as if the wrathful Sultān would stake everything on resistance to this new demand. But the counter-movements of the English army soon brought him into a calmer frame of mind; and on the 19th March his sons presented to Lord Cornwallis the ratified treaty which placed Coorg, Dindigul, Malabar, and the Bāramahal thenceforth in English hands. A large slice of Tipu's northern frontier along the Tungabhadra was shared between our native allies, who also received each a million of the money fine exacted from Mysore. Thus hemmed in by strong neighbours on every side, the humbled son of Haidar Ali might chafe at the shattering of all his dearest hopes, and brood over schemes of vengeance on his English conquerors. But turn which way he would, failure and disappointment were still to be his lot; and the only light which thenceforth shone upon his darkness was the baleful reflection of his own wounded pride, savage bigotry, and undying hate.

The Marātha gains in Southern India were as nothing to the progress meanwhile made by Māhadajī Sindhia in the north. By the treaty of Sālbai that able and ambitious ruler had been raised to the rank of an independent sovereign. Already the foremost native power in Hindustān, he was bent on rising yet higher, on wiping out the last traces of Marātha failure at Pānipat. His opportunity soon came. Delhi was again torn by rival factions, and the leader of one of them implored his help in the name of his helpless sovereign. Sindhia gladly accepted the offer, and the death of him who had made it soon left him master of the position. For the Pēshwa of Poona, as head of the Marātha League, he obtained from Shah Alam the title of Regent of the Empire. As deputy for the Pēshwa, he himself took charge of the Imperial government, with the supreme command of the Imperial armies, for whose maintenance the revenues of Agra and Delhi were entrusted to his sole keeping.

For the next few years the bold Marātha was engaged in strengthening the foundations of his new sway. His enemies around Delhi were neither few nor weak. The proud Muhammadan nobles chafed under the ascendancy of an upstart Hindu. The high-born princes of Rājputāna begrudged the payment to a Sūdra adventurer of the tribute claimed for the Mughal. His rival, Holkar, bore him no good-will, and the Court of Poona dreaded the soaring ambition of their self-appointed deputy. A powerful weapon, however, was already forging for Sindhia's benefit. With the help of Count de Boigne, a Savoyard who had lately entered his service,* he got together a disciplined force of 20,000 men, mostly infantry, officered largely by Europeans, and strengthened by a formidable array of guns. To the sturdy courage of these troops and the skill of their leaders he owed his final deliverance from more than one perilous strait. Defeated by the Rājputs and hard pressed by the Muhammadans in 1787, he looked in vain for help towards Poona, and was fain to seek timely shelter with the Jāt prince of Bharatpur. Ere long, the foolish old emperor himself took open part against his defeated minister.

But Sindhia's turn for triumph came at last. His defeat of Ismael Beg under the walls of Agra, in June, 1788, paved the way for his return to Delhi. He was still

* This adventurer, after serving in the French and Russian armies, became an ensign in the 6th Sepoy Battalion at Madras. Thence he went round to Calcutta, was employed by Hastings on an embassy to Delhi in 1784, and finally took service under Māhadajī Sindhia.

loitering on his road thither, when he heard of the horrible outrages inflicted on the emperor and his household by the ruffianly grandson of the able and upright Najib-ud-daula, who had fought so bravely for the Mughal at Pānipat. This Rohilla savage, Gholām Kādir by name, had retreated to Delhi in company with Ismael Beg. The frightened emperor closed the gates of the city on his defeated allies; but Gholām Kādir bribed his way in, and a Muhammadan army was once more loosed for plunder in the Mughal capital. Disappointed, it seems, of the treasures he had hoped to find within the palace, and enraged beyond bearing at his repeated failures to search out an imaginary secret, the pitiless ruffian put the Princes of Delhi to the torture in the presence of the emperor himself.* In the depth of his anguish the old man cried out, "Take my sight rather than force upon it scenes like these!" In a moment, Gholām Kādir sprang upon his victim, pinned him to the floor, and blinded him with his own dagger. But his hour of triumph was soon to be cut short. On the appearance of De Boigne's battalions before Delhi, he fled thence, after a vain attempt to fire the palace. On his subsequent flight from Meerut he fell into the hands of Sindhia's horsemen, and his crimes were requited by Sindhia's order with the poetic justice of a horrible and lingering death.†

Thenceforth the deputy's greatness knew no check. He replaced the blind old emperor on the throne of Delhi; but the whole powers of government remained in his own hands, and Shah Alam became a mere pensioner on Sindhia's bounty. His old opponents, one after another,

* One of the tortured princes lived to witness as emperor the massacre of English women and children at Delhi in 1857.

† Keene's "Mughal Empire," chap. 5. The wretched man was first led through Muttra on an ass, with his face to the tail. His tongue was then torn out, his eyes blinded, his nose, ears, hands, and feet cut off; after which he was hanged upon a tree.

took arms against him only to ensure their final defeat. Too wise to embroil himself in a second war with the English, he yet steadily set his face against the policy which led his countrymen in Southern India to aid Cornwallis in humbling Tipu. At length, when all was peaceful in Hindustān, Sindhia set out for Poona in 1792 to invest the young Pēshwa, Madhu Rāo, with the dignity thrice conferred on him by the head of the house of Bābur. Such at least was the outward purpose of his journey; but in all likelihood his real aim was to counteract the intrigues of Nāna Farnavīs, and render his own influence supreme in Southern as well as Northern India.

The Pēshwa's investiture was the most splendid ceremony which Poona had ever seen. Sindhia himself rode upon his elephant at the head of a gorgeous retinue; but with an artful show of humility he took the lowest place among the assembled chiefs. When the Pēshwa would have placed him on the seat next his own, he displayed a pair of embroidered slippers, in token of the office he had inherited from his father, and reverently placed them on the Pēshwa's feet. With well-feigned reluctance he at length took the seat of honour which none there present had nearly so good a right to fill.

From that time his Brahman rival, Nāna Farnavīs, began to lose all hold on the youth in whose name he had hitherto governed without a check. Another heavy defeat inflicted on Holkar by De Boigńe left Sindhia virtual master of nearly all India, outside the English possessions and the few native states which owned the English for their allies. In despair at his own darkening prospects the Nāna was about to give up the struggle by retiring to Benāres, when Sindhia's death from fever in February, 1794, removed out of his path the only danger he had hitherto failed to overcome.

By this time Cornwallis himself had disappeared from

the scene of his past labours. But he left behind him a legacy whose value, however highly rated by the statesmen of his own day, has long been regarded by a large class of thinkers with less approving eyes. If the boldness of his foreign policy, in spite of its success, brought him into discredit with a small but noisy class of politicians at home,* his great measure for settling the land revenues of Bengal was hailed by the bulk of his own countrymen with a satisfaction largely owing to his well-earned fame as an upright, clear-headed, successful governor. It is needless here to discuss the question whether private property in land was or was not unknown to Indian usage, and contrary to the spirit of Indian laws.† For the present purpose it is enough to say, that the rents from land in India had come to be divided between the village communities, the *Zamindars* and *Talūkdars*, who farmed the revenues of their several districts, and the State itself, which claimed from one-half to three-fifths of the yearly produce from the soil. In Bengal the rights of the old village communities had been swallowed up in the growing power of the Zamindars or middlemen, whom Hastings everywhere found claiming entire ownership of the land their fathers had mostly held on lease. The ousted Rayats or husbandmen had become mere tenants at will of the usurping Zamindars. These latter Lord Cornwallis had from the first been enjoined to treat, for fiscal purposes, as the only rightful lords of the soil.

Accordingly in 1789 a new assessment of the land-revenue was carried out for ten years on the terms prescribed by the Court of Directors. In 1793 this

* Sir Philip Francis, Hastings' old enemy, was at the head of them.

† The true theory seems to be that private property in land had always been the rule in India, limited only by the sovereign's immemorial right to a certain share in the produce of the soil. The whole question is clearly handled in "Notes on the North-Western Provinces of India," by a "District Officer." (See also the works of Mr. B. H. Baden-Powell.)

settlement was declared perpetual. In spite of the reasons urged against such a measure by Mr. Shore, and other men of long Indian experience, it was decreed that thenceforth the Zamindars of Bengal were to hold their lands for ever at the rent-rates charged upon them in 1789. Three things were involved in this momentous enactment. The Zamindars were formally acknowledged as lords of the soil. The rent-charge on their estates was fixed for ever at a certain rate. And lastly the rate itself was taken at a fixed sum of money, without reference to future changes in the selling value of land and its yearly harvests.

It will thus be seen that the weak points of this permanent settlement lay chiefly under the first and third heads. To turn a body of revenue-farmers into actual landowners was a measure which, however excusable and even expedient, was sure to entail some hardship on the old peasantry whose right to hold their ancestral acres was now swept away at one blow. It is true that some attempt was made to secure to the Rayats their ancient holdings by means of leases, which the Zamindars were bound as a rule to grant them at the former rents. Other steps were also taken to guard their interests from unfair encroachments on the part of their new landlords. But there, as in so many other cases, the weakest went to the wall. The new landowners abused their powers at every turn. Their luckless tenants found their leases withheld, their rents raised under any pretext, their goods liable to distraint without any notice, and themselves ground down by ever new and illegal demands.* To the courts of justice they were free to appeal; but what justice could they hope to win, even if they had the means of seeking it,

* It was not till some years afterwards that the Zamindar was compelled to give due notice of his intention to distrain, and was forbidden to seize the Rayat's cattle and farming tools. Kaye's "East India Company," part ii. chap. 2.

against oppressors powerful from their rank, wealth, and readiness to gain their own ends by any means, however crooked? Every avenue to legal redress was blocked up by pilfering policemen and venal underlings of the law, by whose influence the eyes of well-meaning English magistrates were too often blinded to the truth.

The Zamindars, on the other hand, might plead some excuse for wrong-doing in the high rates at which they were assessed by the government, and the summary powers of sale under which the government demands were enforced. It is certain that under the new system many of their estates were brought to the hammer, and that in 1799 some attempt was made to abate the evil effects of summary sales, by a rule which decreed that sales of land for arrears of revenue should be deferred to the end of each year. It was also alleged that a defaulting Rayat could sometimes evade the demands of a needy or grasping landlord more easily than the latter could put off his payments to the State. On the whole, however, it is pretty clear that the balance of wrong-doing, as Sir John Kaye puts it, "must have been greatly on the side of the Zamindar." He and his agents were far more likely to plunder and oppress the Rayat, than the Rayat, for all his cunning, was likely to outwit them.

If undue haste was shown in fixing the new settlement for ever, before the question of land-tenures in Bengal had been thoroughly sifted and the value of the land assessed had been clearly ascertained, it was still more unfortunate that the boon of a fixed assessment should have been clogged by the State's surrender of its prescriptive right to readjust the land-tax to its own fiscal needs in the future. The main source of revenue in India had always been the land. A certain share of the landholder's yearly profits, whether payable in kind or coin, had been taken by successive governments, Hindu or Muhammadan, for the public use. According as the land rose in value, or the purchasing power of money declined, the State charge on the land was also raised. Under English rule payment in kind had gradually been replaced by payment in money; but it was left for Lord Cornwallis to fix the money payment at a rate which could never more be raised or altered. His successors were thus for ever debarred from replenishing the public purse by adjusting the land-tax to the increasing profits of those who paid it. Had the money payments been fixed at a given proportion to the average rental of the land from time to time, the land revenue of Bengal would now have been double what it is, and the government would not be driven to devise new and often questionable means of taxation in order to arrest the gradual decline of its old fiscal resources.

In some respects, however, the new settlement worked well. After a season of dire confusion and distress, during which many old families passed away from their ancient holdings, or tilled as mere serfs the fields which had once been theirs, while many even of the Zamindars were sold out of the estates conferred on them by English rulers, a new class of landed gentry, enriched by trade and money-lending, rose upon the wrecks of their neighbours' fortunes into a position of assured importance, if not of much political power. Waste lands were gradually brought under the plough; the growing wealth of the province encouraged the growth of its population, and opened out new channels of trade and industry, as well as new sources of public income. If the land-revenue showed no sensible increase, its collection at any rate became easier and the amount less fluctuating. All this, however, might have happened under a system of periodical settlements. Meanwhile, whoever else profited, the Rayats were mostly on the losing side. Their rents were raised without mercy by their new masters, their old rights over-ridden without scruple, and new exactions levied on them at every turn.*

Another important measure carried out by Lord Cornwallis was the reform of the civil and criminal courts. The duties of revenue-collector were for the first time separated from those of the civil judge. Civil courts for the trial of native suits were established in every district. In the criminal courts of each district the higher civil judges held their sessions at different places in turn.† Sir Elijah Impey's Code of Regulations was re-modelled but hardly improved by the addition of intricate rules and idle formalities. Yet more unfortunate was the ordinance which shut out the natives of India from all but the lowest ranks in the public service. The highest office to which a native could thenceforth aspire was that of a police Darogah on twenty-five rupees a month, or that of a Mūnsif or petty judge, who obtained only a small percentage on the cost of civil suits. The good thus wrought in one direction was counterbalanced by evil in another. If a higher moral tone began thenceforth to prevail among the English servants of the Company, their native underlings were driven to eke out their scanty wages by every form of jobbing and extortion. Let the English magistrate be never so upright, he had no means of checking the corrupt tendencies of ill-paid subordinates, who abused to their own profit the power which many circumstances combined to place in their hands. Whatever good might come of English example in high places, it

* "Not a child can be born," wrote the Joint Magistrate of Rangpur in 1815, "not a head religiously shaved, not a son married, not a daughter given in marriage, not even one of the tyrannical fraternity dies, without an immediate visitation of calamity upon the Rayat." On every such occasion the Zamindar or his agent levied a fresh tax on the Rayat's goods. (Raikes's "Notes on the North-Western Provinces of India.")

† Muhammadan law, tempered by English punishments, was still to be administered in Bengal.

Emery Walker, Ltd. photographer.

THE MARQUESS CORNWALLIS, K.G.

FROM THE PAINTING BY THOMAS GAINSBOROUGH, R.A., IN THE NATIONAL PORTRAIT GALLERY

p. 270

was clearly unwise to block up all those avenues to preferment by which the ambition of the higher classes in the country had been wont to seek its natural food.

Before leaving India Lord Cornwallis sailed for Madras in order to command the force he had got together for the siege of Pondicherry, a task imposed upon him by the outbreaking of another war with France. But the timely surrender of that place to Colonel Braithwaite left him free to pursue his voyage homewards, in October, 1793, after a useful, firm, and prosperous reign of seven years. He was succeeded by Sir John Shore, a Bengal civilian of long standing, high character, and approved conversance with revenue affairs.

CHAPTER VI

SIR JOHN SHORE AND MARQUESS WELLESLEY—1793-1800

THE new Governor-General had not long taken up the reins of empire, when a storm of war once more burst upon Southern India. At the death of Māhadajī Sindhia the Marātha power may be said to have reached its zenith. His nephew and successor, Daulat Rāo Sindhia, was still a boy; but Nāna Farnavīs once more reigned at Poona without a rival, and his influence made itself felt from the foot of the Himālayas to the southernmost bounds of Māhārashtra. Quick to avail himself of Sir John Shore's inaction in the field of foreign politics, he began to make threatening demands upon the Nizām, who turned for help to the English Government under the treaty of 1790. But Shore could see no reason for helping one old ally against another, and the Marāthas took their own way unchecked.

Early in 1795 the hostile armies took the field. A hundred and thirty thousand Marāthas, gathered from all parts of India, followed the standard of the young Pēshwa, himself under the actual leadership of Pareshrām Bhao, while the Nizām's forces, 110,000 strong, included a contingent disciplined by French officers under M. Raymond, who had served with Lally many years before. Sindhia's contingent on the Marātha side was also commanded by a Frenchman, M. Perron. The battle which ensued on the 11th March at Kharda, on the Nizām's western frontier, was lost to the Muhammadans mainly by the cowardice of

Nizām Ali himself. Two days afterwards the defeated monarch put his seal to a treaty which condemned him to pay the victors three millions sterling and yield up territory worth £350,000 a year.

The wily minister, Nāna Farnavīs, had now reached the height of his power. Supreme at the court of his nominal master, he was held in awe at every capital where ruled a prince of the great Marātha League. Even the young Sindhia paid him the deference due from youth to a successful veteran in the field of statescraft. But the fate which had frowned so darkly on him a year before the victory of Kharda was ere long to hold him fast in its toils. In October, 1795, the young Pēshwa, Madhu Rāo, slew himself in a fit of despair at the utter thraldom in which his all-powerful minister was bent on keeping him at an age when other princes were deemed fit to govern for themselves. The rightful heir to his throne was Bājī Rāo, son of that Raghuba whose chequered fortunes had closed in peace and privacy after the Treaty of Sālbai. Distrustful of the Nāna's real purpose, Bājī Rāo secretly applied for help to Daulat Rāo Sindhia. When this became known at Poona, the Nāna, who had just been plotting on behalf of Bājī's younger brother, Chimnajī, suddenly resolved to forestal Sindhia by espousing the cause of Bājī himself. The game of intrigue which followed has no parallel even in the history of Marātha politics. As a thing of course Sindhia and the Nāna take opposite sides, and change them whenever it suits their purpose. At one moment the Nāna is an exile and Bājī a prisoner. Ere long the former gains the upper hand, and Bājī Rāo is seated on the throne, which his brother had meanwhile occupied against his own will. Sindhia turns against his own nominee, and casts his own minister, Balloba Tantia, into prison. Bājī Rāo then plots the ruin both of Sindhia and Nāna Farnavīs. The former escapes death through

Bājī's timely indecision, but the latter is treacherously seized, with Sindhia's connivance, and hurried off a close prisoner to Ahmadnagar, whence he is afterwards set free by Sindhia on payment of a heavy bribe.

Meanwhile Sir John Shore had been engaged in dealing with a serious mutiny among the officers of the Company's Indian army. The soreness caused by the late improvements in the pay of the Civil Service, and by the threatened amalgamation of the king's and Company's troops, spoke out at last in a combined movement of the aggrieved officers for their own protection from alleged encroachments on their just rights. Daunted by the growing danger, or loath to use force against men whose claims he could not deem unjust, the Governor-General gave way. The double batta, which had lately been withheld from the Company's troops, was restored in full; brevet rank was largely granted; and an improved scale of pay for officers of every rank was drawn up. Shore's concessions so displeased Dundas, that he besought Lord Cornwallis to return at once to his former post; but the "milk-and-water" policy of the Court of Directors towards their mutinous servants speedily decided him to refuse the offer, and Sir John Shore's concessions were finally confirmed.

If Sir John laid himself open to the charge of acting weakly on this occasion, a later conjuncture showed him to be far from wanting in quiet courage. On the death of Asaf-ud-daula, the Nawāb-Wazir of Oudh, in 1797, he was led by faulty information to acknowledge Wazīr Ali, the Nawāb's reputed son, as his successor. But further inquiry taught him to uphold the stronger claims of Asaf's brother, Sādat Ali. That prince was therefore raised to the throne on condition of surrendering Allahābād to the English, and maintaining ten thousand of the Company's troops in Oudh. The treaty was concluded while Sir

John was yet encamped at Lucknow, in imminent danger of an attack at any moment from the numerous and reckless followers of the prince he was about to depose. But he held his ground with quiet firmness until the troops who were charged to escort the new Nawāb arrived at Lucknow. At their appearance the followers of Wazir Ali dispersed without firing a shot, and in January, 1798, Sādat Ali was proclaimed Nawāb amidst the general rejoicing of his new subjects. Wazir Ali was pensioned off at Benāres, and Shore, who had just been made Lord Teignmouth, set sail for England in March of the same year.

His successor was the Earl of Mornington, elder brother of the great Duke of Wellington, a friend and a follower of Pitt, a trained statesman from his youth up, a ripe scholar, and for four years a leading member of the Board of Control. In the middle of May, 1798, Lord Mornington landed at Calcutta, charged from home with strict injunctions to keep the peace, to abstain from meddling in the affairs of native states, and to use all lawful means of replenishing the Company's exchequer. On his way out, however, he had touched at the Cape; and there by a happy chance he had learned, through various channels, enough to convince him that a policy of peace and retrenchment was far less feasible than it seemed at home. He had not been three weeks in India when the hour for action proved to be already ripe. In a proclamation which had found its way to Calcutta, General Malartic, Governor of the Mauritius, announced that Tipu had proposed a close alliance with the new French Republic against the English in India. Other tidings from trustworthy sources strengthened Lord Mornington's newly-formed design to forestall the plotting ruler of Mysore. The Madras Government, unready as ever, was for temporising with its former foe; but Lord Mornington would take no excuse for unwise delay, and General Harris was ordered to get the Coast Army, as that of Madras was called, ready for the coming march on Seringapatam.

Meanwhile the new Governor-General set himself to win the alliance or secure the neutrality of the Marāthas and the Nizām. From the Pēshwa, whose counsels were once more guided by Nāna Farnavīs, he got little but fair words and fair assurances; nor would Sindhia pledge himself to aid the English against the threatened advance from Kābul of Ahmad Shah's successor, Zamān Shah. With the Nizām, on the other hand, Lord Mornington was more successful. By the 10th October a strong brigade from Madras was encamped at Hyderābād, and a few days later the whole of the French officers in the Nizām's service had gotten their dismissal from the Nizām himself. The twelve thousand Sepoys, whom M. Raymond had trained on the French system, laid down their arms, and the Nizām concluded a treaty which placed six thousand English Sepoys at his disposal, and made English influence for ever dominant at Hyderābād.

Tipu, on the other hand, was steadily rushing upon his doom. To all Lord Mornington's warnings, remonstrances, demands, proposals, he sent nothing but evasive or misleading answers, while he was engaged in sending messages for help to Zamān Shah, to the French Government, and to General Bonaparte, who had already landed in Egypt. Neither Nelson's great victory at Aboukir, nor the alliance of Turkey with England against the French, opened his eyes to the rock on which his consuming hatred of the English was about to hurl him. At last, by the beginning of February, 1799, the Governor-General's forbearance could hold out no longer. The English army was ordered to advance. If Tipu were yet willing to treat for peace, he might send an embassy to General Harris, who was now on the road to Seringapatam, at the head of six thousand white troops, about fifteen thousand Sepoys, and a hundred guns, to say nothing of the twenty thousand horse and foot furnished by the Nizām, and commanded in part by English officers.

"Citizen Tipu," however, as his French friends from the Mauritius called him, would not be warned in time. With the courage of his race and the craft of an old soldier, he left part of his army to watch the English advance, while he hurried westward with the flower of his troops to overwhelm Stuart and Hartley on their advance with the Bombay column from Cannanore. In spite of the timely warning received from the Raja of Coorg, it was all that Hartley's brigade could do to hold the hill of Sidasīr on the 6th March against Tipu's repeated onsets, until General Stuart could hasten up to the rescue. Half-an-hour afterwards the assailants fell back with the loss of two thousand men. A few days later the baffled Sultān went off to meet General Harris advancing by way of Bangalore.

Again defeated at Malavalli on the 27th, Tipu fell back to a strong position in front of his island capital. But the English general declined to fall into his opponent's trap. Instead of marching straight forward through a country laid waste by Tipu's orders, General Harris led his troops round across the Cauvery by a ford lower down the stream. The Bombay column was thus enabled to join him, and the troops obtained supplies from fruitful districts untouched by the ravages of war. Tipu's rage at being thus outwitted passed ere long into sheer despair as the invaders slowly neared Seringapatam.

On the 17th April the siege began. Three days later Tipu asked for terms. Two millions sterling and the cession of half his remaining dominion was the price named. His proud spirit rose in revolt against such an issue to the dreams and efforts of many years. "Better," he exclaimed, "to die fighting than live dependent on the mercy of infidels." On the 3rd May 44,000 English troops advanced under General Baird, a former prisoner in Seringapatam, to storm the city through a breach made by the English guns. A short but sharp struggle placed the stormers on the top of the breach. The two columns then turned off in opposite directions, pushing forward through every obstacle until they met again at the eastern gateway, thinned in numbers, but flushed with entire success. The Sultān's palace was in their hands, and his troops were become a flying mob. But Tipu himself could not be found. At length from amidst a gateway heaped with dead his lifeless body was dragged out under the guidance of a wounded servant, and duly recognised by one of his chief officers. It was buried the next day with all military and religious honours in the tomb which held the remains of Haidar Ali. The guns which boomed their last tribute to the brave but savage bigot who had lost all that his father had won, were strangely echoed by the dreadful thunder which crashed that evening over Seringapatam.

The loss of the English in this memorable siege amounted to 1,164 killed or wounded. A vast store of guns and booty to the value of a million sterling fell into the victors' hands. General Harris was raised to the peerage, and Lord Mornington became Marquess Wellesley in the peerage of Ireland, an honour which he regarded as no more than a "double-gilt potato," in return for the blow thus stricken at the fiercest enemy our arms had ever encountered in Southern India. Part of Tipu's conquered kingdom was divided between the English and the Nizām, Bājī Rāo having declined the conditions on which he also would have received his share. The remainder was reserved under English commissioners for the child-heir of the former Raja, whom Haidar Ali had dispossessed. Tipu's family were removed as state-pensioners to Vellore. Seringapatam itself was placed under the wise control of Colonel Arthur Wellesley, who, as commander of the Nizām's infantry, had borne a prominent part in the siege.

If the timely triumph of our arms in Mysore had crushed one foe, it deferred the day of settlement with another. While General Harris was besieging Seringapatam, Sindhia and the Pēshwa were plotting to aid Tipu and hamper the English by an inroad into the dominions of Nizām Ali. But the happy issue of Lord Wellesley's vigour and his General's soldiership struck them with alarm, and they hastened to congratulate the Governor-General on successes which not only deprived them of a useful ally, but established a closer union between the Nizām, their intended victim, and the English, their most dreaded rivals. A year after the conquest of Mysore, the Nizām's immunity from Marātha aggression was finally assured by a treaty which placed at his disposal a strong Sepoy contingent, commanded by English officers, in exchange for his share of the country won from Tipu in the last nine years.

Another blow to Marātha influence had meanwhile been dealt by Lord Wellesley. In 1799 the little State of Tanjore, founded by Shahjī, father of the great Sīvajī, in the middle of the previous century, passed under English rule with the consent of its rightful Raja, who retained the outward show of a sovereignty whose burdens were transferred to his English friends. A like course was taken with the little Muhammadan State of Surat. This was presently followed by the absorption of the Carnatic, whose late Nawāb, the son of our old nominee Muhammad Ali, had been caught secretly plotting with our deadliest enemy, the late Sultan of Mysore. His successor refusing the terms offered by Lord Wellesley, a titular Nawāb was set up in his cousin's place on a handsome pension, but without a shadow of his grandfather's power. Strong-handed measures these may be called; but no one who has carefully read the foregoing narrative need shrink from allowing to Lord Wellesley and his masters at home the full benefit of the pleas on which those measures were carried out. Had English statesmen been less scrupulous the Carnatic might fairly have been absorbed many years earlier, whether as a stroke of policy or an act of justice. Our countrymen in India had long been drifting into a position from which they could never with any safety recede. Each step forward in self-defence brought them nearer some new danger, with which common prudence forbade them to palter on pain of losing the ground already won. It was Lord Wellesley's great merit, that, foreseeing the danger, he at once proceeded to pluck from that nettle the flower of safety. Knowing that the last great struggle with the Marāthas must soon come, he took care that the rulers of British India should not be drawn into it unprepared or half-hearted. With him at any rate forewarned was to be forearmed.

BOOK V

THE ENGLISH PARAMOUNT

CHAPTER I

MARQUESS WELLESLEY—TO 1805

NOT long after the conquest of Mysore the peace of the kingdom was for a while disturbed by the movements of Dhūndia Wāgh, a Marātha freebooter, who, with the help of a few thousand horsemen recruited from Tipu's army, defied or baffled his pursuers, until Colonel Arthur Wellesley, in September, 1800, brought him to bay. With the utter rout of Dhūndia's force and the death of its leader ended a rising which, but for Wellesley's unflagging pursuit, might have involved the Deccan in grave disorders at a very critical time. Lord Wellesley's hands indeed were just then full of work. A strong force of Europeans and Sepoys under General Baird was shipped off to aid the Turks in driving the French out of Egypt. Baird's march through the Desert of Suez was a feat of which any army might have been proud; and the mere announcement of his approach decided the French commander to sue for peace. But for the disloyal conduct of the English Admiral commanding in Eastern waters, Wellesley would have forestalled the conquest of the Mauritius by nine years, and most of the losses inflicted on our shipping by French privateers would thus have been prevented.

To counteract French intrigues in Persia, and to keep

Zamān Shah from troubling India, was another scheme on which Wellesley had set his heart. A native Indian Wakīl, or envoy, had already sounded the Shah of Persia, and sown dissensions between the Afghan monarch and his brother, which compelled the former to retire across the Indus, leaving Lahore, and the surrounding country under the rule of his chosen lieutenant, the great Sikh warrior Ranjīt Singh. In 1800 a splendid embassy, laden with choice gifts and friendly overtures, was led to Teherān by Captain John Malcolm, the young Sepoy officer who had disarmed the French contingent at Hyderābād and shared in Colonel Wellesley's advance to Seringapatam. The descendant of Nādir Shah readily agreed to befriend the English, commercially and politically, to the best of his power, to expel every Frenchman from Persia, and to aid his new friends in keeping all invaders from the north-west out of Hindustān.

Lord Wellesley's forecasting statesmanship had also employed itself in the direction of Oudh. After half a century of varying fortunes, the Sikh followers of Gūru Gofind had come to sway a wide tract of country from the Indus eastward to the Sīwālik Hills.* A Sikh alliance with Sindhia against the English or the Muhammadans was once more upon the cards, and the Governor-General was resolved to make Oudh contribute its due share to the maintenance of English rule against all assailants. The murder of his agent, Mr. Cherry, at Benāres by the followers of the pensioned rebel Wazīr Ali, revealed at once the political weakness of the reigning Nawāb of Oudh, and the readiness of his subjects to invite help from Kabul. Wazīr Ali was soon hunted down, but thenceforth Wellesley made up his mind to place the military defence of Oudh on a much firmer footing than heretofore.

* Cunningham's "History of the Sikhs," chap. 5.

His demands to this end—demands fully justified by the terms on which alone the Nawāb held his kingdom as an English fief—were parried for a time by evasive offers and sounding remonstrances. These in their turn were answered by a judicious mixture of threats and warnings, until, in November, 1801, Sādat Ali signed the treaty which placed under our absolute sway the districts of Kora, Allahābād, Rohilkhand, Gorakhpur, and Azamgarh, in return for the guaranteed defence of his dominions from foreign attack.*

Amidst the cares and entanglements of foreign politics, Wellesley found time for matters nearer home. His own energy braced up all around him for the work entrusted to their hands. His reforms in the Company's chief civil and criminal courts followed the lines first traced by Warren Hastings, and freed those courts from their old connection with the Calcutta Council. His encouragement of private trade between England and India in India-built ships, however gratifying to the English Ministry and advantageous to the English nation, gave sore offence to the Court of Directors, whose old dislike to "interlopers" no arguments could overcome. His noble scheme for the founding of a great college in Calcutta, at which the young "writers" destined for the Indian Civil Service might complete the training best suited alike to English gentlemen and to the future rulers of a great English dependency, was marred in its working by the same authorities, who restricted the new college to the teaching of the native languages, and founded at Haileybury a separate college for the instruction of young men going out as writers to the East. In his choice of public servants for high or difficult posts Lord Wellesley found his own efforts for the public good continually thwarted by the jobbery or the

* The Hon. Henry Wellesley, afterwards Lord Cowley, was employed by his brother to conclude the treaty.

prejudices of East India Directors at home. Annoyed at all these tokens of ill-will or blindness on the part of his official employers, he wrote home to resign his office in 1802. But the Court of Directors were loath at the last moment to lose the services of a great and successful ruler, and Wellesley was entreated to stay out in India another year.

The answer reached him early in 1803, on the eve of a decisive fight for empire between the English and the Marāthas. After the death of Nāna Farnavīs in 1800, the great Marātha power, which for so many years he had striven to weld together in the Pēshwa's name, began at once to break up under influences always active in Indian history. As with the Greeks of old and the Italians of the Middle Ages, so it happened now with the princes of Māhārashtra. The Sindhia and the Holkar of that day—the latter, Jeswant Rāo, was a bastard son of the upright and able Tūkaji—brought great armies against each other, which were defeated each in its turn. Ere long the Pēshwa, Bājī Rāo, paid with defeat and temporary exile the penalty of espousing the cause of Sindhia. A rival Pēshwa was set up in his stead. In this strait Bājī Rāo no longer rejected the English alliance on the terms already offered by Colonel Close. By the Treaty of Bassein, concluded in December, 1802, he agreed to maintain an English contingent, to assign for their support the revenues of certain districts, and to wage no war nor advance any claims on other powers without leave from the Governor-General.

In May of the following year Bājī Rāo returned to Poona under the escort of his new allies. By this well-timed stroke of policy, which made the English paramount in Southern India, Lord Wellesley strengthened his own hands for the coming struggle with his Marātha neighbours. It was not long before the collision came. Sindhia

Emery Walker, Ltd., photographers

THE MARQUESS WELLESLEY, K.G.

FROM THE PAINTING BY J. PAIN DAVIS IN THE NATIONAL PORTRAIT GALLERY

p. 281

had already formed a league with the Bhōsla Raja of Berār against the Pēshwa. Holkar still held aloof from either side, waiting to see how matters would turn out. But Sindhia's threatening movements and his insolent answer to Colonel Collins, the English Resident at his court, convinced Wellesley that no more time should be lost in idle negotiations. The Pēshwa himself, with his usual treachery, was urging Sindhia to move at once upon his capital. General Wellesley, as great in politics as in war, made one last appeal to the confederate chiefs, but in vain. At length, on the 3rd August, 1803, Collins turned his face from Sindhia's camp, and war was formally declared.

The first blow was struck by General Wellesley against Ahmadnagar, which surrendered on the 12th August, the same day on which General Lake laid siege to the fortress of Aligarh, on the road from Agra to Delhi. On the 23rd September General Wellesley, on his march from Aurangābād, found 50,000 of the enemy strongly posted around the village of Assaye. His own troops were only about 4500 in all, but their leader knew his men, and would lose no time in waiting for the rest of his army. His trained soldiers marched steadily forward across the Kaitna under a heavy fire from Sindhia's guns, overbore the sturdy resistance of Sindhia's best infantry, and carried all before them by dint of hard fighting and cool pluck. The Marātha hosts broke and fled in all directions, leaving thousands dead or wounded on the field, and ninety-eight guns with much booty in the victors' hands. This splendid victory if brought at a heavy price in killed and wounded, gave the death-blow to Sindhia's hopes in Southern India.

Meanwhile in Gujarāt one strong place after another had fallen to our arms. In the following months the province of Cuttack on the borders of Orissa was conquered from the Raja of Berar. At the same time the conqueror of Assaye was pressing forward without a check into the heart of the Raja's kingdom. The capture of Asīrgarh by Colonel Stevenson had already deprived Sindhia of his last stronghold in Khandēsh. By the victory of Argaon on the 28th November, and the subsequent capture of Gawilgarh, General Wellesley drove Ragujī Bhōsla to sue for peace, which he was fain to purchase with the cession of Cuttack, and all Berar to the west of the Wardha river.

Lake's campaign in Upper India had been equally successful. The fall of Aligarh on the 29th August, one of the most brilliant feats in the annals of war, was followed up by Lake's victorious advance on Delhi. Crushing the resistance of a Marātha force outside the capital, he entered it on the 11th, took the blind old emperor out of his prison, and once more placed him on his nominal throne. On the 10th October the Marāthas were heavily beaten near Agra, and the glorious city of Akbar and Shah Jahān surrendered a few days after to its bold assailant. On the 1st November at the village of Lāswāri occurred the hardest fight of the war. Lake's cavalry were hurled in vain against entrenchments bristling thick with guns, and defended by the flower of Sindhia's army, the trained battalions of De Boigne. At length his infantry, who had been marching ever since midnight, came upon the field, and after a brief rest swept forward on their fateful errand. Sindhia's soldiers fought like heroes, and fell in heaps around their guns. But the shattered ranks of Englishmen and Sepoys still held their way under the leader whom they loved, until the crowning victory of the war was theirs, and seventy-one guns had been counted among its fruits. Their own loss was great; but the strength of Sindhia was broken, and before the year's end he had concluded a treaty which stripped him of all his possessions between the Jumna and the Ganges, of nearly all his conquest in Rājputāna, of the districts around Broach and Ahmadnagar, and wiped out all his claims on the Pēshwa, the Gaikwar of Gujarāt, and the Nizām.

Of the provinces thus wrested from Sindhia and the Bhōsla, Cuttack was incorporated with Bengal; the Doāb between the Jumna and the Ganges became the North-Western Provinces; and the Broach district was annexed to Bombay. The fortress and district of Ahmadnagar were handed over to the double-dealing Pēshwa; and the new Nizām, who had just mounted the throne of his father Nizām Ali, was placed in possession of western Berār. Thus, in less than five months, Wellesley had overthrown the fabric of Marātha power, and placed all India from the Sutlej to Cape Comorin at the feet of an English company which less than fifty years earlier had been chased with ignominy out of Bengal. Relieved by the fruits of English valour from their forced allegiance to Marātha lords, the Jāt and Rājput princes of Rājputāna were glad to accept the milder guardianship of their English neighbours. The Sikh chiefs of Sind likewise transferred their allegiance from the Marāthas to Lord Wellesley; and the Marātha Gaikwar of Gujarāt readily placed his own dominions under the partial control of that power which alone could shield him from foreign attacks.

It only remained to deal with Holkar, whose ambition had been fed by the plunder of Sindhia's territory during the late campaign, and by the possession of an army largely recruited from the troops of his defeated rival, until he began to talk of fighting Lake for the lordship of Hindustān. At length his insolence reached so lofty a pitch, that Lord Wellesley was driven to fight him in self-defence. By the middle of April, 1804, the armies of Lake and Wellesley began moving from opposite quarters against their new foe. Holkar at once fell back from Jaipur across the Chambal, but the approach of the rainy season ere long sent Lake into cantonments ; and Colonel Murray, who commanded the southern or Gujarāt column in the absence of General Wellesley, soon followed his example. A few thousand of Lake's Sepoys under Colonel Monson still kept the field. At length that officer's rash advance into the heart of Holkar's country became seriously hindered by want of supplies and the harassing attacks of Holkar's numerous horse. An ill-judged retreat, continued for nearly two months through a flooded country, from an enemy less to be dreaded for courage and soldiership than mere numbers, brought him back to Agra by the end of August with a scanty remnant of his brave Sepoys ; their guns, baggage, and supplies all captured or left behind them on the road.

Emboldened by this disaster, Holkar sent his horsemen swarming across the Chambal up to Muttra and even to Delhi. On the 7th October 20,000 of his best troops with 100 guns suddenly appeared before that city, into which nothing barred their way but a Sepoy garrison far too small for the works they would have to defend. But for ten days the brave Colonel Ochterlony held his perilous post, until Lake himself came up from Agra to his relief. Balked of his prey, Holkar turned off to plunder the Doāb and lay waste its fruitful fields. The English, however, kept him moving at his best pace. While Lake with his "galloper" guns and light horse was in full chase of Holkar's cavalry, General Fraser on the 13th November came up with the enemy's main body drawn out under the guns of Daig, a fortress belonging to the revolted Raja of Bharatpur. The rout of the Marāthas and the capture of half their guns once more attested the prowess of English troops against formidable odds, the Sepoys vying with the famous 76th Highlanders in deeds of daring.

Four days later the dashing Lake burst upon Holkar's camp at Farrukhabad on the Ganges. The surprised

Marātha had barely time to escape with a few followers, while the rest of his troops were ridden down and scattered with heavy loss. The fall of Daig on the 23rd December tempted Lake to enter on the siege of Bharatpur itself, where Holkar's infantry and his Jāt allies had resolved to make their last stand. But even Lake's heroes failed to atone for the want of heavy guns and skilled engineers. Four desperate assaults, resulting in the fruitless massacre of his best troops, at length convinced him that one of the strongest fortresses in all India was not to be taken by heroism alone. By this time, however, the Raja of Bharatpur had grown weary of fighting for his new friends. His prayer for peace was granted on payment of a moderate fine, and Lord Lake—for such he had now become —returned to his former business, the pursuit of Holkar.

For a time it seemed as if Sindhia also, in revenge for the transfer of his late capital, Gwalior, to another chief, was again to be reckoned among our foes. The march, however, of an English force into Bundelkhand made him pause on the road to ruin ; and Lord Wellesley was about to strengthen his wiser learnings by the timely cession of Gwalior, when a new Governor-General landed at Fort William on the 30th July, 1805; and "the glorious little man," who in seven years had by force of arms or treaties placed all India within the Sutlej at his feet, went home to give account of his stewardship to those who had sent him out. A series of attacks in Parliament and a vote of censure from the Company whose possessions he had doubled, whose power he had raised to the highest pitch, were the immediate rewards of a career as statesmanlike as that of Hastings, as all-subduing as that of Lord Dalhousie. The attacks in Parliament were merited and signal failures, but it took the Company thirty years to discover their mistake, and to cancel the outrageous verdict of 1807 by voting a statue and a grant of £20,000 to the great man, whose "ardent zeal to promote the well-being of India, and to uphold the interests and honour of the British empire," ought to have been acknowledged many years before. In Calcutta, Government House, an impressive building, with fine rooms for the State functions, remains as a monument to his love of splendour and dignity.

CHAPTER II

LORD CORNWALLIS AND LORD MINTO—1805-1813

AT the urgent prayer of the India House, Lord Cornwallis resumed his former post with the avowed intention of turning back upon the footsteps of his bolder predecessor. The prevailing "frenzy of conquest" had to be subdued, the Company's treasury to be saved from utter exhaustion. But the climate of Bengal played havoc with the old man's weakened frame; and he died in October, leaving Sir George Barlow, the Senior member of his council, to carry on the mistimed and unseemly task of unpicking the web so carefully woven by Lord Wellesley. Sir George Barlow was a strong minded man and, with whatever reluctance, he felt bound to obey the orders of the Directors. A policy of self-repression, of retreat from fancied dangers and real responsibilities, took the place of that bolder, wiser, more merciful system, by which Wellesley had striven to raise up in India a power strong enough to keep the peace among its turbulent neighbours, and to rescue vast tracts of country from the miseries of chronic strife.

A fresh treaty concluded with Sindhia in November not only yielded everything he had asked for, but released him in part from the restraints imposed by that of Anjangaon. Jeswant Rāo Holkar, whom the unflagging Lake had chased across the Sutlej, was glad to make peace on any terms with his pursuers; but even the mild conditions granted by Lord Lake were yet further tempered by Sir

George Barlow, who gave Rāmpur back to Holkar and left the hapless Raja of Būndi to his fate. In the same spirit our good friend the Raja of Jaipur, in spite of pledges received from Lake and Cornwallis, was abandoned to the ruthless inroads of the Marātha chief whose final overthrow he had helped to hasten. It was a sore trial for the conqueror of Jeswant Rāo to bear the upbraidings and disregard the prayers of the Raja's envoy; but his orders were too clear, and all that he could do to show his indignation he did, by resigning his civil powers into the hands of the Governor-General.

The fruits of this retrograde policy were not long in showing themselves. No sooner had Lord Lake turned his back on the Punjāb than Holkar resumed his plundering habits at the expense alike of friend and foe. His bands of freebooters swept the country clean from the Beas to the Jumna. Hariāna was laid waste. From the helpless Raja of Jaipur he extorted large sums of money; and the Raja of Būndi had cause to rue the day when he held out to Monson's soldiers a helping hand against their ravenous pursuers. Rājputāna itself was ere long torn to pieces by intestine strife, and the ruin caused by the quarrels of Rājput princes was completed by the ruthless raids of Sindhia's Marāthas and Amīr Khan's Pathāns, whose progress was everywhere marked by blazing villages and wasted fields. In the midst of a career of boundless rapine and wanton bloodshed Holkar fortunately went raving mad from drink, and his death in 1811 relieved Central India of one of the worst scourges which his country had ever produced.

Even the Pēshwa began to kick against the barriers set to his ambition by the Treaty of Bassein. The demand for chauth was heard again from Poona, and Bājī Rāo claimed his share of the spoils which Sindhia and Holkar were carrying off from the plundered princes and peoples of Rājputāna. The Nizām, also, who had succeeded his father, Nizām Ali, in 1803, was already intriguing with the Marātha princes against the power to which he owed his throne. But there was a point in his policy of forbearance beyond which Sir George Barlow would not go. Both the Nizām and the Pēshwa were compelled to retrace their steps, and to learn that the bolder spirit of Lord Wellesley had not quite departed from the counsels of his successor.

Meanwhile a new and unforeseen danger threatened the government of Madras. With more than the usual folly of military martinets, Sir John Cradock issued a set of orders regarding uniform, which the Sepoys of Madras read as a wilful attempt to tamper with the creed and customs of their race.* It was about the time when the first English missionaries had entered in Bengal on the work which St. Francis Xavier had begun, and the Protestant Swart,† after a long interval, had continued in Southern India. The Company's servants looked on the new movement with dread, as a likely danger to the public peace ; and the labours of Carey, Ward, and Marshman had to be carried on from the Danish settlement of Serampore on the Hūgli. Idle or evil tongues thereupon spread through Southern India the report of a set design on the part of the English against the creeds and customs of their native subjects. The spirit of distrust and disaffection thus engendered among the Sepoys was carefully formed by the Muhammadans in Vellore where Tipu's family were allowed to dwell at no great distance from the Mysore frontier. One of the Sepoy regiments in that

* The Sepoys were forbidden to wear earrings on parade, and were ordered to shave their chins, and exchange their turbans for a kind of shako.

† He was one of the most remarkable of the missionaries employed by the S.P.C.K. at the end of the eighteenth century, and won the respect and confidence of Haidar, as well as of Cornwallis, Macartney and Coote, and did a remarkable work for more than forty years at Tanjore.

fortress had been largely recruited from the ranks of Tipu's own army.

In the early morning of the 10th July, 1806, the two native regiments at Vellore rose in sudden mutiny, attacked the European barracks, where some 370 men of the 69th Foot were yet sleeping, poured volley after volley into their helpless victims, and shot down thirteen officers coming out of their rooms. Happily for the survivors, help was soon to reach them in their desperate need from the garrison of Arcot, eight miles off. At the head of a squadron of his 19th Dragoons and a few galloper guns, Colonel Gillespie rode at his best pace to the scene of massacre, blew open the gate of the fortress, and with the help of those inside dealt heavy destruction on the mutineers, hundreds of whom were shot, sabred, or taken prisoners. Of the 69th, however, ninety-five men and officers lay dead, and ninety-one wounded. Lord William Bentinck, Governor of Madras, was summarily ordered home without a hearing, as an abettor of Sir John Cradock in the measures which directly provoked so dire a disaster; and the Mysore princes incurred no other penalty for their mischievous intrigues than a compulsory change of abode to Calcutta.

In the following July Lord Minto, a statesman of some promise and of twelve months' special experience at the Board of Control, took his seat as Governor-General in the room of Barlow, transferred to Madras. Enjoined to uphold the policy of peaceful isolation, he soon found cause to unlearn the lessons dinned into his ears at home. The great Sikh leader, Ranjīt Singh, was already seeking to extend his strong sway over the independent Sikh and Mussulman princes of Sind. Twice within as many years he had crossed the Sutlej in furtherance of his ambitious schemes. But at length the boldness of his movements and the prayers of his intended victims for English aid decided Lord Minto to enforce the powers ascribed to him by the suppliant chiefs themselves. To this course he was all the more strongly impelled by Bonaparte's brilliant successes in Europe, and the peace he had just concluded with the Russian Emperor. Mr. Charles Metcalfe, one of Lord Wellesley's ablest pupils, was sent to talk over matters with the bold but clear-headed ruler of the Punjāb ; and when Ranjīt Singh would have shaken himself free from English dictation by another raid across the Sutlej, Colonel Ochterlony marched to the protection of the Sind chiefs. Thanks to this movement and Metcalfe's patient firmness, a treaty was concluded in April, 1809, by which Ranjīt Singh withdrew all claims to sovereignty over the Sikhs on the south bank of the Sutlej. At the same time the outposts of his new allies were advanced from the Jumna to the borders of the Punjāb.

Other missions were despatched about this time to the Shah of Persia and to Shah Shujā, brother and successor to Zamān Shah of Kābul. The latter came to nothing by reason of the Afghān monarch's flight from before the arms of his victorious brother.* Colonel Malcolm's second mission to Teherān for the purpose of thwarting French intrigues was forestalled by that of Sir Harford Jones sent out direct from England. The Shah, however, greeted Malcolm as an old friend, and the rival envoys had become rivals only for the common good, when a new ambassador was sent out from England to supersede them both.

Meanwhile Lord Minto had put forth a hand of power to save the Raja of Berar from the attacks of the turbulent Rohilla chieftain Amīr Khan, who, in Holkar's name, had led out a host of armed freebooters to spread havoc through the fairest provinces of Central India. The invader was driven back to Indore, and his own capital

* The Hon. Mountstuart Elphinstone, afterwards Governor of Bombay, was at the head of this mission.

occupied by Colonel Close. But either from misplaced lenity or undue deference to the supposed desires of the India House, Lord Minto withdrew his troops from the conquered country, and the work which he had well-nigh completed had to be taken up afresh on a larger scale by his successor.

In the same year, 1809, a vigorous onslaught was made on the plague of piracy in Eastern waters. The chiefs of Kolhāpur and Sāvantvadi were forced to surrender their ports on the Malabar coast, whence pirate vessels had long been wont to prey upon the smaller trading craft that passed within their reach. In the Persian Gulf, where swarmed the Arab pirates who had lately murdered the crew of an English merchant ship, a British force from Bombay beat up their chief haunts, burnt their vessels, and stormed the great pirate stronghold of Ras-al-khaima.

A like success rewarded Lord Minto's efforts to protect English trade from the French privateers in Eastern waters. The island of Bourbon was captured with little loss in 1810, and before the year's end the Mauritius also, after a brief struggle, submitted to our arms. The turn of Java came next. Its Dutch possessors, aided by their French allies, made a gallant defence; but Gillespie's timely daring and the strength of the army led by Sir Samuel Achmuty soon overcame their resistance, and Java for a few years passed under the Company's rule.*

Meanwhile Sir George Barlow's government had been harassed by an outbreak in Travancore and a serious mutiny among its own officers. The former was suppressed in the beginning of 1809, and the country placed under English management. The mutiny, which had been provoked by the Madras governor's headlong zeal in a good cause, and fanned by his ill-timed severity, blazed up to such a height that the officers at Seringapatam turned their guns

* Sir Stamford Raffles was appointed Governor.

on the troops sent against them. At last, however, the mutineers returned to their senses. A few of the ringleaders were cashiered or dismissed, and the remainder were glad to sign a pledge binding them to obey and support the government of Madras. Sir George Barlow was recalled.

Not long after the conquest of Java, Lord Minto found himself confronted by a new foe. For some time past the Pindāris, a vast brotherhood of mounted freebooters, who were ready to fight under any standard for the chance of unbounded plunder, had been playing a more and more prominent part in the wars of native princes. As free lances, they had fought for the Pēshwa at Pānipat, had shared in the frequent struggles of the Sindhias and Holkars in Hindustān and Southern India, and made war on their own account with every native prince whose weakness at any moment seemed to invite attack. Daulat Rāo Sindhia himself was fain to purchase immunity from their plundering raids by the cession of several districts to one of their most daring leaders, Chītu, a Jāt by birth and a robber from his earliest childhood. Another chief, the Rohilla Kharim Khan, had become a terrible thorn in Sindhia's side before that potentate could succeed in crippling him. Amīr Khan himself was in league with the Pindāris, by whose help he had risen to power. From the hills and glens of Central India thousands of armed ruffians sallied forth year after year in quest of plunder, sparing no cruelty to gain their ends, and widening the circle of their ravages with each new raid, until in 1811 the smoke of their camp-fires could be seen from Gaya and Mirzāpur.

Had Lord Minto deemed himself free to act as he chose, this last outrage would have been speedily avenged. But his hands were tied by the Court of Directors, and while he was waiting for leave to punish the Pindāris according to their deserts, the order for his recall—a measure forced upon the India House by the Prince Regent—was already on its way to Calcutta. In October, 1813, he set sail for England, to enjoy the earldom which he had fairly earned; and the Earl of Moira went out as Governor-General in his stead.

In the course of the same year the question of renewing the Company's charter, under fresh conditions, for another twenty years provoked some warm debates in Parliament. In vain did the Company and their friends plead for the maintenance of all the privileges secured to the former in 1793. Against them were arrayed the whole strength of Lord Castlereagh's ministry and the growing influence of the trading classes throughout the country. The trade with India was thrown open to all Englishmen alike; but the Company were allowed for twenty years longer to keep in their own hands the sole right of trade with China. At last the Church was allowed to have a Bishop, for the control of its work in India, and Dr. Middleton was consecrated to the see of Calcutta in 1814. In respect, however, of their political power, the Company escaped the doom which some of the leading statesmen in England would have enforced against them even then.

CHAPTER III

MARQUESS OF HASTINGS—1813–1823

THE peace which Lord Minto had left behind him was not to remain long unbroken. Among the legacies bequeathed to his successor was a deepening quarrel with the Gūrkha rulers of Nepāl, a long tract of Himālayan upland overlooking the fertile plains and forests of Oudh. In the course of four centuries the Rājput settlers in Nepāl had brought under their sway the old Mongol dwellers in the hills, and out of their several conquests arose one Gūrkha kingdom, whose power in the nineteenth century was felt from the highlands of Bhutān to the banks of the Upper Sutlej. For some years past the Gūrkhas had carried their inroads across the Oudh frontier, even at last into the districts which the Nawāb had ceded to Lord Wellesley. Lord Minto's demands for restitution of the conquered villages had been treated with contempt, and when Lord Moira reached Calcutta, the quarrel was already swollen to a dangerous head.

He renewed the former demand in terms whose meaning could not be mistaken. A murderous attack on the police at Botwal, in Gorakhpur, was the only yet decisive answer from Katmandū. In the autumn of 1814 a strong British force, in four columns, marched on as many points of the Nepālese frontier. The campaign, which had been skilfully planned, was to be cruelly blundered in the prosecution. Gillespie's headlong valour before the hill-fort of Kalanga cost him his life, and involved his troops in heavy losses. Not till after a second assault, attended with issues yet more fatal, did the remnant of the Gūrkha garrison make their escape from a post no longer tenable. Gillespie's successor wasted months in blockading another fort, which a little more energy would have placed much earlier in his hands. General Wood and General Marley vied with each other in losing great opportunities and throwing discredit upon the British name. But for Ochterlony's successful advance from Ambāla into the troubled sea of green hills about Simla, and his brilliant capture of Malaun, on the Upper Sutlej, from the ablest of the Gūrkha leaders, Amar Singh, this first campaign against a foe weak in numbers, but strong in native courage and natural resources, would have ended in utter failure, if not in something worse.

The capture of Malaun, however, following on Colonel Gardiner's successes in Almōra, changed the face of affairs, not only in Nepāl, but all over India. The native princes, who were all but ready for one more struggle against the English power, drew back at the last moment from a course so dangerous to themselves; and the Gūrkha Raja of Nepāl was about to make peace with Lord Moira, when the fiery Amar Singh persuaded him to renew the war. It was not long, however, before he had reason to repent his rashness. Early in 1816, Sir David Ochterlony, who had just gained his knighthood, marched at the head of a powerful army on Katmandū. After a brief but vain resistance, the Gūrkha Government saved their capital by signing a treaty which stripped them of nearly all their lowland possessions, turned Kumaun into an English province, and placed an English Resident, for the first time, at the Nepālese court. For his successful conduct of the war Lord Moira was created Marquess of Hastings.

Ṭo thwạrt Marāṭha intrigues and punịsh Ṗindāri

aggressions was the Governor-General's next aim. In spite of hindrances offered by his own Council and the Court of Directors, he set himself to revive and extend Lord Wellesley's policy of securing peace and order throughout India by means of treaties, which placed one native prince after another in a kind of vassalage to the paramount power that ruled from Fort William. The Pathān ruler of Bhopāl, in Mālwa, claimed and received the formal protection of a power to which his successors have proved their loyalty under every trial. In 1816, Appa Sahib, the Regent of Berar, agreed to maintain a British contingent at his own cost. By means of a little timely compulsion, the able and accomplished Elphinstone baffled for a while the plots which the Pēshwa, Bājī Rāo, and his villainous accomplice, Trimbakji Danglia, had woven against their English allies. The treaty of June, 1817, left Lord Hastings master of Sāgar and Bundelkhand, while it bound the Pēshwa to renounce his friend Trimbakji, his own claims to the headship of the Marātha League, to make no treaties with any other native prince, and to accept in all things the counsel and control of the Company's Government. Hard as these terms may seem, there was no choice, averred Lord Hastings, between thus crippling a secret foe and depriving him of the crown he had fairly forfeited.

Meanwhile Lord Hastings' fearless energy had already saved the Rājputs of Jaipur from further suffering at the hands of their Pathān oppressor, Amīr Khan, and forced from Sindhia himself a reluctant promise to aid in suppressing the Pindāri hordes, whose fearful ravages had at length been felt by the peaceful villagers in the Northern Circars. In the autumn of 1817 Hastings took the field at the head of an army which, counting native contingents, mustered nearly 120,000 strong, with some 300 guns. From east, west, north, and south, a dozen columns set forth to hunt down the merciless ruffians who had so long been allowed to harry the fairest provinces of India. In spite of the havoc wrought among our troops by the great cholera outbreak of that year, and of a sudden rising among the Marātha princes for one last struggle with their former conquerors, our arms were everywhere successful against Marāthas and Pindāris alike. The latter, hunted into the hills and jungles of central India, found no safety anywhere except in small bodies and constant flight. Chītu, one of their boldest leaders, was chased from Rājputāna into Gujarāt, from Gujarāt into Mālwa, where for several months he roamed through the dense jungles with hardly a companion, until one day his body was found half-eaten by tigers in the heart of the Sātpūra Hills. The other leaders were all slain or captured, their followers dispersed, and the famous robber-league passed into a tale of yore.

Not less swift and sure was the punishment dealt upon the Marātha leaders who joined the Pēshwa in his sudden uprising against the British power. His late submission had been nothing but a mask for renewed plottings. Elphinstone, however, saw through the mask which had taken in the confiding Malcolm. Before the end of October an English regiment, summoned in hot haste from Bombay, pitched its camp at Kirkee, about two miles from Poona, beside the small Sepoy brigade already quartered there. In the first days of November Bājī Rāo began to assume a bolder tone as his plans grew ripe for instant execution. On the 5th, a body of Marāthas attacked and destroyed the Residency, which Elphinstone had quitted in the nick of time. A great Marātha army then marched forth to overwhelm the little garrison at Kirkee, before fresh troops could come up to its aid from Sirūr. Elphinstone, however, who knew his foe, had no idea of awaiting the attack. Colonel Burr at once led out his men, not 3000 all told. A brilliant charge of Marātha horse was heavily repulsed by a Sepoy regiment, and the English steadily advancing drove the enemy from the field.

A few days later General Smith, at the head of a larger force, advanced on Poona, occupied the city, and pursued the frightened Pēshwa from place to place. The heroic defence of Koregaom, a small village on the Bhima, by Captain Staunton and 800 Sepoys, with only two light guns, against 25,000 Marāthas during a whole day, proved once more how nobly native troops could fight under English leading.*

Happily for Staunton's weary and diminished band, Smith came up the next morning, and the desponding Pēshwa continued his retreat. Turn where he would, there was no rest for his jaded soldiers. Munro with a weak force, partly of his own raising, headed him on his way to the Carnatic, took several of his strong places, and drove him northwards within reach of General Smith.

On the 19th February, 1818, that officer overtook and routed the flying foe at the village of Ashti. Bāpu Gokla, the Pēshwa's staunchest and ablest follower, perished on the field, while covering the retreat of his cowardly master. For some weeks longer Bājī Rāo fled hither and thither before his resolute pursuers. But at length all hope forsook him as the circle of escape grew daily narrower; and in the middle of May the great grandson of Bālajī Vishvanāth yielded himself to Sir John Malcolm at Indore, on terms far more liberal than he had any reason to expect. Even for the faithful few who still shared his fortunes due provision was made at his request. He himself spent the rest of his days a princely pensioner at Bithūr, near Cawnpore; but the sceptre which he and his sires had

* Only three English officers remained unhurt out of eleven. Of the men 175 were killed and wounded.

wielded for a hundred years passed into English hands, while the Raja of Satāra, the long-neglected heir of the house of Sīvajī, was restored to the nominal headship of the Marātha power.

Meanwhile Appa Sahib, the usurping Raja of Berar, had no sooner heard of the outbreak at Poona, than he, too, like the Pēshwa, threw off his mask. On the evening of the 24th November, 1817, his troops, to the number of 18,000, suddenly attacked the weak English and Sepoy force of 1,400 men with four guns, posted on the Sitabaldi Hills, outside Nāgpur. A terrible fight for eighteen hours ended in the repulse of the assailants, with a loss to the victors of more than 300 men and twelve officers. A few weeks later Nāgpur itself was occupied after another fight. Even then the Raja might have kept his throne, for his conquerors were merciful and hoped the best. But they hoped in vain. It was not long before Appa Sahib, caught out in fresh intrigues, was sent off a prisoner towards Allāhabād. Escaping from his captors, he wandered about the country for several years, and died at Lahore a pensioner on the bounty of Ranjīt Singh.

The house of Holkar had also paid the penalty of its rash resistance to our arms. After the murder of the great Tulsi Bhai, Regent of Indore, a wise stateswoman famous among Indian rulers, by the chiefs of her own army, in 1817, they spurned all Malcolm's offers of peace, and from a strong position at Mehidpur, on the banks of the Sīpra, awaited the attack of a Madras column led by Sir Thomas Hislop. Under a withering fire from the Marātha guns Hislop's Sepoys crossed the river in the face of 20,000 foes, and carried all before them with the bayonet, after a hard struggle which cost the victors 778 men. Sixty-three guns with all the camp stores fell into their hands. On the 6th January, 1818, the young Holkar was glad to sign a treaty which placed him and his heirs under English protection at the cost of his independence and of some part of his realm. Luckily for himself, Sindhia had remained quiet, if not quite loyal, throughout this last struggle between the English and his Marātha kinsfolk.

Thus in one short and decisive campaign, the great Marātha power, which had survived the slaughter of Pānipat, fell shattered to pieces by the same blow which crushed the Pindāris, and raised an English merchant-company to the paramount lordship of all India. The last of the Pēshwas had ceased to reign, the Raja of Berār was a discrowned fugitive, the Raja of Satāra a king only in name, while Sindhia, Holkar, and the Nizām were dependent princes who reigned only by sufferance of an English Governor-General at Calcutta. The Mughal Empire lingered only in the palace of Delhi; its former viceroy, the Nawāb of Oudh, was our obedient vassal; the haughty princes of Rājputāna bowed their necks, more or less cheerfully, to the yoke of masters merciful as Akbar and mightier than Aurangzeb. Ranjīt Singh himself cultivated the goodwill of those powerful neighbours who had sheltered the Sikhs of Sind from his ambitious inroads. With the final overthrow of the Marāthas a new reign of peace, order, and general progress began for peoples who, during a hundred and fifty years, had lived in a ceaseless whirl of anarchy and armed strife.

With the capture of Asīrgarh in April, 1819, the fighting in Southern India came to an end. The country conquered from the Pēshwa was placed under the fostering care of Mountstuart Elphinstone, who afterwards, as Governor of Bombay, completed the healing work which he and his able subalterns had begun from Poona. Sir Thomas Munro, one of the ablest soldier-statesmen of his time in India, became ere long Governor of Madras, and reformed the land-revenue system of that Presidency in accordance with the lessons he had learned in the Ceded Districts.* About the same time Mr. Holt Mackenzie entered on the task of reassessing the land in the North-Western Provinces, on the basis of a settlement neither with the Rayat as in Madras, nor with the Zamindar as in Bengal, but with the head-man of every village community. In Orissa, on the other hand, a popular outbreak, caused by excessive demands for land-revenue, had to be put down by force, and the assessments to be curtailed by nearly one-half.

Free at length from warlike cares, Lord Hastings threw himself with unflagging zeal into the task of governing his broad dominions. His great capacity for hard work was enhanced by a thorough mastery of details and the liberal spirit of his measures for the good of his native subjects. He helped to found schools for the teaching of native children and youths. A native newspaper—the first of its kind—started by the Serampore Mission, received his steady support. The English press in India became for a time practically free. He restored the canal which had once supplied Delhi with water from the Upper Jumna. Calcutta itself was sweetened with broad streets and shady squares, and adorned with a noble strand. In 1819, with the help of Sir Stamford Raffles, he made up for the loss of Java, given back to the Dutch, by purchasing from its native ruler the neighbouring island of Singapore. His own example did much to raise the tone of the Indian services, and to strengthen their hold on the goodwill of the people at large.

The only cloud upon these later years was caused by the embarrassed state of the Nizām's affairs. The great banking firm of Palmer & Co. had become a power at

* The Rayatwāri system, of which Munro was the chief advocate, was, broadly speaking, a yearly settlement of the land-revenue with each *rayat* or cultivator.

Hyderābād—a power which Sir Charles Metcalfe at length pronounced so dangerous, that Lord Hastings was compelled to step in between the impoverished Nizām and his more and more grasping creditors. The claims of the former to a yearly tribute for the Northern Circars were wiped out for ever by the payment of a large sum down, most of which went to extinguish the loans due to the English bankers. A year afterwards the house of Palmer & Co. stopped payment, while the Nizām appears to have reaped no lasting good from a compromise which placed him more than ever at the mercy of his turbulent barons, and of native usurers far less scrupulous than those from whom he had been rescued.

Lord Hastings' services to the Company were crowned by his marked success in matters of finance. In spite of costly wars and other sources of increased outlay, the Indian revenues before his retirement were yielding a yearly surplus of two millions, and the Company's credit stood at a premium of fourteen per cent. All this, however, added to his former deserts, failed to avert from Lord Hastings the attacks which awaited him on his return to England in 1823. The coolness of the India Board became open hostility in the Court of Proprietors, whose vote of virtual censure for his conduct in the affairs of Palmer & Co. was only softened by his acquittal of any corrupt intent. It was not till after his death in 1827 that the India House made some amends for its past unfairness by voting the payment of £20,000 to his son.

CHAPTER IV

LORD AMHERST AND LORD WILLIAM BENTINCK—1823-1835

FOR the next few months after the departure of Lord Hastings, the government of British India rested in the hands of Mr. Adam, senior member of the Calcutta Council. His rule was chiefly memorable for the harsh treatment of Mr. Silk Buckingham, the able and independent founder of the *Calcutta Journal*, whose comments on official acts and persons provoked Lord Hastings' narrow-minded successor to decree his banishment and virtual ruin. The press of India, as if unfit to exercise its newborn freedom, was once more placed under close supervision by a ruler bred in the despotic traditions of other days. Meanwhile the suicide of Lord Londonderry—the Lord Castlereagh of earlier times—had determined George Canning, the most eminent statesman of the day, who had accepted the office of Governor-General, to resume his place in the English Ministry, instead of giving India the benefit of his commanding talents. At length Lord Amherst, the late ambassador to China, was appointed to the vacant post, and reached Calcutta on the 1st August, 1823.

His arrival proved to be the forerunner of a new war. The conquest of Assam by the Burmese in 1822 had inflamed the ambition of a power which, from small beginnings, had in the last seventy years established its sway over the neighbouring provinces of Arakān, Pegu and Tenasserim. The successors of Alompra had even begun to dispute our right to various provinces of Bengal; and an insolent letter to Lord Hastings in 1818—so insolent that he treated it as a mere forgery—was ere long followed by an inroad into Cachar. At length, in 1823, English forbearance gave way before a Burman attack upon Shahpūri, a British Island off the Arakān coast. It was soon recovered by a British force; but the warnings addressed to the Court of Ava were answered only by the despatch of Māha Bandūla, the great Burman general, with an army intended for the conquest of Bengal and the capture of the Governor-General himself.

In February, 1824, Lord Amherst declared war in his turn against the insolent barbarians who had mistaken forbearance for fear. Bandūla's progress in Bengal was soon checked. Before the middle of May a strong force from Madras, under Sir Archibald Campbell, captured with unexpected ease the important town of Rangoon, near the mouth of the Irrawaddy. After the long inaction caused by the heavy rains of a tropical summer—inaction relieved only by the capture of several places on the Tenasserim coast, and of a few stockades near Rangoon—Campbell's army marched out to attack Bandūla, who barred the way inland with 60,000 of his rabble warriors, mostly entrenched behind strong stockades. By the middle of December the last of these had been carried, and the boastful Burman retired with all haste to his stockaded fortress of Danubyū, forty miles up the Irrawaddy. The repulse of a weak brigade from this place in March of the following year was retrieved by its capture in April, under the eyes of Campbell himself, who brought back his troops and heavy guns betimes to Cotton's aid.* Before the end of April, Prome itself, the capital of Lower Burma, was

* The death of Bandūla during the attack contributed greatly to Campbell's success.

occupied by an English garrison, and the Burmese began to treat for peace.

By this time Colonel Richards had driven the Burmese out of Assam, and gained firm possession of its capital, Rangpur. On the other hand an attempt to reach Manipur from Cachar had been utterly baffled by the hardships of a march in the rainy season through an unbroken succession of steep hills and hollows, covered with pathless forests and beset with deep quagmires. Yet more disastrous was General Morrison's march from Chittagong into Arakān in 1825. Precious time was lost upon the road; the May rains involved a halt at the town of Arakān; and the subsequent sickness among our troops slew one-fourth of the whole number, and disabled nearly all the rest. The country was conquered, but of the 10,000 men who invaded it, very few were fit for duty when the order came for their return home.

Once more, towards the end of 1825, Sir A. Campbell moved out against the Burmese, for their haughty monarch would not yet stoop to make peace on the only terms which Campbell was empowered to offer. After carrying a few more stockades and routing a fresh Burman army near Prome, the English general marched on to Yandabo, within sixty miles of Ava itself. At length the king, thoroughly frightened, agreed to purchase peace by the cession of Assam, Arakān, and Tenasserim, and the payment of a million sterling towards the expenses of a war which had cost the victors nearly thirteen millions. Even at that price, however, the conquered provinces have proved well worth the conquering. The rice of Arakān and the tea of Assam are important staples of Indian commerce; and the goods that pass through Moulmein, the chief port of Tenasserim, already amount in value to nearly a million a year.

One sad incident sprang out of this prolonged and

mismanaged war. The Madras Sepoys went cheerfully across the sea to fight the new enemy, but their high-caste brethren of Bengal, with their religious dread of the "black water," could only be forwarded to the field by land. Several regiments had already started in 1824, and others were waiting the order to start. But the arrangements for their march involved them in expenses to which they had never been accustomed. The news from the eastern frontier of Bengal, magnified by distance and transmission from mouth to mouth, struck terror into the hearts of the Sepoys waiting for their turn at Barrackpore. Their reasonable complaints unheeded by the Government, they began to nurse all kinds of unreasonable fancies. They believed that Government, in default of baggage-cattle, was about to carry them to Rangoon by sea. Discontent soon ripened into open mutiny, in which the 47th Regiment took the lead. Its officers, new to their men, for the whole native army had just been remodelled, failed to check the mutinous spirit which now found vent in open refusals to attend parade. On the morning of the 2nd November, the 47th Regiment were confronted by the troops which Sir Edward Paget, the Commander-in-Chief, had brought up overnight to Barrackpore. The Sepoys, like passionate children, refused either to march or to ground their arms. The two English regiments wheeled aside to let the guns come forward, ready loaded with grape. At the first discharge, the frightened Sepoys cast away their unloaded muskets, and fled like scared sheep, followed by the troopers of the body-guard. A good many were shot down, sabred, or drowned in the Hūgli; the ringleaders were afterwards sentenced to death or hard labour; and the regiment itself was struck off the list of the Bengal army. There was no more mutiny for many years to come; but the verdict of a court of inquiry betokened the general sympathy with men whose unsoldierly outbreak had been largely owing to their master's own fault.*

While the Burmese war was yet on foot, the growing insolence of the new Raja of Bharatpur had led to a second siege of that renowned fortress, with happier issues than those of 1805. In December, 1825, 20,000 men, with a hundred guns, marched out under Lord Combermere—the Sir Stapylton Cotton of the Peninsular war—and the fortress which Durjan Sāl had deemed impregnable, and on which our heaviest guns could make no impression, was carried by storm after a wide gap in its defences had been opened by the bursting of a great mine, on the 18th January. Durjan Sāl atoned for his rashness with the forfeiture of his realm, which was handed over to the nephew he had supplanted: and the dismantling of Bharatpur itself once more proclaimed to the native princes the irresistible, if sometimes dormant, strength of their new masters.

In 1827 the East India Company lost one of their ablest servants, and Madras her most popular governor, by the death of Sir Thomas Munro. In the same year Elphinstone was succeeded in Bombay by the soldier-statesman, Sir John Malcolm. It was in 1826 that Reginald Heber, the scholarly, pious, gentle, and justly-beloved Bishop of Calcutta, passed away to his rest, after three years of unwearied labour throughout a diocese then comprising the whole of British India. His letters and journal, afterwards published, throw much light upon the social life of India, among natives and Europeans, during this period. In this year also died Daulat Rāo Sindhia, leaving his dominions to be ruled by his widow, in the name of her adopted son, Jankajī Sindhia. About the same time the government of Nāgpur was handed over to its young Raja,

* "The mutiny," said the Court, "was an ebullition of despair at being compelled to march without the means of doing so."

whose subjects soon found cause to regret the change of rulers. The death of the gallant Ochterlony in 1826 had led to the removal of Sir Charles Metcalfe from Hyderābād to Delhi, and the good effect of his wise counsels soon passed away from the feeble government of the Nizām. After a farewell progress through the upper provinces, Lord Amherst himself retired from office and from India in February, 1828.

Lord Amherst was succeeded by that Lord William Bentinck whose career as Governor of Madras had closed so abruptly after the mutiny of Vellore. Coming out again to India full of humane intentions, and charged with strict orders to keep down the public expenses, he had the good fortune to achieve his twofold mission during a period of general peace. Before the end of 1829 he had issued the decree which made *Sāti*, or widow-burning, thenceforth punishable as murder throughout British India. In the following year he began a merciless war against the Thags, a brotherhood of secret murderers who, in the name of their goddess Kāli, were wont to strangle in lonely places the unwary travellers whom they had agreed to rob. The task of hunting down these ruffians was entrusted to the active Major Sleeman, who, aided by a staff of picked subordinates, and the clues supplied by one of their own number, tracked them into their secret haunts, caught several thousands of them in a few years, and succeeded in utterly suppressing their dreadful trade.

William Henry Sleeman (1788–1856) was one of the most valuable servants ever employed by the East India Company. Between 1825 and 1835 he did most important work in the Central Province, and from 1839 he was commissioner for the suppression of Thagi and dacoity, and it was due to him that the terrible organization for murder ceased to exist. His "Rambles and Recollections of an Indian Official" (1844) is a delightful book which has frequently been reprinted. He was made a K.C.B. just before his death.

In unwilling obedience to orders from England, Lord William Bentinck carried out the ungracious task of cutting down the pay of his native troops in Bengal. Officers and men were alike indignant at a measure which seemed to them a wanton breach of faith, a measure which applied only to the stations nearest Calcutta. But the Court of Directors paid no heed to their just complaints, and Lord William Bentinck saw no way of shirking the enforcement of a cheese-paring thrift which saved his masters about twenty thousand a-year, and rendered himself for a time the worst abused Englishman in all India. In curtailing the allowances of civil servants, his lordship acted with much less reluctance, and his masters with better excuse. Another of his reforms laid him open to just censure: the abolition of flogging in the native army, while the punishment was still retained for our white troops, did honour to his humanity at the expense of his political foresight.

His humanity was employed to better purpose in opening to the natives those higher ranks of the civil service from which Lord Cornwallis had shut them out. Native judges sat once more in civil courts; native Christians were encouraged to take office; and the old Hindu laws of inheritance were shorn of the provisions which virtually forbade the descent of Hindu property to heirs of another creed. Some useful reforms were made in the administration of justice, and the native languages of India supplanted Persian in the courts of law. A medical college for the natives was founded in Calcutta, and the study of Western lore and science was encouraged by the introduction of English teaching into the State-aided schools—a measure largely due to the zeal of such men as Mr. Macaulay and Sir Charles Trevelyan.

In 1833 Lord William Bentinck gave the word for a revised settlement of the North-Western Provinces on the lines laid out in 1822. Under the able lead of Mr. Robert Mertins Bird, the work of surveying and reassessing the land of a province larger than England and Wales, and more populous than Great Britain, was carried through in eight years, with all the care and thoroughness demanded for the survey of a private estate. The trade of the country received a new impulse from Lord William Bentinck's efforts in its behalf. In 1830, English steamers, built at Calcutta, made their way for the first time up the Ganges to Benāres and Allahābād. The same year also witnessed the successful voyage of a Government steamer, the *Hugh Lindsay* from Bombay to Suez, at the top of the Red Sea. Had Lord William Bentinck's efforts to shorten the journey from England to India been properly seconded by the Court of Directors, twelve years would not have been lost in following up the issues of an experiment which marked out the Isthmus of Suez as the best available road for the Indian mails.

In his dealings with native princes, Lord William Bentinck combined the utmost forbearance with a certain share of firmness on fit occasions. The Raja of Jodhpur was replaced on the throne from which his rebellious barons had ousted him. The mother of the young Sindhia was bidden to hand over the reins of government to her son. In the affairs of Jaipur and Bhopāl, the Governor-General declined to interfere for the maintenance of order and the protection of their rightful lords. But the reckless and incapable Nawāb of Oudh was sharply rebuked for his shortcomings, and plainly warned against persistence in misrule. An armed force under General Fraser was sent to punish the refractory Raja of Coorg, and his little state was brought under English rule. Cachar was annexed on the death of its childish ruler. A serious outbreak in Mysore, provoked by the misrule of its incapable Raja, had to be put down by a strong force from Madras; and the power which he had abused, in spite of repeated warnings, passed into English hands, in accordance with the terms laid down by Lord Wellesley.

A rising of Muhammadan fanatics at Barasat, not far from Calcutta, disturbed the peace of the empire in 1831. Inflamed by the preaching of one Tītu Mīr, a disciple of Saiyid Ahmad, founder of the new Wahābi sect in the Punjāb,* they proclaimed a holy war against the infidels in Bengal, and launched into all manner of outrages on their Hindu neighbours. Their suppression was followed in the next year by a rising among the Kōls, an aboriginal race in the hills of Western Bengal. These rude foresters fell upon the Hindu settlers and underlings whose encroachments and hard dealings had aroused their wrath; and many fields were wasted, villages burnt, and people slain, before the revolt was put down, and their country placed under a special commissioner. A few years earlier, the brave young soldier, Outram, had reclaimed the Bhīl tribes in the forests of Khandēsh from a state of lawless savagery into one of peaceful industry and loyal submission to our rule.

About the same time Captain Hall was engaged in taming the Mairs who inhabited the hills of Merwāra, on the borders of Ajmēr. Another wild race, the Khānds of Goomsur in the Northern Circars, was being gradually weaned by the labours of Captains Campbell and Macpherson from the time-honoured practice of manuring their fields with the flesh of human beings offered up

* In 1827 Saiyid Ahmad attacked Peshāwar, which Ranjīt Singh had lately won from the Afghāns. The attack was renewed in 1830 with more success, but he was soon driven out again, and was slain in Kashmīr in 1831 by the Sikh troops.

as a sacrifice to the Earth-goddess. Noble efforts were also made by several of our countrymen, with the warm encouragement of Lord William Bentinck, to check the prevalence of female infanticide among the Rājput tribes in various parts of India. But a practice born of caste-pride, and of hard social customs which forbade the marriage of a Rājput girl with one of lower rank, which made her marriage with an equal ruinously expensive, and which exposed her to the deep disgrace of remaining unmarried, was not to be uprooted all at once; and the good work begun by Mr. Duncan in the first years of this century was very far from completion when Lord William Bentinck left India.

Meanwhile, however, the results of two wars between Russia and Persia had made Russian influence supreme at Teherān,* and reawakened among English statesmen those fears of coming danger to India which Lord Wellesley's and Lord Minto's efforts had lulled to sleep. It was resolved to send a mission to Ranjīt Singh by way of the Indus, with the twofold object of strengthening our relations with an old and useful ally, and of bringing the Amīrs of Sind within the pale of Anglo-Indian diplomacy. The Tālpur chiefs from Balūchistān, who had wrested Sind from the Afghāns in 1786, did all they dared to thwart the policy of their English neighbours; but Lieutenant Burnes succeeded in passing up the Indus and delivering his presents to the ruler of the Punjāb.† Ranjīt Singh received him with open arms, and the good results of their friendly intercourse were followed up by a formal interview between the ambitious Sikh and the Governor-General at Rūpar, on the upper Sutlej, in the same

* The treaty of Turkomanchai in 1828 had given Russia a large slice of Persian territory in addition to the conquests of 1812.

† He was accompanied by Captain Wood of the Indian navy, who afterwards explored the sources of the Oxus.

year. Sixteen thousand of his best soldiers, drilled by French and Italian officers, attended the former to the place of meeting, while a choice brigade of English troops discharged the like duty for Lord William Bentinck.

With his usual good sense, the great Sikh ruler fell in with the views of his English ally, and Shikārpur, for which he had been hankering, was saved to the Amīrs of Sind. The treaties concluded with him and the Amīrs opened up the Indus and the Sutlej for the first time to English trade, and the Maharaja of Lahore found fresh employment for his restless soldiery in resisting the attempts of the Afghān, Dost Muhammad, to regain possession of Peshāwar.

At length in March, 1835, Lord William Bentinck sailed for England, leaving behind him the memory of a wise, humane, and successful governor, who had made the welfare of his subjects his foremost aim, struck heavy blows at barbarous usages, reformed the civil service, encouraged modern enterprise, and restored the Indian revenues to a state of health. The last years of his rule were memorable for the debates in the English Parliament which issued in the extinction of the Company's last remaining privileges in respect of trade. With the renewal of their charter in 1833 for another twenty years, the China monopoly ceased to exist, and the trade with Chinese ports was thrown open to Englishmen of every class. From that time also our countrymen became free to settle and buy lands in any part of India, while no native could any longer be debarred from public office by reason of his religion, birthplace, colour, or descent. The legislative control of the Governor-General in Council over the minor governments was for the first time secured by the same act, and an English lawyer of acknowledged repute was added as a fourth member to the Calcutta

Council. The first holder of this new office was Mr. Macaulay, the brilliant essayist and historian of a later day, whose Indian labours were ere long afterwards to bear rich fruit in the penal code first drafted by his own hands.

CHAPTER V

LORD AUCKLAND—1836–1842

MR. MOUNTSTUART ELPHINSTONE having declined on the plea of ill-health to take Lord William Bentinck's place, the Government of India was for a time entrusted to the able hands of Sir Charles Metcalfe. But his very first measure, the passing of an Act which made the press of India as free as it is in England, gave such deep offence to the Court of Directors, that all his past services were forgotten ; and the Government of Madras, which had just fallen vacant when Lord Auckland went out to India, was refused to one whom the directors a few months before would have confirmed in his acting appointment, if they could. In March, 1836, Lord Auckland reached Calcutta and soon afterwards Sir Charles exchanged the service of the Company for a useful and distinguished career under the Crown.

The first two years of Lord Auckland's rule were marked by nothing more important than his interference at Lucknow on behalf of the rightful heir to the throne of Oudh, against a rival set up by the widow of the late Nawāb. In 1839 the intrigues of the Raja of Satāra, whom Lord Hastings had restored to freedom and kingly honours, were brought to a final stop by his dethronement and removal to Benāres.

By this time, however, Lord Auckland's policy had committed India to a war, whose ultimate fruits were to be gathered amidst vain regrets for the loss of many lives, millions of money, and much of our national honour. In 1837 Captain Burnes, Lord Auckland's envoy, was kindly received at Kābul by Dost Muhammad, the Barakzai chief, who had avenged his brother's cruel death by overturning the dynasty of Zamān Shah. Not content with governing the unruly Afghāns, Dost Muhammad was eager to enlist our aid in his efforts to recover the rich Peshāwar valley from the Sikhs. A Russian emissary was then at Kābul. The English envoy's mind was sedulously filled with warnings of the danger which threatened India from Russia's progress in the East. But Burnes's errand was purely commercial: and Lord Auckland answered the Amīr's overtures by a plain demand for the dismissal of his Russian visitor, and a flat refusal to aid him in any way against our Sikh ally.

Meanwhile the Shah of Persia, with the help of Russian money and Russian officers, was laying siege to Herāt, the Gate of Afghānistān. Dost Muhammad's brothers, the princes of Kandahār, were treating for a Persian alliance; and the Amīr of Kābul himself was ere long turning to the same quarter for the help denied him from Simla. In this state of affairs Lord Auckland chose the very worst of the courses which lay open to him. He resolved to aid Shah Shujā in recovering the kingdom from which he had been more than once expelled by Dost Muhammad. By a treaty concluded with the royal exile and Ranjīt Singh he bound himself to support the latter in his efforts to replace the imbecile Shah Shujā on the throne of his father, Ahmad Shah. In the teeth of every argument, of warnings from every quarter against the folly of waging an unprovoked war at such a distance from his own frontier, in a barren and difficult country peopled with hardy, warlike mountaineers, Lord Auckland prepared to assemble an army for the invasion of Afghānistān. The Calcutta Council, the Court of Directors, nearly all the foremost statesmen in both countries, every one, in short, except Lord Auckland, his secretaries, a number of young Indian officers eager for distinction or adventure, and Sir John Hobhouse, President of the Board of Control, was against a move not more impolitic than unjust. But the Governor-General had taken it into his head that Russian intrigues could be thwarted only by the dethronement of Dost Muhammad; nor could even the successful defence of Herāt by the daring Lieutenant Pottinger avail to turn him from his purpose. The treaty with Ranjīt Singh had pledged the English to help Shah Shujā with nothing more than money and English officers, and all danger on the side of Persia had been removed by the retreat of the Persian army from Herāt. Shah Shujā himself had no wish to re-appear among his former subjects as a king who owed his crown to British bayonets. But Lord Auckland had made up his mind to act with vigour, and before the end of November, 1838, the "Army of the Indus" lay encamped on the sandy plain of Ferozepore.

For some time all went swimmingly enough. The Amīrs of Sind were coerced into forwarding the designs of the Governor-General. From Karāchi and Ferozepore the two divisions of the invading army held their way towards the passes in the Sulaiman Hills, which lead from the Sind frontier into Afghānistān. The long march through dreary deserts and dangerous defiles was accomplished painfully but successfully under the supreme command of Sir John Keane. Before the end of April, 1839, Shah Shujā at the head of his own troops had entered Kandahār, where early in the following month he was joined by both divisions of Keane's army.

After a rest of some weeks the army resumed its march. On the 22nd July the gates of the strong fortress of Ghazni were blown in by our engineers, and the place itself stormed by a bold rush with little loss to the victors.

Dost Muhammad sued for peace, but the offer of a dignified retreat on Indian ground was spurned by a king who had ruled his subjects with marked ability for more than ten years; and he fled, hotly pursued by Outram, to the wilds of Bamiān. On the 7th August his victorious rival rode through the streets of Kābul, escorted by British troops, amidst the silence or the muttered curses of the people he had not seen for thirty years, to his palace-citadel the Bāla Hissār.

Meanwhile the Sikh and Afghān force under Colonel Wade had won its way from Peshāwar through the Khyber Pass to Jalālabād, reaching Kābul on the 3rd September. Ranjīt Singh himself, the old one-eyed "Lion of the Punjāb," had died in June at Lahore, after a masterful reign of about forty years, leaving his sceptre in the nerveless hands of his son Karak Singh. Thus far the army of the Indus had done its work; and the honours showered on Lord Auckland, Sir John Keane, Colonel Wade, Mr. Macnaghten, and other chief actors in the late events, marked the high if not excessive value placed on their deserts. In September the Bombay troops began their homeward march, capturing on their way the town of Kalāt, whose Baluchi master had been caught intriguing against Shah Shujā's allies. Some ten thousand Bengal troops remained behind to garrison the chief places in Afghānistān, while the care of our political interests was made over to Lord Auckland's Chief Secretary, Sir William Macnaghten.

For some time longer matters in the conquered country went on as smoothly as could be desired. Dost Muhammad, hunted from place to place, yielded himself a prisoner to Sir William Macnaghten in November, 1840, and withdrew to India on a handsome pension. A few disturbances about Kandahār, Kalāt, and elsewhere, were easily suppressed. In 1841, however, the storm of popular discontent began to blow more meaningly. A great rising among the Khilji tribes near Kandahār was quelled only after two battles and much loss of life. Later in the year they rose again, attacked our convoys, and spread the flame of revolt from the Khyber to Kābul. Sale's brigade on its way to India fell back to Jalālabād. The Afghān hatred of the infidel, fed by the loose behaviour of English officers towards Afghān women, could no longer contain itself. At length, in the beginning of November, Macnaghten and Sir Alexander Burnes, who had been knighted for his many services, were roughly awakened from their dreams of a security in which clearer-sighted officers had long ceased to believe.

On the morning of the 2nd, Burnes was attacked and murdered in his own house by a mob of furious Afghāns, in revenge for the offence he had given an Afghān noble. No effort, worth the naming, was made either by Macnaghten or the English officers who commanded in the cantonments to save their helpless countryman, or to avenge his death. The insurrection, which might easily have been quelled at once, spread fast and far. In the teeth of every military dictate the Bāla Hissār was left to the sole charge of Shah Shujā, and five thousand English soldiers and Sepoys were shut up in a weak cantonment, while swarms of well-armed Afghāns cut off their chief supplies, and beat back the troops sent out to dislodge them. The blundering of the leaders cowed their men, the supplies ran short, the sharp Afghān winter was setting in, and the enemy grew bolder day by day. Macnaghten did his best to avert by diplomacy the disastrous issues of his own blindness and of General Elphinstone's unfitness for such a need. But English honesty was no match for Afghān cunning. On the 11th December it was agreed that all our troops should be allowed to quit the country, the Afghāns finding supplies and carriage for that purpose; that Dost Muhammad should be set free; and that the Kābul garrison should march out in three days, leaving four officers as hostages in the hands of Akbar Khan, the son of Dost Muhammad, and the acknowledged leader of his revolted countrymen. A more disgraceful treaty had never perhaps been signed by Englishmen; but Macnaghten, a brave man of soldierly instincts—he had once been a soldier himself—saw no other means of escape from utter ruin, and the word went forth for the evacuation of all our chief places in Afghānistān.

Days passed, however, and still the promised supplies were not forthcoming. In despair Macnaghten strove by secret negotiations to sow discord among the Afghān leaders. Akbar Khan got scent of what was passing, and laid a trap into which the ill-fated envoy fell but too readily. At the interview to which he had been invited on the 23rd December, the officers who went with him were suddenly seized by some of Akbar's men, and Macnaghten himself, after a brief struggle with the angry chief, was shot dead by Akbar's own hand. The deed appears to have been done upon the spur of the moment, and it is only fair to suppose that the seizure rather than the death of so important a leader was the real object of his murderer's attack.

Not an effort was made to avenge Macnaghten's death. Matters only grew from bad to worse. There was no lack of brave hearts and cool heads in the luckless garrison, but the folly or the helplessness of their leaders would have paralysed the bravest troops. In vain did Pottinger urge a stand for life or death in the Bāla Hissār. The negotiations were resumed, and Afghān insolence rose with each fresh default of English honour. At last, on the 6th January, 1842, General Elphinstone marched out of his cantonments, leaving behind him all his treasure, stores, and ordnance, except six guns, while four officers remained as hostages in Akbar's hands. The snow lay thick on the ground, and the neighbouring hills swarmed with Afghān marksmen thirsting for English blood.

On the 13th January one Englishman, Dr. Brydon, half dead from wounds and exhaustion, was seen guiding his jaded pony towards the gates of Jalālabād. Of all the five thousand soldiers, with twice as many camp-followers, who had set out a week before, he alone succeeded in reaching an English garrison, to tell the dismal tale of his companions' fate. With the exception of a hundred and twenty men, women, and children, whom Akbar Khan had taken prisoners on the way, and a few score Sepoys who afterwards straggled into Peshāwar, none else had survived the horrors of a retreat in mid-winter, without due supplies of any sort, through mountain-passes crowned with hostile Afghāns, and blocked with a mob of helpless fugitives, who fell at every step under the falling snow from cold, hunger, or the deadly rain of Afghān bullets. Thousands perished in the Khūrd Kābul Pass alone. In the Jagdalak Pass the slaughter was renewed, until every trace of a disciplined army had disappeared. Some sixty officers and men reached Gandamak; but these too, with the one exception of Dr. Brydon, perished on the road thence to Jalālabād.

The tidings of this great disaster, the heaviest which had yet befallen our arms in Asia, struck dismay for the moment into every English heart in India itself. They became the talk of every Indian bazaar, and inspired our ill-wishers throughout the country with vague hopes of yet worse things to come. No outward stir, however, gave form to the feeling of the hour, nor do any of the native princes seem to have renewed their old intrigues against our rule. Happily for England, her honour was still upheld by such men as Nott and Rawlinson at Kandahār, Sale and Broadfoot at Jalālabād, Clerk, Mackeson, and

Henry Lawrence in the Punjāb. While Lord Auckland and his Commander-in-Chief, Sir Jasper Nicholls, were feebly paltering with the new danger, Nott and Sale bravely held their ground, deaf to the orders they had received from Kābul and undismayed by the annihilation of Elphinstone's force. Instead of waiting behind his defences, Nott marched out and beat the enemy whenever he got a chance, and even sent out one of his two Sepoy brigades under Colonel Wymer to show the backward General England the way into Kandahār.

Meanwhile Mr. George Clerk, as Governor-General's agent, was straining every nerve for the succour of General Sale. But the failure of Colonel Wild's attempts to carry his Sepoys through the Khyber threw Sale back upon his own resources for some months longer; while the misconduct of our Sikh allies, the apathy of Sir Jasper Nicholls, and the mutinous spirit which had spread from the Sikhs to our own Sepoys at Peshāwar, reduced Clerk and his able helpmates to the verge of despair. A fresh brigade, however, was already on its way to Peshāwar under Colonel George Pollock, a Company's officer of acknowledged worth; and other troops were getting ready for the same service at Ferozepore.

By this time Lord Auckland had resigned his post into the hands of Lord Ellenborough, who reached Calcutta in February, 1842. One of his last acts had been to sever the old connection between the Government and the national faiths. The revenues derived from Hindu temples and religious rites were made over to the care of Hindu priests; the tax on pilgrims was abolished on grounds still open to question; and the Company's troops were forbidden thenceforth to parade in honour of native festivals. It is however by his Afghān policy that Lord Auckland is best remembered, and the results of that policy were equally hurtful to his own fame, to his country's honour, and to the finances of our Indian Empire. The sad catastrophe in the Afghān snows could never have occurred but for the ill-judged invasion of Afghānistān; and more than twenty millions were added to the debt of India, before the disgrace of Elphinstone's retreat from Kābul had been wiped out by the victories of Nott and Pollock.

CHAPTER VI

LORD ELLENBOROUGH AND LORD HARDINGE—1842–1848

A FEW weeks before Lord Ellenborough's landing General Pollock had reached Peshāwar. The outlook at that moment was dark enough. Half his Sepoys were in hospital, and the rest were deeply tainted with the mutinous spirit of Avitabile's Sikhs. They had no mind to face the dreadful Khyber, and some of their English officers shared the feeling. The Sikhs were insolent and unmanageable by their own commanders. Sher Singh, the successor of Karak at Lahōre, had little power to enforce compliance with Clerk's demands for the promised succours and supplies. The Khyberīs, deaf to all Mackeson's offers, prepared to defend the pass with all their might. But Pollock's patience, well seconded by the energy of Clerk and Lawrence, overcame all hindrances. In two months the quiet, cool-headed artillery-officer, who had served in two sieges and three great wars, had so far recruited the health and discipline of his troops, that the timely arrival of English gunners and dragoons enabled him on the 5th of April to attempt the passage of the far-famed Khyber.

The attempt was brilliantly successful. The tremendous cliffs on either side of the pass were soon swept clear of the astonished foe, while Pollock with the centre column held his way unchecked through the long gloomy gorges between. By the 15th April the relieving army had exchanged greetings with the brave defenders of Jalālabād, fresh from their last victorious sally against the troops of Akbar Khan, who had been closely besieging them for more than a month past. With the utter rout of the Afghāns on the 7th April Sale's heroic garrison found rest from their prolonged toils, and perfect freedom from any immediate danger. Not till three months after their rescue did Pollock's pleadings for an advance on Kābul, in behalf of English honour and English captives, wring from Lord Ellenborough a half-hearted consent to the only course which policy and patriotism alike dictated. Pollock and Nott were at last permitted to withdraw at their own risk from Afghānistān "by way of Kābul and Ghazni."

Those brave men, however, were quite prepared to take all the risk on their own shoulders. On the 7th August Nott led out his Sepoys from Kandahār. On the 30th he took Ghazni, which had been tamely surrendered to the Afghāns some months before. The fortifications were blown up, and the famous sandal-wood gates of Somnāth carried off from the spot where they had rested for eight centuries. One last victory on the 14th September cleared the road to Kābul, where three days afterwards Nott found Pollock already encamped.

The latter general had set out from Jalālabād on the 20th August, driving the Afghāns before him at Jagdalak on the 23rd, and routing Akbar Khan's best troops on the 13th September at Tezin. Two days' marching brought him to Kābul, and on the morning of the 16th the British ensign once more floated proudly from the top of the Bāla Hissār. One thing only was wanting to crown the triumph of our arms—the recovery of the captives whom Akbar had sent off towards Bamian. The honour of rescuing them fell to Sir Richmond Shakespear, and by the 22nd September they were all safely lodged in Pollock's camp.*

* General Elphinstone had died in captivity. Among the released prisoners were nine ladies and several children.

After the capture and destruction of Istalīf and Charīkar by General McCaskill, one last deed of vengeance for past humiliations remained to do. The great Bazaar of Kābul, where Macnaghten's mangled body had been exposed to every insult, was blown up and utterly destroyed, while a maddened soldiery, bursting through all control, revelled for three days in the plunder of the city itself. At last, on the 12th October, the whole army set out from Kābul on their march homeward through the Khyber, carrying with them the family of Shah Shujā, who had been slain by his own subjects some months before. His eldest brother, the blind old Zamān Shah, who had dreamed of conquering India in the days of Lord Wellesley, and been driven from his throne in 1801 by a brother of Dost Muhammad, was now glad to close his days on English ground, a pensioner on the bounty of his ancient foes.

A splendid gathering of troops at Ferozepore, in honour of Pollock's safe return, gratified Lord Ellenborough's taste for pageantry, and proclaimed to all India the complete success which had rewarded the efforts of his commanders to wipe out the stain of Elphinstone's miscarriage. After a narrow escape from adorning Lord Ellenborough's triumph, Dost Muhammad was set free to govern the people who had once flung aside the dynasty of Shah Shujā. A bombastic manifesto from Simla announced the removal of the Somnāth Gates to India, and "the insult of eight hundred years" was "avenged" by the possession of a trophy which proved to be no more than a modern forgery. For their splendid services in the late campaign—services performed in spite of Lord Ellenborough's virtual opposition—Pollock and Nott received each a knighthood, with a handsome pension from the Court of Directors. It was not till nearly thirty years later that Sir George Pollock was made a baronet, in reward for his achievements which not only stamped him as the greatest soldier of his day, but had probably saved our Indian empire from perils of the gravest kind.

Pax Asiæ restitutæ—"Peace restored to Asia"—was the high-flown legend of a medal struck by Lord Ellenborough's order in memory of the late events. A few weeks afterwards he had entered on a war with Sind. The Amīrs of that country were rewarded for their co-operation in the late campaigns by a demand for further concessions, which they were loath to yield. The demand was enforced by a movement of British troops under Sir Charles Napier towards Hyderābād on the Indus. On the 12th February, 1843, the treaty was signed; but the Baluchi followers of the Amīrs were stirred to uncontrollable rage on learning that half the country had been ceded to the English Government. A furious attack on the Residency at Hyderābād ended in the retreat of Major Outram and his weak escort to an armed steamer on the Indus.

On the 17th February Sir Charles Napier won the hard-fought battle of Miāni against seven times his own numbers. The capture of Hyderābād was ere long followed by another great victory at Dabha, which placed all Sind at the conqueror's mercy. The despoiled Amīrs were hunted into exile or borne into captivity; their conquered kingdom was annexed to the Bombay Presidency; and Sir C. Napier became the successful governor of a province won by the sword, on grounds which Outram did not stand alone in condemning.

It was not long before the Marātha kingdom of Gwalior was once more to feel the weight of our arms. On the death of Jankaji Sindhia in February, his uncle, the Nāna Sahib, became regent, with the Governor-General's express sanction. But Jankaji's widow intrigued with the troops against him, and ere long a favoured rival was set up in his place. This defiance of the Paramount Power was made more serious by the growing turbulence of the Gwalior army, and by the danger which seemed to threaten India from the restless ambition of the great military power beyond the Sutlej. Even before the murder of our ally Sher Singh in September, the army of the Khālsa had begun to rule the Sikh state, and the men whom Ranjīt Singh had hardly kept in hand might be tempted at any time through fear and wantonness to pick a quarrel with their English neighbours.

An English army, under the veteran Sir Hugh Gough, began its warning march towards the Chambal in December, 1843, accompanied by Lord Ellenborough himself. All chance of a peaceful settlement vanished on the 28th, when the Marāthas opened fire on an English outpost near Maharājpur. Next morning Sir Hugh Gough carried with the bayonet a strong position, armed with powerful guns and defended with a stubbornness which cost him dear. On the same day General Grey's division fought and routed another large body of Marāthas at Paniār, twelve miles from Gwalior.

These two victories ended the brief campaign. The Queen-mother and her young son the very next day placed themselves at the mercy of Lord Ellenborough, who had shared in the perils of the day before. The former was pensioned off; a council of regency was set up under the virtual control of the Resident, Colonel Sleeman; the Gwalior army was cut down to 9,000 men; and a contingent of 10,000 men, largely recruited from the old Rājput soldiery who had fought so well at Maharājpur, was placed under the command of picked English officers.

While the Governor-General was thus engaged on the frontier, his deputy at Calcutta, Mr. Wilberforce Bird, carried out Lord Auckland's humane designs by an Act which abolished slavery throughout India. A few months later Lord Ellenborough learned the tidings of his own recall by a vote of the India House, in spite of the resistance offered to such an exercise of the Company's privilege by the Board of Control. In the minds of the Directors the alarm awakened by his warlike tendencies went hand in hand with deep resentment of his insolent behaviour towards themselves and their favourites in the Civil Service of India. In July, 1844, his brother-in-law, Sir Henry Hardinge, landed in Calcutta, and took up the vacant post. The very last months of Lord Ellenborough's brief rule had been clouded by a mutiny among the Bengal Sepoys. Several of the regiments which had been ordered to garrison Sind stood upon their right to receive extra pay for foreign service, and refused for a time to march on. Their claims were at length conceded; but one regiment, the 34th, had gone so far towards open mutiny that nothing short of its disbandment could be allowed to atone for its offence. Even in Madras there were symptoms of a like spirit during the same year.

A rising in the Southern Marātha highlands about Kholāpur broke the lull of Indian politics in October, 1844. The task of suppressing it brought out in a new field the skill and energy of Colonel Outram, worthily seconded by the courage and endurance of his troops. A brilliant campaign against the Baluchi raiders on the Sind frontier in 1845 bore fresh witness to Napier's soldiership, and secured the peace of his new province. Meanwhile the new Governor-General kept his eye upon the darkening storm-cloud in the Punjāb. With the death of Sher Singh the anarchy beyond the Sutlej grew worse and worse. A powerful army, restless, greedy for more pay or plunder, filled at one moment with wild mistrust of Anglo-Indian statesmanship, at another with ignorant scorn of English forbearance, had to be wooed and humoured by successive leaders, each of whom in his turn paid with a bloody death the price of his own folly or of his soldiers' fickleness. Even the brave, well-meaning Hīra Singh, who ruled for a time in the name of the boy-king, Dhulīp Singh, failed to escape the common doom. Twice in two years had a large Sikh army set out from Lahore, as if for the invasion of Hindustān. Sir Henry Hardinge quietly massed his troops in Sind, ready for the struggle whenever it might come. At last, in December, 1845, a great Sikh army for the third time began its march towards the Sutlej.

That the Sikhs were in earnest on this occasion no one in Hardinge's camp appears to have believed. It is even doubtful whether they themselves had quite made up their minds until the last moment to dare the issue of a struggle which Ranjīt Singh would never have provoked.* Be that as it may, Sir Henry Hardinge, an old soldier who had earned his laurels in Spain under Wellington, was not to be caught asleep. Before the enemy had crossed the Sutlej our troops were hurrying by double marches towards the frontier,† commanded by the war-loving Sir Hugh Gough himself. On the 12th December the Sikh army, about 60,000 strong in regular troops alone, with 150 guns, began to cross the river, and by the 16th were encamped in threatening neighbourhood to Ferozepore. Sir John Littler, with half of his 10,000 men, marched out to meet them; but the Sikhs, declining the challenge, turned aside to entrench themselves at Ferozeshahr, while 20,000 of them pushed on towards Mūdkī in hopes of taking Gough's troops by surprise.

On the 18th Gough's wearied soldiers were resting near that place, when the gallant Broadfoot gave timely warning of the Sikh advance. The battle of that afternoon was

* See Sir Henry Lawrence's "Essays, Military and Political."

† They marched 150 miles in six days.

waged on both sides with equal courage, but nothing could withstand the repeated onsets of the English horse, followed up by the steady advance in line of our brave infantry. By nightfall the Sikhs had fled, leaving seventeen guns in the hands of the victors, whose own loss had not been slight.

Reinforced by half of Littler's men and some fresh troops from Ambāla, Gough on the 21st led his army, now 17,000 strong, against the Sikh array of more than 40,000 good troops entrenched at Ferozeshahr, behind breastworks guarded by a hundred guns. Sir Henry Hardinge, who had placed himself under Gough as second in command, led the centre of the English line. Late in the afternoon the battle began. On the English right and centre all went fairly well in spite of the havoc wrought by the steady fire from guns far heavier than our own. But on the left, where Littler commanded, his infantry, after a bold dash forward, fell back in utter disorder. When night fell upon the scene of carnage, a few thousand English soldiers and Sepoys lay on the ground they had already won within the entrenchment, worn out, hungry, thirsty, pinched with cold, and harassed by the frequent fire from still uncaptured guns. One of these tormentors had to be silenced by a charge of infantry under Hardinge himself. There was even talk of a retreat on Ferozepore, but neither Gough nor Hardinge would hear of a move so fatal to English honour.

Once more with returning daylight our rallied regiments advanced to complete their work. Lal Singh's battalions wavered, broke, and fled; battery after battery fell into our hands; and the foe were already out of sight, when Tej Singh, coming up with a fresh army of 20,000 men and 60 guns, spread new anxiety in our shattered ranks. But the Sikh leader had no mind to dispute the issue of those two days' fighting; and he too withdrew from the field, after firing a few shots, which the English guns for want of ammunition could not return.

The victory thus hardly earned had been dearly bought. Out of 17,000 brought into the field, 2415 had been killed or wounded, including ten of Sir Henry's aides-de-camp. For the next few weeks, while the English were awaiting fresh succours and the heavy guns from Delhi, the Sikhs lay idle on their own side of the Sutlej. At length, towards the end of January, 1846, Ranjōr Singh recrossed the river and threatened Ludhiana. On his march thither with a few thousand troops, Sir Harry Smith lost his baggage near the fort of Baduwāl. But a few days later, the brilliant victory of Aliwāl, in which the Sikhs last 67 guns, more than atoned for the previous mishap; and the Sikhs, from behind their strong entrenchments at Sobraon on the Sutlej, awaited the next move in the English game. At last, on the 10th February, Gough's warriors, 15,000 strong, dashed forward, after a fierce but fruitless cannonade, to storm a position held by 35,000 of the best Sikh troops, and armed with 67 heavy guns. Under a withering fire they struggled onwards, recoiling only to renew the attack, until the entrenchments were fairly entered, and the Sikhs, still fighting manfully, were driven back before the British bayonet.

Ere long the retreat became an utter rout. The English guns played havoc among the masses of flying Sikhs, who crowded towards the bridge of boats, or threw themselves into the swollen Sutlej. A river red with blood and choked with corpses seemed more than a figure of speech on that day of slaughter, when some 10,000 followers of Gofind perished in the field or in their flight. The loss of the victors in killed and wounded amounted to 2383; but the whole of the enemy's guns and stores on the left bank of the river had fallen into their hands, and no army now stood between them and Lahore.

Ten days afterwards the victorious English were encamped in view of the Sikh capital. On the 23rd February, the ministers of Dhulīp Singh signed the treaty which transferred Jullundur and the Sikh states on the left bank of the Sutlej to English rule, and bound the Sikh Government to pay a heavy fine for the costs of the war. It was afterwards agreed that the bulk of the fine should be paid off by the sale of Kashmīr to Gūlāb Singh, the Rājput lord of Jammū, who had borne no part against us in the late struggle. The remnants of the old Khalsa army were disbanded, and Lahore was held for a time by English troops. Colonel Henry Lawrence, who had been summoned from Nepāl on the death of the gallant Major Broadfoot, was appointed to act for the Viceroy at the Lahore court.

For these great successes, achieved in two months, the Governor-General and Sir Hugh Gough were raised to the peerage. It was not long before Lawrence had to place a curb on the intrigues of the Lahore government. At the head of 10,000 of our late foes, he forced the unruly Shaikh Imām-ud-din to surrender Kashmīr to its new master. Lāl Singh, the Queen-mother's favourite, was removed from his office of wazir and banished to Benāres. Before the year's end the treaty of Bhairowāl made Lawrence virtual master of the Punjāb, aided by a council of Sikh Sardārs or chiefs, and a picked staff of English officers, who looked for guidance to the Resident alone.

Successful in war, Lord Hardinge turned his attention to works of peace. The crusade against Satī, infanticide, and slavery, was carried with good results into the dominions of native princes. The great Ganges canal, ordained by Lord Auckland after the dreadful famine of 1837, and suspended by Lord Ellenborough, was pushed forward in the spring of 1846, with renewed vigour, under the able management of Major Cautley, seconded by the zeal of Mr. Thomason, Lieutenant-Governor of the North-Western Provinces. The question of railways in India found in Lord Hardinge an eager advocate, and the surveys for two great lines went steadily forward. Private enterprise opened out new fields of trade in the factories of Western India and the tea-gardens of Assam. To the cause of native education Lord Hardinge proved from the first an enlightened friend. New schools of various kinds were opened in many places; and the new-born native impulse towards wider fields of learning and mental growth was encouraged by the preference given in the public service to those natives who had passed through a government school or college.

A few local disorders, such as the Muhammadan plot at Patna, an anti-Christian riot at Tinnevelly, a civil war in Bhopāl, armed strife in Oudh and the Deccan, and a rising among the Khānds of Goomsur, marked the closing years of Lord Hardinge's government. The worst of these, however, happened in native states, where disorder was still the rule; and the Khānd rising was put down with little bloodshed, if not without some trouble to the troops employed. At length, in March, 1848, Lord Hardinge turned his face homewards amid the general regret of all classes, after making over the seals of office to his great successor, James Ramsay, Earl of Dalhousie.

BOOK VI

CONSOLIDATION OF ENGLISH RULE

CHAPTER I

LORD DALHOUSIE—1848–1856

WHEN Peel's able President of the Board of Trade arrived in India at the beginning of 1848, the country was in almost perfect peace. But for a commercial crisis in Calcutta and a flickering little war in the Khānd jungles, not a cloud appeared on the political horizon. In a few months, however, all was changed. While Colonel Lawrence was seeking health and rest in England, a new storm of war was gathering in the Punjāb. Mulrāj, the Governor of Multān, had agreed to resign his post; and Mr. Vans Agnew, with Lieutenant Anderson and a small body of Sikh troops, was directed by the Lahore Government to instal Khan Singh in his place. But the two Englishmen were treacherously attacked in Mulrāj's presence, and afterwards foully murdered by his men.

Sir Frederick Currie, who was then acting for Lawrence at Lahore, instead of moving troops with all speed to the scene of outrage, as Lawrence would have done, awaited the issue of an appeal for help to the Commander-in-Chief. But Lord Gough was against moving a large force at the hottest season of the year; and Lord Dalhousie, being new to office, concurred in his reasons for an ill-timed delay. It remained for one of Lawrence's best subalterns, the young Lieutenant Edwardes, who was engaged in settling the province of Bannū beyond the Indus, to set his countrymen an example of prompt action. With the help of his own levies, of some troops under Colonel Cortlandt, and of others presently furnished by the loyal Nawāb of Bahāwalpur, Edwardes thrice defeated the rebel Mulrāj, and finally shut him up in Multān.

By this time matters in the Punjāb looked so serious, that General Whish was ordered to undertake the siege of Multān with a regular force of eight thousand English and Sepoys. On the 4th September he pitched his camp before that city. Edwardes' little army had already been reinforced by a few thousand Sikhs under the Raja Sher Singh. Hardly had the siege begun, when the latter made common cause with the rebels and marched away to kindle fresh revolts elsewhere. His desertion caused the suspension of the siege, pending the arrival of fresh succours from Bombay and Ferozepore.

It was soon evident that a new fight for empire was on our hands. The Sikh leaders everywhere joined the revolt, and a holy war was proclaimed against the infidel "Faringi." Nothing remained but to take up the challenge. "The Sikh nation," said Lord Dalhousie at the farewell banquet given him at Barrackpore, "has called for war, and on my word, sirs, they shall have it with a vengeance." While he hastened up the country, a powerful army was mustering on the Sutlej under Lord Gough. Its march did not begin too soon. Sher Singh was already menacing Lahore, with a large army of the veterans who had rallied to the Khālsa war-cry; and Dost Muhammad was bargaining for Peshāwar as the price of his co-operation with our Sikh foes.

On the 27th December, Whish was enabled to renew the siege of Multān. On the 22nd January, 1849, his troops stormed the city, but Mulrāj still held the citadel with the obstinacy of despair. At last, on the 22nd January, when the fortress inside had become a mere wreck, and two great breaches invited an easy entrance to our troops, he and the remnant of his brave garrison surrendered at discretion.

His followers were allowed to go their own way, while Mulrāj himself was carried off a close prisoner, to await the trial which ended in dooming him to a felon's death. His life, however, was ultimately spared, but death alone cut short his term of lifelong imprisonment.

Meanwhile Lord Gough had encountered Sher Singh at Rāmnagar on the Chenāb, and again in the jungles of Chiliānwāla on the Jhelum. The repulse of the Sikhs at the former place was marred by the headlong valour of Havelock's dragoons, many of whom, with their brave leader and General Cureton, perished in vain efforts to retrieve their blunder. On the 2nd December a part of Lord Gough's army under Sir Joseph Thackwell crossed the Chenāb higher up the stream, and engaged the Sikhs at Sadūlapur, forcing them to retreat towards the Jhelum. Thither Lord Gough slowly followed them, until, on the afternoon of the 13th January, he suddenly felt the fire of their outposts from amidst the jungle around Chiliānwāla. It was late in the day, but the fiery old soldier would not wait for the morrow. His troops, about 11,000 strong, advanced to attack some 30,000 Sikh veterans with sixty guns strongly posted on the plain behind a thick belt of intervening jungle.

Before night-fall the Sikhs had been driven back to the Jhelum with a heavy loss in men and guns. But the victors also had suffered heavily. One brigade of Campbell's division had been hurled back in utter disorder,*

* It is a well-attested fact that General Campbell made his division advance through the jungle with unloaded muskets. One brigade under

and the cavalry on the right wing had fled in sudden and mysterious panic before a small body of Sikh horse. The rest of the troops, however, fought with their wonted daring, and another hour of daylight would probably have renewed the slaughter of Sobraon. But night came on; our troops fell back a little for want of water; and the Sikhs, returning later to the field, cut up many of the wounded and carried off most of the captured guns. Twelve only were secured by the victors, whose own loss in killed and wounded amounted to 89 officers and 2357 men, besides four guns and three sets of colours.

For several weeks the two armies lay almost within sight of each other, while Lord Gough waited for reinforcements from the camp of General Whish. While these were yet on their way, the Sikh army under Sher Singh and his father Chattar Singh marched round the English General's right flank towards Lahore. But the blow thus aimed fell short of its mark. British troops held the fords of the Chenāb, and the Sikhs turned off to take up a strong position on the plain in front of Gujrāt. There, with 50,000 men and sixty guns, the Sikh leaders awaited the final onset of Gough's army, now swollen to 20,000 men and a hundred guns.

On the 21st February the fight began with such a fire from the English heavy guns as had never before been witnessed on an Indian battle-field. For more than two hours the English batteries, light and heavy, played upon the foe with ever-increasing havoc. At last the Sikh gunners, who had manfully returned shot for shot, slackened their fire and began to fall back. The British infantry were then let loose upon the wavering Sikhs. One of Gilbert's brigades under Penny swept forward against the strong village of Kālra, still held by the pick

Colonel Hoggan, however, advanced firing, and swept the enemy before them. The other obeyed the order, and suffered accordingly.

of the Sikh infantry. Under a scathing fire the 2nd Europeans stormed the place, while a smaller village was attacked and carried by the 10th Foot. A spirited charge of Malcolm's Sind horse ere long drove the best of the Sikh cavalry from the field. Sir Joseph Thackwell with the whole of his fine cavalry and light horse guns took up the pursuit of the beaten foe, driving them before him with heavy slaughter, until night found him fifteen miles from the field, which our troops had won with a loss of less than 800 men. Fifty-three guns, many standards, and the whole of the enemy's camp betokened the completeness of a victory which laid the Sikh power for the last time in the dust.

It only remained to gather up the after-fruits of that day's work. Early next morning Sir Walter Gilbert, with 12,000 men and forty guns, set off in pursuit of Sher Singh's broken army. The chase was kept up with so much vigour, that by the middle of March the last of the Sikh leaders had surrendered, and the last of their wearied soldiers had laid down their arms to the pursuing column at Rāwal Pindi. Forty-one more guns were added to the spoils of Multān and Gujrāt, and Sher Singh was carried off a prisoner to Lahore. His Afghān allies, who had shared the disasters of Gujrāt, still kept ahead of their unwearied pursuers; but only a few hours before Gilbert reached Peshāwar, they fled back, as it was said, "like dogs" into the mountain passes whence they had ridden out "like lions" a few months before.

On the 29th March the last blow was struck by order of Lord Dalhousie at the independence of the Sikh kingdom. In the presence of the boy-sovereign, Dhulīp Singh, was read the proclamation which made him a pensioner of the East India Company, and annexed his country to British India. The conquered province passed under the rule of a Board of Three, at the head of which Sir Henry

Lawrence, who had come out again from England with a knighthood, deservedly took his place. Conspicuous among his colleagues was his brother John Lawrence, who, with the aid of a few irregular troops and Sikh levies, had kept Jullundur in comparative quiet during the war. For the next few years the two brothers, with the help of Mr. Mansel, and afterwards of Mr. Montgomery, ruled the Punjāb with light but firm hands, restoring order, suppressing crime, revising the revenue system, enforcing a simple code of laws, freeing the trade of the country from its former shackles, making roads, canals, and other useful works, and winning alike the respect and the affections of a conquered but brave and high-spirited people. Sir Henry's mild influence fell like balm on the hearts of the humbled Sikh Sardārs, and did much to counteract the harsher tendencies of a rule which recognised no distinction between class and class in respect of their common rights, duties, and burdens. To the Marquis of Dalhousie—for such he had now become—belongs much of the credit due to all concerned in the pacification of the Punjāb. His eyes were everywhere during his frequent travels through the country; no details of Government were too small to escape his notice; and the measures taken for guarding the Punjāb frontier were the direct offspring of his own brain.

Meanwhile the new Commander-in-Chief, Sir Charles Napier, was dealing in his own stern fashion with a mutiny among the Bengal regiments told off to garrison the new province. Some of them had refused to take their ordinary pay, and the 66th Sepoys went so far towards open mutiny, that Napier took upon himself to disband the regiment and put a Gūrkha battalion in its place. This and other measures, decreed by him on his own authority, brought him into collision with the Governor-General, who had no mind to let another usurp his lawful power. The quarrel ended in Napier's resignation; but the mutinous spirit which had been rife in the Bengal army ever since the Afghān wars kept smouldering beneath the surface, ready to burst forth again on the smallest provocation. The Government saw no pressing danger, and Delhi, the great centre of the Mussulman intrigue and the chief arsenal for Upper India, was still left under the sole protection of Sepoy bayonets.

In 1852 another war was forced on Lord Dalhousie's hands by the continued insolence of the Burmese. The rude treatment of English Residents at Ava had been followed by a series of outrages on English merchants and shipping at Rangoon. Dalhousie's demands for redress were made in vain, and those who bore them subjected to open insult. At length Commodore Lambert was driven to blockade Rangoon and silence the batteries which had opened fire on his frigate. Dalhousie at once prepared for war. On the 2nd of April, 1852, a powerful British fleet, including many war-steamers, and carrying a strong force under General Godwin, anchored off Rangoon. Martaban, on the Salween river, had already been attacked and taken by Bengal Sepoys. Before the middle of April the English, in spite of a brave resistance, were masters of Rangoon itself. Bassein was taken in May, and Pegu in June. The road to Ava lay open; but Godwin declined to expose his small force to the risks and discomforts of the rainy season.

His advance to Prome in October, and the relief of Hill's small garrison in Pegu, were followed early in the next year by the capture of Danubyū and the rout of the Burman leader, Miā-Tun, by Sir John Cheape. Thenceforth the war was virtually over. With the whole province of Pegu occupied by our troops, it was deemed needless to push on after an enemy who declined to fight. To negotiate with the King of Burma proved to be a waste of time and words. The Peguers on their part seemed perfectly willing to exchange the Burman for the British yoke. Dalhousie, therefore, boldly resolved to fill up the British seaboard between Arakān and Tenasserim by the annexation of Pegu, with or without the consent of the Burman sovereign. His intention indeed had already been made public in December, 1852; but it was not until the following June, when the obstinate King of Burma had virtually yielded to all our demands, that peace was finally proclaimed and Pegu freed from all fear of Burman aggression.

While the conquest of the Punjāb brought all India within the Sulaimān Hills and the Himālayas under our virtual rule, the annexation of Pegu made the Company masters of all the coast country on the eastern side of the Bay of Bengal, from Chittagong to the borders of Siam. Under the wise rule of Colonel Phayre, Pegu itself became a model province, easily held by a few troops, its people steadily advancing in wealth and numbers, and its chief port on the Irrawaddy becoming ere long the populous seat of a thriving trade.

Meanwhile the work of annexation had been going on within the bounds of our Indian empire. In 1848 the Raja of Satāra died without an heir. Was the boy whom, according to Hindu custom, he had adopted two hours before his own death to be recognised as his successor to kingly title and power, as well as to all his personal estate? In spite of the arguments of Sir George Clerk, then Governor of Bombay, Lord Dalhousie held that the Government was not bound to accept the consequences of an act whose validity it had never acknowledged. The State of Satāra, as created by an English viceroy, had lapsed to the Company through default of heirs; and the Government was "bound to take that which was legally and justly its due, and to extend to that territory the benefit of our sovereignty, present and prospective."

Emery Walker, Ltd., photographer.

THE MARQUESS OF DALHOUSIE

FROM THE PAINTING BY SIR J. WATSON GORDON, R.A., P.R.S.A., IN THE NATIONAL PORTRAIT GALLERY

p. 348

Armed with the approval of the India House, Dalhousie struck Satāra out of the list of native states, bestowing liberal pensions on the Raja's widows and his adopted son.

Five years later died the Bhosla Raja of Berar or Nāgpur and the Raja of Jhānsi in Bundelkhand. As the former had neither left nor named a successor, and the people under the fostering care of Mr. Jenkins had learned to value aright the benefits of our rule, Nāgpur also was speedily annexed. The ruler of Jhānsi, on the other hand, had left an adopted heir, in whose name his widow claimed to govern. But the absorption of Satāra furnished the Governor-General with ample grounds for rejecting her claims, and placing Jhānsi also directly under British rule. The Rāni, an ambitious woman, brooded in secret over the imagined wrong, until the moment for taking a terrible revenge seemed to have come.

Karauli, in Rājputāna, was another state whose sovereign had left no direct heir. But the question of its disposal was referred to the Court of Directors, who decided in favour of acknowledging the adopted son of a protected ally. Another question which came before Lord Dalhousie concerned the claim of Dhūndū Pant, the infamous Nāna Sahib of after-years, to the handsome pension which Lord Hastings had bestowed on his adoptive father, the erewhile Pēshwa Bājī Rāo. It was decreed on just, if not politic grounds, that the ex-Pēshwa's princely income had lapsed to the Company on his death in 1853. In vain did the angry Nāna plead his cause at the India House. It was decided that he had no claim to a pension granted only to Bājī Rāo and his family; but by way of balm for his wounded feelings, he was allowed to hold the lordship of Bithur, on the Ganges, not far from Cawnpore.

About this time also the Nizám's province of Berar

was virtually transferred to British rule in payment of the heavy debts he had incurred to the Indian Government. To this concession the Nizām unwillingly agreed as the only means of retaining the services of his useful but ill-paid contingent. The weak-minded successor of Chīn Kilich was thus rescued from the worst results of a misrule prolonged for many years past; while the ceded province, over which he still retained a portion of his sovereign rights, throve apace under a rule which brooks no internal disorders, and has always laboured for the well-being of the people at large.

Three years later, in 1856, the dethroned Raja of Mysore renewed his prayer for restoration to the government of which he had been justly deprived in 1831. Through all that time his forfeit kingdom had been ably governed by General Mark Cubbon, in spite of some resistance from the Raja's friends. Lord Dalhousie saw no good reason to grant a prayer which Lord Hardinge had found good reason to reject; and it was not till ten years later that an English minister was rash enough to reverse the wiser policy of successive governors-general, and hand over a flourishing province to the doubtful blessings of native rule.

Meantime the misrule in Oudh had been growing yearly worse and worse, ever since Lord William Bentinck had solemnly warned the king of the Company's firm resolve to interfere, if he made no effort to mend his ways and govern his people in closer harmony with the counsels of the English Resident. In 1847 the warning was repeated by Lord Hardinge. But the long-suffering of the Indian Government proved of no avail. The king amassed money at the expense of his subjects, only to waste it on women, fiddlers, and buffoons. Justice was openly bought and sold. The great land-holders, like many a baron of the Middle Ages in Europe, openly defied the royal power from their well-armed forts, and throve on the plunder of their weaker countrymen. The king's troops made up for their scanty and irregular pay by living freely on the people they were supposed to protect. Colonel Sleeman, who became Resident in 1848 and undertook a three months' tour through the country in 1849–50, for all his sympathy with native princes, avowed that the misgovernment had reached an unbearable pitch, and advised his masters to place the country under British rule. His successor, the high-souled General Outram, pronounced in favour of a like course. All the best-informed statesmen in India argued to the same effect.

It only remained to settle the conditions on which English rule should be established in Oudh. On this point Lord Dalhousie was nearly at one with Colonel Sleeman. Both agreed in wishing to leave the king his nominal sovereignty, but the Governor-General was for employing the surplus revenues that might accrue to him under the new form of government, not for the king's benefit, but for that of India at large. Some members of his Council argued strongly for the entire absorption of Oudh into British India, and their views found most favour with the Government at home. In compliance with positive orders from the India House, Lord Dalhousie prepared to annex the country, and dethrone the dynasty which Lord Hastings had set up. On the 7th February, 1856, Sir James Outram announced to the king that he had ceased to reign. The tidings were received with a burst of tears, and a flat refusal to sign the treaty which transformed him into a discrowned pensioner of the Indian Government. It was useless, however, to struggle against his fate. He withdrew to Calcutta on a handsome pension, and the whole kingdom submitted without a blow to its future masters.

A few months earlier, in July, 1855, the peace of

Bengal had been broken by a sudden rising of aboriginal Santals in the hill ranges of Rājmahal. Maddened by the extortions of Bengali money-lenders, who worked the law-courts for their own ends, these simple savages marched forth in a vast body to lay their grievances before the Calcutta Council. Provisions failing them, they began to plunder the villages on their way, to attack police-posts, to murder native officials and stray Englishmen, and even to threaten the safety of important stations. The few troops that first encountered them were driven back or slain by their poisoned arrows. It was not till the cold season of 1855 that their power for mischief was checked by the advance of fresh troops, who hemmed them in on all sides, and hunted them down with little mercy. By the year's end the rising had been quelled with the death of its ringleaders; and the wrongs for which they had sought so wild a redress were shortly remedied by the appointment of a Commissioner, who ruled the Sāntāl districts on a simpler system than that which had long prevailed throughout Bengal.

We have yet to mention those peaceful services which have shed so bright a lustre on Lord Dalhousie's Indian career. No Governor-General has ever been so fortunate in his opportunities, or so successful in turning them to account. His genius for governing embraced a rare mastery of details, a clear conception of the work that lay before him, a thorough knowledge of his tools, and a strength of will which triumphed over the drawbacks of a sickly frame yet further enfeebled by prolonged toil in a very trying climate. In every department of the State his strong hand wrought some change for the better. Both in the army and the civil service individual over-looking was substituted for that of Boards; even the Punjāb Board under Sir Henry Lawrence giving place in 1853 to the rule of a Chief Commissioner, Sir Henry's brother John. In 1852 was established a new Department of Public Works, which furnished India with a staff of civil engineers fit to carry on the great projects which a time of peace and a full treasury encouraged Dalhousie to set on foot or bring to an early completion. The greatest of these was the Ganges Canal, perhaps the noblest work of its kind in the world, with its five hundred miles of navigable main stream and many hundreds of irrigating branches. Thanks to Lord Dalhousie's unwearied efforts, the waters of the Upper Ganges were let into this mighty work on the 8th April, 1854, amid crowds of wondering natives; and its chief engineer, Colonel Cautley, received the Order of the Bath for his success in carrying out the scheme which he himself had planned fifteen years before. Of only less importance was the network of canals which Colonel Napier had meanwhile begun to weave for the parched but not unfruitful plains of the Punjāb.

Dalhousie's name, indeed, is inseparably linked with the whole history of India's progress during the last twenty-five years. To him India owes the removal or the lowering of almost every remaining barrier to trade, industry, social well-being, and mental growth. From the planting of trees in dry places to the building of railways, from reforms in jail discipline to the diffusion of aids to knowledge among the people, nothing seemed too small or too great for his far-reaching powers. He was the first to endow India with a cheap uniform rate of postage, whereby a letter from Peshāwar to Cape Comorin, or from Arakān to Karāchi, could be carried for half an anna, or three farthings. Under his zealous encouragement Dr. O'Shaughnessy was enabled in the course of a few years to cover India with 4,000 miles of telegraph wires. Dalhousie succeeded in cheapening the rates of postage from England to India. Under his orders the first yearly reports were sent in from the heads of every province on all things connected with its administration. To him also India owes the general planning and first instalments of those 4,000 miles of railway which now join Bombay to Madras, Calcutta, Allahābād, and Lahore. To the scheme of cheap popular instruction which Mr. Thomason first set on foot in the North-Western Provinces he lent his eager countenance; and, fortified by Sir Charles Wood's Education Despatch of 1854, he began at once to organise that improved system of State-aided schools and colleges under which more than three million scholars are now taught, at a yearly cost of £1,300,000 to the State.

In 1853 the question of renewing the East India Company's Charter was again the subject of parliamentary debate, which resulted as before in fresh curtailments of the Company's power. The days of its rule were, in fact, already numbered. Of the eighteen members of the Court of Directors, six were henceforth to be chosen by the Crown. India might still be governed in the name of the Company, but all power became practically vested in the Board of Control. A heavy blow was dealt at the Company's patronage by an Act which opened the Civil Service of India to public competition. A heavy burden, on the other hand, was taken off the shoulders of the Governor-General by the arrangement which gave a Lieutenant-Governor to the populous province of Bengal Proper. New members with enlarged powers were also added to the Supreme Council in Calcutta.

With the annexation of Oudh, Dalhousie's term of office, twice prolonged by the Court of Directors, came to a glorious, but for him much-needed end. Worn out with eight years of hard work, the great marquis gave the last touches to the farewell minute—the master work of a pen as clear, direct, and polished as Cæsar's or Wellington's—which contains at once the history and the best defence of his memorable career. In another set of minutes he enlarged on the policy of reducing the overgrown Sepoy army and strengthening the European force in India. At length, on the 6th March, 1856, he embarked for England, followed by impressive tokens of the esteem and admiration which all classes had learned to feel for a ruler perhaps as great as any since Warren Hastings. But his part in life, as he himself declared, was already played out; and the death which awaited him in 1860 was even then written on the face of one who had landed in India at the early age of thirty-six.

An able and determined man, with a burning zeal for good government, his work yet left seeds of serious trouble. The judgment of Sir John Kaye will probably be accepted as just by future historians.

CHAPTER II

LORD CANNING—1856–1862

LORD CANNING, son of the great English Minister whom Pitt had first brought into notice, found India for the moment in perfect peace. To follow in the footsteps of his great predecessor, and carry forward his unfinished schemes for the good of the people, was all the task which seemed then cut out for the erewhile Postmaster-General of Great Britain. The Penal Code, in which Macaulay had sought to furnish a simple uniform system of law for all creeds and classes in India, was entrusted to the revising hands of another great jurist, Mr. Barnes Peacock. Recruits for the Bengal army were henceforth required to take the same oath of general service as their brethren in Bombay and Madras; a measure intended, like the introduction of Sikh recruits into Bengal regiments under Lord Dalhousie, to counteract the domineering spirit of the high-caste Sepoys in Bengal. Dalhousie's scheme for removing the Mughal princes from Delhi on the death of the reigning king, Bahādur Shah, was furthered by the recognition of his lawful heir, on terms which expelled the dynasty of Timūr from the palace where they had hitherto retained a certain semblance of independent power.

By this time, however, Lord Canning's attention was turned towards Persia, whose sovereign, in breach of former treaties, had sent an army to capture Herāt from the Afghāns. In obedience to orders from home, the Governor-General prepared for war. Early in December, 1856, a

British force under the brave General Outram, aided by the fire of Leeke's ships, gained swift possession of Bushire, on the Persian Gulf. Ere long a Persian army began its march towards the conquered place; but Outram hastened forward to stay its approach, and its retreat from Barāsjūn on the 5th February was followed by its utter rout on the 8th at Khūshāb. The strong fort of Muhamrah, on a branch of the Euphrates, was easily taken on the 26th March; and the flight of the Persians a few days later from Ahwāz may be said to have finished the campaign. Its close was doubtless hastened by the treaty of alliance which Sir John Lawrence, Sir Henry's fit successor in the government of the Punjāb, had formed with our old foe, Dost Muhammad, in January, 1857. By the Treaty of Paris, which had already been signed on the 4th March, the Shah of Persia pledged himself to withdraw his troops from Herāt and renounce all claim to sovereignty over any part of Afghānistān.

It was a happy thing for India that the war ended when it did, in good time to enable Lord Canning to meet the heaviest blow which has ever yet been struck at English supremacy in Hindustān. By whom that blow was planned is still a matter for conjecture; but there is ample evidence that a spirit of unrest was abroad throughout the country in the beginning of 1857, that rumours of evil bode to India's rulers were everywhere rife, and that many causes combined to bring about the disaster to which those rumours seemed to point. It is always difficult for foreign rulers to guess at what is passing through the minds of their subjects; and the gulf which parts our countrymen in India from the millions among whom they come and go is one which few Englishmen can quite bridge over. Some of them, indeed, were warned of mischief brewing, but few even of these paid any heed to the hints or counsels of their native friends, and those who smelt danger beneath the surface found small encouragement to speak out.

In the Imperial Palace at Delhi, in the Nāna's castle at Bithūr, in the pleasant quarters occupied near Calcutta by the deposed King of Oudh, in every place where people cherished a grudge against their English rulers for some real or fancied wrong, plots were quietly hatching against the Power which, according to native soothsayers, had already entered on the last year of its reign. Emissaries from native courts were roaming the country, inflaming the minds of the discontented, and spreading everywhere dark rumours, none the less potent for their general absurdity, of a great English plot for abolishing caste and converting the whole of India, by fraud or force, to its masters' creed. The air grew thick with falsehoods, none of which were too wild for the popular belief. The fears alike of the Hindu and the Muhammadan were fed with omens and idle tales. An outbreak of cholera, a bad harvest, a jail riot, a heavy flood, anything served as a handle for the most outrageous slanders against a Government guilty only of a well-meant desire to keep the peace, to advance the general welfare, and to imbue its subjects with a taste for Western civilisation.

The time seemed propitious to our foes in India. Our English garrisons had been weakened to furnish troops for the campaign against Russia in the Crimea; nor was their place filled up by other troops from England, in spite of the warnings uttered by Dalhousie before and after the annexation of Oudh. Fresh regiments were shipped off from India for the Persian war. It was given out by the Nāna's emissaries that our army in the Crimea had perished almost to a man, and that England needed every soldier she could muster for her own defence, to say nothing of fresh embarrassments caused by another Chinese war. It was certain that only one English regiment lay between Calcutta and Agra, and that all India was held at that moment by about thirty thousand English troops, more than half of whom were quartered in or near the Punjāb.

The Sepoys also in Bengal were growing restless. Their discipline had been weakened by doubtful measures of military reform, by the moral effects of Afghān and Sikh campaigns, by the growth of new social habits among their English officers; their caste pride was sorely hurt by the admission of Sikhs and other low-caste men into their ranks, and their prescriptive rights were scattered to the winds by the new rule which compelled all recruits to enlist for general service, whether by land or sea. While the Nāna's agents tampered with the Hindu Sepoys, the minds of the Mussulman soldiery were inflamed against their masters by the preaching of Wahābi fanatics and the intrigues of the Delhi princes, wroth at their coming expulsion from the seat of their forefathers.

About the beginning of 1857, a new cause of alarm began to spread among the Sepoys. A rumour, born of chance gossip in the Dam-dam Bazaar, but, as it proved, not wholly destitute of foundation, flew about the country declaring that the cartridges of the new Enfield rifles had been greased with the fat of pigs and cows, in order to bring about the defilement alike of Muhammadans and Hindus. No such intention of course was at the root of what was no more than an unintentional, though foolish and disastrous, blunder. Before the end of January the Sepoys in Barrackpore were holding nightly meetings on the subject; several bungalows * were set on fire, and a marked change was seen in the men's bearing towards their officers. The same thing occurred at Rāniganj, the furthermost station on the new railway. On the 26th February, the 19th Sepoys at Berhampore refused to

* One-storied houses with steep roofs of thatch or tiles.

receive the suspected cartridges, and were hardly restrained from firing on their own officers. The mutiny was quelled, but no mercy was shown to the mutineers, who were marched down to Barrackpore and there disbanded by General Hearsey, in the presence of comrades no less guilty in spirit than themselves. Two days earlier, on the 29th March, a Sepoy of the 34th N.I. at Barrackpore seized his musket and called on some of his comrades to rally round him in defence of their religion. He attacked and wounded two officers before help came, which led him to turn his weapon against himself. The wound, however, was not fatal; he lived to undergo his trial and be hanged a few weeks afterwards.

All through March and April the tokens of disaffection grew more and more rife. Night after night fresh fires, whose origin remained a mystery, broke out in the great northern station of Ambāla; and the men who handled the new cartridges were marked out for the jeers and persecutions of their numerous comrades.* In Meerut the Sepoys readily came to believe that the wells had been defiled, that animal fat had been boiled up with the *ghee*, or liquid butter, sold in the bazaars, and that ground bones had been mixed up with the flour they ate. Meanwhile all over India a mysterious signal, in the shape of a *chapathi*, or flat cake of flour, was passed on from village to village, like the fiery cross in Scotch history, as if to prepare men's minds for some great scheme on foot.

In April the disaffection spread to Oudh, where Sir Henry Lawrence had taken up the post of Chief Commissioner in the room of Mr. Coverley Jackson. It was too late even for the successful ruler of the Punjāb to

* It seems that beef fat had really been used in greasing the cartridges; but the use of these was countermanded by the end of January; the Sepoys were then allowed to grease their own cartridges, and to tear off the ends instead of biting them off with their teeth. (See "*Incidents of the Sepoy War*," by Sir Hope Grant and Captain Knollys. Blackwood & Sons; 1873.)

repair the mischief done by his predecessor, or to avert the great storm of mutiny and rebellion whose warning murmurs were already falling on men's ears. On the 2nd May a native regiment quartered near Lucknow broke out into open mutiny. Sir Henry's prompt advance scattered the mutineers, some forty-five of whom were seized, tried, and sentenced to imprisonment for various terms. For some weeks longer all seemed quiet in Lucknow; but the frequent firing of bungalows and Sepoys' huts warned Sir Henry against setting too mueh faith in passing appearances and the soothing magic even of his own high name.

At last, on the 10th May, the storm burst over Meerut, where 1800 English soldiers lay in the midst of 2900 native troops. On the 24th April, 85 troopers of the 3rd Bengal Cavalry had openly rejected the very sort of cartridges which they had been using for some time past. On the 9th of the following month the mutineers were marched off in irons from the parade-ground, to undergo their several sentences of imprisonment with hard labour; a heavy punishment for Muhammadans of good family, for soldiers of any spirit a terrible disgrace. Next evening, while our countrymen were at church, the native regiments rose in arms with one consent, shot down some of their officers, set fire to their lines, emptied the jails, and spread sudden panic throughout the European quarters. General Hewitt and most of those around him were utterly paralysed by an outbreak which prompt action on their part would soon have quelled. The rabble of the bazaars joined with the released convicts in the work of murder, pillage, and general havoc; and the moon rose on blazing bungalows, on men and women dead, dying, or fleeing for their lives from ruffians thirsting for yet more blood. When the European troops were at length brought upon the scene of horror, night was already closing round them, and the mutinous regiments held their way unchecked and unpursued to Delhi.

The early morning of the fatal 11th May saw some troopers of the 3rd Cavalry riding into that city, eager to continue the work they had begun at Meerut. In a few hours all Delhi was up against the bewildered English, who had heard nothing of the mischief wrought the day before, and little dreamed that not a hand from Meerut would now be stretched forth to help them. English men, women, and children were foully butchered within the Palace itself, under the eyes, if not with the express permission, of the old king, who owed to English forbearance all the dignities and comforts he still enjoyed. Many an officer was shot down by his own men. Before sunset all Delhi was in the hands of the mutineers; the gallant Willoughby and his eight heroic followers having blown up the arsenal which they could no longer defend against hopeless odds.* Of those who had escaped death in the city, some were struggling on their perilous way to Karnāl, while others had joined the little band of officers who, under Brigadier Graves, still clung to the Flagstaff Tower on the heights overlooking the northern side of Delhi, in vain hope of the help that never came from Hewitt's garrison.

At last, when the ruffians from the city were renewing the work of plunder in the cantonments outside, the English watchers on the Ridge had to seek their only safety in flight. The more fortunate soon made their way to Meerut or Karnāl; but some of their number, including women, ran the gauntlet of every possible hardship and danger, in a hostile country under the fierce May sun, before they found rest and shelter among their friends.

Happily for our countrymen elsewhere, the dreadful

* Willoughby died soon afterwards of his wounds. Scully, who fired eht train, was never seen again.

deeds doing at Meerut and Delhi had been telegraphed to Ambāla and Agra before the rebels had time to cut the wires. From thence the tidings were at once flashed on to the Punjāb and down the country to Calcutta. Sir John Lawrence and his trusty subalterns proved equal to every need. Two days after the Delhi massacre Colonel Corbett had quietly disarmed the Sepoys at Lahore. Amritsar, the Sikh Benāres, was speedily made safe. Timely succours were thrown into the fort of Phillaur on the Sutlej. At Peshāwar, Brigadier Cotton and Colonel Edwardes planned and carried out the disarming of four native regiments out of the five there posted. Of the insurgent Sepoys at Mardān very few escaped the doom that dogged them, whether from English or Afghān hands. Betrayed by the hillmen of the border or hunted down by Edwardes's police, numbers of them were afterwards shot or blown away from guns, while many more paid the forfeit of their treason with life-long labour on the roads.

It was fortunate also for our cause that Lawrence and his brave helpmates could reckon upon the loyalty of the Sikhs on either side the Sutlej, in his efforts to meet a danger, at thought of which even the boldest sometimes held their breath. Not only Sikhs but the wild Muhammadans of the border flocked into the new regiments raised by the Lahore Government. The ruler of Kashmīr proved himself a friend in need. From the Cis-Sutlej chiefs of Patiāla, Jind, Nabha, and Kapurthala, came ready promises of aid in men, arms, and money; promises which in every case were loyally fulfilled. Many chiefs and gentlemen of less mark in the Punjāb offered their best services to the same effect. Nor was our old foe, Dost Muhammad, backward in assurances of goodwill. His hands thus strengthened, the Chief Commissioner of the Punjāb was left free by the spread of revolt below Delhi to employ his best energies in defence of Upper India. While a movable column of picked troops marched out from Jhelum to keep the peace in his own province, regiment after regiment was sent across the Sutlej to aid in punishing the mutineers, and to strengthen the little force which General Anson had led to the siege of Delhi.

All through May and June the revolt kept spreading, from Ferozepore to Allahābād and Benāres, from Ajmēr to Rohilkhand, involving hundreds of Englishmen in the same bloody doom. If some regiments spared their officers, others shot them down or saw them massacred by less scrupulous men. The Rāni of Jhānsi took a bloody revenge for the loss of her late husband's realm, by ordering the massacre of nearly a hundred men, women, and children, whose lives she had just sworn to spare. Before the end of June not a station in Oudh, except the capital, was left in English hands; and the garrison of Lucknow itself was cut off from all communication with the outer world. At Cawnpore Sir Hugh Wheeler and his luckless followers were vainly fighting for their lives within weak intrenchments, under roofless and crumbling walls, against thousands of merciless rebels commanded by the infamous Nāna Sahib. In many districts of the North-Western Provinces the mutiny had widened into a general revolt; station after station was abandoned by those civil officers who had time to escape; and the last traces of English law and order were swept away in a flood of rapine, bloodshed, and general lawlessness. Outside the fort of Agra, where English folk of all classes found passing refuge, the power of Mr. Colvin, the Lieutenant-Governor, was openly defied. A reign of terror had begun for all well-wishers to our rule.

Meanwhile the news from Meerut and Delhi had roused Lord Canning into taking measures more or less worthy of so great a need. Messages for aid were sent in all directions, to Bombay, Madras, Rangoon, and Ceylon; special powers were entrusted to the Lawrence brothers; and Lord Elgin was entreated to bring on to Calcutta the troops destined for the Chinese war. By degrees the expected succours flowed in; but much time was lost in forwarding troops by driblets to Benāres and Cawnpore; and the delay in disarming the Sepoys at Barrackpore and enrolling volunteers in Calcutta led to a disgraceful panic in the capital of British India. Early in June the brave Colonel Neill and his Madras fusiliers reached Benāres in time to save that city from the worst issues of a Sepoy rising. On the 11th his presence at Allahābād gave fresh heart to his countrymen in the fortress at the meeting of the Jumna with the Ganges, and cleared the way for some dashing onsets against the rebels in that neighbourhood. He had got all ready for a final march on Cawnpore, when General Havelock came up to relieve him of the chief command, and to carry on the noble enterprise which he had so well begun.

On the 7th July Havelock's little army set out from Allahābād. At Fatehpur, and again by the Pāndū stream, the troops of Nāna Sahib strove to arrest his progress, but in vain. On the night of the 16th his weary soldiers slept on the parade-ground of Cawnpore, still unprepared for the crowning tragedy, whose tokens on the morrow were to meet their eyes. They knew that, after weeks of terrible suffering, Wheeler and his wasted garrison had surrendered to the treacherous Raja of Bithūr, that volley after volley had been suddenly fired into the boats prepared for their promised voyage down the river, and that nearly all the men who survived this cowardly attack were afterwards taken out of the boats and shot. But not until the morrow did they learn the whole truth; how on the 15th July, the day of his second defeat, the ruthless Nāna had caused the remnant of his captives, men, women, and children, to be shot down, hacked, stabbed, or beaten to death, within the bungalow where they had been shut up for a fortnight past, and how next morning their mangled bodies had been stripped and tumbled in the nearest well.* Of all the 900 who had entered the intrenchments of Cawnpore, four only, two officers and two privates, escaped almost by a miracle to tell of the horrors they had seen and suffered.†

* Among the victims of the Nāna's butcheries were a number of men, women, and children, who had escaped the slaughter of Fatehgarh. Two hundred in all are said to have perished in the bungalow. The well at Cawnpore was afterwards bricked over, and a handsome memorial built upon the site.

† These were Lieutenants Thompson and Delafosse, Privates Murphy and Sullivan, who, after many hairbreadth escapes, found rest and shelter at last with a friendly Oudh chief, Raja Dig Bijai Singh, until they were able to join Havelock's force on the march to Lucknow.

CHAPTER III

LORD CANNING—(*continued*)

WHILE Havelock was making desperate efforts to relieve Lucknow, and the flames of revolt were spreading into Central India, a few thousand English and native troops were engaged in the momentous work of besieging Delhi, the one great stronghold of the mutineers. After the death of General Anson, his little army, reinforced by a part of the Meerut garrison who had fought two battles on their way to Delhi, drove the rebels before them at Badli Serai on the 8th June, and encamped on the ridge overlooking the tall red towers and long walls of the Mughal capital. There, week after week, they lay like a forlorn hope in front of a city held by 30,000 Sepoys, themselves just able by dint of heroic efforts to hold their ground under every kind of danger and difficulty against repeated onsets from the walls. All through the heats of June and the rains of July the besiegers were in fact themselves besieged. Sally after sally from the city wasted their numbers, still further thinned by disease and overwork. Sir Henry Barnard, their brave commander, died of cholera in the beginning of July, and his successor, General Reed, was soon forced by illness to make over the command to Brigadier Wilson of the Bengal Artillery. But the road from the Sutlej was kept open by the loyal princes of Sind, and Sir John Lawrence strained every nerve to reinforce his countrymen from his own province. All through July and August fresh troops came streaming or dribbling into Wilson's camp. At last, by the middle of August the gallant Nicholson, fresh from the slaughter of armed mutineers on the Rāvi, near Gurdāspur, led into the camp before Delhi the last brigade of troops which Lawrence could well spare from his already scant resources.

Nicholson's rout of the rebels at Najafgarh on the 25th finally cleared the way for the approach of the heavy guns destined to batter down the walls of the rebel stronghold. With their arrival on the 6th September the siege began in earnest. It did not begin a moment too soon. Partial risings had taken place in the Punjāb itself. From Saharanpur to Meerut the country was overrun by bands of lawless villagers, or armed rebels following the standard of some ambitious chief. The hard-pressed defenders of Lucknow were beginning to despair of the help which Havelock had twice failed to bring them. Large bodies of rebels from Indore, Gwalior, and the neighbouring provinces were gathering for a march on Agra, and all Sindhia's efforts were growing powerless to keep the Gwalior Contingent from joining in the game of havoc. The most loyal of the native chiefs could hardly count on the faithfulness of his followers to what seemed already a losing cause.

On the other hand, succours from Ceylon, the Cape, and other quarters, were steaming up the Hūgli ; Peel's naval brigade was hastening up the country ; Outram, in himself a host, was preparing for another march from Cawnpore to Lucknow ; and the gallant Major Eyre, an old Kābul prisoner, had just been scattering the rebels, who had besieged his countrymen at Arrah, and striven to bar his way among the jungles of Jagdispur. In Southern and Western India, where the Sepoys with one or two exceptions continued faithful, all was quiet ; and the Nizām's able minister, Salar Jang, maintained under very trying circumstances the peace of a province filled with warlike Arabs and fanatic Muhammadans of every class. Lastly, inside Delhi itself the rebels were disheartened by past defeats; they had no leader in whom all could trust; their own countrymen grew weary of a yoke far heavier than that from which they had been rescued; and the old strifes of race and creed broke out among men who had little in common besides the knowledge of their common guilt.

On the 11th September the new heavy batteries showered forth their iron rain on the walls of Delhi. In vain did the enemy strive their best to cope with the rising danger. In three days the battered walls were a heap of ruins, and Wilson's heroes were only waiting for the word to rush up the breaches made by their guns. On the early morning of the 14th September, the great rebel stronghold was stormed in three places by as many columns, numbering in all not quite three thousand men. The Kashmīr Gate was blown in under a deadly fire, while Nicholson's stormers mounted the main breach. Two hours of hard fighting left our soldiers firmly lodged within the walls; but their success was dearly bought by the fall of the gallant Nicholson, the leader of the storming columns, the hope and pride of all India. He lingered for nine days of a mortal wound; but his last hours were cheered by the knowledge that he had not died in vain. After six days of hard fighting not one armed mutineer or rebel remained alive within the captured city. On the 21st September the old king himself, in whose name the city had been defended, was brought back a close prisoner to his former home. His intriguing wife, Zīnat Mahal, and her son, Jamma Bakht, shared his confinement. Two more of his sons were slain next day by their captor, the daring Captain Hodson, in the sight of a great crowd, who seemed bent on rescuing them from his small escort,

Several other of the Delhi princes were afterwards taken, tried, and hanged for the part they had borne in the murder of English women and children on the 11th and 12th May. In March of the next year the wretched old king was doomed to death by a military court for waging war against the English and ordering the murder of forty-nine Christians within Delhi. But death was exchanged for transportation, and the white-haired felon died a few years afterwards in a remote corner of Pegu. A cry for vengeance went forth against Zīnat Mahal and her son; but Lord Canning, as firm as he was merciful, gave no heed to the cry, and both queen and prince were allowed to share the fortunes and cheer the last days of Muhammad Bahādur Shah.

In all the history of British India, so fruitful in great deeds, no greater achievement was ever recorded than the capture of a strong walled city, seven miles round, by about six thousand Englishmen and Sikhs, arrayed against many times their number of desperate and well-armed foes. After three months of watching and hard fighting for the very ground on which they stood, their numbers steadily thinned by wounds and sickness, Wilson's heroes had planted their batteries within grapeshot of bastions heavily armed and stoutly defended, had scaled in broad daylight walls twenty-four feet high, and cleared out the foe in six days from a town where every large building was itself a stronghold, and every street had to be won by the bayonet or the pickaxe. And all this was done, as Lord Canning proudly declared, "before a single soldier of the many thousands who are hastening from England to uphold the supremacy of the British power, has set foot on these shores," and even before any of the troops shipped off from the nearest colonies had made their way into Wilson's camp. For this memorable feat of arms, which cost the victors a total loss of nearly four thousand from the beginning of the siege, and of 1674 from the 8th to the 21st September, no small share of England's gratitude was due to Sir John Lawrence, whose bold counsels and unflagging efforts had enabled the Forlorn Hope before Delhi to hold the ridge against all comers, until the moment came for striking a death-blow at the rebel cause. With the fall of the old imperial city the neck of the mutiny was fairly broken, although many months were yet to elapse before the monster breathed his last.

While some of Wilson's victorious troops were engaged in scouring the country between Delhi and Agra, beating up rebels and restoring order as they marched along, the timely presence of Outram and Havelock at Lucknow had rescued its war-worn garrison from imminent destruction, if not yet from absolute danger. Down to the end of June Sir Henry Lawrence had been employed in strengthening the one post which still remained to the English in Oudh. But his failure on the 30th to check the advance of a strong rebel army on Lucknow was closely followed by the siege of the English Residency, wherein some fifteen hundred Europeans and faithful Sepoys were hemmed in for months by a well-armed, numerous, and determined foe. His own death, on the 4th July, from a mortal wound deprived the garrison of a leader whose many public services were enhanced by virtues of the highest order, and whose whole life may be summed up in the sentence carved upon his tomb—"Here lies Henry Lawrence, who tried to do his duty."

Happily his spirit still lived in those who carried on the defence for which his foresight had so well prepared. Under every drawback of scanty numbers, sickness, hard fare, incessant work, in spite of a weak position, of hopes continually disappointed, of prolonged resistance to fearful odds, the defenders of the Lucknow Residency upheld for more than three months the honour of their flag and the safety of their countrywomen against the banded forces of a whole province in revolt. Men and women alike toiled, watched, and suffered in their several ways under a ceaseless hail from guns and musketry, varied by the noise of bursting mines and the yells of desperate onsets daringly repelled. At last, in the beginning of September, Outram led forth his succouring brigade from Allahābād. On the 19th, some three thousand soldiers, chiefly English, marched out from Cawnpore under Outram, Havelock, and Neill, to cut their way at all hazards into Lucknow. On the 23rd, Havelock's army—for, thanks to Outram's generous self-denial, he had retained the chief command—stormed the Alambāgh, or summer-palace of the queens of Oudh, under a furious fire from the enemy's guns.

Two days later they fought their way through streets of loopholed houses, over barriers bristling with death, into the half-ruined Residency itself. Nearly five hundred slain or wounded was the price which Havelock paid for his success, and the joy of victory was further damped by the death of General Neill within a few yards from the British entrenchments. But the deliverers had not come too soon, for the enemy had carried two mines under the Residency, and a very few days more might have seen the last of its defenders buried beneath its ruins. Even as things were, the relieving force, once more commanded by Sir James Outram, could do little more than carry on with ampler means the defence of the position so hardly won, until a new army could march up to aid them in withdrawing the old garrison to Cawnpore.

In due time a fresh army, under Sir Colin Campbell, of Crimean fame, began its march towards Lucknow. By the 12th November it was encamped at the Alambāgh. On the 14th Sir Colin resumed his advance, carrying one strong post after another at the point of the bayonet, with due help at need from his heavy guns. On the 16th

RUINS OF THE RESIDENCY, LUCKNOW

two thousand rebels were mercilessly slain by the troops who stormed the massive walls of the Sikandar Bagh. The storming of the Shah Najaf Mosque, after Peel's naval guns had vainly battered its strong masonry for three hours, closed that day's work with brilliant promise of triumphs yet to win. A few hours more of steady fighting on the morrow, in which Outram's soldiers played their part, brought the besieged and their deliverers face to face. A few days later the last of the Lucknow garrison slept once more in peace and safety on the pleasant camping ground of the Dil-Kushā. There, on the 25th November, Sir Henry Havelock, worn out by toil and sickness, breathed his last.

Leaving Outram strongly posted at the Alambāgh, Sir Colin Campbell marched off with the rest of his troops and the rescued women and children for Cawnpore, where his presence was already needed by those he had left behind. The powerful Gwalior Contingent, having at last broken loose from Sindhia's control, had crossed the Jumna, and with numbers swollen by the remnants of the Nāna's forces, marched on towards Cawnpore. After a vain attempt to bar their progress, Windham's small force fell back in some disorder into an entrenched position near the Ganges. Here for two days the rebels, twenty thousand strong, under their ablest leader, Tāntia Topi, pressed him so hard that the bridge of boats was in imminent danger of destruction, when Sir Colin's soldiers on the 28th November reappeared betimes on the opposite bank.

As soon as the sick and wounded, the women and children of the Lucknow garrison had been sent off towards Calcutta, Campbell proceeded to settle accounts with the foe. Their utter rout on the 6th December, with the loss of seventeen guns and all their stores, was crowned on the 9th by their pursuit and final dispersion, with the capture of all their remaining guns. During the same month fresh victories were gained by English columns over the rebels in Rohilkhand and the districts bordering the Ganges. Rewah, in Bundelkhand, was cleared of rebels by the gallant Lieutenant Osborne. The mutineers of Nimach were routed by Brigadier Stuart near Mandasōr. Saugor, in Central India, was still held by faithful Sepoys, and order was restored in the dominions of Holkar.

Several of the leading rebels had by this time been caught and hanged, nor was any mercy shown to those who had taken part in the murder or ill-treatment of English people. It must even be confessed that in some places the work of vengeance and repression had been carried by civil and military officers to a length which neither past provocation nor present danger could fairly excuse. The cry for blood went forth from all quarters, and many innocent perished, or were brought to ruin along with the guilty. It is greatly to Lord Canning's honour, that he boldly and firmly set his face against deeds of wanton cruelty wrought in the name of justice by some of those whom he had necessarily entrusted with special powers. From the first he denounced the folly of dealing with the people at large as mere rebels or abettors of rebellion; and all the abuse showered upon him, both in India and England, for his noble interference failed to turn him from his purpose of tempering just retribution with open-handed and politic mercy. Even in the darkest days of 1857, it came out more and more clearly that the Sepoy revolt had widened into a popular uprising, mainly in districts new to our rule, or peopled largely by robbers and Muhammadans, or held by unruly and disaffected chiefs. Many a life was saved by the devotion of native servants, as well as the active loyalty of native gentlemen. In putting a stop betimes to the wholesale burning of suspected villages, and the indiscriminate slaughter of suspected criminals, Lord Canning rendered a signal service not only to his own countrymen, but to the people of India, who learned that their masters, however quick to strike and stern to punish, could yet stay their hands when the worst of the danger had blown over. Englishmen and natives alike may thank him for preventing a formidable outbreak from flaring up into a war of race against race.

While Outram held his post at the Alambāgh against repeated onsets of many thousand rebels, and Hope Grant was gaining fresh victories in Rohilkhand, and Franks, with a force partly composed of Gūrkhas from Nepāl, was driving the enemy before him into Lucknow, and other officers were doing good work in Central and Western India, Sir Colin Campbell was making ready, in his own cautious fashion, for one last overwhelming advance on the capital of Oudh. At length, on the 2nd March, 1858, the van of his fine army, 25,000 strong in all, including 16,000 good English troops, with a powerful siege-train, halted after a brief fight on the old camping-ground at the Dil-Kushā. On the 6th, Outram crossed the Gumti to play a leading part in the capture of Lucknow. By the 16th the two commanders had won their way, not without some hard fighting, into the heart of the rebel city, while the Nepālese Jang Bahādur cleared out the enemy from the southern side, and rescued two English ladies who had survived the murder of their friends and kindred some months before. A few days later not an armed rebel remained in or near Lucknow. The trifling loss sustained by the victors was heightened by the death of the daring Hodson; and Captain William Peel, whose sailors had been foremost in every fight, died in April of small-pox, which attacked him just as he was recovering from his wounds.

The conquerors of Lucknow had still to deal with the insurgents in Rohilkhand, whose numbers were swollen by fugitives from all parts of Oudh. Shahjahānpur was taken on the 25th April, and Bareilly on the 6th May. The insurgent forces, beaten and broken up in every fight, still roamed about the country, causing their pursuers much trouble and some little loss from the heat and hardships to which they were exposed. Rohilkhand, indeed, was virtually reconquered before the end of June; but the rising in Bihār under Koer Singh involved weary marches amid deep jungle, and the reconquest of Oudh was only completed on the last day of December, when the high-mettled Begam of Oudh, and the outlawed Nāna Sahib led the last of their hunted followers across the Rāptī into the forests of Nepāl. Even of this poor remnant many fell by the swords of their pursuers; while others, including the Nāna himself, are believed to have perished of disease.

One leader, Prince Firoz Shah of Delhi, cut his way with a few followers through Oudh across the Ganges, to share the fortunes of Tāntia Topi, who, driven out of Gwalior by Sir Hugh Rose, still held a few troops together in the wilds of Rājputāna, doubling on his pursuers like a hunted hare. How he had been brought to this plight, it remains to tell.

In the beginning of 1858 several columns of troops from Bombay and Madras were marching on various points of the country lying to the west and south of the Jumna, from the Aravalli to the Vindhya Hills. A Madras column under General Whitlock, after doing good service about Jubbulpore, moved on to defeat the rebels in Bundelkhand. Yet harder work awaited the Bombay column which Sir Hugh Rose led first of all to the relief of Saugor. On the 11th February the strong fort of Garhakotah fell into Sir Hugh's hands. The rout of the rebels at Madanpur opened the way to fresh successes. On the 17th March Stuart's brigade stormed the fortress of Chandēri. Jhānsi itself was invested. Twenty thousand men under Tāntia Topi crossed the Betwa in hopes of raising the siege. On the 1st April they were routed with heavy slaughter by 1200 of Sir Hugh's force, and two days afterwards the fierce Rāni's rock-perched stronghold was carried by storm; herself with a few followers escaping into the jungle. Again the Rāni and her Brahman ally barred the way against their old assailants at Kūnch on the 7th May. Once more driven from the field of their own choosing through Sir Hugh's masterly tactics, they fell back with a loss of several guns on Kalpi, a strong fortress overlooking the Jumna, not far from Cawnpore.

Sir Hugh, however, was not to be thwarted. On the 19th May, with the aid of a column from Cawnpore, he began the attack. Twice the rebels sallied out against his wearied soldiers, but in vain. By the 23rd May they were off to Gwalior, and Sir Hugh became easy master of a fortified arsenal containing fifty guns and large store of arms and ammunition. By this time, both he himself and his heroic little army were in sore need of rest after so many months of constant marching and hard fighting under an Indian sun,* across many hundred miles of very broken ground. But the state of affairs at Gwalior forbade more than a brief halt at that moment. On the 1st June the brave young Sindhia and his able minister Dinkar Rāo were flying for their lives to Agra from a capital already filled with victorious rebels. Among these Tāntia Topi at once took the lead, in the name of the Nāna, whom the Marātha soldiery were bidden to accept as their future Pēshwa. Leaving Whitlock, the captor of Banda, to guard Kalpi, Sir Hugh Rose lost no time in marching upon Gwalior, where some 18,000 rebels, strongly posted around a rock-fortress of vast strength, awaited his attack. Nothing, however, could long withstand the determined

* Sir Hugh Rose himself had suffered from five sunstrokes in a few days, and many of his soldiers died from the same cause.

efforts of disciplined veterans led by the most brilliant general whom the mutiny had produced. Three days of bold manœuvring and successful fighting, in the course of which the bloodstained Rāni of Jhānsi met a soldier's death, placed all Gwalior outside the citadel in Sir Hugh's hands. On the 20th June a handful of Sepoys scaled the far-famed citadel itself, already abandoned by most of its defenders; and the young Maharāja rode back in triumph through the streets of a city which British valour had won back for its rightful lord. Next day Brigadier Robert Napier, with a few hundred horsemen and six light guns, caught up and scattered by a daring charge several thousand of Tāntia's beaten troops. Twenty-five guns fell into the victors' hands, and the army of the Pēshwa, broken up into small flying bands, no longer existed as an organised force.

Thus ended one of the most brilliant and masterly campaigns of which history has any record. In less than six months Sir Hugh Rose had led his few thousand warriors, English and native,* over more than a thousand miles of rugged country, bristling with arms, and dotted with strongholds, each capable of a stout defence. From Indore to Saugor, to Jhānsi, to Kalpi, at length to Gwalior, they had marched without a check in the fierce heats of an Indian summer, from victory to victory, across rivers, over mountain passes, through intricate jungles, into the strongest forts, in the teeth of armies well fed, fairly disciplined, not badly equipped, and always far outnumbering their own. Their bravery, devotion, and discipline, under hardships, dangers, and temptations of every kind, had well earned the hearty thanks of the skilful leader, who, with their help, had placed himself by that one campaign on a level with some of the first names in the annals of modern warfare.

* Among these were some of the Hyderābād Contingent, whose loyalty had remained proof to all temptations.

BOOK VII

INDIA UNDER THE CROWN

CHAPTER I

LORD CANNING—(*continued*)

WITH the recapture of Gwalior ended the last serious struggle against our arms. In the most unquiet districts order was being gradually restored, and the rule of the civil officer was fast replacing that of the military chief. A passing outbreak in the Southern Marātha country had been suppressed betimes, before it came to a serious head. Delhi and the adjacent districts had been added to the Government of the Punjāb. Order reigned in the North-Western Provinces. In Oudh the mild influence of Sir James Outram and his successor, Mr. Montgomery, was fast winning over the rebellious Talūkdars or land-holders to accept the only terms on which Lord Canning would reinstate them in their forfeit domains. By the end of the year the last of the Oudh insurgents were driven, as we have seen, into the jungles at the foot of the Nepālese Hills. Tāntia Topi was still at large in Central India, leading his pursuers a weary chase from Rājputāna to Berar; but he, too, on the 7th April, 1859, was caught at last in the jungle near Sipri, betrayed, like another Wallace, by one of his most trusty followers. His trial and speedy death as a proven accomplice in the Nāna's crimes cut short the career of the one able leader on the rebel side, and marked the close of a mutiny which had drenched all Upper India in blood. His comrade, Firoz Shah, once more escaped; but the last embers of revolt had been trodden out. The great Sepoy Army of Bengal had been swallowed up in the storm of its own raising. The massacres of Cawnpore, Delhi, and Jhānsi, had been requited a hundred-fold. Of the surviving mutineers thousands were doomed to hard labour in Indian jails, or to lifelong imprisonment in the Andaman Islands. Of the leading rebels who fell into our hands, some were put to death; others, less criminal, were banished or imprisoned; while the remainder, with the bulk of their followers, were allowed to go free.

In the last months of this momentous struggle, the great Merchant Company, which had subdued all India in less than a hundred years, underwent the doom which had been hanging over it ever since the days of Pitt. On the 2nd August, 1858, Queen Victoria gave her assent to the Bill which, drawn up by Lord Stanley and carried with few amendments through both Houses, decreed the transfer of all sovereign power in India from the hands of the East India Company to the Crown. Thenceforth the government of India was vested in one of Her Majesty's Ministers, aided by a Council of Fifteen, eight of whom were to be chosen at first from the old Court of Directors. One of the last acts of the discrowned Company was to vote Sir John Lawrence a handsome pension for services unsurpassed in Indian history.

Thus in the very zenith of its outward greatness passed away from the historic scene a power whose services alike to India and England might have seemed to deserve a better fate. Englishmen might well be proud of a body whose fame had filled the world, whose servants in a hundred years had borne the Company's flag from one end of India to the other, fighting always against heavy odds, overthrowing many great dynasties, and proving in peace as well as in war their right to rule the two hundred and odd millions whom successive conquests, made for the most part in self-defence, often in the teeth of orders from England, had finally placed under their charge. But the tree, in fact, was rotten before it was cut down. The Company's sovereignty had long been undermined by the powers entrusted to the Ministerial Board of Control; and its patronage, the last remaining source of its political life, was fast slipping out of its hands, when the great storm of 1857 revealed the weakness of its friends to withstand the widespread demand, raised both at home and in India, for its entire suppression as a ruling power.

On the 1st November all India was made aware of the change which had befallen her late masters. On that day Lord Canning, as the new-made Viceroy under the new rule, issued from Allahābād the famous proclamation which announced in the Queen's name the final transfer of India's sovereignty from the Company to the Crown. Throughout the chief cities of British India the new era of national progress was solemnly proclaimed to eager and rejoicing crowds, amidst the booming of guns, the clang of martial music, and the cheers of paraded troops. In the words of the royal manifesto there might be nothing absolutely new beyond the fact that another hand would henceforth wield the sceptre hitherto entrusted to a private Company. No new principles were really involved in the assertion of Her Majesty's resolve to govern her new subjects with a tender and scrupulous regard for the rights, dignities, usages, and well-being of each and all. But a certain sense of relief from past troubles and secret fears for the future inclined the people at large to hail the new edict as a timely message of peace, forgiveness, and good will, a sure promise of better days to come, a formal charter of rights hitherto begrudged or disregarded in fact, if not in words.

Honours and rewards were freely distributed among all who had done good service during the late revolt. Lord Canning became an earl; Sir John Lawrence, General Wilson, and Sir James Outram baronets; Sir Colin Campbell won his peerage as Lord Clyde; the son of General Havelock succeeded to the baronetcy conferred upon his dying father. Nicholson's widowed mother was not forgotten, nor the family of the daring Neill. A host of deserving officers, civil and military, were endowed with the Order of the Bath. Every soldier who shared in the siege of Delhi or the defence of Lucknow was allowed to reckon another year's service towards his pension. Estates were conferred on unofficial Englishmen who, like Boyle, the defender of Arrah against thousands of armed Sepoys, had done things worthy of remembrance.* Every native known to have saved English lives or property received a liberal reward. On those native chiefs and princes who had stood loyally by the Government all sorts of honours and gifts were ungrudgingly bestowed. The Nizām himself got back a part of his former territory, and the balance of his debt to the State was wholly remitted. His able minister, Salār Jang, in addition to a knighthood of the new Star of India, was handsomely rewarded in other ways. New rights, grants

* The defence of Mr. Boyle's bungalow at Arrah by 18 Europeans and 50 Sikh police, for seven days, against 3000 armed mutineers, aided by two guns, was one of the most brilliant episodes in the war of 1857. It was conducted by Mr. Wake of the Bengal Civil Service, but its success was mainly owing to the foresight of Mr. Boyle, a railway engineer, who had fortified and provisioned his house weeks before the revolt of the Sepoys at Dinapore. One attempt to relieve the defenders from Dinapore was beaten back with heavy slaughter. The supply of drink ran short, but the Sikhs found fresh water by digging through the floor. At length, on the 3rd August, Major Vincent Eyre, with 200 English soldiers and three guns, scattered the besiegers, saved the little garrison from further danger, and cleared the road from Bengal to Cawnpore.

of land, and privileges, were secured to Sindhia and Holkar, and in yet larger measure to the loyal Sikh princes without whose aid Delhi could not have been retaken, nor the adjacent provinces so speedily subdued. The noble Raja of Patiāla was the first native who took his seat in the Viceroy's Legislative Council, as remodelled in 1861.

One concession by which the native princes set most store was made by Lord Canning, in the Sanads or patents which acknowledged, with due restrictions, the right of every native feudatory to adopt an heir on the failure of male issue in his own line. In some cases a special provision was even made for the appointment of a fit successor to a prince who left neither a natural nor an adopted heir.* The spirit of the Royal Proclamation was also visible in the process of doing away with the old distinctions between Supreme and Sadr Courts. The right of sitting in the new High Court of each province was for the first time thrown open to qualified native judges of a lower grade. About the same time the Penal Code first drafted by Macaulay became the law of the land for all creeds and classes. For the first time also since the days of Cornwallis native gentlemen were empowered to serve as magistrates under the Crown.

The last years of Lord Canning's rule were employed in repairing the mischief caused by the great mutiny. In 1859 Mr. James Wilson was sent out from England to devise new ways and means of replenishing an exhausted treasury and reducing the public outlay. On his untimely death in 1860 his place was taken and his task successfully carried on by Mr. Laing. A few small local outbreaks ruffled for a while the general peace, and riots in the indigo districts of Bengal reduced some of the planters for a time to serious straits. But all these were

* "Rajahs of the Punjāb," by Sir Lepel Griffin. 1873.

trifles compared to the great famine which wasted Upper India in 1861, causing the death of half a million sufferers, and throwing back for several years the process of recovery from the disasters of 1857. Foremost in the efforts made by his countrymen to allay the consequent misery was Colonel Baird Smith, who had borne no trifling part in the siege and capture of Delhi. He died on his way home, a victim to overwork in a baneful climate.

In 1859 Lord Canning's Government passed a law which aimed at fulfilling the pledges made by Lord Cornwallis in 1793. The Bengal Rent Act secured for one class of rayats almost absolute ownership of their lands, and for another class the right of holding at a rent which no zamindar could enhance at his mere pleasure. A yet wider measure of tenant-right was carried, as we shall see, by a later Viceroy.

On the 1st November, 1861, a splendid gathering of English officers and native chiefs ranged itself round Lord Canning at Allahābād, to take part in the investiture of some among them with the order of the Star of India. Chief among those who received the badges of the new order from the hands of its first Grand Master, the Viceroy himself, were the Rajas of Gwalior and Patiāla, the Nawāb of Rāmpur, and the stout-hearted Bēgam of Bhopāl. A few months later Lord Canning, worn out with cares and failing health, left Calcutta on his way home. On the 17th June, but a few weeks after his landing in England, the heirless son of George Canning had ceased to breathe.

He had already lived down the unpopularity which his earlier measures during the mutiny had provoked. Whatever may have been his shortcomings at the outbreak of a storm which found him still new to his work, surrounded by advisers no abler nor clear-sighted than himself, his cool courage and firm adherence to his own views of duty and justice won him the respect even of those who found most fault with his seeming blindness to the true purport of passing events. Undismayed by the panic around him, unswayed by the impulses of popular clamour, he worked away at his post with the calmness of conscious rectitude, and kept his own head clear when all around him were fast losing theirs. The bold stand which he made against the popular cry for indiscriminate revenge forms perhaps his highest claim to historic remembrance; and the name of Clemency Canning, once fastened on him in keen reproach, has already become the fairest tribute to his public worth.

Before Canning left India he could point to the great progress already made in works of national usefulness. By the beginning of 1862 thirteen hundred and sixty miles of railway had been opened, half of that total in the last two years. The great trunk road from Calcutta had been completed to Peshāwar, and many hundred miles of new roads had been opened throughout the country. New canals were begun, continued, or completed in several provinces, and other public works were pushed steadily forward. The whole foreign trade of India had increased from 32 millions in 1850 to 80 millions in 1861. In Bengal the customs revenue had nearly trebled itself in ten years. In the last four years the foreign trade of Bombay had been increased by ten millions, to the enrichment of the cotton growers and merchants in Western and Southern India, who had begun to furnish the mills of Lancashire with the cotton no longer obtainable from the war-burdened States of the American Union.

CHAPTER II

LORD ELGIN AND SIR JOHN LAWRENCE—1862-1869

LORD CANNING'S place in India was worthily filled by Lord Elgin, whose successful diplomacy had just secured the fruits of Sir Hope Grant's victorious march to Pekin. The sometime Governor of Jamaica and Canada had already won for himself a name of statesmanship of a high order; and the work awaiting him in India was far from light. His first year of office was spent mainly in Calcutta, in the quiet discharge of his new duties. Early in 1863 he set out for the upper provinces, holding State *Darbārs* at Benāres, Agra, and Ambāla, on his way up to the hills. Towards the end of September he started again from Simla on an exploring journey through the mountain tracts of the Punjāb. But the keen air of the wild Kūlu passes proved too much for a frame already weakened by the climate of Lower Bengal; and on the 20th November Lord Elgin died of heart disease at Dharmsāla in the Kāngra valley, in the midst of plans for a great military and official gathering at Lahōre, and for checking the movements of Wāhābi fanatics in the hills westward of the Indus.

Before his death the Sitāna campaign had already begun with the advance of a British force under General Neville Chamberlain into the Ambēla Pass. But the fierce mountaineers fought hard in their native hills; Chamberlain himself was badly wounded in November; and his troops held only the ground they had won after days of incessant fighting. The Council at Calcutta were on the point of ordering an ill-timed retreat, when Sir William Denison, Governor of Madras, reached Calcutta as Lord Elgin's acting successor, in time to overrule their feebler counsels, and to support Sir Hugh Rose, the Commander-in-Chief, in his efforts to strengthen the hands of Chamberlain's successor. The needful reinforcements soon reached Garvock's camp. Ambēla was stormed in December, and some of our late foes were glad enough to show their victors the way to Malka, the chief seat of the Sitāna fanatics. With the utter destruction of that place the war was over, and a wholesome fear of English prowess kept the rude highlanders of those regions quiet for years to come.

In January of the following year Sir W. Denison made over the seals of government to Sir John Lawrence, the first Bengal civilian who had ever been formally appointed Governor-General of India since the days of Sir John Shore. His return to the country where he had lived and laboured for so many years was hailed by his countrymen as a just reward for his splendid services in 1857. After spending the summer months at Simla, Sir John proceeded to meet his old friends and followers at Lahore. In simple but impressive terms he told the assembled Sikh chiefs and gentlemen of the interest which the Queen of England took in their well-being, and passed in brief review the efforts made by successive English rulers, from Sir Henry Lawrence to Sir Robert Montgomery, to further that well-being in every possible way.

Meanwhile a little war was unwillingly opened with the rulers of Bhutān, a little Himālayan state to the north of Assam. For some years past the Bhotia highlanders had made frequent inroads into British ground lying at the foot of their hills, and claimed by their chiefs as part of Bhutān. In 1863 the Hon. Ashley Eden had been sent to treat with the Bhutān government on behalf of the British subjects who had been kidnapped in these raids. The utter failure of the mission was crowned by the insults heaped upon the envoy himself. In fear of his life he had to sign a treaty surrendering the very lands in dispute. After some vain attempts to patch up the quarrel and gain redress for the outrage, Sir John Lawrence in November, 1864, declared war against Bhutān. A small force entered the hills; but mismanagement and a sickly season delayed its progress; some of our troops on one occasion were disgracefully defeated, and not till some months later was the enemy driven to sue for peace and give sure pledges for its maintenance.

From that time no other warlike movement disturbed the general quiet, until 1868, when a rising of lawless Wāghirs in Kathiawār had to be quelled by an armed force. Later in the year the Afghān tribes of the Black Mountain, not far from Sitāna, egged on by Wāhābi refugees from Patna, provoked speedy punishment for a daring outrage on the Punjāb frontier. Determined this time to do nothing by halves, Sir John ordered a strong force under General Wylde to march towards the Black Mountain. In three weeks the invading columns had dealt the hill-tribes such a blow, that chief after chief threw himself and his clansmen on the invader's mercy, and the plotters who had stirred them up to acts of violence were glad to seek safer hiding-places elsewhere.

The history of Sir Robert Napier's well-planned and thoroughly successful march to Magdāla, the capital of King Theodore, the headstrong ruler of Abyssinia, is not to be told in these pages. It must not, however, be overlooked that the troops whom Napier led to victory in 1868 were largely composed of Sikh regiments from

India, that the task of equipping them and feeding them on the march devolved on officers of the Indian Government, and that Napier himself, as an officer of Bengal Engineers, had won his laurels in many an Indian field. In the preparations for this campaign the Viceroy himself played a useful and important part.

A steady friend to peaceful progress, Sir John Lawrence withstood all temptations to meddle in the affairs of his Afghān neighbours. On the death of Dost Muhammad in 1863, a long struggle for the throne of Kābul ensued between his sons Muhammad Afzul Khan and Sher Ali Khan. The latter, whom his father had chosen for his heir in preference to either of his eldest sons, applied to the Indian Government for help against his insurgent brother. Beyond acknowledging Sher Ali as king for the time being, Sir John Lawrence declined to interfere. A just dread of embroiling India in the domestic quarrels of a turbulent neighbour decided him to watch the progress of events across the frontier, and do nothing which could give either party fair cause for complaint. The strife between the brothers raged with varying fortune, and victory for a moment seemed to have finally turned the scales against Sher Ali Khan. Afzul Khan in his turn was acknowledged as the actual ruler of Kābul and Kandahār, while Sher Ali retained possession of Herāt. Once more, however, fortune smiled on the latter. On the death of Afzul Khan his next brother, Azīm Khan, took his place at Kābul, but not for long. The dethroned Sher Ali set out from Herāt, and, fighting his way back to Kābul, once more became the acknowledged ruler of his father's realm. Before the end of 1868 he was firmly seated on the throne from which he had been driven three years before; and Sir John's successor was enabled to reap the fruits of a policy which the event had fully justified.

The five years of Sir John's rule were years on the

whole of peace and marked prosperity. In Western and Central India new sources of wealth had been opened up to many classes by the great demand for Indian cotton which sprang out of the American war. For several years a golden stream kept flowing fast into the country. Cotton and railways brought untold plenty to millions who had hitherto earned their three or four rupees a month. The poorest Rayat became suddenly rich. His old mud hut was replaced by a roomier dwelling of brick or stone. His wife and daughters decked themselves in jewels of price. Earthenware pots gave way to vessels of brass, copper, and even silver. Every coolie—said one who lived among them—"took to dressing like a Brahman." In many cases old caste-distinctions were broken down by the growing self-esteem that comes of growing wealth. Bombay itself went mad over new schemes for making money; and the great commercial crash of 1865, the natural result of reckless gambling in trade matters, dealt sudden ruin among many households. But the ruin did not spread far outside the western capital. Most of the new wealth remained in the country, enriching the mass of traders, husbandmen, and artisans, turning the waste lands into fruitful fields, giving new life to the cotton-looms of Nāgpur, and increasing the public revenue in divers ways. Bombay itself, when the storm blew over, could still export more than a million bales of cotton in one season, and point to a foreign trade worth about forty millions a year.

Under the active rule of Sir Richard Temple the Central Provinces, which had been formed in 1861 out of Old Bengal districts and later annexations, rose in a few years to a rare height of well-ordered prosperity. By 1868 their foreign trade had swollen in value from two and a half to thirteen millions, and the number of schools had risen from four to 249. A line of railway linked Nāgpur with Bombay and the cotton-fields of Berar, while rich streams of traffic from nearly all parts of India found their meeting-point at Jubbulpore. In British Burma the mild sway of Sir Arthur Phayre did much to further the well-being of that young, loyal, and rising province. In twelve years its population was doubled, partly by immigrants from across the Burman frontier; its revenues had increased to the same extent, and its foreign trade risen to the value of ten millions a year.

Oudh, the granary of Upper India, had little cause to repent the old days of Muhammadan misrule. The people at large were prosperous and contented; new schools sprang up everywhere; railways and canals were flinging abroad the seeds of golden harvests; and its rulers found willing and enlightened helpmates in the Talūkdars, whose submission to our rule had been rewarded by the restoration of their former rights and powers. What causes of difference at first lay seething between them and the tenant-farmers of a certain standing, were dispelled or abated by the measure which Sir John Lawrence carried in 1866 for securing the right of hereditary cultivators to hold their lands at the old accustomed rates.

The Punjāb, Dalhousie's model province, had thriven steadily under the rule of Sir Robert Montgomery and his widely-loved successor, Sir Donald McLeod. In no other part of British India did the people show equal readiness to pluck the best fruits of Western civilisation. The North-Western Provinces were fast recovering from the combined effects of the great Mutiny and the famine of 1861. Railways and public works gave a new impulse to trade and labour, while irrigation doubled and trebled the produce of the fruitful plains between the Ganges and the Jumna. When drought once more visited these provinces in 1868 its worst horrors were averted by the new growth of railways and canals. Distress there was, of course, in some places, but the great Ganges Canal, with its 650 miles of main stream and 3000 of branch channels, saved nearly a million acres from drying up. A like service on a smaller scale was rendered by the Eastern Jumna Canal and the channels that water Rohilkhand and Dēhra Dūn, while the surplus grain of Oudh was poured by rail into those districts where the drought was sorest.*

Less fortunate were the sufferers in Orissa during the great famine of 1866. A scanty rainfall in the previous year had been followed by a widespread dearth. The Lieutenant-Governor of Bengal shut his eyes to the tokens of coming disaster, until it was too late to pour in supplies of food by sea. Before relief came with the close of the next rainy season, nearly a million souls had died of hunger or disease in a province containing about four millions. In the neighbouring province of Madras a like disaster was averted by the zeal with which its governor, Lord Napier, took timely measures to relieve his suffering people. Mysore also in the following year was saved by the efforts of its English rulers from much of the suffering threatened by a sudden drought.

During these years the whole foreign trade of British India rose to about a hundred millions sterling a year, or nearly four times as much as the total for 1848. The revenues of the country had increased in eleven years from thirty to nearly fifty millions, about five of which went to pay interest on the public debt. More than 1500 miles of new railway had been laid down in the last five years on the lines projected by Lord Dalhousie. In almost every province new works of irrigation were steadily carried forward, or new embankments raised to lessen the mischief caused by sudden floods. The warm interest which Sir John took in the well-being of his European soldiers displayed itself in the building of new

* In Rājputāna, however, there was great distress from the drought of 1868.

barracks at a heavy cost, while the safety of the empire against future revolts was ensured by the construction of fortified posts, which might serve at once to protect our arsenals, overawe the surrounding country, and furnish shelter for our countrymen in time of need.

In each of the three presidencies a sanitary commissioner was for the first time entrusted with the duty of planning measures for improving the general health of the people and guarding the military and civil stations from attacks of preventible disease. In aid of the former object municipal committees, formed largely of natives, and headed by the civil officers of districts, were for the first time established in the chief towns of the North-Western Provinces, with power to raise taxes for sanitary purposes on the towns and villages placed under their control. Important reforms were also carried out in the police of each province and in the management of the central jails.

Great progress had meanwhile been made in the work of popular education. The State outlay on schools and colleges had risen in ten years from £100,000 to £800,000, the number of pupils from 40,000 to 70,000 and the number of schools and colleges, supported wholly or in part by public funds, from a few hundred to nearly 19,000. Every province had its own staff of paid teachers, from the chief director to the humblest of village schoolmasters. The vernacular, middle, and high schools in each district were linked together by means of scholarships, which enabled the best pupils to work their way up from the village school to the local college. Normal schools were training the youth of one generation to become the teachers of the next. 54,000 girls were already learning their lessons in 2000 schools, while training schools for women sprang up here and there under English ladies. Mission and private schools added thousands of scholars to the general sum. In many districts natives of rank and wealth came forward with large subscriptions for the diffusion of knowledge among their countrymen. Some of the native princes—notably those of Jaipur, Kolhapur, and Travancore, were already following the good example of their neighbours within the British pale.

Much of the impulse so given to the spread of popular instruction may be traced to the universal efforts and strong personal influence of Sir John Lawrence himself. To him also was largely owing the first successful attempt to bring the management of Indian forests under the nursing care of the State. In some other directions his hand was equally visible. He placed the cotton-culture of India under the charge of a special commissioner. Many hundred miles were added to the telegraph lines, and a message could be flashed from one end of India to the other for a uniform charge of one rupee. The ruler of Kashmīr was persuaded to abolish or reduce the tolls which hampered the growth of Indian trade with Ladākh and Turkestān. Like concessions were at length obtained from the headstrong King of Burma; and the first attempt at opening Western China to our Indian trade was made in 1868, when Captain Sladen set off from Mandalay, the new Burman capital, on his exploring mission to Bhāmo and Momein (Teng-yueh). Had the Burmese officers proved as friendly as the Panthay rulers of Yun-nan, that journey might have solved the question of carrying English wares from the Irrawaddy to the Yangtse.

Early in January, 1869, Sir John Lawrence took his final leave of the country in which he had spent the best years of a useful and eventful life. One of his last acts was to double the standard weight of letters carried for half an anna. At the last sitting of his council he passed a Bill enabling the Talūkdars of Oudh to borrow money from the Government in time of need, on the principles already applied in Bombay. On his return to England, worn out with ceaseless toiling for the public good, he obtained the peerage to which no living Englishman could have shown so strong a claim, and which the general voice of his countrymen would have awarded him ten years before.

CHAPTER III

LORD MAYO AND LORD NORTHBROOK—1869-1873

LORD LAWRENCE was succeeded by the Earl of Mayo, a statesman of some mark in Lord Derby's Government. A few weeks after his landing at Calcutta the new Viceroy set out to exchange greetings with Sher Ali, whose crowning victory over his brother's troops at Ghazni had once more placed him firmly on the throne of Dost Muhammad. At the magnificent Darbār of Ambāla, in the last days of March, 1869, the war-worn Amīr of Kābul gave Lord Mayo a rare opportunity of playing at once the powerful patron and the winning host. For ten thousand pounds a month and a few thousand muskets Sher Ali agreed to be the friend of our friends and the enemy of our enemies. The lessons learned by him during that visit were not forgotten after his return home, and the friendly motives which had brought him so far away from his own dominions were not a little strengthened by Lord Mayo's kindly bearing and graceful words.

The famine of the past year was still sore in Rājputāna. In spite of the relief-measures ordained by Colonel Keatinge, and promoted by some of the native princes, half a million beings were said to have died of hunger or disease, while nearly all the cattle perished or were driven beyond the border. The summer rains fell just in time to save the Punjāb and Central India from a like fate. Later in the year fever raged among the marshy jungles of Hūgli and Burdwān. Trade declined, and the public revenue fell far short of the estimated yield. Lord Mayo set himself to the work of retrenchment with more perhaps of zeal than discretion. The outlay on public works was cut down in all directions. The income tax was doubled in the autumn of 1869, and trebled in the spring of 1870. By this measure. which aimed at drawing money from the pockets of the wealthier trading-classes, the Viceroy and his finance-minister, Sir R. Temple, succeeded in restoring the balance between outlay and income at the cost of their own popularity and of untold oppression on the part of their native underlings. For every rupee which reached the Treasury, at least three or four were squeezed by native harpies for their own profit from the fears or needs of their helpless countrymen. The rich gave bribes to escape their due share of the hated impost; the poor were frightened into paying unlawful demands, or punished for their resistance by the seizure and forced sale of their few goods. Meetings against a tax denounced for one reason or another by all classes and colours were held in nearly all the chief towns and stations of India; petition after petition was sent up by the Chambers of Commerce, and other bodies representing European or native interests: the newspapers teemed with instances of hardship or extortion; and the Government found itself at issue with some of its oldest and ablest officers, notably with Sir William Muir, the enlightened ruler of the North-Western Provinces.

All this, however, failed for the time to secure the removal or abatement of an impost utterly at war with native usages and modes of feeling. Lord Mayo lived, indeed, to own his error; but loyalty to his ministers and the India Office stayed his hands, and for his successor was to be reserved the credit of doing away with the obnoxious tax.

The landing of Prince Alfred, Duke of Edinburgh, at

Calcutta, in the last days of 1869, served for a time to draw people's minds away from their fiscal grievances to the progress of their princely visitor through his mother's Indian realms. His welcome everywhere was all that his own countrymen could have desired. Lord Mayo's taste for pageantry shone out in the great Calcutta Darbār, at which the Prince was invested with the Star of India amidst a picturesque and splendid gathering of English officers and native chiefs. The Prince was royally feasted by the native gentry of the capital. Hospitable Rajas found sport for him on his upward journey. The great cities of Upper India received him with all befitting honour. His visit to Lucknow was greeted by a brilliant gathering of loyal Talūkdars. On the 7th March he played his part in the formal opening of the railway that links Jubbulpore with Bombay and Allahābād. The capital of Western India entertained him with becoming splendour for several days; nor was Madras at all behindhand in her efforts to amuse and honour the departing guest.

In spite of his economical efforts, Lord Mayo gave his best energies to the pushing forward of useful public works. On the score of cheapness a new system of State railways was set on foot, to continue and complete the work begun by the guaranteed companies. The first of the new lines, the Khamgaon Railway, which links the cotton marts of Berar to the port of Bombay, was opened early in 1870 by the Viceroy himself. Other lines destined to tap the salt-bearing districts in Oudh, the Punjāb, and Rājputāna, were begun or projected. The first sod of a State railway from Lahore to Peshāwar was turned in 1870. On the older lines steady progress continued to be made. The opening of the great bridge over the Sutlej in October completed the line of railway from Bombay, through Allahābād and Delhi, to Lahore. Only a link or two was yet wanting in the iron chain which bound

Madras to Bombay. On the last day of 1870 the Eastern Bengal Railway was completed to Goalundo in Assam. New roads and canals were making everywhere, new schools were founded in every province, a new department of trade and agriculture was called into being, and the opening of coal-mines in the Wardha Valley gave promise of a time when the railways in Western India would cease to depend on English coal.

The year 1871 opened with the untimely death of Sir Henry Durand, whose long and able services had only seven months before been crowned by his promotion from a seat in the Viceroy's Council to the government of the Punjāb, in the room of Sir Donald McLeod. Before the end of January the peace of India was once more broken by bands of Lushai savages, whose murderous raid across the Bengal frontier spread havoc among the outlying tea-gardens of Cachar. Troops and policemen were sent off to guard the frontier from further ravages; but, owing to the lateness of the season, no attempt could then be made to pursue the raiders into their pathless jungles. In November, however, two columns, under Generals Bourchier and Brownlow, set out from different points on their toilsome march through a land of swamps and dense bamboo jungle, broken by a succession of steep hills, each crowned by a stockaded village. Both columns slowly forced their way through all obstacles, beating the enemy wherever they made a stand, and bearing hardships of every kind with the cheerfulness of soldiers confident in their leaders and in themselves. By the end of February, 1872, their work was over, the Haulong and Sailu chiefs had yielded at discretion, and the troops quietly marched back across their own frontier before the rains set in. Their success was largely owing to the careful arrangements planned at the outset by Lord Napier of Magdāla, the Commander-in-Chief.

Meanwhile the Wāhābi plotters in Bengal had received a severe check from the trial and condemnation of Amīr Khan and some of his accomplices. In the Punjāb a new danger to the public peace revealed itself in a number of murderous outrages inflicted on harmless Mussulman butchers by Sikh fanatics of the new Kūkā sect, whose leader was Rām Singh. Condign punishment overtook the murderers; but some of their brotherhood had yet to learn the folly of defying a powerful Government. In the middle of January, 1872, while British troops from Upper India were massed in the Camp of Exercise near Delhi, a few hundred of these fanatics sought to raise the Punjāb by a sudden rush into the fort of Malodh, and a daring attack on the town of Malair-Kotla in Sind. Baffled in the latter attempt, they were speedily hunted down by the Deputy-Commissioner, Mr. Cowan, and the disarmed remnant were blown away from guns, with a merciless contempt of rules which evoked the just censure of the Indian Government.

In his foreign policy Lord Mayo was equally cautious and successful. When civil war raged between Sher Ali and the unfilial Yākūb Khan, the Viceroy's friendly counsels bore fruit in the timely reconciliation of the combatants, and in a large concession to the just demands of Sher Ali's ablest and most popular son. An old boundary dispute between Persia and Kalāt was finally settled by Sir Frederick Goldsmid, acting as umpire for the Indian Government. A like dispute between Persia and Afghānistān regarding Seistān was in course of settlement by the same officer. The King of Burma was at length persuaded to proclaim free trade throughout his dominions. In the quarrels of petty potentates on the Persian Gulf, Lord Mayo interfered only when they seemed to imperil the interests of British subjects. Over the Indian chiefs and nobles who thronged to his frequent

Darbārs, his fine tact and courtly breeding conspired with a certain taste for pomp and splendour to strengthen the influence naturally due to his viceregal rank and powers.

Like many of his predecessors, he displayed a keen appetite for hard work, and a searching eye for details, however trifling. One of his rides before breakfast would have been for most men a good day's work. Now hurrying from one frontier post to another, anon inspecting the site for a new hill-station; one while opening a new line of railway in a cotton district, at another exchanging courtesies with the high-born princes of Rājputāna or political talk with the Mahārāja of Kashmīr; he went everywhere, saw and heard everything for himself, and turned his new knowledge to the best account. The abuses he discovered in the department of Public Works were exposed and repressed with a single eye for the public good. Few Viceroys have ever taken a keener or more intelligent interest in all schemes for developing India's productive wealth; nor did even Lord William Bentinck show greater zeal in the task of keeping down the growing outlay at the least possible sacrifice of the public needs.

During these years many useful and important measures became law. A Hindu Wills Act, framed by Mr. Fitzjames Stephen, Law Member of the Council, gave a legal sanction to practices more or less conflicting with old Hindu usage. The Punjāb Tenancy Act defined and guarded the rights of occupiers under former settlements. A new amendment of the Penal Code assimilated the Indian law against sedition to that of England. Bills for legalising the marriages of Brahmists and other dissenters from the prevailing creeds were carried after much debating. An important measure for dealing with the criminal tribes of India, and an Act for checking the nuisance of European loafers, were likewise passed. In the Bengal Legislature fresh safeguards were enacted on behalf of Coolie emigrants to the tea-gardens of Assam. The Government of Bengal was for the first time empowered to raise cesses on the land for the extension of roads and schools. In England an Act was passed in 1869 which limited the service of members of the Home Council to ten years, and took away from the Council itself the right of appointing half its own number.

A yet more important measure of administrative reform was applied in 1871, when the local governments were for the first time entrusted with the management of all revenues required for local purposes. By this arrangement a due proportion of the imperial revenues was yearly allotted to the several provinces for disbursement on roads, schools, jails, police, and some other items hitherto supervised by the Central Government. Thenceforth each local governor was free to frame his own budget, to spend as he might deem best the money assigned him from the common fund, and to raise new taxes at need from his own province in aid of the purposes for which that money was to be assigned. A new guarantee for thrift in provincial outlay was thus supplied by the transfer to provincial rulers of a part of the power hitherto wielded by the Central Government alone.

Lord Mayo's active and useful career was suddenly cut short by the knife of an assassin on a remote island in the Bay of Bengal. On the 24th January, 1872, he embarked from Calcutta on a tour of inspection whose promised goal was Orissa. Some days of busy sight-seeing were spent at Rangoon and Moulmein. On the 8th February he reached Port Blair, to examine for himself the new convict settlement in the Andaman Islands. After a hard day's work he reached the pier, where a boat was waiting to carry him and his party aboard their vessel.

The brief twilight of the tropics had already faded into

night. In a moment an unseen convict, a Pathān who had been transported for murder done in the Punjāb, sprang out of the darkness, and, before help could reach his victim, the stroke had been dealt which deprived India of an able ruler, and the native princes of a wise and honoured friend. In another moment the murderer was pinned by those around him, but his sharp knife and strong arm had done their work. Half-an-hour afterwards Lord Mayo breathed his last, a victim to the frenzy of a young savage soured by brooding over his fancied wrongs, and reckless of the means he took to gratify at once his thirst for vengeance and his fanaticism.

The tidings of Lord Mayo's death thrilled all India with horror and genuine grief. All classes of his subjects mourned the loss of a ruler whose winning manners and honest zeal for the public good had secured the affection or the respect even of those who disliked some parts of his public policy. Hindus and Muhammadans alike came forward to express their loyal sympathy with the widow of a Viceroy whose strong good sense had bidden fair to undo the mischief caused by his earlier fiscal measures, and whose efforts to redress or abate Muhammadan grievances were already bearing fruit when the hand of a Mussulman savage laid him low. On the princes and nobles of India his death came like a personal bereavement. Sindhia's exclamation, "I have made and lost a friend," bore touching witness to the kindly tact and skill with which Lord Mayo won the hearts and moulded the policy of the native rulers. As a personal friend, indeed, he was mourned not only by the highest in the land, but by all who had ever felt the charm of personal intercourse with perhaps the most genial statesman of his day.

For a few months his place was worthily filled by Lord Napier, the retiring Governor of Madras. Early in May, however, the new Viceroy, Lord Northbrook, took up the reins of government at Calcutta, laden with the fruits of a long previous training in the India Office, the Admiralty, the War Office, and one or two other departments of the State. His new career may be said to have begun at Simla, where, in compliance with recent usage, he and his Council passed the hot and rainy season of 1872. One of his first acts betrayed a becoming care to walk in the steps of his latest predecessors. The Russian conquerors of Bokhāra were about to punish the Khan of Khiva, the ancient Kharizm, for the many outrages inflicted year by year on Russian subjects by his man-stealing and murdering Turkmans. An envoy from Khiva besought Lord Northbrook to step in between his master and the coming danger. Lord Northbrook answered by a friendly message counselling the Khan to offer timely amends for the misdeeds laid to his account. Had his advice been honestly followed, perhaps the Russian advance to Khiva in 1873 might never have taken place.

After some months spent in useful if unobtrusive work, the new Viceroy set out in October on a tour of inquiry through nearly all the chief towns of Northern, Western, and Central India, from Lahore to Bombay and Jubbulpore. Darbārs were held at several places on his road, which brought him into friendly contact with a host of princes and great nobles north of the Tāpti, from Patiāla to Indore. The two great Marātha feudatories, Holkar and Sindhia, vied with each other in the splendour of the welcome given by the one at Bombay, by the other at Barwai, to their viceregal guest. In those two months of constant travel Lord Northbrook laid in fresh stores of practical knowledge on all the leading questions of the day.

Foremost among these was the question of taxation. In a populous country ruled by a handful of strangers from afar, it behoves the rulers above all things to abstain from laying heavy or unwonted burdens on the subject millions. The murmurs provoked throughout India by the fiscal experiments of late years, especially by the income-tax of 1870, had not been silenced by the subsequent lowering of that unpopular impost. Even Lord Mayo's concession of larger powers to the local governments became, in the popular fancy, a mere blind for further inroads on the tax-paying classes. From the first, however, Lord Northbrook set himself to grapple with the salient causes of popular discontent. A careful inquiry into all the taxes and cesses levied throughout India issued in the collection of a large body of facts and opinions, which served to guide and strengthen the Viceroy's efforts in the field of financial reform. The lessons he had thus been learning emboldened him in March, 1873, to abolish the income-tax altogether, to proclaim the early enforcement of a road-cess in Bengal, and to warn the local governments against any further increase of the local burdens.

In the early part of the same year the excitement lately caused, both in India and at home, by the progress of Russian arms and influence in Central Asia, was in some measure allayed by the readiness of the Russian Government to acknowledge and respect the new line of frontier laid down by the India Office for Afghānistān, as the limit of English influence in the regions bordering the Punjāb. Later interviews between Lord Northbrook and a special envoy from Kābul issued in a renewal of the friendly assurances exchanged between Lord Mayo and Sher Ali at the Ambāla Darbār. In the interests of Indian trade with Turkestan, Mr. Forsyth in 1873 led a second embassy to the court of our good friend Muhammad Yākub, the firmly established ruler of Kashgar, Khotan, and other provinces not long wrested from Chinese rule. Forsyth's success on this occasion was to bear no lasting fruit, for a few years later fortune turned against our new ally, and a Chinese Viceroy once more ruled over Eastern Turkestan. Another mission, headed by Sir Bartle Frere, had set out from England, towards the close of 1872, for the purpose of checking the rampant slave-trade along the eastern coast of Africa, by means of fresh treaties with the Sultān of Zanzibar and the adjacent chiefs. It was not till after the leader of the mission had returned home that the reluctant Sultān was coaxed or frightened into joining the new crusade against a traffic which his own connivance and the cunning of not a few Indian traders had done so much to foster and extend.

In the midst of his official labours Lord Northbrook found himself confronted by a great and growing danger. During the rainy season of 1873 the greater part of Bengal and Bihār was suffering from a drought which boded a wide-spread failure of the autumn crops. Early in September the warning notes of impending famine were sounded by Sir George Campbell, the energetic Lieutenant-Governor of Bengal. Lord Northbrook hurried down at once from Simla to aid his lieutenant in fighting against a famine which might else rage unchecked among twenty-five million souls. The fight was long and arduous, for the winter rainfall proved too partial to do much good; but the Viceroy was determined to spare no effort in the task of bringing food to the hungry and saving human lives. When Campbell's health, long failing, broke down under the strain, Sir Richard Temple, then Finance Minister, took his place. Vast stores of rice, bought up by Government officers in Burma, were shipped to Calcutta and distributed through the suffering districts; relief committees sought out the weak and helpless, and those who were ashamed to beg; and relief-works were promptly opened in every centre of distress. Temple himself spared no pains and knew no rest in the discharge of his multifarious duties; while a picked staff of officers, white and dusky, worked away like heroes in aid of the object which their leaders had most at heart.

In May, 1874, the famine reached its height. But the Viceroy's forethought, aided by Temple's supervising energy and the zeal of all who worked under him, kept the people alive, until the monsoon rains of July and August sent the most of them flocking from the relief-works back to their wonted labours in the fields. By the middle of October all fear of further suffering was dispelled by the tokens of returning plenty. For once no epidemic disease followed in the famine's wake. Only twenty-two persons in all were known to have died of sheer starvation; a result which loudly testifies to the thoroughness with which Lord Northbrook's policy of saving life at whatever cost was carried out. Of the six millions sterling spent on famine relief, no small part went towards the making of new roads, branch railways, and embankments for canals. In another twelvemonth all traces of the mischief caused by the famine had disappeared. The foreign trade of Bengal was steadily increasing, and her land revenue yielded its normal amount.

As Lieutenant-Governor of that great province, Sir G. Campbell had proved himself a wise statesman and a vigorous reformer. He was the first to carry out in Bengal those principles of popular instruction which had already borne good fruit in Bombay and the North-West. In the course of three years and a-half his province was covered with primary schools, each furnished with trained masters, at a trifling increase of the total cost to the State. Tests of bodily as well as mental fitness were applied to candidates for the Native Civil Service. His scheme of "promotion" in the higher ranks of the Covenanted Service left every civil officer free to rise in that branch of the service which best suited his own tastes or his previous training. He carried through his Council a bill which compelled the Zamindars of Bengal to contribute something towards the maintenance of roads and schools. Under his able guidance the first regular census of the people in his province was carried out in 1872. The agrarian troubles in Eastern Bengal brought out alike his sympathies with a rack-rented peasantry, and his firmness in repressing overt disorder. Of the administrative burden which had lain upon Campbell's shoulders some part was lifted from those of his successor; for in 1875 the border provinces of Assam, Cachar, and Sylhet, were handed over to a chief commissioner responsible only to the Viceroy himself.

In the same year Sir John Strachey took over the government of the North-West Provinces from the scholarly and zealous Sir William Muir. The Revenue and Rent Acts, which Muir had lately carried through the Viceroy's Legislative Council, besides other improvements in the land-law of the province, secured to a large class of tenants the right of holding at a fixed rent for ten years. The timely action of the Indian Government averted a Santhal outbreak against the money-lenders of Bengal. Risings of peasantry against the village usurers of Poona and Ahmadnagar troubled for a time the peace of Bombay, then governed by Sir Philip Wodehouse. The report of a Commission ordered by Lord Northbrook to inquire into the cause of these outbreaks showed what reason the peasants of the Deccan sometimes had for turning upon those who plundered them in the name of the law. In due time they also were to obtain a lawful remedy for the wrongs thus brought to light.

Early in 1875 the Gaikwar of Baroda, Malhar Rāo, whose misrule had sorely taxed the Viceroy's endurance, was at length arraigned before a mixed Commission of Englishmen and Natives of high standing, on the charge of attempting to poison his Resident, Colonel Phayre. At the end of a long trial the three English Commissioners found him guilty, while their Native colleagues pronounced more or less confidently in the Gaikwar's favour. In compliance with orders from Lord Salisbury, then Minister for India, Lord Northbrook formally deposed the Gaikwar, not for the outrage on Colonel Phayre, but for all his past misconduct, and his late disregard of former warnings. A new Gaikwar was installed at Baroda, under the regency of Jamna Bai, and one of the ablest of Native statesmen, Sir Madhara Rāo, who had done good service in Travancore and at the court of Holkar, was appointed to rule the State as Chief Minister, with Philip Melville for his Resident.

The misrule in Baroda formed a rare exception to the good things reported from most of the Native States. These were no longer as they had been in Dalhousie's days. The sons and nephews of Rajas and Sardars were learning to ride and play cricket in schools managed by English masters. In the high schools and colleges English teaching was steadily making its way. Many of the Native princes were learning to spend money freely on schools, hospitals, and public works. In several States of Rājputāna and Central India justice was administered on pure English principles. Holkar was zealous in founding cotton mills, and otherwise developing the natural resources of Indore. The rulers of Travancore were liberal patrons of all Western culture, and the schools in that southern kingdom might bear comparison with those of any province in British India.

In the higher offices of the State Native agency was steadily gaining ground. Native judges took their seats in the High Court of more than one province; Native gentlemen appeared on Municipal Committees, on the bench of magistrates, and in the Legislative Councils. Natives thronged the higher ranks of the Uncovenanted Service, and two or three Native Candidates passed by open competition into the favoured Civil Service itself. On the other hand, Western Ideas and influences were gradually leavening the Native mind. Societies were founded in many places for the purpose of discussing questions of social or political reform. The great Brahmo reformer, Keshab Chandra Sen, taught his followers a religion deeply permeated by Christian modes of thought. Many Natives readily sent their children to Mission schools. Scholarly Natives wrote in good English on subjects which few Western writers could have handled more ably. Some of the leading Hindus had begun to educate their daughters in the learning of modern Europe, and Native ladies began to exchange visits with their English female friends. Brahman Pandits discovered that a Hindu might cross the sea without losing caste, that the eating of flesh was not forbidden by the Vedas, and that a Hindu widow might marry again without deadly sin.

By the untimely death of Lord Hobart in April, 1875, Madras lost a Governor whose services to his people it would be hard to overrate. He had opened schools for the special use of Muhammadan children, and had fought, not wholly in vain, against the Viceroy's scheme for enhancing the salt-duties of his province in order to lower those of Upper India. Later in the year Lord Northbrook's Council ordained a large reform of the Customs Tariff. Thenceforth export duties were to be levied only on indigo, rice, and lac; of the import duties some were repealed and the remainder greatly reduced. In spite of famine charges and a falling exchange, the revenue for this year was to yield a net surplus of a million and one-third over an outlay of 49⅝ millions.

The visit of the Prince of Wales to India towards the close of 1875 was an event which stirred large classes of the people to unwonted enthusiasm. They welcomed him as their future sovereign, the heir of that royal lady who had first claimed their homage in the proclamation of 1858. His progress everywhere from Bombay to Kashmīr was one long triumph. Never had Calcutta beheld a pageant so gorgeous as the Chapter of the Bath held by His Royal Highness on the great Maidan. The princes and nobles of India vied with each other in the costliness of their presents and the splendour of their hospitalities. Their intercourse with a guest so gracious quickened their sense of personal loyalty towards the British Crown.

In his dealings with the Border States Lord Northbrook showed himself a friendly and forbearing neighbour. He succeeded in restoring peace between the Khan of Khalat and his unruly Sardars. His attempt to send a Mission through Burma overland to Shanghai was early frustrated by Chinese treachery. Sher Ali, the Afghān Amīr, kept him duly informed of every letter that passed between him and the Russian Governor at Turkestān. But the Viceroy's views on Afghān policy were not those of the Home Government. Their proposal to place a British Resident at Herāt was met by Lord Northbrook with grave remonstrances and well-reasoned warnings against a course so hateful to our Afghān ally. When Lord Salisbury finally urged him to find or make some pretext for sending a Mission to Kābul, Lord Northbrook declined to embark on an enterprise which involved so dangerous a departure from the policy of twenty years past. Having to chose between a breach of discipline and the breach of treaty pledges, Lord Northbrook resigned office on some plea of ill-health, and turned his face homewards in April, 1876, amidst the outspoken regrets of all classes. As a leading Native journal well said, he "could not be considered a brilliant ruler, for he made no war, annexed no territory, committed no plunder; but he gave the land rest."

CHAPTER IV

FROM LORD LYTTON TO THE MARQUESS OF LANSDOWNE—1876–1889

ON the 12th April, 1876, the new Viceroy, Lord Lytton, landed in Calcutta, and entered with a light heart on the task cut out for him by the Government at home. Faithful to the instructions sent out by Lord Salisbury, he at once requested Sher Ali to receive a British envoy at Kābul or elsewhere. The arrival of a new Viceroy and the assumption of a new title by the Queen of England were the pretexts assigned for a move so contrary to all existing pledges. In spite of the Amīr's reluctance to walk into the trap thus laid for him, Lord Lytton continued to press him with new demands backed by veiled menaces and fine-sounding offers. Sher Ali was reminded that the British Government "could break him as a reed"; that his true position between England and Russia was that of the earthen pipkin between two iron pots. At last the Amīr agreed to the holding of a conference at Peshāwar.

In the last days of January, 1877, the two envoys, Sir Lewis Pelly and Nur Muhammad, opened a conference, the very bases of which remained in dispute. The Afghān envoy pleaded long and earnestly against the formidable risks involved in the admission of British officers into Herāt and Kandahār. Sher Ali's throne would be endangered, and the British officers might be killed. Pelly insisted on compliance with Lord Lytton's demands. After his envoy's death in March, Sher Ali was on the point of giving way, when Pelly, by the Viceroy's orders, brought the conference to a sudden close. Soon afterwards the Viceroy's Vakil, or Native agent, was recalled from Kābul.

Meanwhile Lord Lytton had taken another long step in furtherance of the new policy favoured by the powers at home. In November, 1876, a British garrison was finally planted in the fortified town of Quetta, which overlooks the Shal valley and commands the road from Kandahār to Sind through the Bolan Pass. The right to occupy such a post was implied in the Treaty of 1854; but the wisdom of occupying a place so far beyond the wild mountains which guard our Sind frontier had been strenuously denied by nearly all the best judges from Lord Lawrence to Sir Harry Lumsden and Sir Herbert Edwardes. Nor can it be doubted that the presence of a British outpost in such a quarter deepened the Amīr's distrust of British friendliness and good faith.

On the first day of 1877 the Imperial Assemblage, in honour of the assumption by the English Queen of the title, justified by present facts as well as of historic usage, of Empress of India, was held on the memorable ridge that looks over the city of Delhi. Amidst a vast and gorgeous array of princes, grandees, British officers and ladies, Lord Lytton took his seat in the huge pavilion, to hear the proclamation of the new imperial title which the Queen had deigned to assume. Its last words were caught up by a grand salute of guns and musketry and the crashing music of thirty regimental bands. The proclamation was read aloud amidst smaller gatherings in all the chief cities and stations of India. Honours were showered in all directions; a new Order of the Indian Empire was proclaimed; the rulers of Gwalior and Kashmīr were gazetted generals in the British army; and fifteen thousand prisoners were set free.

Amidst all this splendour and excitement a dark cloud of famine was breaking over Southern India. By the end of 1876 vast numbers of people in Madras, Bombay, and Mysore were already feeling the pinch of a calamity far more prolonged and widespread than the recent famine in Bengal. In July, 1877, two million people in the Madras Presidency alone were receiving State relief in the shape either of wages for special work, or of food and alms. By September the numbers were still greater. The distress continued even into the following year. In Mysore it became almost unmanageable. In spite of the vast machinery organised everywhere for famine relief, in spite of the help afforded by the railways, of all the precautions taken by the supreme and local governments, of the zeal and self-devotion displayed by a whole army of hard-working overseers, the total of deaths from famine and disease amounted to five millions and a quarter, while the whole cost of famine relief was reckoned at eleven millions sterling. At one time the scarcity spread over parts of Northern India, accounting for the loss of another million lives in the North-West Provinces alone.

In order to provide against future famines Lord Lytton's Government of 1878 decreed the levying of a licence tax on trades, and of a special cess on the land in Northern India, while they enhanced the salt tax in Bombay and Madras. The proceeds of the new imposts were to form a famine insurance fund of a million and a half a year, not a rupee of which should be applied to other uses than the payment of famine debts or the making of "protective" works, such as canals and branch railways.

Unfortunately the new fund was soon to be swallowed up in the expenses of another Afghān war. In the spring of 1878 a picked force of 8000 Sepoys was shipped off from India to Malta, as a kind of menace to Russia, whose armies were encamped within easy reach of Constantinople. The Russian countermove was made from Samarkand, in the shape of an embassy to the Amīr of Kābul. Before Colonel Stoletoff arrived in Kābul, the treaty of peace between Russia and Turkey had already been signed at Berlin. Nothing came of the embassy to Kābul but an exchange of mere civilities. Lord Lytton, however, demanded that Sher Ali should forthwith receive an English embassy also. In spite of the Amīr's protests and pleadings for delay, Sir Neville Chamberlain with a strong escort set forth in September from Peshāwar. At Ali Masjid in the Khyber Pass, one of his officers was firmly but politely required to turn back by the Afghān commandant.

This rebuff was telegraphed to England as the forcible repulse of a British embassy from an Afghān outpost. Lord Lytton prepared for war, but by orders from the Home Government the Amīr was granted a few weeks' grace. His letter of apology miscarried, and on the 21st November three columns of British troops advanced from three different quarters into Afghānistān. Before the winter had set in, Jalālabād and Kandahār were in British keeping. Sher Ali fled from Kābul and died soon afterwards in a corner of his realm. In the following April his son Yākub Khan signed the Treaty of Gandamak, which gave India a new frontier beyond the passes, and guaranteed the safety of a British Resident at Kābul.

For a few months all went smoothly in Afghānistān; but it was only "the torrent's smoothness ere it dash below." On the 3rd September, 1879, the British Residency, where Sir Louis Cavagnari had been installed in July, was attacked by a furious Afghān mob, including hundreds of the Amīr's soldiers. The Amīr himself was, or seemed to be, powerless to interfere. In a few hours the Residency was gutted and all its inmates and defenders dead. Early in October Roberts led his troops from the Kurram Valley on Kābul, while Stewart once more marched to Kandahār. The victory of Charasiah gave Roberts full possession of Kābul. More than once that winter his troops were fiercely assailed by swarms of insurgent Afghāns. Yākub Khan gave himself up to Roberts and was sent off a State prisoner to Peshāwar. His brother Ayub held Herāt in his name, while other chiefs rallied to the cause of Yākub's infant son. Anarchy and violence reigned everywhere outside Kābul and the province of Kandahār. On his march from Kandahār to Kābul in the spring of 1880, Stewart had much ado to beat off a large body of Afghān fanatics in the fight of Ahmad Khel.

He had hardly joined hands with Roberts at Kābul when a new Ministry came into power at home, pledged to undo Lord Lytton's aggressive policy in Afghānistān. Lord Lytton therefore at once resigned his post in April, 1880, leaving behind him the legacy of a heavy debt incurred for no good reason, and the memory of a severe law passed against the Native Indian Press. In March, 1878, he had forced through his Council an Act which placed Native newspapers under an almost Russian censorship. Of other measures enacted during his rule, the most beneficent was the Act of 1879, which insured to the peasantry of Southern India a sensible relief from the greed of ruthless money-lenders, and the one-sided action of the civil courts. Thenceforth, for one thing, the peasant's holding could not be wholly taken away from him, even for a term of years, until all means of inquiry and arbitration had failed; nor might the peasant be imprisoned in execution of a decree for debt. In 1879 the right of natives of India to a larger share in the government of their own country was acknowledged by the creation of a Statutory Civil Service, the candidates for which were to be selected by the Local Governments. A number of appointments hitherto reserved for the Covenanted Service were to be allotted yearly to civilians of the new class.

Lord Lytton's place was filled by the Marquis of Ripon, who, as Lord De Grey, had once for a few months been Secretary of State for India. Sher Ali's nephew and old antagonist, Abdur Rahman Khan, had already been summoned from his place of exile to the vacant throne of Kābul. In July the new Amīr was installed by British officers, and our troops were ordered to prepare for leaving his capital. By that time, however, Ayub Khan was marching with his Herātis across the Helmand. A British brigade sent out against him from Kandahār was routed with heavy slaughter at Maiwand, and great fear was felt for the safety of Kandahār itself.

Happily the troops which Stewart had brought to Kābul were still there. Nine thousand of these under the dashing Frederick Roberts marched off without delay, traversed three hundred miles of rugged country in twenty days, and on the 1st September drove Ayub's army, after some sharp fighting, in wild rout from the neighbourhood of Kandahār. In the following year Lord Ripon withdrew the last of his troops from Afghān territory. The Treaty of Gandamak became almost a dead letter. No successor to Cavagnari was ever forced upon the Afghān Amīr, nor was any return attempted to the vexatious policy of Lord Lytton's day. Ere long Ayub was driven out of Herāt, and Abdur Rahman reigned in peace over all the realms of Dost Muhammad. Of the twenty millions which India had expended on the late war, one-fourth was repaid her from the Imperial treasury.

Under Lord Ripon's peaceful and progressive rule

India moved briskly forward along all the lines of organic growth. A series of good seasons fostered agriculture, stimulated trade, and enabled the Government to fill its treasuries without recourse to new taxes. Public works of all kinds were prosecuted with increasing vigour and with every promise of ultimate advantage. The railway system was steadily developed, especially in respect of new State lines. Several of the old guaranteed lines had begun to yield a substantial profit. India's foreign trade rose in value from a hundred and twenty to a hundred and fifty millions a year. A general lowering of the salt-duties to one uniform rate in 1882, entailed no permanent loss of revenue, while it proved a real boon to millions .of poor rayats. In the same year were abolished the last of those duties on cotton imports, some of which had disappeared in Lord Lytton's time. The import duties on all articles except arms, alcoholic drinks, salt, and opium, were also done away. Of exports since 1880 rice alone continued to pay duty.

In everything that concerned the moral and social well-being of his subjects Lord Ripon took a lively interest. In 1882 a select commission, with Dr. William Hunter (afterwards Sir William Hunter, one of the most eminent modern writers on Indian history and the creator of the Imperial Gazetteer of India) for its president, was appointed to inquire into the working of the educational system first organised in 1854. The inquiry resulted in a well-considered scheme for limiting the State outlay on the higher education, in order to improve and develope the still backward system of primary and middle schools. The training of the people for the due management of their local affairs was the object of a radical reform in the municipal system of India. The Municipal Committees in almost every province were remodelled on a basis of popular election, such as the great capitals had long possessed. By another enactment the Native Press was restored to its former freedom.

Lord Ripon's zeal for even-handed justice brought him, once at least, into sharp collision with the bulk of his own countrymen. Several Natives had lately made their way into the Covenanted Service. With the Viceroy's sanction Mr. Ilbert, Law Member of his Council, drew up a Bill which extended to Native rural magistrates the right of trying all criminal cases that came before the district courts. The Europeans in India raised a furious outcry at this new attack on the privileges of the dominant race, and a storm of obloquy raged loud and long against the Viceroy himself. Lord Ripon saw the need of some compromise, and the Ilbert Bill in a modified form at length became law. The rancour of his assailants endeared him all the more visibly to Natives of every class. The spontaneous outburst of popular gratitude which everywhere cheered his last journey through Upper India in 1884 far surpassed in cumulative strength and fervour anything seen or heard by any former Viceroy.

Three years earlier the province of Mysore, which had flourished for half a century under British rule, was formally handed over, by command of the India Office, to a youthful scion of the old Native dynasty, which Lord W. Bentinck had to all seeming dethroned for ever. Towards the end of 1884 Lord Ripon's place was filled by the Earl of Dufferin, who had already won high honours both as a statesman and a diplomatist. For the new Viceroy was reserved the credit of carrying through its last stages a long-debated measure of reform in the rent law of Bengal. The Bengal Tenancy Act of 1885 gave clearer sanctions and a much wider scope to the principle of tenant-right enforced by the Rent Act of 1859. Fixity of tenure and fair rents were secured thenceforth, as a rule, to every rayat who had retained his holding for three years, while a tenant of twelve years' standing could not have his rent enhanced on any pretext. Two years later a fair measure of tenant-right was secured to the rayats of Oudh.

Matters of less peaceful import were already engrossing Lord Dufferin's attention. English and Russian officers had been commissioned to define the northern boundaries of Afghānistān. Between the two parties arose disagreements and misunderstandings which at one time threatened the peace of Asia and Europe. Happily the storm-clouds were dispelled by prudent statesmanship. The Amīr of Kābul gave due heed to the Viceroy's counsels; and the marking out of the Afghān frontier was finally carried through without any further hitch. Meanwhile fresh trouble had been brewing on the side of Upper Burma, where the long misrule and virtual hostility of the savage king Theebaw had brought matters to a deadlock. The need for British interference was accented by the rumour of French intrigues and the progress of French arms towards the Burmese border. Before the end of 1885 Mandalay, the capital, was occupied by British troops, the king himself was prisoner in our hands, and the greater part of his country was held by British garrisons. In February, 1886, the issue which Dalhousie had long since foreseen became an historic fact. The Alompra dynasty ceased to rule over the wide tracts of mountain and forest which divide Pegu from the Chinese frontier; and the half-conquered country was declared a British province, to be ruled by the Viceroy through a Chief Commissioner, aided by a select staff of British officers. It was no easy task to establish peace and order in a province as large as France, infested with rebellious chiefs and an armed banditti of unemployed soldiers. In three years, however, that task was nearly accomplished, and when Lord Dufferin quitted India the foundations of civilised order and social well-being were already laid in the youngest province of his empire.

But for the lingering troubles in Burma, and the small campaigns of 1888 in the Black Mountain and on the borders of Tibet, the peace of India remained unbroken during the last years of Lord Dufferin's rule. The Burmese war, with all that came of it; the need of strengthening the defences of the North-Western frontier; a large increase of the Indian Army; and a steady fall in the exchange value of the rupee—all this involved an outlay of many millions sterling, a part of which had to be defrayed by new or increased taxation, and by the appropriation of funds designed for local and special purposes. In spite of a growing revenue, of a flourishing export trade, and of a strict economy in administrative details, there was a deficit of six millions on the total income of four years. Several of the Native princes proved their loyalty by offering large sums of money in free gift towards the cost of the frontier defences, or by granting loans on liberal terms to the Supreme Government. In the Jubilee year, 1887, some of them, including Holkar, crossed the sea to pay their homage to the great Queen-Empress, and to bear their part in the ceremonial pomps and festivities which crowned the first half-century of her benign rule. In India the Jubilee festival was marked by the release of 25,000 prisoners from the jails, while Sindhia's heart was gladdened by the free surrender of that historic fortress of Gwalior which our troops had garrisoned ever since the Mutiny.

Meanwhile the leaven of English influence and example was working more and more freely upon Native habits and institutions. The princes and chiefs of Rājputāna pledged themselves to curtail the ruinous cost of marriage and funeral rites among their own people, and to fight against the time-honoured practice of child-marriage. Englishwomen were doing good work as teachers or as doctors among the inmates of many a Zenāna. Numbers of young Indians flocked over to England for the purpose of studying law or medicine, or other branches of practical knowledge, or of gaining an insight into the social and political life of Englishmen at home. Two or three men of ripe culture and strong ambition stood forth as candidates for seats in the British House of Commons. In India a great "National Congress," composed of several hundred delegates—Hindu, Muhammadan, Parsi—from all parts of the country, met once a year in one of the great Indian cities, to discuss important questions, social and political, in a spirit by no means hostile to the British rule. If some of their language wanted measure, if their demands were not always reasonable, they expressed at any rate the thoughts, desires, ambitions of a class which for many years had been nourished on the strong mental food supplied by their English teachers—a class which was yearly growing in numbers and self-respect, and which had already learned from our example the policy of concerted action for a common end. The National Congress, however misleading its title or faulty its methods, was becoming a fact which no prudent Viceroy could overlook.

That the time was ripe for anything like true representative government, Lord Dufferin would not allow. But the time, he held, was come for giving the Natives a larger share in the government of their own country. Acting on the report of a special commission, he threw open to Native candidates three hundred of the higher posts hitherto reserved for the Covenanted Service. And before leaving India he had strongly advised the Home Government to admit more Native members into each of the legislative councils. During his rule a careful inquiry, begun under Lord Lytton, had been completed, into the condition of the people in every province; an inquiry which tends to show that nearly all classes are somewhat better off now than they had been thirty years before. The growth of population in the more crowded districts has become a source of far greater anxiety than the recurrence of a widespread famine. The true remedy for overpopulation can be found only when the habits and feelings of the people have undergone a radical change.

Early in December, 1888, the Marquis of Dufferin and Ava made over the reins of power to his successor, the Marquess of Lansdowne. He had done his duty well and faithfully amidst untoward circumstances; and he left behind him a fair prospect of unclouded peace, with all the blessings which peace, upheld by a strong but kindly despotism, can bring to birth.

CHAPTER V

THE MARQUESS OF LANSDOWNE—1889–1894

THE Viceroyalty of Lord Lansdowne was marked by satisfactory progress in many fields of peaceful activity. During each cold season he visited some portion of his wide dominions, from Baluchistan in the west to the easternmost frontier of Burma, and from Kashmīr southward to Mysore. In 1889, he received in public Darbār at Quetta, the Khan of Kalat, and many chiefs and Sardars of Baluchistan. On his tour through the Punjāb in 1890, Lord Lansdowne installed the young Maharāja of Patiāla, whose grandfather had stood so bravely by us in the dark days of the mutiny. On his way through Rājputāna Lord Lansdowne distributed prizes to the students of the Mayo College, which Rājput liberality had enabled Lord Mayo to found at Ajmēr. At Udaipur he opened the Victoria Hall, which the loyal Rana had built in honour of the Queen's Jubilee.

At Jodhpur the Viceroy found a marked improvement in the general administration of a State which in former times had been among the least progressive in Rājputāna. In the beautiful city of Jaipur he laid the foundation of the twenty-seventh new hospital which had been founded in the State of recent years; and he paid a just tribute to the rapid progress of education among its people.

In the autumn of 1891, Lord Lansdowne visited Kashmīr and restored to its ruler some of the powers which that prince had resigned two years before. Turning southward to Gwalior he exchanged courtesies with its youthful Mahārāja, who was entrusted two years later with a probationary share in the government of his kingdom. From Gwalior the Viceroy journeyed to Bhopāl, whose Bēgam renewed her offer to place a portion of her troops at the disposal of the Indian Government.

In the following year the Viceroy spent some days at Hyderābād counselling the Nizām to look more carefully after his finances, and to get rid of a large proportion of his useless and expensive troops. At Mysore he complimented the young Sovereign of that State on the good work which his government had already achieved in many directions during the last ten years. "He has proved himself," said Lord Lansdowne, "an intelligent and upright Ruler . . . alive to the duties of his position. There is probably no state in India where ruler and ruled are on more satisfactory terms, or where the great principle that government should be for the happiness of the governed has been more thoroughly carried out."

Lord Lansdowne's last tour in 1893 carried him to Mandalay, the old Capital of Upper Burma. During his Darbār at that place, he spoke with just complacency of the success which had attended British rule in Burma; especially in the work of suppressing the numerous bands of dacoits, by which that province had long been infested. From Mandalay the Viceroy passed on up the Irrawaddy to Bhamo, where he assured the Chinese traders of his desire to leave them no just cause for complaint. To the Kachin chiefs from the adjacent hills he promised the friendly countenance of his Government in return for their abstinence from all attacks on British officers, and the peaceful dwellers in the plains.

During these five years Lord Lansdowne was more than once compelled to enforce the principles of British order on recalcitrant Native States. In September, 1890, the reigning Chief of Manipur, a small protected State on the eastern borders of Assam, was deposed by his brother, the Senapati, or Commander-in-Chief, who set up another of his brothers in the Chief's place. As the deposed Prince had been a weak and incompetent ruler, the Viceroy decided to acknowledge his successor, but to banish the Senapati. In March, 1891, Mr. Quinton, the Chief Commissioner of Assam, set out with an escort of 400 Gurkhas to carry out the Viceroy's orders at Manipur.

On the 24th, an attempt was made by Mr. Quinton's orders to arrest the Senapati, who had refused to attend the previous Darbār. The attempt was defeated by the Manipuris themselves, and after a fight of several hours our troops retired into the Residency, which afforded sorry shelter from the fire of the enemy's guns. In the course of the evening, Quinton and his assistant, Grimwood, with Colonel Skene were inveigled under a flag of truce into the Palace, and treacherously put to death. That night the Residency was abandoned by its diminished garrison; but succour and revenge were soon at hand. A British force occupied the country, and stormed the capital. The Senapati and five others who had taken part in the murders were promptly tried, and paid with death the penalty of their crime. The Regent was transported for life, a heavy fine was inflicted on the State, and a child belonging to the ruling family was raised to the Chiefship. During his minority the State was administered by a British officer.

In the course of 1893, the Khan of Kalat was relieved at his own request of the sovereign powers which he had in various ways outrageously misused. With the hearty approval of the Khan's chief Sardars, Sir Robert Sandeman, the British Agent, installed the Khan's son in his father's stead.

At Gilgit on the northern frontier of Kashmīr, Lord Lansdowne in 1889 re-established the British Agency which Lord Ripon had withdrawn in 1881. Westward of Gilgit lies the hill-state of Chitral, whose Mehtar, or ruler, had sought and obtained the feudal protection of Kashmīr. The Mehtar's death in 1892 was followed by a period of intestine strife before his eldest son, Nizām-ul-Mūlk, won his way to the disputed throne. A British officer was appointed to reside at the new Mehtar's Court, and the independence of Chitral against Afghānistān was guaranteed by the Viceroy's treaty with the Afghān Amīr.

It was not until 1893 that the Amīr of Kābul, Abdur Rahman Khan, found himself free to receive the mission which Lord Lansdowne had long desired to send him for the purpose of settling matters of importance to both parties. In September of that year, the mission, headed by Sir Mortimer Durand, was escorted by Afghān troops across the Afghān frontier towards Kābul, where it was cordially received by the Amīr himself. A series of friendly conferences between our envoy and the Amīr resulted in a settlement which defined the respective spheres of influence for the two powers; and transferred from Kābul to India the right of controlling certain frontier tribes. The Amīr's subsidy was also increased from twelve to eighteen lakhs of rupees, and he was allowed to import arms of all kinds at discretion into Afghānistān. The signing of the treaty was followed by an exchange of friendly assurances between the Amīr and Sir M. Durand, ending with the Amīr's expression of his desire to see our envoy again some day at Kābul.

"Spheres of influence" was the name given to the new policy which the government of Lord Lansdowne had set itself to pursue. This policy aimed at surrounding India's natural frontier with a belt of country within which British influence should alone prevail. With the dwellers along this political frontier no foreign power, Russian, French, or Chinese, should be allowed to interfere. The independence of the tribes within this belt was to be carefully respected, while the Indian Government claimed for itself the right of making roads through any part of it, and maintaining posts at need for their protection.

Towards the close of Lord Lansdowne's Viceroyalty, an important military reform, which had long been called for, was carried into effect. The three armies of Bengal, Madras, and Bombay were formed into one army under one Commander-in-Chief, with four large divisions, each commanded by a Lieutenant-General. The three separate Staff Corps were also amalgamated into one great Corps, thenceforth called the Indian Army. During the same period some thousands of picked troops from the armies of the Native Princes were enrolled for purposes of Imperial defence on the strength of Her Majesty's regular forces. These "Imperial Service" troops have since played their part with high credit in the customary camp of exercise, and have at need done excellent service in the field.

By an Act of Parliament passed in 1892, the right to discuss questions of financial policy was fully conceded to the Viceroy's Legislative Council. The new rule appears to have worked well in the interests both of the public and the Indian Government. By the same Act, Lord Lansdowne was empowered to increase the numbers of the supreme and local Legislative Councils by means of a direct appeal to the votes of certain elective constituencies. "I earnestly trust," said Lord Lansdowne to his Imperial Council, "that this Council, strengthened as it has lately been by the extension of its functions, and by the addition to its ranks of a larger number of representative members, some of whom will owe their presence to the recommendation of their fellow-citizens, will enjoy an ever-increasing share of public confidence, . . . and that it will prove to be a new source of stability and usefulness to the institutions of this country."

One of the beneficent measures passed by the Viceroy's Legislative Council, was an Act which limited to eleven hours the women's working-day in every Indian factory, and that of children to half-time. It also secured a weekly holiday for every factory hand. An Act of 1890 imposed certain penalties on all persons convicted of cruelty to animals, captive as well as domestic.

The peace of the country was broken for a time by serious riots born of religious fanaticism. A social Hindu movement for the protection of cows from wanton ill-treatment, soon degenerated into a lawless agitation against the slaughter of kine for food or sacrificial purposes. The Muhammadans fiercely resented any interference with their customary ritual. Riots resulting in much loss of life took place in many parts of India, and for three days the wealthy and populous city of Bombay was given up to virtual anarchy. Order was everywhere speedily restored by the prompt action of the local authorities. At the Viceroy's invitation, the leaders of the people in the disturbed districts formed conciliation committees to ascertain and record the existing usage as to the slaughter of kine, and to make due provision against the recurrence of all such outbreaks in the future.

During the five years of Lord Lansdowne's rule, education made some noteworthy progress both in primary and secondary schools. The revenue derived from school fees increased by more than 23 lakhs; a result which showed the growing desire of the people to rely more upon their own resources, and less upon contributions from the State. A marked increase was also recorded in the number of girls reading in schools of both classes; and thirteen females took the degree of Bachelor in Arts, while one woman was found duly qualified for the degree of Master.

Workshops were attached to the Schools of Art in each of the great provincial centres, with results that justified their introduction. The teaching of science was carried on with equal success in most of the English and vernacular schools, while sanitation was made a compulsory subject in many parts of the empire. New industrial schools were established, and agricultural classes were formed in some of the high schools.

The right of selecting a certain number of qualified men for University Fellowships was bestowed at the Viceroy's own suggestion upon the graduates of each University, an experiment which was justified by its practical results. At the same time the beginning of a great Imperial Library in Calcutta supplied a manifest want in the intellectual development of India. The establishment of a Central Record Office was another of the boons conferred by Lord Lansdowne's government.

The census returns for 1891 showed the total of 287¼ millions of souls, of which about 66 millions belonged to the Native States. In the ten years since 1881 the population of British India had increased by 22 millions, and that of the Native States by about 11 millions.

During these years a vigorous attempt was made to grapple with the epidemic diseases to which millions of cattle fall yearly victims. Careful attention was also paid to all matters connected with the productive tillage of the soil. It appears that the Indian husbandman has after all not much to learn from the practice of other countries. "At his best," writes Dr. Walcker, "the Indian cultivator is quite as good as, and in some respects the superior of the average British farmer, whilst at his worst it can only be said that this state is brought about largely by the absence of facilities for improvement, which is probably unequalled in any other country." The same authority points out that the Rayat is always ready to adopt any improvement which may seem to offer him a fair return for his outlay.

Irrigation works and railways have largely contributed to the development of India's agricultural wealth; the peasant has been enabled to cultivate fields which had lain barren for ages, while the spread of railways tends to secure markets for his surplus produce. During this period the area of irrigation was increased by about 1,878,000 acres, while nearly 4000 miles of new railway were opened for traffic. Important sanitary improvements were also carried out in many places. In many of the chief cities in Upper India new waterworks were constructed with most beneficial results on the health of the millions concerned. A large extension was also given to Lady Dufferin's noble scheme for supplying medical aid and education to the women of India, by means of special hospitals and dispensaries.

The first three years of Lord Lansdowne's government showed a considerable surplus of revenue over expenditure. In the next two years, however, various causes, and especially the fall in silver values, resulted in unavoidable deficits. In 1893 the Home Government consented to a modified form of the Viceroy's scheme for restricting the free coinage of silver by the Indian Mints; and in the middle of that year the Mints were accordingly closed to the general public. At the same time the public treasuries were empowered to receive gold at the rate of one sovereign for fifteen rupees, and currency notes were issued in exchange for gold at the rate of 1*s.* 4*d.* the rupee. By this means some check was placed on the serious fluctuations in the exchange value of gold and silver. As the exchange value of the rupee fell at one time to less than fourteen-pence, it is easy to see how heavy a burden was laid on the Indian Exchequer in respect of the home charges of the Indian Government.

Early in 1894, the Marquess of Lansdowne was succeeded by the Earl of Elgin, son of that Lord Elgin whose vice-regal career had been cut short in 1863 by his untimely death.

INDIAN EMPIRE
IN
1914.

CHAPTER VI

THE EARL OF ELGIN—1894–1898

DURING the year 1894, the process of marking out the new frontier between India and Afghānistān was interrupted for a time by need of punishing the Mahsud Wazirs, whose raids into Bannu had cost the lives of two British officers, and several sepoys. In the course of December, three strong columns under Lieutenant-General Sir William Lockhart, entered the wild Waziri hills, destroyed a number of Mahsud towers and villages, and made the offending clansmen pay very dearly for their murderous outrage.

On the 1st January, 1895, Nizām-ul-Mūlk, the new chief of Chitral, was slain at a hunting party by the emissaries of his half-brother, Amīr-ul-Mūlk. Before the latter was firmly seated in the vacant chiefship, one of his brothers, and the chief of a neighbouring state, raised the standard of revolt and were quickly joined by the tribesmen of Chitral. Dr. Robertson, the British Agent, had to take refuge in the fort, which he prepared to hold to the last with a garrison of 370 men. After a fruitless sally on the 3rd March, Robertson was closely blockaded for the next six weeks before help could reach him from Kashmīr.

On the 1st April a strong British force under Lieutenant-General Sir Robert Low marched from Peshāwar into the Swāt valley for the purpose of attacking the insurgents from the south, while a smaller force under Colonel Kelly moved out from Gilgit towards Chitral. On the 3rd April Low forced the Malakand Pass. Pushing its way across the Panjkora river Low's force on the 17th defeated Umra Khan, one of the insurgent chiefs, in the neighbourhood of Jandol.

The tidings of Low's advance served to relax the pressure upon Chitral at the moment when the small Gilgit column was drawing near the beleaguered garrison. On the 20th April the brave Colonel Kelly entered the fort of Chitral at the head of a few hundred Gūrkhas and Punjābis, after three weeks of toilsome and perilous marching over 200 miles of rugged mountainous country. Starting from Gilgit with only four officers and two hundred men while the snow still covered the ground, he forced his way over a pass about 12,000 feet high which lay between him and Laspur. On the 9th April he reached Mastuj, where he increased his numbers by some four hundred men and two guns. From Mastuj to Chitral Kelly's advance was a brilliant and unbroken success, and before the 20th the last of the insurgents had disappeared.*

The relief of Chitral thus brilliantly accomplished, it became a question for the Home Government whether it was worth our while to maintain an outpost in a remote corner of the Hindu Kush, nearly two hundred miles beyond our Punjāb frontier. The only possible excuse for a British garrison at Chitral was an unreasoning dread of Russian intrigues among the neighbouring hill tribes. To the Government of Lord Rosebery no such excuse carried any weight against the teachings of past experience and the opinions of the best military experts. On the 13th June, 1895, Sir Henry Fowler, then Minister for India, telegraphed to Lord Elgin clear instructions that

* Dr. Robertson was afterwards made a K.C.S.I., and Colonel Kelly a C.B. and A.D.C. to the Queen; Sir R. C. Low was created a G.C.B.

no British agent or garrison should be retained at Chitral, that the state should be handed over to its new Mehtar, Shujā-ul-Mūlk, and that no attempt should be made to connect Chitral with Peshāwar by means of a road across the Swāt valley. Before Lord Elgin could carry out these orders, a Conservative Ministry came into power, and early in August the New Secretary of State for India, Lord George Hamilton, sent out a telegram countermanding the previous orders. Chitral therefore remained under the charge of a British Resident, aided by a sufficient military force.

The failure of the monsoon rains in August, 1896, was followed by a serious failure of the harvest over a wide extent of country in Western, Central, and Southern India, and even in Upper Burma. From October onwards for more than a twelvemonth, famine more or less sharp spread by degrees over an area of 570,000 square miles, peopled by 130 million souls. The number of starving folk who were kept alive by the public relief works rose at one time to nearly five millions. In spite of railways, roads, canals, of public supervision and private charity, great numbers died of starvation and disease. This great famine, the most widespread of the century, cost the Government in one shape or another about Rx. 18,000,000, or about ten million sterling. But for the splendid contributions sent from all parts of the British Empire, and from some foreign countries, the cost, both in life and in expenditure, would have been much heavier.

The year 1897, which brought to a happy close the sixtieth year of Queen Victoria's reign, was fraught for India with other calamities besides famine. Nearly fifty thousand natives perished in Western India of the plague, which had found its way thither from China in the previous autumn. The unceasing efforts made by Government officers to stamp out this new and terrible scourge were rewarded on the whole with marked success. But modern sanitary ideas came once more into open conflict with ancient Hindu customs, and the search for infected houses may not always have been carried out with due regard for popular prejudices. At Poona, the great centre of Brahmanic influence among the Marātha people, two British officers were murdered on the 22nd June; and some of the native newspapers inflamed the popular mind by unmeasured attacks upon the local Government. Several editors, including a native member of the Bombay Legislative Council, were tried and sentenced more or less heavily under the Indian Penal Code.

On the 12th June, Assam and Lower Bengal were visited by the most disastrous earthquake ever recorded in the history of modern India. In Calcutta alone many public buildings were badly damaged. Several church spires and towers, including the spire of Calcutta Cathedral, fell to the ground. Numbers of private houses from Chauringhi to the native town, were reduced to wreck. The same shock was severely felt at Darjeeling, and less severely at Simla, Agra and Bombay. Great damage was also done to several lines of railway in Bengal.

For some time after the relief of Chitral, in 1895, things went on tranquilly enough along the Punjāb frontier. The intervening tribes seemed to acquiesce in the making of roads and the planting of British posts between Peshāwar and Chitral, while Afridi levies loyally garrisoned the road through the Khyber Pass. But in June, 1897, the peace of the frontier was rudely broken by a murderous attack on the escort of a political officer passing through the Tachi valley, a few miles beyond the Bannu border. Three British officers were killed and as many wounded, of whom one afterwards died. Of the Sikh troops forming the escort, twenty-three were killed and twenty-five wounded. A strong British force under General Bird marched a month later into the Tachi valley and made the customary reprisals upon the offending tribesmen.

Meanwhile, towards the end of July, another rising, due to the fanatical preaching of a mad Muhammadan fakir, took place among the Pathān tribes of the Swāt valley. Their attacks on the British post at Malakand were, after some hard fighting, successfully repulsed, and other posts threatened by the insurgents were promptly relieved and strengthened. But the preaching of fanatic Mullas fanned the flames of popular discontent at the movements of British surveyors, engineers, and working parties, in a country peopled by independent and warlike tribes. By the end of August a general rising of tribes along the Punjāb frontier involved the gathering of a powerful British army for its suppression. All the forts and fortlets in the Khyber Pass were captured by Afridi kinsmen of those who had lately guarded them. Mohmands, Afridis, Urakzais, Sheoranis, Wazirs, Mamuzais, Swatis, and several other tribes and clans, all from time to time did their best to harass and hinder the march of our troops into their highland fastnesses.

For over four months several British columns under the supreme command of General Sir William Lockhart were engaged in fighting their way through a wilderness of hills and valleys held by swarms of well-armed riflemen, whose bullets seldom missed their mark, and who never lost an opportunity of taking our troops at a disadvantage. After many weeks of hard incessant fighting, and of hardships bravely borne by officers and men, the hostile tribes, one after another, were fain to accept the terms imposed by the Indian Government; and the long campaign was brought to a partially successful close in the first days of 1898. Fines were levied from all the insurgent tribes, and many hundred rifles were quietly surrendered into our hands. The losses on both sides had been very great, but the Khyber was once more re-opened to peaceful traffic, and the bulk of our countrymen were glad of a decent pretext for closing a profitless and costly war.

In 1896 an important change was made in the Indian cotton tariff. All cotton yarns, whether home-made or imported, were free from duty, while the uniform duty of 3½ per cent. was imposed on all woven cotton goods whether imported or produced in Indian mills. Owing to famine, plague, earthquake and war, the Indian exchequer had been burdened with an outlay of Rx. 24,313,000; but the actual deficit for 1897 amounted only to Rx. 6,095,000.

In September, 1897, Lord Elgin's Government urged the rejection of a proposal made by France and the United States for re-opening the Indian mints to the free coinage of silver, as part of an international scheme for establishing a joint gold and silver standard at a fixed ratio. The scheme therefore fell through.

The first two years of Lord Elgin's administration resulted in a total surplus of more than Rx. 2,000,000, on a revenue rising from 95 to 98 million tens of rupees. By the close of the next year, 1896–97, an estimated surplus of Rx. 463,000 had been converted into an actual deficit of Rx. 1,594,000. For the year 1897 there was a deficit of Rx. 6,095,000, which was met by another loan.

By the end of March, 1897, the total number of miles of railway throughout British India amounted to 20,390, while 4000 miles of new railway were in course of construction during the next two years. The net earnings of all these lines soon averaged about 5 per cent. yearly, in spite of the large yearly loss due to the low rate of exchange. In 1895 the irrigation works then opened throughout the country yielded a net income of 4·1 per cent. to the State. During the next two years of scarcity and famine the net yield was still greater on eleven million acres of irrigated land.

The Forest Department also showed satisfactory progress during the next few years. On 75,000 square miles of forest reserved and worked by the State there accrued in 1895 a nett revenue of Rx. 749,000. Before the close of 1896, 46,375 miles of telegraph lines were in full work, yielding a net revenue of $5\frac{1}{4}$ per cent. on a total cost of nearly Rx. 6,000,000; and the Post Office was carrying 413 millions of letters, post-cards, newspapers, etc., at a net profit to Government of Rx. 70,000. It is worth noting, by the way, that in India the postal service has been carried on solely with an eye to the public convenience, and not as a means of enriching the State Exchequer.

Salt and opium still continue to be two of the richest sources of revenue for British India. In 1896 the salt duties yielded a net revenue of nearly Rx. 9,000,000 on rates varying from 1 rupee a maund of 82 pounds in Burma to Rs. 2, 8 annas for the rest of India. On the other hand there has been a gradual decline in the exports of Indian opium to China, owing to the increased consumption of the home-made drug by the Chinese themselves.

The total yearly value of India's foreign trade has continually risen. The exports, which cover about two-thirds of the total trade, include tea, coffee, cotton, raw and manufactured, jute, rice, wheat, oil-seeds, opium, hides, and skins, sugar, silk, indigo, saltpetre, spices, manures, wools, teak-wood, and several other staples of more or less value.

Perhaps the most striking feature in this connection is the rapid growth of India's tea industry during the last fifty years. The people of England who once drank nothing but China tea, now drink hardly any tea save that which comes from India and Ceylon. The export of Indian wheat, on the other hand has greatly declined. The

Indian imports include cotton goods, metals, hardware, petroleum, silk, raw and woven, machinery, chemicals, drugs, dyes, and alcoholic liquors.

Owing to the development of Indian coal-fields there has of late years been a steady decline in the imports of English coal. Ninety per cent. of the coal used on all Indian railways is now supplied by India herself.

Among other incidents of Lord Elgin's rule was the appointment in 1897 of a Lieutenant-Governor for the great province of Burma in the place of a Chief Commissioner. The new functionary was furnished with a Legislative Council of nine members, five official and four non-official. In the same year a similar Council was attached to the Lieutenant-Governor of the Punjāb.

Among the laws passed by the Viceroy's Council was an Act of 1897 for preventing the spread of epidemic diseases. Another Act of the same year enabled local authorities to borrow money for temporary emergencies, such as the recent famine. In 1895 an Act was passed for improving the sanitary arrangements on board the ships that carried Muhammadan pilgrims to Mecca. An emigration Act of the following year did away with some of the abuses which had marked the working of the old Act of 1883. The laws affecting the land revenue and municipalities of the Punjāb were amended by two new statutes in 1896. In 1897 amendments were also made in the Criminal Tribes Act of 1871, while the same year saw the passing of an Act for the protection of Indian fisheries.

In the autumn of 1898, the Honble. George Curzon (created Lord Curzon of Kedleston in the Peerage of Ireland), who had lately served with much credit as Under-Secretary in the English Foreign Office, was selected by Lord Salisbury to succeed Lord Elgin as Viceroy and Governor-General in the following year.

CHAPTER VII

LORD CURZON OF KEDLESTON—1899–1905

LORD CURZON of Kedleston came to India with a knowledge of its politics and problems greater than that possessed by any of his predecessors who had not actually worked in the country as servants of the Company or the Crown. He had made long tours in the East, in the course of which, after a visit to Ceylon, he landed at Tuticorin in November, 1887. On this occasion he stayed over four months in the country, going eastwards as far as Darjeeling, and northwards to the Khyber Pass. In the next year he spent some time in Russian Central Asia, and in the year after he stayed some time in Persia, and thence came to India by way of Baghdad and the Persian Gulf. A later visit enabled him to "examine, in a comparative light, the political, social, and economic conditions of the kingdoms and principalities of the Far East." On Persia and on the Far East he published important and valuable books. Again, in 1894, he visited India, going through Kashmīr to the Pamirs, and winning the gold medal of the Royal Geographical Society by discovering the source of the Oxus. On his return he saw the Hunza and Nagar states, among the mountains of Kashmīr and Chitral, soon to become a centre of interest and danger. Afghānistān also he visited, and studied the opinions of Abdur Rahman and of Habibullah, who was to be his successor. Thence he rode to Kandahār and on to Baluchistan. It is known that the results of these travels were embodied in a volume which was ready for publication when he became Viceroy, but was suppressed in deference to the wishes of Lord Salisbury, the Prime Minister, who considered that no Governor-General ought to write a book on subjects with which he would be called upon to deal.

Lord Curzon was indeed exceptionally fitted for his task. Not only had he studied the problems of Indian government on the spot, but he had dealt with them as Under-Secretary for India and, less directly, as Under-Secretary for Foreign Affairs. He regarded English work in India as the touchstone of imperial greatness. He saw that we were employed on a task which no other people had ever attempted. He believed that the attraction and importance of the East to England would continue to increase, and he hoped that parliament would come to take as much concern in India as it took in Europe. Towards this consummation it was his good fortune to lead the way.

On January 6th, 1899, he formally assumed office at Calcutta. He had declared, in his first speech at Bombay, that his aim would be "to hold the scales even," a motto worthy of a Viceroy with the highest aims and of the British administration in India. His first Budget speech, on March 27th, showed a desire to view all sides of the financial position before embarking on definite changes; and his tours through India during the year were designed to make him acquainted with the latest developments and difficulties, especially in the districts affected by plague and famine. At Poona, in November, he strongly advocated inoculation as a preventive of the bubonic scourge.

During the first fifteen months of Lord Curzon's viceroyalty he had three finance ministers. Sir James Westland, whose was his first budget, had managed the finances with much skill, and was able to report a considerable increase of revenue. The railway system was being continually and profitably increased. But a remission of taxation was not yet found possible.

The Indian Currency Committee reported in favour of a gold standard, and of fixing the rate of the rupee. On September 8th, Mr. Clinton Dawkins, the new financial member of the Council, on the instructions of the home government, introduced the Currency Bill, and it was passed on September 15th. By this the rupee was fixed at 1*s.* 4*d.*, and the British sovereign was made legal tender in India. Mints were to be opened in India and gold was to be coined there, as soon as possible, for use in the country. Mr. (afterwards Sir) Clinton Dawkins only held office till March, 1900, when he was called, with the consent of the Government, to important financial work elsewhere. He was succeeded by Sir Edward Fitzgerald Law, K.C.M.G., who had obtained a high reputation by his financial work at Constantinople, and was a man of great ability and personal charm. The second Budget speech of Lord Curzon, March 28th, 1900, eulogised the work of Mr. Dawkins, advocated sparing legislation, and dwelt upon the disappointment of financial hopes by the sad recurrence of famine. Plague and famine indeed were disastrously severe during Lord Curzon's first year. Official figures gave the total mortality as not less than a quarter of a million since the beginning of the outbreak of plague. Great relief works were organised to help the poor during the famine, and generous help was given by native rulers, especially the Nizam of Hyderābād and the Mahārājā of Gwalior.

On the frontiers there were slight operations due to the predatory attacks of Waziris and Mahsuds; but the relations with Afghānistān remained cordial. Abdur Rahman in his Autobiography, published in November,

1900, showed no special attachment to Great Britain, but, on the other hand, he observed the treaties more strictly than his predecessors, and showed no sign of encouraging any Russian advance. He died in October, 1901.

In 1900 frontier troubles were resumed, the Mahsud Waziris being especially active. In November, Mr. Merk, Commissioner of Derajāt, brought them to submission under threat of a blockade.

In this year a famine of unparalleled magnitude spread over India, particularly Bombay and the Central Provinces. This affected over twenty-five million people in British India, and thirty millions in native states. It was calculated that the loss in crops amounted to £50,000,000 in British territory alone. Lord Curzon stated that it was "not merely a crop famine, but a fodder famine on an enormous scale, followed, in many parts, by a positive devastation of cattle—both plough cattle, buffaloes, and milch kine. In other words, it affected, and may almost be said to have annihilated, the working capital of the agricultural classes." It attacked native states, ill-prepared to meet it. "It laid its hand upon primitive hillmen, unused to discipline or restraint, impulsive, improvident, lazy, living in an almost barbarous state in wild and inaccessible jungles. It sharpened the lurking nomadic instinct of wandering tribes, and sent them aimlessly drifting about the country, a terror to the famine country and an incubus in the camps." The Viceroy travelled through the famine districts, organising and superintending relief, and large sums were subscribed throughout the empire to provide the necessaries of life for the starving people.

Lord Northcote, now Governor of Bombay, gave valuable aid, and the people noticed with awe that the Viceroy's visits to stricken districts were frequently followed by the much-needed rain. In Gujarāt the cattle were saved by the action of Lord Northcote, who collected the best in herds. It was said that "Lord Northcote did many beneficent things during his period of office in Bombay, but nothing he did is held in more grateful remembrance than his salvation of the cattle in Gujarāt."

The mortality among the population was enormous. In British districts alone it seems that about a million and a quarter died: in native states the deaths were much more numerous. A Commission under Sir Antony (now Lord) Macdonell afterwards considered the famine works, and came to the conclusion that deficient organisation had led to considerable waste. The Famine Codes were thereupon revised, to provide work for the able-bodied, and the experience of 1907–8 seems to show that famines can now be dealt with much more successfully.

During the year 1900, the Viceroy, accompanied by his wife, an American lady whose charm, ability, and goodness made a deep impression wherever she went, paid visits over a very wide area. Assam was visited for the first time by a Viceroy, and the keenest interest was shown in the work of the planters, those "independent pioneers of progress." At Quetta the northern chiefs were addressed on the duty of loyalty and defence of the frontier. From Karachi Lord Curzon went to Kathiawār, to Surāt, to Bombay, and thence to Bijapur and on to Goa. The visit to the flourishing Portuguese dependency illustrated the most cordial relations between the British Empire and its oldest ally. Southwards, through Travancore and Cochin, Tinnevelly, Trichinopoly, and Mysore, the Viceregal party went to Madras, where Lord Ampthill had now succeeded Sir Arthur Havelock as Governor, and thence returned to Calcutta, after a journey of about 6000 miles all round India.

The year 1901 was chiefly important for the creation

of a new frontier province. This was prepared by the establishment of a definite policy with regard to Chitral, where the maintenance of British troops was left undecided by Lord Elgin. Lord Curzon decided to maintain a small garrison at Drosh, with a guard for the Political Resident at the capital. A good road was made and a telegraph wire constructed. A force of scouts was raised among the Chitralis, to undergo periodical training, with a view to frontier defence.

From Chitral Lord Curzon passed on to consider the condition of the Pathān frontier in general. In a minute addressed to the Secretary of State, Lord Curzon severely criticized the administration of this district of the Punjāb government. He declared himself against a forward movement, and was thought to be a disciple of the policy inaugurated by the Lawrences half a century before. He advocated the "withdrawal of British forces from advanced positions, employment of tribal forces in defence of tribal country, concentration of British forces in British territory behind them as a safeguard and a support, and improvement of communications in the rear." But in this policy he was careful to show that he was not endeavouring to revive a dead past, but to meet the exigencies of the present and the future. The policy of Lord Lawrence he considered as dead "from the complete change in the situation and from the effluxion of time," and a forward policy was so elastic and pliable a phrase as to mean much too much or much too little. Lord Curzon's was a "common-sense" policy of concentration and conciliation.

The new province was formed because the administration of the frontier by the Punjāb government had proved ineffective and unsatisfactory. The Punjāb officials had enough to do in the districts that were properly their own, and had, as a rule, no frontier experience. Of late years they had committed palpable blunders. It had long been seen that a change was necessary, and several Viceroys had approached the subject with a view to the creation of a new system. Lord Lansdowne had expressed himself desirous of "a single frontier charge." Lord Elgin, listening to the opinions of conservative officials, had done nothing. Lord Curzon saw clearly and acted decisively.

On November 9th, 1901, the new North-West Frontier Province was called into being. The *Annual Register* for 1901 states its geography thus: "Its territorial limits include the districts of Hazara, Peshāwar, Kohar, Bannu (except Isakhel and Mianwali), and Dera Ismail Khan (except Leia and Bhakkar), and the trans-border territory up in the Durand line. The four tahsils taken from Bannu and Dera Ismail Khan are formed into a new Punjāb district." A commissionership of Multān was created in the Punjāb, those of Rawal Pindi and Lahore being rearranged. The old North-West Province now received the name of "the United Provinces of Agra and Oudh." The first Commissioner, Sir Harold Deane, was succeeded in 1908 by Sir George Roos-Keppel, and he by Mr. W. R. H. Merk (see above, p. 444).

The policy of Lord Curzon in the creation of this new province was subjected to severe criticism, and the past action of the Punjāb government was defended notably by Sir Dennis Fitzpatrick and Sir Charles Roe. Difficulties in regard to the administration of land revenue arose, as had been foreseen. But, on the whole, the statement made in 1911 was justified, and still remains true. Lord Curzon "gave India the longest peace upon her North-West Frontier she has ever known, and the system he devised is still unshaken." *

In his budget speech of 1901, Lord Curzon was able to point to a practical and business-like session as concluded. Much needed relief in respect of inheritance and of

* Lovat Fraser, "India under Curzon and after," p. 63.

succession duties in regard to native Christians had been given, and the Assam Labour Bill and the Mines Bill had been carried. Sir Edward Law had won a surplus of one and three-quarter million pounds sterling. A reform had been made in the rules as to leave, with a view of securing closer continuity of administration, and preventing "the frequent removal of officers upon leave at short and insufficient intervals, with a consequent chain of transfers and far-reaching dislocation." An even more welcome reform was that which drastically curtailed the immense quantity of written reports which it had been the custom to require from overworked civil servants of every grade. A new set of Rules of Business for the Secretariat of the Government of India provided for "greater simplification of procedure, less penwork, more frequent verbal consultations, superior despatch." Within a year the amount of printed pages of reports had fallen from 18,000 to 8600. During the year railway extension on a large scale had been inaugurated.

At a time when India was itself providing the cost of rearming and reorganising the Army out of current revenue, and the pay of British troops in the country was being increased, it was natural that special attention should be directed to the relations between British soldiers and the natives of India. A revision of the rules under which soldiers could "go out shooting" the game of the country had been undertaken; and this was but one illustration of the endeavour of Lord Curzon and his government "to draw closer the bonds of friendly feeling that should unite the two races whom Providence has placed side by side in the country."

A year later, on March 26th, 1902, the Viceroy was able to announce definite progress on the lines sketched in 1901. More than 3000 additional miles of railway had been laid down during his period of office, and 2000 more were in progress. Relief had been given to the cultivators, who had suffered severely from the famine, by remission of large arrears of land revenue. A Resolution on Land Revenue policy, issued in January, 1902, written by Lord Curzon, had examined the assessments of various parts of India and laid down lines for future treatment in a generous spirit.

In foreign policy during the year 1902 it is to be noted that the relations with the new Amīr of Afghānistān remained satisfactory. Some raids from over the border had been met by the Kurram Militia. The border towards Tibet had been rectified, with the addition of 350 square miles to British India.

The year 1903 opened with a great Darbār at Delhi. The death of Queen Victoria on January 22nd, 1901, had not passed unnoticed in India. On the contrary, the mourning had been marked and widespread. Though the Empress was doubtless a very dim and distant figure to the vast majority of the Indian peoples, yet her personal share in the great events of her reign was well known among, and indeed beyond, the educated classes. She was personally associated with the great proclamation at the close of the Sepoy War, the Magna Carta of Indian liberty under Great Britain as it was often called. Her deep interest in India and the Indians was evidenced by the number of Indians she had in her household and by her study of Hindustāni in her old age. She had constantly advised her servants in the Peninsula, and she had shown the deepest concern in the welfare of the people whom they governed in her name. A Memorial Hall, the splendid services of which to the history, the commemoration, the education of India, past, present, and future, were eloquently prophesied by the Viceroy in several speeches when he initiated the scheme, was built at Calcutta. It was to be devoted to the commemoration of notable events and remarkable men, both Indian and European, in the long history of the country. It was to contain paintings, sculptures, enamels, manuscripts, personal relics of all sorts. With a history and an art so magnificent as that of India, it should be possible to create a museum which, for interest and value, would be unsurpassed in the world.

While the commemoration of the first Empress of India was proceeding, the coronation of her successor was being prepared. Edward VII. had himself visited India, in 1875, and he was known to not a few of the ruling chiefs. His dangerous illness postponed his coronation at Westminster till August 9th, 1902. At this many Indian princes were present. On January 1st, 1903, a great Darbār was held at Delhi, on the spot where Lord Lytton had announced, a quarter of a century before, the assumption by the British Crown of the imperial title. The King was represented by his brother, the Duke of Connaught, and the Viceroy announced to the vast assemblage the coronation of Edward VII. A hundred of the ruling chiefs attended, and some 173,000 people. The Viceroy's speech, renewing to the princes and peoples of India the Emperor's promise to respect their liberties and rights and to serve their welfare, impressively summed up the objects of British rule.

The Budget of 1903 gave welcome evidence how these objects were being attained in several and not unimportant points. Lord Curzon, on March 25th, was able to announce a considerable reduction in taxation. The classes most in need—though it cannot be said that, judged by the standards of Europe or by those of the Mughal government of centuries before, India was at all highly taxed—were relieved. The income tax, which in all countries presses so heavily on the wage-earners of the middle class, and the salt duty, felt by the cultivators, were now appreci-

EARL CURZON OF KEDLESTON K.G.

ably reduced. In announcing this, Lord Curzon expressed the hope that critics who professed doubts as to the financial stability of the Indian Empire would see that steadily improving revenues, coupled with a reduction of taxation, afforded proof of the economic vitality of the country. Perhaps the new agreement with the Nizām may be regarded as looking the same way. This, concluded shortly before the Darbār, marked an important step in the confirmation of British power in Central India. The position of Berar had long been anomalous: the Nizām's ancient claims over it had not for centuries been effective rights. Lord Curzon made an arrangement by which the British Government obtained a perpetual lease of Berar for the annual payment of twenty-five lakhs of rupees to the Nizām, and the district was incorporated for administration with the Central Provinces.*

During 1904 the plague still raged, but two good harvests had greatly benefited the country, and the yield of the taxes showed a real increase in national prosperity. Indian cotton had found wider markets, and the export of tea had greatly increased. Finance bore similar witness. The estimates for 1904–5 showed a revenue of £80,148,600, and an expenditure of £79,229,000, the surplus being thus not far from a million pounds.

It will be convenient to reserve some of the more important works of Lord Curzon as Viceroy, and notably his foreign policy as a whole, for consideration at the time when his final resignation of office is recorded. But in the summer of 1904 he returned to England, during the interval between his first and second terms of office. In accordance with the Act of 1861, Lord Ampthill, as the senior of the two Governors of Presidencies, was appointed to act as Viceroy during the interim.

Lord Curzon had a warm reception in England, and

* See below, p. 466.

he took occasion to deliver several speeches which threw much light upon his aims, his endeavours, and his successes. On July 20th he received the freedom of the City of London, and he spoke twice at the Mansion House. On July 28th he received the freedom of the borough of Derby and addressed a large audience from his native county. In all the speeches he sounded a note of confidence in the future, and he emphatically dwelt upon the need of keeping India outside the party quarrels of England. He spoke of the isolation of India from ordinary English interests, and lamented that the average man at home seemed to care more for a football or a cricket match, a motor trial, or a wrestling encounter, than for "the greatest responsibility that has been undertaken by his fellow-subjects on the face of the earth." What was our record? "Where else in the world has a race gone forth and subdued, not a country or a kingdom, but a continent, and that continent peopled, not by savage tribes, but by races with traditions and a civilisation older than our own, with a history not inferior to ours in dignity or romance; subduing them, not to the law of the sword, but to the rule of justice, bringing peace and order and good government to nearly one-fifth of the human race, and holding them with so mild a restraint that the rulers are the merest handful among the ruled, a tiny speck of white foam upon a dark and thunderous ocean?"

Indian problems were like some of those at home, but magnified; but also there were other problems remote from all our home experience. This involved ceaseless anxiety and unending toil, but the duty was cheerfully undertaken and proudly borne.

Lord Curzon described the work of the last five years as one of reform and reconstruction, and he illustrated this in its different aspects. He was especially interesting when he spoke of the native princes and chiefs, and declared his desire that they should share the responsibilities as well as the glories of British rule. He spoke of the Imperial Cadet Corps, which he had founded, "where we give military education to the pick of the Indian aristocracy, which will eventuate, as time goes on, in the bestowal for the first time of commissions as British officers upon Indian chiefs, nobles, and gentlemen." After a sketch of the foreign policy of the last few years, Lord Curzon emphasised the fact that the basis of British rule was not military force, or civil authority or prestige alone, but, above all, the eternal moralities of righteousness and justice; and he repeated his determination that our Indian fellow-subjects should be recognised as truly our equals in the eyes of God and the law. And on this he based the assurance that "our work is righteous, and it will endure."

In another speech he paid a noble tribute to the administrative ability, the industry, and the self-sacrifice of the officials, from the high Empire-builders to the "men in the plains," the "real organisers of victory."

At Derby he remarked how strange it was that the three most eminent persons in purely British political life who had given serious attention to Indian problems should have been so wrong in their verdicts: Burke, Macaulay, and John Bright—and he showed that the union which the last deemed impossible is "neither a chimera nor a dream." The extraordinary diversity in Indian civilisation may long stand in the way; but the ideal is there, and we are approaching continually nearer to its realisation. "The one thing in governing an Asiatic country," said Lord Curzon, "is to break down the barriers between the hearts and consciences of men." A striking passage from this same speech may well be quoted at length, for no better description exists of the India which Lord Curzon governed, or of its difference from the past.

"I remember hearing of an English sportsman in India who examined the arrows in the quiver of a native shikari belonging to one of the aboriginal tribes. He found the first arrow tipped with a stone—a relic of the neolithic age; the next arrow was tipped with electric telegraph wire—a theft from the twentieth century. That story is typical of the whole of India. It conveys to you the amazing synthesis of anthropology, of history, of human experience, which is gathered within the boundaries of that great area. You may imagine that with a people so diversified, representing such opposite poles of creed and civilisation, complete unity is a thing which we cannot aspire to produce. India must always remain a constellation rather than a single star, must always be a continent rather than a country, a congeries of races rather than a single nation. But we are creating ties of unity among those widely diversified peoples, we are consolidating those vast and outspread territories, and, what is more important, we are going forward instead of backward. It is not a stationary, a retrograde, a downtrodden, or an impoverished India that I have been governing for the past five and a half years. Poverty there is in abundance. I defy any one to show me a great and populous country, or a great and populous city, where it does not exist. Misery and destitution there are. The question is not whether they exist, but whether they are growing more or growing less. In India, where you deal with so vast a canvas, I dare say the lights and shades of human experience are more vivid and more dramatic than elsewhere. But if you compare the India of to-day with the India of any previous period of history—the India of Alexander, of Asōka, of Akbar, or of Aurangzeb—you will find greater peace and tranquillity, more widely diffused comfort and contentment, superior justice and humanity, and higher standards of material well-being, than that great dependency has ever previously attained."

On his return to India, Lord Curzon had the experience, unique for a Viceroy, of welcoming the presentation to the Legislative Council of a seventh budget. He congratulated Mr. E. N. Baker, the successor of Sir Edward Law, on the culminating point of a process of financial recovery. It marked at once an increase in administrative outlay and a reduction in the burdens on the people. The increase was largely due to expenditure on railways and on the army. The pending reduction of taxes had prevented what would have been a surplus of nearly three and a half millions sterling. Taxation to the amount of £1,371,000 had been remitted, increased postal facilities had cost £47,000, and administrative reforms £1,077,000; the balance was £903,800. Considerable progress had been made with great schemes of irrigation. The Chenāb Canal, which cost 280 lakhs of rupees, gave a large district to cultivation which had hitherto been little better than a desert, and produced a revenue of 65 lakhs per annum. A similar canal from the Jhelum promised equally well.

This was Lord Curzon's last Budget speech. Within a few months he had resigned office, and before the end of the year, after welcoming the Prince and Princess of Wales, he left India. The cause of his resignation was a difference of opinion with the Home Government, and with Lord Kitchener, the Commander-in-Chief in India, as to army administration. The point at issue was distinct and simple. Lord Kitchener claimed that the Commander-in-Chief, when he submitted proposals on military matters to the Viceroy (who was at liberty to accept or reject them as he thought fit), should be regarded as the expert adviser of the Indian Government, and should not be subject to the criticism of the military member of the

Council. It seemed to the Viceroy that this view would deprive him of the counsel which he might need, and that it was essential to the formation of wise decisions that he should be able to rely upon the advice of the military member of the Council when he had to consider the views of the Commander-in-Chief. The matter, of course, came ultimately before the Home Government (that of Mr. A. J. Balfour). A committee was appointed consisting of the Hon. St. J. Brodrick (afterwards Lord Midleton), Secretary of State for India, the Marquis of Salisbury, Earl Roberts, Sir George White, Sir James Mackay, Sir Edward Law, and General Gordon. Its report was unanimous, and to the effect that the strictly military parts of army administration should be controlled solely by the Commander-in-Chief, and the departments not exclusively military by another member of the Viceroy's Council; and that, while a second purely military expert opinion in the Council was not desirable, a member of the Council should have charge of the subsidiary and less exclusively military business. The military member then sitting (Sir Edmond Elles) was to retire, and Lord Curzon was invited to propose a successor. He proposed Sir E. Barrow. Mr. Brodrick stated that his transfer from a military command was undesirable, and that his training made it likely that the old system would soon return. Lord Curzon declined to withdraw the suggestion, and as the Home Government would not give way he resigned office. He truly said, in his last speech in India, that no man would resign such a post for any but the strongest reasons. What these reasons were had best be stated in his own words: "I resigned for two great principles. Firstly, the hitherto uncontested, the essential, and, in the long run, the indestructible subordination of military to civil authority in the administration of all well-conducted states; and, secondly, the payment of due and becoming regard to

Indian authority in determining India's needs. I am making no vain boast when I say that in defending these principles as I have sought to do, and in sacrificing my position sooner than sacrifice them, I have behind me the whole of the Civil Services in India, the unanimous weight of non-official English opinion in this country, an overpowering preponderance of Indian opinion, and I will add, which is more significant still, the support of the greater part of the Indian Army."

We may now review Lord Curzon's administration in regard to those policies which were spread over several years, and are most conveniently to be taken as a whole. First of these may be taken that which aroused the most public comment, the partition of Bengal.

While Calcutta was the centre of British official and commercial life in India, much of Bengal had remained in comparative neglect. Eastern Bengal was almost unknown: well watered, beautiful, with ancient cities and a contented peasantry, it seemed to have escaped for centuries the attention of its rulers. Dacca, its capital, was important in commerce, and the Government had endeavoured to make it important in education. The population was largely Muhammadan, and it was loyal. But the territory was vast, the officials were few, and the police system over considerable districts was impotent.

It was to deal with this state of affairs, to lighten the burden on the higher officials, and to make good government possible, that after long consideration Lord Curzon's Government presented proposals to the Secretary of State which were eventually sanctioned, and on July 19th, 1905, were carried into effect. That scheme was published on September 1st, 1905. A new province was created, called Eastern Bengal and Assam. It consisted of Assam, and the districts of Dacca, Mymensingh, Faridpur, Backergunge, Tippera, Noakhali, Chittagong with the hill district near it, Rajshahi, Dinajpur, Jalpaiguri, Rangpur, Bogra, Patna, and Malda, in Bengal. Mr. (afterwards Sir) Bampfylde Fuller was the first Lieutenant-Governor, with a council of fifteen.

On October 16th the new system began its work at Dacca. It was not destined long to survive, so it may be unnecessary to write of it in detail. It will be well, however, to record the aim of its creation, and to discuss the criticism to which it was subjected. The aim was undoubtedly to remedy defective administration. Sir Andrew Fraser, who became Lieutenant-Governor of Bengal in 1903, stated, in a review of the circumstances after he had left India, that the partition "was passed after the fullest consideration, after public and private discussion with representatives of all the interests concerned, and from no other motive than the real and permanent benefit of the people of the two provinces. I have never known any administrative step taken after fuller discussion and more careful consideration." But this was not heeded, in the agitation which instantly sprang up and was not quelled till the partition was revised eight years later. It was alleged that in the new province the Hindus would be made subject to the Muhammadans: figures and facts refuted the charge. But the Native Bar at Calcutta foresaw that it would ultimately suffer, and the native newspapers saw that they too would suffer, from the creation of a new Province which must soon have its own High Court and its own Press.

The agitation was fostered by members of the Calcutta University who had not forgiven the Universities Act, passed in March, 1904. This Act was the result of Lord Curzon's prolonged investigation into the educational system of India, and of the report of a Commission which visited the Universities in 1902, under the chairmanship of

Sir Thomas Raleigh, Legal Member of the Viceroy's Executive Council. Lord Curzon approved of the introduction of European learning and English education into India, but he considered that English models had been too slavishly copied, and he desired to emancipate the system from the tyranny, though not from the assistance, of examinations. Primary education had especially suffered. "Ever since the cold breath of Macaulay's rhetoric passed over the field of the Indian languages and Indian text-books, the elementary education of the people in their own tongue has shrivelled and pined." The Act was aimed to begin the reform from the top, by raising the standard of higher education, and, through that, working downwards. Thus the Universities were given new powers of government, and the policy of supplementing examinations by thorough general teaching was placed before them. The Senates of the Universities, Allahābād, Lahore, Calcutta, Madras, and of Bombay (the largest of all, of over three hundred members) were unwieldy and ill-regulated: the syndicates of each needed remodelling, and the affiliation of colleges to the Universities needed some central control. All this was given by the Act. The colleges to be affiliated were placed under regulation and inspection, and the candidates for University examinations, if they were not already members of the University, were required to have completed a course of instruction certified by it. The educational effect of the Act was undoubtedly good, but all who were affected by the reforms vigorously protested, and their opposition was thrown into the scale when the new Province came into view.

In elementary education Lord Curzon secured a permanent annual grant (besides special benefactions when needed) of £230,000 for the schools, which led to the opening of thousands of new schools. He was not himself in favour of a bureaucratic control; he thought a department would be "packed with pedagogues and crusted with officialism": he well knew what had happened in England. But in 1910 a Ministry of Education was created, obtaining the wise control of Mr. (now Sir) Harcourt Butler, an eminent member of a family whose services to education are famous. Lord Curzon had laid foundations, and, of the battles fought over his educational reforms, he said he was "firmly convinced that out of them had been born a new life for Higher Education in India."

We may now turn to Lord Curzon's foreign policy. A few words will suffice to conclude what is to be said about Afghānistān. Habibullah may be said to have kept the English for a long time at arms' length. He did not take the subsidy given to his father: he entered into no treaties with the Government: he was angry when he was not allowed to import munitions through British India. In 1904, when Lord Ampthill was Viceroy during the absence of Lord Curzon in England, a mission under Mr. (later Sir Louis) Dane was sent to Kābul. It remained for three months, and was ended by the signature of a treaty accepting both the claims of the Amīr, to arrears of the subsidy and free admission of munitions. A visit of the Amīr to India in 1907 was no more than a friendly act: he was given the designation of "Majesty," which he claimed through a telegram from Edward VII. The Amīr returned home, holding a strong position, and he has made considerable reforms within his kingdom. The alliance between England and Russia now secures both powers against his separate intrigues with either.

In the Persian Gulf, and Persia itself, Lord Curzon acted with special knowledge. Persia may be regarded as outside the limits of Indian history. It needs therefore only to be said that Lord Curzon did his best to encourage the introduction of a telegraph system into Persia and maintained friendly relations with the country and with border chieftains. With the Persian Gulf the concern is more direct. While Russian activity there died away, German efforts—the object of which has since then been clearly revealed—were continuous during the early part of Lord Curzon's rule. There were innumerable attempts, sometimes under the cloak of Turkish claims, sometimes by application of commercial companies, to acquire control over the Gulf, with a view to the acquisition of political power on the completion of the Baghdad railway. Commerce was the pretext, territorial status the end.

Koweit was the first point of attack, where the Sheikh was, in the words of Mr. Balfour (April 3rd, 1904), "under our special protection and with whom we have special treaties." An attempt was also made to plant pearl fisheries under German control. The Hamburg-Amerika line sent a vessel to the Gulf every month. Then the Sultān of Turkey claimed suzerainty over Koweit and sent a ship to enforce it. But a British ship was there before the Turks, and they promptly retired. Before long they instigated a land attack, which was at least kept at bay. British protection, though the Foreign Office seemed tepid in the matter, was so far effective as to prepare allies for the Great War of 1914. In Bahrein also there was trouble, but a British gunboat watched the fisheries. All along the Gulf Lord Curzon was vigilant. He had the surveys revised and completed, the canals increased, the residencies rebuilt or founded. The culmination of his action was the Viceroy's own visit to the Gulf in 1903. He came from Karachi to Muscat with a fine assemblage of warships, and decorated the Sultān in Darbār. Thence he went to Shargah, Bunder Abbas, Lingah, Bahrein, Koweit, and Bushire. On his way back he called at Sask and Pasni. No such visit had ever been paid by an English Viceroy. Important at the time, it is impossible to calculate its value in view of the desperate and world-wide struggle towards which the Empire was so rapidly, though unconsciously, approaching. Mr. Lovat Fraser has very truly stated that "British supremacy in India is unquestionably bound up with British supremacy in the Persian Gulf. If we lose control of the Gulf we shall not long rule in India." * Lord Curzon's far-sighted and determined action served to preserve that control at a moment which the future showed to be critical indeed.

Since the time of Warren Hastings, who inaugurated or foresaw so many of the wisest developments of British rule in India, little had been known of Tibet. His mission, of Mr. Bogle, had not been allowed to lead to intercourse which might have been of great service to the civilisation of Central Asia. When Darjeeling had become a British outpost, and the frontier line lay but a few miles beyond it in the valley, the traveller gazing from Tiger Hill to the magnificent range of eternal snows looked eagerly for the thin dark line which marks the single road to the city which remained sacred, inaccessible, and mysterious for a century and a half after the embassy which that great Governor had sent had returned to Calcutta. The Chinese had stepped in and checked every venture of English trade. Then Tibet played against China, China against Tibet, both against Great Britain. Sikkim remained under the protection of our Empire, and Nepal was our ally. But Tibet was closed even to trade, and a Joint Commission failed to achieve any result. In 1903 Lord Curzon sent Colonel Young-husband, but he was met by continual delay. The Dalai Lama was believed to be under the control of Russia. A Russian agent, Dorjiev, was suspected of having made a treaty which practically handed over Tibet to Russian rule. This was denied, and probably rightly. But,

* Lovat Fraser, "India under Curzon and after," p. 112.

LHASA

THE POTALA VIEWED FROM INSIDE THE WESTERN GATE

p. 452

however advised, the Tibetans were guilty of encroachment and attack, and of neglect of treaty obligations. It was resolved to send a mission to Gyantse, about halfway to Lhasa, and the mission was protected by a considerable force. There was a treacherous but ineffective resistance at Gura on March 31st, 1904. Of the expedition it has been said that, "No army in the world has ever before conducted a campaign at an altitude frequently as high as the summit of Mont Blanc. At the engagement in the Karo Pass the Gūrkhas were operating at a height of 19,000 feet. The whole enterprise was a triumph of organisation and daring, and at no time was its success more creditable than during the return journey." * Lord Curzon expressed his admiration at the expedition "getting back again."

Lord Curzon's first term of office came to an end when the British force was still at Gyantse. Lord Ampthill, after the Tibetans had attacked our camp, ordered an advance to Lhasa. The sacred city was entered on August 3rd, 1904. On September 7th a treaty was signed in the great monastery, by which the Tibetans agreed to pay a lakh of rupees annually till £500,000 was reached, and during that time the important strategical position of the Chumbi valley was to be held. The Secretary of State for India refused to sanction Colonel Younghusband's action; the indemnity was reduced to £166,000. The conclusion of the whole matter will be recorded later.

The Tibetan expedition was a remarkable and romantic one. If Lord Curzon had remained in India, doubtless it would have led to an opening of the country. But darkness has now settled down again upon the mysterious land.

British troops and native regiments had done gallantly among the snows. No less gallantly did they support

* Lovat Fraser, *op. cit.*, p. 141.

the Empire in Natal during the Boer War and in Somaliland. The English troops from India saved Natal. Lumsden's Horse, a corps composed largely of Calcutta business men and the tea-planters of Assam, did splendid service, and its return to the capital in 1901 was the occasion of a brilliant and moving display, civic, ecclesiastical and imperial. The welcome accorded in the cathedral by Dr. Welldon, then Metropolitan of India, was singularly impressive, and a tablet, erected by the Viceroy, records the "wonderful movement which ran like a thrill through the whole heart of the Empire," and had its individual contributions from the traders of Calcutta and the planters of the East. The Indian troops upheld the honour of their country amid difficulties and dangers the most severe.

The military tie is perhaps the strongest which binds the native states to the sovereign and imperial power. Sindhia had sent his contingent to join the British troops which sailed to relieve the besieged Legations in China. And whatever may be the political interests which bind the states together, there can be no doubt that a large part of the enthusiasm which is felt for the sovereign is due to the common service of his subjects in war. This has been abundantly shown in 1914 and the years that followed. But the political and commercial ties are strong also. The agricultural needs, the village systems of cultivation or of government, the dangers of famine and plague, all form links between the states, large and small, and the paramount power. There are more than six hundred native princes, of every grade of rank and every diversity of intelligence, education, civilisation, interest. Lord Curzon probably entered more intimately into the aims of the native states than any Viceroy before him. Again and again he visited them, on occasions of public or of semi-private concern.

He frequently admitted to the exercise of their authority young rulers, such as the Nāwab of Bahawalpur, the Maharāja of Alwar, the Maharāja Holkar, the Maharāja of Kashmīr, the Maharāja of Mysore. He brought the native rulers more and more into association with the central government. And this association became, in his hands, not only official but personal. He himself paid visits to more than forty native states, several of which had never been seen by a Viceroy before. But the military side of the connection still remained in obvious prominence. Lord Dufferin had formed a scheme for Imperial Defence, in which native troops should be inspected by British officers and placed, when their rulers thought fit, at the service of the British Government. As thus organised, there were some 18,000 men. In 1903 the Aga Khan, the recognised representative of the Muhammadan powers in India, suggested in the Imperial Council that these troops should be placed more definitely under the control of the Commander-in-Chief while still remaining clearly the soldiers of their own states. The matter was much discussed, but no systematic organisation on these lines was reached. Lord Curzon's institution, the Imperial Cadet Corps, formed of the young sons of noble families who desired military training, was a further link between the sovereign power and its subject states. The creation of chiefs' colleges at Ajmēr, Lahore, and Rajkote was a similar step, for it was designed to train the sons of chiefs for their future work, and the Daly College at Indore was given the same status and endowed by the chiefs on a generous scale. Many instances of Lord Curzon's personal interest in the chiefs could be given, but the most important event of his time in the relations between the Imperial power and the subordinate states was the settlement of the ambiguous and long-unsettled relations between Hyderābād, Berar, and the Government of India. After personal negotiation between Lord Curzon and the Nizām in 1902, the British Government received a perpetual lease of Berar for £168,000 a year. The Nizām's own finances were also rehabilitated by the capable supervision of Mr. Casson Walker. Lord Curzon's policy towards the native states may be summed up in his words of November 12th, 1903—

"When the British Crown, through the Viceroy, and the Indian princes, in the person of one of their number, are brought together on an occasion of so much importance as an installation ceremony, it is not unnatural that we should reflect for a moment on the nature of the ties that are responsible for this association. They are peculiar and significant; and, so far as I know, they have no parallel in any other country in the world. The political system of India is neither feudalism nor federation; it is embodied in no constitution, it does not always rest upon treaty, and it bears no resemblance to a league. It represents a series of relationships that have grown up between the Crown and the Indian princes under widely differing conditions, but which in process of time have gradually conformed to a single type. The sovereignty of the Crown is everywhere unchallenged. It has itself laid down the limitations of its own prerogative. Conversely, the duties and the service of the states are implicitly recognised, and as a rule faithfully discharged. It is this happy blend of authority with free will, of sentiment with self-interest, of duties with rights, that distinguishes the Indian Empire under the British Crown from any other dominion of which we read in history. The links that hold it together are not iron fetters that have been forged for the weak by the strong; neither are they artificial couplings that will snap asunder the moment that any unusual strain is placed upon them; but they are silken strands that have been woven into a strong cable by the mutual instincts of pride and duty, of self-sacrifice and esteem. It is scarcely possible to imagine circumstances more different than those of the Indian chiefs now from what they were at the time when Queen Victoria came to the throne. Then they were suspicious of each other, mistrustful of the paramount power, distracted with personal intrigues and jealousies, indifferent or selfish in their administration, and unconscious of any wider duty or Imperial aim. Now their sympathies have expanded with their knowledge, and their sense of responsibility with the degree of confidence reposed in them. They recognise their obligations to their own states and their duty to the Imperial throne. The British Crown is no longer an impersonal abstraction, but a concrete and inspiring force. They have become figures on a great stage instead of actors in petty parts.

"In my view, as this process has gone on, the princes have gained in prestige instead of losing it. Their rank is not diminished, but their privileges have become more secure. They have to do more for the protection that they enjoy, but they also derive more from it; for they are no longer detached appendages of Empire, but its participators and instruments. They have ceased to be the architectural adornments of the Imperial edifice, and have become the pillars that help to sustain the main roof."

How this ideal was translated into fact was shown as it were in illustration of the magnificent Darbār of 1903, which was held to proclaim the accession of Edward VII. to the throne of Victoria. It has been declared that this was in several respects without precedent in the history of Asia. The princes were given their due honour, and their honour was laid, ceremonially and dramatically, at the foot of their Emperor's throne. Of Lord Curzon's personal share in this great historic event

—for such it was—Lord Milner, than whom no living English statesman could be better qualified to judge, has quoted with approval an eloquent description—

"The public never knew the enormous amount of labour Lord Curzon devoted to the Darbār. It came in the midst of absorbing preoccupations; it was only an incident of his Viceroyalty, but the work he did for it would have served some men for a lifetime. The task of preparation on the spot occupied a considerable staff for a whole year. Four times Lord Curzon visited Delhi to inspect, revise, and improve the arrangements. He planned every detail, and saw every detail executed. From first to last, the whole gathering was his own conception, and the driving force which made him a human dynamo during his sojourn in India alone rendered the scheme possible of execution. Everybody predicted failure, and yet there was never the slightest semblance of a breakdown. The secret of the work which Lord Curzon accomplished in India was that from early manhood he had trained himself to be absolutely methodical in all he undertook. No Viceroy, save Dalhousie, ever wrote so much with his own hand. His papers were a miracle of orderliness. Some one has said that his capacity for work is almost inhuman, and certainly to unmethodical men he seemed to toil with the unswerving certitude of a machine; but it was only by this rigid persistence that he left behind him such an astonishing record of labours completed. In no undertaking did his talent for organisation shine so brilliantly as in the Delhi Darbār."

The indefatigable industry which created the magnificence of the Delhi Darbār was no doubt a labour of love. So it certainly was when it was devoted to the archæology of India. Lord Curzon knew more of the art and the antiquities of India than any Viceroy before him, and he certainly cared for them with a more intelligent and appreciative supervision. After personal inspection of a vast number of the artistic remains of ancient India, Lord Curzon embodied his proposals for the removal of the horrors which had defaced them, and the conservation of the beauties which had remained or had been renewed, in the Ancient Monuments Bill which was passed in 1904. In 1901 he had appointed a Director-General of Archæology (Mr. J. H. Marshall), whose work in advising and supervising the provincial governments soon bore abundant fruit. Lord Curzon himself had a close personal concern in all that was done. To record it would be to write an account of the greatest archæological and artistic treasures of India. It may suffice to say that no one who has visited Delhi or Agra can fail to have been impressed by the beauty and splendour of the ancient memorials and the charm of the setting in which each is seen. They form a splendid memorial of the age-long greatness of the Indian races and their rulers. And that they preserve these memories, it may now be hoped for ever, is due to the administration of Lord Curzon.

These services to the Indian peoples were appreciated by every rank in Indian society, and they had a special personal interest for the Viceroy who inaugurated them. But it may well be that nearer still to his heart was the policy of his Government towards the dwellers and workers on the soil. "The peasant," he said, "has been in the background of every policy for which I have been responsible, of every surplus of which I have assisted in the disposition."

This feeling was embodied in constant and beneficent legislation, such as the Suspensions and Remission Resolution, regulating the non-collection of revenue in time of famine, the Punjāb Land Alienation Act, which checked the depredations of the money-lender and helped the hereditary landholders and cultivators to retain their property, and the institution of land banks by the Co-operative Credit Societies Act, which has gone far to revive and establish agricultural prosperity in many parts of India. But more direct measures were also taken. Lord Curzon stated that the aim of his administration had been "for the first time to apply science on a large scale to the study and practice of Indian agriculture." In 1901 an Inspector-General of Agriculture was appointed, in Mr. J. Mollison. An American millionaire, Mr. Henry Phipps, gave the Viceroy £30,000 which with Government addition was used to found an Agricultural Research Institute at Pusa in Bengal; and £130,000 a year was granted by the Government for the support of "agricultural research, experiment, education, and demonstration." Practical and theoretical agriculturists were brought from Europe, experimental farms were started, and attention was paid to the breeding of cattle. In every way the position of the cultivator was greatly improved. There could be no surer test of the prosperity of the land.

Reform of the police, inaugurated by the Commission of 1902, was much needed, and not a little was accomplished. At the same time judges were added to several of the courts, from the High Court at Calcutta downwards, and the Indian Code of Civil Procedure was revised, though this work was not completed till 1908. Lord Curzon's endeavours to form a military force of Eurasians (now called Anglo-Indians) were frustrated by the military authorities in India or at home. But his personal action on behalf of the Civil Service, the "men in the plains," and the men in offices, from the highest to the lowest, had many happy results. What he said about his powers as a final court of appeal on every case may well be recorded here, for it is a motto for much of the work which he did in India. "I can recall long night hours spent in the effort to unravel some tangled case of alleged misconduct resulting in the dismissal of a poor unknown native subordinate. Perhaps those hours have not been the worst spent of my time in India, and the simple letters of gratitude from the score or more of humble individuals whom I have thus saved from ruin have been equally precious in my eyes with the resolutions of public bodies or the compliments of princes."

It was in August, 1905, that Lord Curzon tendered his resignation. He actually left the country on November 18. He had remained to welcome the Prince and Princess of Wales, who began this cold weather a tour of the greatest interest by visiting Northern India.

His successor was the Earl of Minto, the great-grandson of the Viceroy who had ruled some eighty years before. The last words of Lord Curzon in India, two days before he sailed, may well be taken as the motto of the period which now closed—

"A hundred times in India have I said to myself, 'Oh that to every Englishman in this country as he ends his work, might be truthfully applied the phrase, "Thou hast loved righteousness and hated iniquity.'" No man has, I believe, ever served India faithfully of whom that could not be said. All other triumphs are tinsel and sham."

CHAPTER VIII

TO THE DARBĀR OF 1911

IN 1906 the visit of the Prince and Princess of Wales was extended southwards, and the heir to the thrones of the British Empire became the guest of great native princes of the south, at Mysore and Hyderābād. Gwalior was twice visited by the Prince, and an Anglo-Oriental College, for Muhammadan notables, was designed at Aligarh to commemorate the royal visit. At Quetta the Prince attended a great Darbār on March 7th, where the Khan of Kalat and the Jam of Las Bela were present, the new Agent to the Governor-General in Baluchistan, Sir Henry MacMahon, thus inaugurating a valuable work of alliance and protection of frontier tribes, for which his settlement of the disputes on the Helmund, about irrigation and boundaries, had shown him to be well qualified.

Afghānistān remained friendly, and the Amīr, at the end of 1906, started on a visit to Calcutta, which had rather a ceremonial than a political significance, though the review of 30,000 troops at Agra, which he witnessed, may well have impressed him with the power of his great neighbour. An Anglo-Russian convention, concluded in 1907, settled the status of Afghānistān, it may be hoped, for many years; and it may well have marked the beginnings of a better understanding between the two great powers which has since developed into a firm alliance. By this treaty the English Government disclaimed any intention to alter the political position of

Afghānistān or to take any measures there against Russia, while Russia agreed to send no agents thither, to treat with Afghānistān always through the British, and to regard the country as outside the sphere of Russian influence. Equality of commercial privilege was agreed upon. Lord Curzon's treaty of 1905 was declared to bind the English not to annex or occupy Afghān lands. It was a maintenance of the *status quo*, but dictated by a friendly spirit on both sides. The tranquillity of Afghānistān was reflected, both in 1906 and in 1907, on the northwest frontier.

During 1905–6 the revenue showed a considerable improvement generally, and it was anticipated that 1906–7 would show an important increase. This proved to be the case, especially in the land revenue, through the very favourable season on the Bombay side, since which not only current taxes, but arrears had been collected.

Less was spent on the Army, the Financial Member of Council in 1907 reducing the annual grant of two millions by a quarter, owing to the improvement in the general political situation. It was considered that Lord Kitchener's military reforms were now concluded. They had almost entirely rearmed the artillery with quick-firing guns, established munition factories in many places, reorganised the hospital and transport service, and added considerably to the officers of the Indian Army. It was declared that the total military expenditure from 1904–5 to 1906–7, consequent on these measures, was £5,543,000, of which £2,400,000 was spent on Lord Kitchener's reforms. Railway and navigation schemes were pressed on, and both showed a substantial profit. In 1906 copper coinage ceased and was replaced by bronze, at a very considerable saving.

Plague and famine remained, famine abating where

the rains were plentiful, but still causing many deaths and involving much special relief work. Plague, reduced in 1905-6, increased again the following year, and at the end of 1907, reached the highest point it had ever attained since statistics were accessible. The Commission of investigation had shown that the abandonment of affected areas and sites and the destruction of rats were the most efficacious remedies, but the ignorance of the people still rendered these measures often ineffectual. In 1907 a nickel coinage was added, and it proved highly popular.

If it had been hoped that the rearrangement of Bengal would gradually be accepted by the people, no signs of this were visible in 1906 and 1907. In October, 1905, Sir Bampfylde Fuller, Lieutenant-Governor of Bengal, issued a circular reprobating the interference of scholars in politics, and threatening that schools which disregarded this order would be disaffiliated from Calcutta University. Persistence in this conduct led to the reference of the matter to the University in 1906, but the Government of India, acting, it seemed obvious, on pressure from home, requested him to withdraw his demand on the University, and he in consequence resigned, and was succeeded by Mr. R. Hare. The general agitation continued. In 1907 the Governor-General in Council issued an order empowering local governments to "proclaim" any district, thereby prohibiting public meetings without notice and sanction. This order was eventually embodied in a law, which was to be operative till the autumn of 1910. Extensive riots, with attacks by Hindus on Muhammadans, occurred in Eastern Bengal, and more dangerous ones in the Punjāb, which led to the deportation, sanctioned by Mr. (afterwards Viscount) Morley, the Secretary of State, of the leaders, Lajpat Rai and Ajit Singh.

The "National Congress" continued its meetings, and afforded a less dangerous but almost equally pugnacious outlet for the feelings of discontent. In 1907, the "moderate" party, under Mr. Ghose, declared that its aim was not severance from the Empire, but the attainment of self-government similar to that enjoyed by Canada. The Magistrate at Dacca, Mr. C. B. Allen, was dangerously wounded by some students on December 23rd, 1907. There were signs that sedition was becoming rife in the district.

During this period the Home Government showed considerable firmness, and Mr. Morley declared that he would make no apology for strong measures, such as deportation, legalised by the regulations of 1818. India, he said, must remain under personal and absolute government. But he foreshadowed considerable changes, both in the Governor-General's and the Provincial Councils, quoting the great General Gordon's saying that the only way to govern men was by trying to realise their feelings. British rule in India must continue. The alternative is an anarchy of blood and chaos. In a later speech, in Scotland, Mr. Morley said that it would be folly to govern India like Canada, and that the disorders were not political but racial.

Mr. Morley's solution of the controversy which had caused the retirement of Lord Curzon was that the Military Secretary should hold a similar position to that of the other secretaries and be a member of the Mobilisation Committee: that the military member of Council should serve on the Defence Committee: that the Viceroy should appoint to these Committees.

In September, 1909, Lord Kitchener, having accomplished a most important work, was succeeded by Sir O'Moore Creagh as Commander-in-Chief. His work had been considerable indeed. "He placed the Army of

India on a far sounder footing, he made it a more efficient instrument . . . he did great things in India and he did them well." * He paid much attention to the defence of the country. He rode up and down the Northern frontier, seeing every pass for himself. He seems to have regarded a Russian invasion as not impossible of accomplishment, and his action certainly alarmed the Russian Government. But he more than once explained that the policy of redistribution of troops, to which he paid so much attention, "did not contemplate the massing of troops on the north-west frontier," and that he himself was opposed to such a step. The frontier campaigns were of course under his direction: but he was never in favour of war when it could possibly be avoided. He did a great deal to increase the efficiency of the Indian Army as a striking force. He left it so that nine divisions of infantry and eight cavalry brigades could be placed in the field on mobilisation. In each division there were two brigades of native, one of British, troops. The divisions were concentrated along the main lines of railway, and were grouped under two commands, the Northern with its head-quarters at Murree and the Southern with its head-quarters at Poona. A Staff College at Quetta provided for the education of officers: new methods of training the troops were instituted. The pay of the Indian soldiers was increased, and their allowances were enlarged: pension rules were revised and imposed. Lord Kitchener left India with much sound work done, though the change in the relation of the military department to the Central Government, by the creation of the Supply Department, for which he was responsible, was reversed within three years and before he himself left India. As a practical soldier he had done great good in India; but his theory of the relation of the military to the civil power was not

* Lovat Fraser, "India under Curzon and after," p. 399.

one which was compatible with English ideas of constitutional government.

A considerable change in the keeping of the accounts was ushered in by the Budget statements of March, 1908, from which accounts of local boards were omitted. The revenue showed an increased surplus. The expenditure showed a large increase in the civil departments, chiefly due to the new police regulations; but next year, when a surplus of £571,500 had been expected, a deficit of £3,720,500 resulted from the continuance of famine in Upper India. Plague, however, showed considerable diminution at last.

Afghānistān remained quiet, but the Amīr's consent to the Anglo-Russian Convention was not announced. But in 1908 expeditions became necessary against the Zakka Khels and the Mohmands. Both were led by Sir James Willcocks, and were entirely successful, and the tribes submitted to the English terms. The troops were withdrawn, and tranquillity was only broken by a rapid raid of the Mahsud Waziris. Other raids were defeated in 1909, but tranquillity was only slightly disturbed.

In Bengal there was a great contrast. The agitation, only half real, which had been now going on for some years, showed itself to be in some of its developments distinctly seditious and anarchical. An attempt was made to wreck the train of the Lieutenant-Governor, Sir A. Fraser: he was fired at a few months later: attempts were made on the lives of English officials and residents, some of them successful; and some of the police officials who had been most active were assassinated. Special legislation dealt with disloyal newspapers and with the manufacture of explosives. Mr. Tilak, an Indian journalist, was sentenced to a heavy fine and transportation for six years, but the Governor of Bombay remitted the fine and substituted simple imprisonment. The Indian penal code was strengthened; but the end of the agitation was not yet.

On November 1st, 1908, fifty years after the assumption of the direct government of India by the Crown, the King-Emperor issued a proclamation which was read to the princes by the Viceroy in Darbār at Jodhpur. It eulogised the services of the chiefs, renewed the promises of Queen Victoria's famous letter, and stated that in spite of the excesses of the last few years it was not intended to delay the promised progress and reform. This was explained by the introduction of a Bill into the House of Lords on December 17th. By this, which was severely criticised by several ex-Viceroys, but passed without alterations, in obedience to the wise principle that party politics should not be brought into Indian affairs, power was given to increase the Governor-General's Council by sixty additional members, the Councils of the Governors of Madras and Bombay and of the Lieutenant-Governor of the two Bengals and of the United Provinces by fifty, of the Punjāb and Burma by thirty. Additions may also be made to the ordinary members of the Councils of Madras and Bombay. This would retain the official majority in the Governor-General's Council, but destroy it in the other Councils. The resolutions explaining the new law, issued by the Government of India on November 15th, 1909, explained these points and dealt in detail with the representation which they gave to the different classes of Indian life—the professional, the land-holding, the Muhammadan, and the representative of Indian and of European commerce.

The new constitution, for such it was, may briefly be epitomised as follows. In the Council of the Governor-General thirty-five new members are nominated, twenty-five elected. These latter are chosen, two by the non-official members of the Councils of Madras, Bombay, Bengal, United Provinces; one by those of the Punjāb, Eastern Bengal, Burma; one each by certain district and municipal councils, one each by five Muhammadan communities. Similar arrangements were made with regard to the Provincial Councils.

While these reforms were welcomed generally in India, the "National Congress" denounced them, and the anarchist schemes continued with but little check. Three murders of prominent persons were committed by students, and a bomb was thrown at the Viceroy, happily without effect. Where sedition showed itself in Native States the rulers promptly suppressed it.

The conclusion of the war with Tibet may have been as good as could be expected, but the Convention which followed it with China and with Russia showed that England had surrendered any benefit she might have expected to win. Chinese suzerainty was recognised. Great Britain would not interfere in Tibet, nor would China allow any other power to do so. Russia and England agreed to treat with Tibet only through China, to send no representatives to Lhasa, and to seek no concession for mines, railways, roads, or telegraphs. But the trading facilities guaranteed in 1904 were to be effectively maintained, and the British troops were withdrawn from the Chumbi valley when these facilities had become secure. A Convention with China, in April, 1908, confirmed the stipulations. The Dalai Lama, after a long residence in India, paid a visit to China, when the Chinese suzerainty was reasserted. The Chinese Amban became a real Viceroy of Tibet, and when the Dalai Lama returned to Lhasa he was expelled by the Chinese and fled for his life.

The relations between China and the Indian Empire became of special interest during this period in two directions. In 1902 Lord Curzon had been able to record in his Budget speech, with laudable pride, that it was "an Indian General (Sir A. Gaselee) commanding native troops from India that relieved the Legations at Peking" when they were in grave danger from the Boxer rebellion. A force of about 20,000 men was sent, which remained in China for a considerable time.* Later on, the opium trade, which had long linked India to China, came into final question, leading, it was hoped, to eventual extinction. In 1908 the Government, influenced no doubt by many years of anti-opium agitation, agreed to help the Chinese reformers in the attempt to suppress the opium traffic. It was decided to limit the export of opium from Bengal for the year, and thenceforth to reduce the number of chests each year. The area under cultivation was also reduced. In subsequent years the revenue from the sale was greatly diminished. In 1909-10 it was estimated to be about a million and a half pounds sterling less than in 1908-9. The agreement was confirmed in 1911. The limit of ten years from March 31, 1907, was decided upon for the total end of the opium traffic.†

Lord Curzon's policy with regard to the native princes

* See above, p. 464.

† The *Times* of March 31, 1917, in recording the conclusion of the period, stated that, "Under this Treaty His Majesty's Government undertook that the export of opium from India to China would be decreased annually by 5100 chests, until its extinction at the end of 10 years, provided the Chinese Government carried out its arrangement for the reduction and consumption of opium in China.

"The use of opium was regarded by the Chinese Government as one of the most acute moral and economic questions which they had to face as a nation. It was estimated that it represented an annual loss to the country of 856,250,000 taels. In 1906 the Chinese had decided to put an end to the use of the drug, and the agreement with Great Britain was eagerly welcomed. An edict was issued on September 20, 1906, forbidding the consumption of opium and the cultivation of the poppy in China, and the culminating act in this plan of national reformation took place in February last when the Chinese Government concluded an agreement with the opium combination for the purchase for medicinal purposes of the surplus of certified stocks of opium remaining on March 31."

has been sketched above. It was probably not intentionally that Lord Minto in 1909, at Udaipur, expressed what seems to be a direct contradiction to his predecessor's aims. He deprecated interfering with native governments, and preferred that reforms should be native-born and "grow up in harmony with the traditions of the states." Administrative efficiency, carried on according to English methods, might well affect the loyalty of the people to their ruler: it might be bought too dear. These views, of course, made his relations with the native states fully as cordial as those of Lord Curzon. In 1910 he installed the new Mahārāja of Patiala and the Rana of Barwani, and announced the recognition of the Mahārāja of Benāres, the successor of the zamindar whose rank had in the days of Warren Hastings been so much misunderstood in England, as one of the Ruling Chiefs of India, with a territory containing a population of nearly 400,000.

During the year 1910 there were several raids on the north-west frontier, but none of serious importance. The Viceroy visited the Kurram valley and addressed several of the chiefs.

The surplus of 1910 proved to be £269,500. The new budget, of Sir Guy Fleetwood Wilson, introduced by an interesting historical survey, anticipated good harvests and good trade, but a reduction in the opium profits. Increase in railway receipts, excise, customs, posts, salt-tax were expected, and a surplus of £245,900 was looked for. New taxes were to be levied on alcoholic liquors, on bills of exchange, and for the transfer of securities. The budget now passed through three stages, of explanation, discussion, and revision.

In 1910, while famine had greatly decreased, plague was still rife. The people were still hostile towards some of the wisest preventive measures.

On November 23rd, 1910, Lord Minto retired from

office and was succeeded by Lord Hardinge of Penshurst. This change coincided with the retirement of Lord Morley of Blackburn from the office of Secretary of State. The two statesmen had worked together throughout their terms of office, and it is impossible to distinguish the personal action of either in any special case. Both were agreed in "making a breach in the walls of bureaucracy." It is too early to criticise the manner in which, on particular occasions, they carried this aim into effect. Considerable interest, however, was aroused by the appointment of a Hindu barrister, Mr. Sinha, as legal member of the Viceroy's Council, and his replacement, on his resignation a few months later, by Mr. Syed Ali Khan, an eminent Muhammadan representative of the same profession.

Lord Minto had kept watch on the northern frontier and the shores of the Persian Gulf. Into the sad and decadent politics of Persia it is not necessary to enter. But it may be noted that by British naval action a great number of rifles were stopped on their way to Afghānistān by the Perso-Mekran coast. On April 10th, 1911, a force of sailors and Indian soldiers was landed at Sirik on the Mekran coast, which in three hours dispersed the troops of Bakrat Khan and the hostile tribesmen. In British Baluchistan, Habibullah Khan, after the murder of his father by soldiers and the usurpation of his uncle, was installed by the British Political Agent as chief of Kharan. Afghānistān was quiet; and the north-west frontier was disturbed only by a few raids. On the frontier of Assam a British official was slain by the savage Abors, and an expedition of punishment was sent.

A satisfactory revenue year left a balance of £680,000 better than the estimates for 1910–11. Famine conditions existed, but were not excessive. The plague unhappily showed a sad increase.

In March, 1911, the decennial census was taken. It showed an increase of population amounting to 7·1 per cent., the total population being 315,132,537. In the same session a valuable Factory Act was passed, limiting the hours of labour to twelve for men, and six for women and children. The Seditious Meetings Act of 1907 was renewed in August, 1910, for six months only. In 1911 a select committee recommended that, with slight amendments, it should be made permanent, and this was done. It was indeed necessary, for during the year a considerable number of political murders were committed. Mr. Ashe, the collector at Tinnevelly, several police officials, and some witnesses in cases of sedition, were killed, at different times, by conspirators. The conspiracy at Dacca, 1910, was punished by long imprisonment or transportation of the criminals.

The year ended, and this record of Indian history may fitly close, with the Darbār at Delhi in December, when King George V., accompanied by Queen Mary, wore his crown as Emperor of India, in the presence of a concourse of almost 100,000 people. He was received at Bombay by the Viceroy, Lord Hardinge of Penshurst, and arrived at Delhi on December 7th. The Marquess of Crewe, Secretary of State for India, was in attendance. The Emperor and Empress were received by the Viceroy, the Governors of Madras and Bombay, the Lieutenant-Governors of Provinces, the Commander-in-Chief, and the Ruling Chiefs, with many officials. After receiving private visits from the chiefs, on December 12th the Emperor met his subjects in a great Darbār. The Emperor addressed the assembly, and homage was done by the chiefs and princes. The Viceroy then, by the Emperor's command, announced the favours by which he marked the great occasion: grants of land to those who had done special service, a gift of fifty lakhs for the education of the people, release of prisoners, extra pay to soldiers of the Native Army and inferior civil servants. The Indian Army was declared eligible for the Victoria Cross. All was well and generously conceived. But the dramatic surprise, the disclosure of a policy which had been kept secret with entire success, was to conclude the great day. The Emperor announced that the capital of British India was to be transferred from Calcutta to Delhi; that the two Bengals were to be reunited under a Governor-in-Council, thus creating what was practically a third presidency; that Behar, Chota Nagpur, and Orissa were to become a Lieutenant-Governorship; and that Assam was to be placed in charge of a Chief Commissioner.

In 1901 Lord Curzon had said, "It is now too late—I sometimes wish it were not—to turn Delhi again into an imperial capital." The Government of 1911 thought differently. The Government of India had recommended the change, the Secretary of State had sanctioned it, and the Emperor announced to his people this return of the supreme power to the home of the Mughal emperors. It was an expression of the desire of the British rulers to identify themselves with the great past of the Indian peoples.

It is too early to judge the effects of this great change. Calcutta has hardly yet settled down to its new position. The new capital at Delhi is not built. But the Great War of 1914, in the splendid outburst of spontaneous loyalty which all India has shown, and the services which her gallant sons have rendered in the field, witnesses to the bonds which link the Great Empire to the British Crown.

This sketch of Indian history, written and revised at intervals during the hundred years which have done so much to confirm and consolidate British rule, may well close with the words of the great Viceroy of the later years—

"If our Empire were to end to-morrow, I do not think that we need be ashamed of its epitaph. It would have done its duty to India, and justified its mission to mankind. But it is not going to end. It is not a moribund organism. It is still in its youth, and has in it the vitality of an unexhausted purpose. I am not with the pessimists in this matter. I am not one of those who think that we have built a mere fragile plank between the East and West which the roaring tides of Asia will presently sweep away. I do not think that our work is over or that it is drawing to an end. On the contrary, as the years roll by, the call seems to me more clear, the duty more imperative, the work more majestic, the goal more sublime. I believe that we have it in our power to weld the people of India to a unity greater than any they have hitherto dreamed of, and to give them blessings beyond any that they now enjoy. Let no man admit the craven fear that those who have won India cannot hold it, or that we have only made India to our own or to its unmaking. That is not the true reading of history. That is not my forecast of the future. To me the message is carved in granite; it is hewn out of the rock of doom—that our work is righteous and that it shall endure."

INDEX

THE END